THE

MAGNIFICENT

MEDILLS

THE
MAGNIFICENT
MEDILLS

America's Royal Family of Journalism

During a Century of Turbulent Splendor

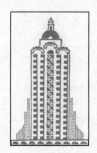

MEGAN McKINNEY

HARPER
An Imprint of HarperCollins*Publishers*
www.harpercollins.com

HarperCollins books may be purchased for educational, business, or sales promotional use. For information, please write: Special Markets Department, HarperCollins, 10 East 53rd Street, New York, NY 10022.

FIRST EDITION

Designed by Fritz Metsch

Library of Congress Cataloging-in-Publication Data
McKinney, Megan.
The magnificent Medills : America's royal family of journalism during a century of turbulent splendor / Megan McKinney.—1st ed.
p. cm.
Includes bibliographical references and index.
ISBN 978-0-06-178223-7
1. Medill, Joseph, 1823-1899. 2. Newspaper editors—United States—Biography. 3. Publishers and publishing—United States—Biography. 4. Journalists—United States—Biography. 5. McCormick, Robert Rutherford, 1880-1955. 6. Patterson, Eleanor Medill, 1881-1948. 7. Patterson, Alicia, 1906-1963. 8. Newspaper publishing—United States—History—19th century. 9. Newspaper publishing—United States—History—20th century. I. Title.
PN4874.M484M35 2011
070.5092'273—dc22
[B]   2011009989

11 12 13 14 15   OV/RRD   10 9 8 7 6 5 4 3 2 1

For Robert Whitfield and our beautiful daughter, Kay

CONTENTS

PREFACE

Printer's ink raged in their veins throughout a century and their legacy prevailed for another five decades. If Joseph Medill and his McCormick and Patterson heirs were individually headstrong, quirky and often thoroughly disagreeable, each was brilliantly creative, and together the achievement was immense. Their era of great city newspapers may have entered a period verging on nostalgia, yet we continue to hear echoes of its thunder rumbling in the publishing titles they left behind, trophies that until recently aroused the lust of twenty-first-century billionaires. The *New York Daily News* was acquired by real estate tycoon Mortimer Zuckerman in 1993, the *Chicago Tribune* by Chicago buccaneer Sam Zell in 2007, and *Newsday* by Cablevision's Dolan family in May 2008—following a bidding war against both Zuckerman and Rupert Murdoch.

Today these newspapers are archaic relics struggling to survive in a digital age, yet for many decades they reigned as the prime source of information for millions of readers while participating in shaping the opinions of the nation's decision makers. And each was created by the publishing dynasty founded by Joseph Medill more than a century and a half ago. No less remarkable were the men and women the dynasty produced, Captain Joseph Medill Patterson, Colonel Robert R. McCormick, Cissy Patterson and Alicia Patterson, among the most vivid American personalities of the past century. With their collective genius for creating, packaging and publishing news, these journalists shared a genetic brilliance that swept across decades, through wars and presidential administrations, bridging periods of prosperity and depression, upheaval and change—always in the forefront of events. The fiery abolitionist Medill was himself a towering figure, a man who personally influenced the political tide that transformed America during the mid-nineteenth century—first as a major force behind the founding of the Republican Party and election of President Abraham Lincoln, then as catalyst for the outbreak of the Civil War. His passion for late-breaking information was so intense that his last words before dying at age seventy-six in 1899 were "What is the news this morning?" And his tradition for compelling journalism is carried on today in the prestigious Joseph Medill School of Journalism at Northwestern University.

Medill's extraordinary newspapering DNA was transmitted through two willful red-haired daughters to a trio of grandchildren who inherited his publishing genius and rose to simultaneously lead three of the most successful American newspapers of the mid-twentieth century, and a great-granddaughter who created a fourth. However, the dark edge of the impulse that drove Medill's heirs to create and shape their groundbreaking and influential publications was a destructive compulsion that left members of the clan crippled by alienation, alcoholism, drug abuse, and even madness and suicide.

The history of the dynasty is also a powerful chronicle of the gains made by and for women in the past century and a potent reminder of a time when even strong women with forceful personalities could be thwarted, leaving them to live unfulfilled and damaging lives—or to exist as shadow performers behind their men. It was within Joseph Medill's wife, Katherine Patrick, daughter of the publisher of an early nineteenth-century Whig paper, that the journalistic passion first erupted; she patiently taught the patriarch to set type and encouraged him in his desire to leave law practice to become a newspaper owner—a role she could never hope to fill.

The Medill daughters, Katherine and Elinor—known as Kate and Nellie—inherited their mother's dynamic personality and possessed characteristics that, had they lived in a later age, might have been channeled into the pioneering careers forged by women of the next generation in two male-dominated fields. Kate's daughter-in-law, Ruth Hanna McCormick, joined Nellie's daughter, Cissy Patterson, in breaking through glass walls and concrete ceilings to become two of the most outstanding women of their time in politics and journalism. Both Cissy and her niece Alicia Patterson were awesome industry pioneers, who forged dazzling careers as two of the greatest entrepreneurs—male or female—in the history of journalism. Alicia refused to accept her father's estimation of her journalist talents and retaliated by founding the most successful paper of post–World War II America. While shattering barriers, each of these trailblazers consciously created opportunities for other women—their contemporaries as well as those who would follow. Within the current extended family, when Madeleine Albright, wife of Alicia's nephew, was spurned by her husband after a twenty-three-year marriage, she refocused her energies to become—as United States secretary of state—arguably the most influential woman in the world.

The dynasty's century spans a period that began with Joseph Medill's agreement to purchase a portion of the *Chicago Daily Tribune* on a spring morning in 1855 and ends with the death of his last surviving grandchild, Colonel Robert R. McCormick, on the first day of April one hundred years later. There have been excellent biographies of Colonel McCormick and Cissy Patterson through the years, as well as a pair of informative books about the *Daily News,* a fine study devoted to *Newsday,* and several massive histories of the *Chicago Tribune;* however, there has not been a comprehensive chronicle covering the sweep of the dynasty, concentrating on its riveting, complex and sometimes relatively neglected personalities—interweaving the personal daily activities of each and their public achievements against a larger historic canvas.

Essential to an understanding of the individual Medills is a thorough knowledge of interactions within the family as a whole throughout the American epoch so powerfully influenced by the dynasty's publishers. *The Magnificent Medills* has been designed to fill this niche.

FAMILY TREE *(Names in italics are siblings)*

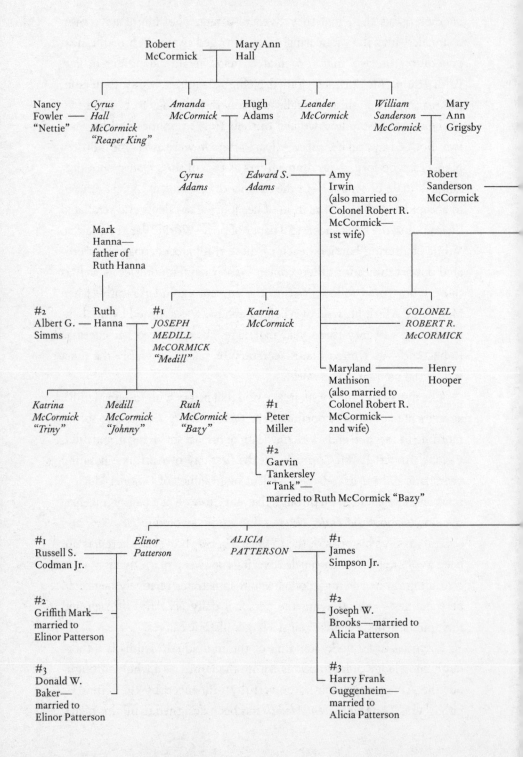

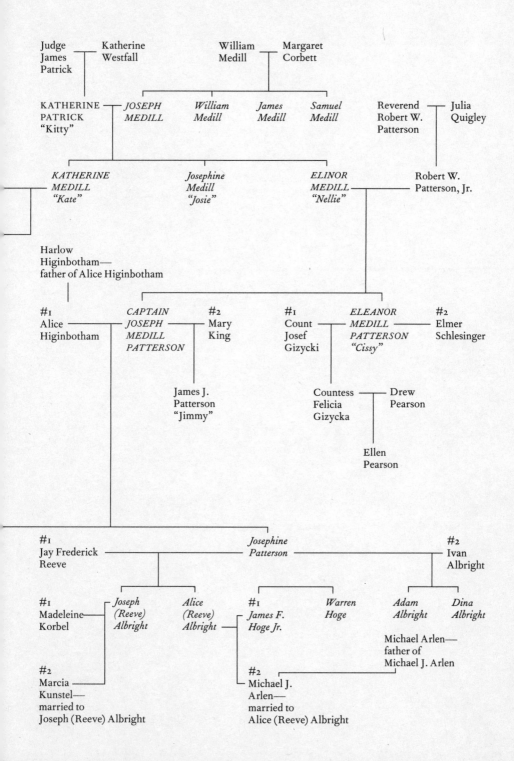

FERTILE SOIL

THE city that shaped the great publishing family is more recent even than the dynasty itself. Founder Joseph Medill was a ten-year-old Ohio boy in 1833, when a pastoral fur trading post guarded by the soldiers of Fort Dearborn was incorporated as the town of Chicago. This tiny community at the far edge of civilization consisted of no more than three hundred and fifty hardy souls who resided in the barracks, wigwams and wood cabins near the muddy banks of the Chicago River; among them were soldiers garrisoned at the fort and their families, a few natives of the Potawatomi tribe and assorted traders of John Jacob Astor's American Fur Company.

Deer sipped serenely from the river in the early morning, wolves howled in the prairie at night and Indians lurked behind trees of the forest on the river's north bank, occasionally venturing across to the fort, where they peered in and startled soldiers' wives. The only diversion for this heterogeneous population was to travel to Wolf Point at a fork in the river, where Mark Beaubien, a gregarious fiddle-playing Creole, owned the Sauganash Hotel, a tavern that throbbed night and day with vitality. As Beaubien himself said, "I plays de fiddle like de debble an I keeps hotel like hell." The Sauganash was a place where all races, ranks and classes gathered for drinking, singing, dancing, card playing and roulette, mixing as equals. And they were there every night.

The soldiers, the Potawatomi, Astor's traders and the dancing parties at Wolf Point were destined to become the stuff of legend when, as the 1830s progressed, eastern money began betting that Chicago—not St. Louis, Milwaukee or even Kenosha or Racine—would become the commercial capital of the northwestern frontier. But only if a navigable link between Lake Michigan and the Mississippi River could be created. While the site was tantalizingly close to the point at which the continent's two crucial water systems might connect, the village was virtually isolated. The Chicago River provided a channel to the Great Lakes, but there was no clear water passage connecting it to the Illinois River and thus with the great Mississippi. Furthermore, a sandbar blocked the mouth of the river, making it impossible for large ships to enter. Removing the sandbar was relatively simple; building a canal was not. To finance construction of the new passage, large chunks of public land designated as "canal lots" were sold in an escalating real estate market as a canal mania that had begun with the astonishing success of the Erie Canal spread westward. Eastern financiers fueled the boom by speculating on the swampy land parcels, which they drained and developed. This fed the upward spiral further, and as property was sold and resold, the land's skyrocketing value attracted even greater investment until the economic reversal created by the panic of 1837.

The long-awaited channel, the Illinois and Michigan Canal, was completed in 1848, placing the port of Chicago at a strategic position in an uninterrupted water passage between the harbor of New York and the Gulf of Mexico. Goods and raw materials flowed smoothly from the East through the Erie Canal and Great Lakes, and from the South via the Mississippi River and the new canal. In the decade that followed, the city became the nation's great rail center and a system of turnpikes was laid. The once isolated village became linked, through water, rail and roadway, to the magnificent riches of lumber, grain and livestock surrounding it. The year 1848 also saw the opening of the Chicago Board of Trade, which created a center for buying and selling those commodities, and in the same year the city's first telegraph connection made possible an exchange of commodities futures with traders in other cities. As the century progressed, Chicago's position as a railroad hub—more than any other factor—caused the city to leapfrog over inland rivals to realize its potential to become the commercial center of the burgeoning northwestern frontier.

THE PATRIARCH

IN May 1860, an immense temporary building rose on the site of
Mark Beaubien's tavern at Wolf Point. Dubbed the Wigwam and
looking nothing like the Potawatomi dwellings dotting the environs thirty years before, it was a pretentious behemoth built for a
gaudy political occasion. Chicago had been chosen to host the second
Republican National Convention, and soon the new building rising
over the bones of the Sauganash Hotel would hold ten thousand boisterous Republicans to select Senator William H. Seward of New York
as their presidential candidate. For all its massive pine-board sham, the
Wigwam would be the setting for a momentous event, one of the most
pivotal in American history, but few participants knew how significant
it would be, and none could have anticipated how differently history
might have played out had the convention gone as most expected.

Delegations from Illinois, Indiana, Ohio and Pennsylvania began
flooding Chicago during the week preceding the convention. The
oom-pah-pah and drum beat of uniformed bands and political clubs
echoed through the downtown streets for two full days before a designated train arrived from New York. Within it was Republican boss
Thurlow Weed, shepherding thirteen cars of confident Seward supporters and seventy official delegates. Boss Weed also brought in his
own marching clubs, "Seward's Irrepressibles," to join similar groups
from Ohio, Indiana, Missouri and other states in a nineteenth-century

custom of supporters marching through the thoroughfares of a convention city to promote their respective candidates. The Irrepressibles were especially effective in adding to the raucous merriment of Chicago's streets and hotel lobbies, where they handed out cigars and champagne to strangers. To stir enthusiasm further, Weed rented the Wigwam for a Seward rally on the eve of the convention, an expensive maneuver disrupted by the Pennsylvania delegation, which took the floor until almost midnight. By then most spectators had wandered out into the rowdy streets in boredom or fatigue.

Five blocks away, at the Tremont House, Joseph Medill sat bent over the marble top of a table strewn with lists and other papers in the hotel's Abraham Lincoln headquarters. It was one of many nights with little sleep that the managing editor of the *Chicago Press & Tribune* and a half-dozen cohorts had spent in the suite, surrounded by the elegant rosewood disorder of rooms littered with stacked papers, cigar stubs and empty coffee cups. Bowed from exhaustion, Medill dipped his pen into an inkwell and made another notation before straightening up to stretch his lanky body. It was quieter now, but not for long. Little time would pass between silence falling on the street below and a fresh stream of morning sunlight flowing over sparkling lake waters into the hotel's east windows. Medill had worked diligently in anticipation of this week and much was dependent on victory. At stake were his ideals, the success of his candidate and the integrity of his country.

Among other prominent party members working beside the editor throughout the long nights and longer days were Illinois Republican chairman Norman Judd and Lincoln's convention manager, Judge David Davis; for weeks they had strategized, bargained and persuaded, calling upon their pooled skills, influence and highly placed connections in quest of the Lincoln nomination, collectively maneuvering powerful affiliations and backroom deals that knew few limits. When a wire arrived from Springfield stating, I AUTHORIZE NO BARGAINS AND WILL BE BOUND BY NONE, it was too late; deals had been sealed and cabinet seats promised. Most recently, the Lincoln team had secured Indiana's twenty-six votes in exchange for a pledge that its favorite son, Caleb B. Smith, would be named secretary of the interior, and its members were in continuing negotiations with other states, particularly the vital state of Pennsylvania.

Voting did not begin until the third convention day, a day that had been engineered with a precision not even the wily Boss Weed could anticipate. Medill and Judd, in charge of logistics, had contrived to isolate Seward's New York constituency by distributing discounted train tickets and bogus convention passes to eager Lincoln supporters who were instructed to arrive at the Wigwam early and commandeer prime seating. The strategy forced New York delegates to be seated off to one side, away from such swing states as Pennsylvania, whose delegates could barely hear them. When Judd placed Lincoln's name in nomination, the pandemonium unleashed by the immense Illinois claque resounded throughout the vast building, shaking its roof. Medill later admitted that packing the Wigwam with Lincoln supporters was "the meanest trick I ever did in my life."

Seward held firm during the first ballot, receiving 173½ of the 233 votes required for nomination. Others in the running were Lincoln, with 102 votes; Senator Simon Cameron of Pennsylvania, 50½; Ohio's Governor Salmon P. Chase, 49; and U.S. Representative Edward Bates of Missouri, 48. On the second ballot, a crucial backroom deal came together. Forty-eight of Pennsylvania's votes went to Lincoln in a questionable deal to give a cabinet seat to Senator Cameron, a man who believed an honest politician was "one who when bought, stays bought."

Medill, a former Ohioan, had been romancing old friends and Chase supporters in the Ohio delegation without success; nevertheless, he moved to sit in their section that day. By the third ballot, he had begun hovering next to delegation chairman David Cartter, a man whose speech when he was excited stuttered as erratically as his name. When Lincoln gained a total of 231½ votes—one and a half from victory—Medill leaned over to Cartter and whispered, "If you can throw the Ohio delegation for Lincoln, Chase can have anything he wants." The surprised Cartter asked, "H-how d-d'ye know?" Medill replied,

"I know, and you know I wouldn't promise if I didn't know." Cartter shot out of his seat, jumped up onto his chair and in a loud stammering voice blurted forth, "Mr. Chairman! I-I-I a-arise to announce a ch-change of f-f-four votes, f-f-from Mr. Chase to Mr. Lincoln." An astonished moment of absolute silence followed, and then mayhem exploded, with ten full minutes of stomping and shouting throughout the floor, and squeals of rapture from the balcony. A cannon atop the Wigwam boomed out, boat whistles sounded from the river, the courthouse bell began tolling, and church bells rang, as though all sensed history in the making. Prairie yells resounded throughout the city as the news spread. The *Tribune* reported, "It is absolutely impossible to describe . . . the delirious cheers, the Babel of joy and excitement . . . strong men wept like children" and two gubernatorial candidates "sank down in excess of joy." Later, with superb understatement, Medill commented, "There was more management in the nomination of Lincoln than history has set down."

A DOZEN YEARS earlier, Joseph Medill's political intrigues had been confined to a one-room schoolhouse in New Philadelphia, Ohio, where he was replacing a teacher who had been cowed by the behavior of more than a few uncontrollable students. Income from a law practice of three years was meager and the teaching job paid a welcome twenty-five dollars a month; nevertheless, cramming rudimentary learning into the heads of a score or so pupils was not a pleasant prospect, especially considering their wide range in age and aptitude. "In the name of common sense," he later fumed, "how can one person be expected to hear a dozen branches recite twice, three, or four times in a single day, out of as many different kinds of schoolbooks? And all this in a single room, densely jammed, wretchedly heated, unventilated, some roasting, others shivering, all breathing an atmosphere foul as a glue factory." When Medill's fury exploded on the first day of school, three soundly thrashed students—one of whom was knocked to the ground with a blow to the ear—would not forget the incident for years to come.

A fourth student would remember it for the rest of her life. She was Katherine "Kitty" Patrick, and the memory of Medill's strong-jawed face that day, flushed with anger and frustration, his soft, reddish-brown hair curling around his ears, and his tall, trim body leaning over one misbehaving rascal after another, would be with her forever. Like Medill, Kitty was a slender, handsome redhead, but with hair so gloriously auburn it glistened in the sunlight and shone brightly even within the dingy schoolhouse. When Medill's anger toward his truculent pupils subsided, he noticed the lovely Kitty. And he would continue to notice her in the coming days, the willowy, nubile girl who was but eight years his junior.

Kitty's father, the Honorable James Patrick, small in stature but large in voice and a fervent orator, was editor of the local newspaper, the *Tuscarawas Chronicle,* a Whig weekly. The Belfast transplant had arrived in Ohio in 1803 to become a land commissioner and the area's Indian agent, by appointment of John Quincy Adams; he was also an elder in the Presbyterian Church, a Whig party leader, and the Tuscarawas county judge. James Patrick was so passionate about journalism that he bought presses in Pittsburgh in 1819 and had them transported by mule-drawn wagon to New Philadelphia, where he founded eastern Ohio's second newspaper. A colorful figure in a fur-collared cape, the judge would not let anyone forget he was the nephew of a professor at the University of Dublin, and he made frequent allusions to the seat of his education, Belfast College, where "sons of gentlemen went" and where his brother remained a professor of mathematics. Books in the library he amassed were ordered from the East and delivered by horseback across the mountains, along with the oysters he fancied. He also fancied fine horses, and bred them. But most of all, Judge Patrick fancied pretty women, or any women, evidenced by the number of children in the environs of New Philadelphia who bore his features.

Kitty's mother, formerly Katherine Van Etten Westfall, was not without her own pretensions and eccentricities. She was quick to enlighten Ohioans about the exploits of her father, Major Abraham Westfall, a gallant veteran of the Revolutionary War, and a grandfather,

Colonel Peter Van Etten, who distinguished himself in the French and Indian War. From these and other Hudson Valley forebears Katherine inherited a sense of privilege so intense it would be embedded in the psyche of her descendants for generations. And, for generations, those descendants would tell of Katherine Patrick's personal signature, the stash of gold dollars she carried with her wherever she went.

Joseph descended from the Medilles, seventeenth-century French Huguenots, who, with the Edict of Fontainebleau, fled France, and, as they moved through the British Isles, the name evolved from Dill in England, to McDill in Scotland and finally Medill in Ireland, where for several generations they worked in the Belfast shipyards. In 1819, Joseph's father, a firm Presbyterian, married Margaret Corbett, whose only boast was a tenuous blood kinship with Sir Walter Scott. Because both sets of parents—the Presbyterian Medills and the Church of England Corbetts—objected to the union on religious grounds, the couple left almost immediately for the New World, where they settled on a small farm on a sliver of northern Maine later awarded to Canada. There, in St. John, New Brunswick, Joseph was born on April 6, 1823, the eldest of the nine children his parents would have. Because of the border change, the little farm's location would forever bar Joseph from being president of the country that would soon be his home.

In 1832, the Medills moved to a farm in Stark County, Ohio, outside the town of Massillon, then to another farm in Pike Township nearby. If Joseph could not control the circumstances of his birth or early financial vagaries, he could manage his own conduct. With the decline in his father's health, years of poor crops and a fire that destroyed the family home, money expected for college was not there. But he applied himself while studying at an academy at Massillon and he read voraciously. He regularly walked a six-mile round-trip to the neighboring farm of A. C. Wales when chores were done at the end of the day. From Mr. Wales, a Quaker and bibliophile, he borrowed and hungrily consumed books, primarily the histories and biographies he so craved. And he devoured the classics. On Saturdays he walked nine miles east to Canton, where a local clergyman tutored him in Latin, logic and natural philosophy. After reading law with a local firm, he was admitted to the Ohio bar in 1846 and formed a legal association with New Philadelphia's George McIlvaine, a future Ohio Supreme Court chief justice. "It was hard work," he said later, "and what education I obtained came by self-denial and application." The self-taught Joseph had become a comparatively cultivated young man, but ultimately it was a passion for journalism that would navigate his life—journalism driven by politics.

NINETEENTH-CENTURY JOURNALISM WAS in effect a branch of politics and the two were intimately entwined with the profession of law; it was a vocational triangle that had existed in small towns throughout America from the time of the first white settlers. The great barons of journalism, foremost among them Horace Greeley of the *New York Tribune*, were basically politicians whose newspapers existed primarily to voice the views of their political parties. Rather than seeking the level of the mass mind as so many of their followers would do, they rose above public thought and sought to shape it. They believed that a newspaper must reflect its editor's character, hence Greeley's *Tribune* and Joseph Pulitzer's brilliant but more populace-focused *New York World* were mirrors of the minds of those men. So it is not surprising that Medill, who began as a lawyer, would never depart from the editor-politician example set by Greeley. His first foray into the Fourth Estate was to sell subscriptions to the *Weekly Tribune*, Greeley's rural arm, a modest beginning to a long and fruitful association with the influential but quirky New York editor. He also peppered area newspapers with fervent letters to their editors concerning current political matters. Medill's tenure as schoolmaster did not last, but his attraction both to Judge Patrick's newspaper—now rechristened the *Tuscarawas Advocate*—and to the judge's daughter did. In an era of personal journalism, newspaper offices were lures for those interested in politics, and Joseph began spending an increasing amount of time in the *Advocate* office, discussing politics with the judge's cronies and writing sporadic articles and editorials. Kitty, as dedicated to newspapers as her father, taught Joseph to set type and showed him the mechanics of operating a hand press. She worked with him as he learned every aspect of producing a newspaper—from reporting, editing, composing and printing to soliciting advertising and even to applying ink to the type. And she encouraged him to switch from law to journalism. He didn't need to be convinced, but accomplishing the career change was no easy task, and the only way of pursuing his dream was to purchase a paper, which required money.

Bolstered by Kitty, in 1849 he approached his father with a proposal, explaining that he wished to spend two years away from practicing law to see if he could make a success as a newspaper editor. Furthermore, a five-hundred-dollar loan would enable him to become a newspaper owner with employment for his three brothers, William, James and Samuel. The scheme worked, and Joseph was able to buy a paper in nearby Coshocton, Ohio. The name "Republican" held an early grip on Medill's imagination and, although there was not yet a Republican political party, his first action was to alter the paper's name from *Coshocton Whig* to *Coshocton Republican*. As soon as he had the press repaired and bought new type, he and his brothers were in the newspaper business. It was an invigorating time for Joseph professionally, but equal to his passion for journalism was his obsession for the young woman he had left in New Philadelphia. The image of Kitty—or Kate, as in his ardor he often called her—was with him always. He had never told her of his love and was not certain of her feelings for him, but nevertheless he brought in the new half century on January 1, 1850, by writing her from Coshocton, "I have determined to make a clean breast of it—to at last confess to what the torture could not wring from me—the secrets of my life, Kate, I have loved you in secret for more than three years."

Thus began Joseph's campaign to press his suit, but he had a grim adversary in Kitty's father, who would have none of it. The judge's stated objection to Joseph as a serious suitor was that he doubted he had the substance to succeed as a newspaperman and therefore provide the life Judge Patrick wished for his daughter. But this was merely a pretext; Kitty's father's far greater wish was that she would remain un-married. Patrick was a selfish, egocentric man who wanted to keep his beautiful, accomplished daughter with him as a companion and hand-maiden for the remainder of his life. Both men were tugging at Kitty and each was determined to have her. Joseph only partially understood the reason for the judge's objection; however, the obstacle intensified his motivation to secure a viable career, and to do so with haste.

In 1851, Medill hoisted his sights by selling the *Republican* and moving on to the larger arena of Cleveland, where he founded the *Daily Forest City*. He wrote Kitty, "My prospects are bright. I would not exchange them with any man's in the state. My highest hopes have been so realized, and more. My future is made and position among men secured. Ten thousand dollars would not buy the 'Forest City' from me." He accelerated his progress by merging the *Forest City* with an existing Free-Soil publication, the *True Democrat,* and christened the resulting paper the *Cleveland Morning Leader.* Soon Medill was known for his fierce antislavery editorials, impressing Horace Greeley, who made him the *New York Tribune*'s Cleveland correspondent. In addition to giving Joseph a national presence, the prestigious sideline solidified a connection between the two men, one that would prove pivotal in Joseph's future.

His career was now flourishing, but Judge Patrick was unbending in his determination to keep his youngest child at home, and his motive for doing so would soon become evident. Late in spring 1852, Kitty wrote Joseph, "Father says he never intended that I should get mar-ried—meant to have me always with him—that is just precisely what I intended to do myself—I fully determined never to fall in love with anyone, more especially with a Mr. M—but *you* have spoiled all our calculations, or are trying your best to do so."

"My God!" Joseph replied in a letter written to her on June 27. "[W]hy have you not told me this before. You have done me a great wrong. Why have you withheld from me your secret determination never to marry '*especially me.*' God forbid that I should do my best to spoil your happiness and fixed plans—No, I love you too well for that, too disinterestedly, generously to be guilty of plotting against you and your dear father's happiness. Your heart is entwined about his, and his very existence is centered in you."

Dramatically passionate in his alleged unselfishness, Joseph followed with "My madly loved Kate! I had rather follow you to your grave, than to the nuptial altar did I think the step you were taking would not promote your happiness as much as mine. . . . So far from wishing to seduce you from your father's love I have always said and now say that unless his free consent is given I relinquish my suit. I would do the same if we were beside the altar. To marry you against his consent would be poisoning your happiness ever after." He concluded by writing, "From henceforth this matter must all rest in your hands. . . . Care nothing for me. I am a man. I can plunge into the struggles of the world and try to forget my loveliness in its cares and strifes and vicissitudes. If an inexorable Fate had decreed that in the flesh we must be twain yet in spirit I am thine forever. Adieu dear love."

By the end of summer, the young journalist had won. On September 2, 1852, despite her father's lack of enthusiasm, Katherine Patrick and Joseph Medill were married, and during their early days together she worked steadily with him on his newspaper. She was in the *Leader* office early every afternoon, her shiny auburn hair pulled back in a neat twist as her tall, graceful body bent over the type she was skilled at setting. With the progression of winter months into spring, the waist of her long full skirt inched higher until the end of June and her retirement from journalism. On July 11, 1853, the Medills' first child was born and christened Katherine. With both his career and his domestic life in place, Joseph actively plunged into confronting the issues of the day boiling around him.

FROM THE BEGINNING, young Medill possessed a sense of destiny, and destiny reciprocated. During his short practice of law in a small Ohio firm, one associate had been Edwin M. Stanton, who would reappear in his life as Lincoln's secretary of war, and another, Ohio governor Salmon P. Chase, whose delegation votes—transferred by Joseph—were to secure the 1860 Republican nomination for Lincoln. This form of synchronicity would occur time and again. The ambitious young men who came of age with Joseph were a small band within a vast population, but their common interests made them part of a budding club; its members, sprinkled throughout a still-developing nation, would continue—throughout their lives—to repeatedly bump into each other, often with mutually advantageous impact. But Joseph's inclusion was not from random gregariousness on his part. He was a man who increasingly seemed never to unbend and spent little time nurturing relationships that would not be fruitful; they were a waste of precious time. As a result, during his lifetime he would have few close friends but many useful acquaintances.

Politics continued to be a Medill passion, one that he monitored daily; the two major political players during the century's second quarter had been the Democrats and the Whigs, with the Free-Soil Party rising as a third option in the elections of 1848 and 1852. Prompted by the extension of slavery into territories acquired from Mexico, Free-Soilers opposed the expansion of slavery without taking a stand on its abolition. The movement's subtext therefore was to keep the new lands to the west free of slavery. And white. Another political group in play during the middle of the century was the Know-Nothing faction, which reacted to the massive flood of Irish Catholic immigrants into the country by fighting to keep America Protestant. In 1852, the Whigs nominated Mexican-American War hero General Winfield Scott, one of the most brilliant warriors of his time, to run against Democratic presidential candidate Franklin Pierce. This meant passing over incumbent president Millard Fillmore, a fellow Whig, with results that were horrific. Pierce slid neatly into an easy victory with 254 electoral votes to Scott's paltry 42, a defeat so devastating it destroyed the Whig Party forever. Predictably, the debacle only spurred Medill to increase the heat of his passionate editorials, in which he repeatedly urged the formation of a new party, one that would bring together diverse political interests in a united thrust against slavery.

The label "Republican" had been lurking in Whig shadows for a quarter century, and although it was anything but innovative, Medill sponsored the name with tenacity. Opposed to the historic and foreign connotations of "Whig" and having no interest in fresh coinage, he called for "Republican" repeatedly in editorials and letters. In response to one missive, Horace Greeley, who had originally resisted the name, wrote, "Go ahead, my friend, with your proposed Republican party and God bless you. . . . If you can get the name Republican started in the West it will grow in the East." Medill kept pressing onward; one evening in March 1854, within a month of a comparable February gathering in Ripon, Wisconsin, he convened a secret meeting in his *Leader* offices that lasted through much of the night. At Medill's meeting, consisting of influential Whigs, Democrats and Free-Soilers—all antislavery advocates—he proposed his choice and, before dawn the following morning, the group had adopted the name National Republican, as well as a platform hammered out during the night. After giving the party its name, Medill would remain devoted to the Republican cause for the remainder of his life.

JOSEPH WAS THOROUGHLY immersed in both the Cleveland newspaper and his new Republican Party, but an alternative enticement was brewing. In autumn 1854, Captain J. D. Webster, an owner of the *Chicago Daily Tribune*, approached him with an invitation to visit his city and extended an offer for him to join the paper as its managing editor. Joseph was mildly intrigued by the offer, enough so to make the trip to Chicago to meet Captain Webster.

What he found on his arrival was the chaos and clamor of a turbulent port, where he was confronted by an unruly mix of barkeeps, gamblers, squatters, prostitutes and itinerant sailors. The foul-smelling river was clogged with a forest of tall masts, springing from ships that had come from as far away as England by way of the St. Lawrence

River. The raucous pandemonium of cargo unloading on wharfs lining the river echoed the hammering of new construction and clanging of metal upon metal from surrounding blacksmiths and small manufacturing shops. While the collective mayhem contributed to a din unlike any Joseph had heard in rural Ohio or experienced in relatively civilized Cleveland, there was an enticing energy about the city. Each day scores of smoke- and cinder-spewing trains roared noisily into town, bringing finished goods, raw commodities and passengers, and roared back out again, exuding a seductive romance the railroad was just beginning to project onto the imagination of the America people.

But Joseph was not tempted. He and Kitty were happily ensconced in the orderly city of Cleveland, and he was making an impact there. Furthermore, they were now a family; Kitty was expecting a second child in January to join fifteen-month-old Katherine. Nevertheless, there was a lingering feeling that remained with Medill after his visit—the persistent memory of the dynamism of Chicago with its intriguing possibilities—and it continued to haunt him after he returned to Cleveland. Then, almost as though he had tapped into Joseph's thoughts telepathically, Horace Greeley reappeared in his life. So precise was the timing that it may have inspired the probably apocryphal legend that it was to Joseph that Greeley directed his immortal phrase, "Go West, young man!" True or not, it was definitely Greeley who convinced Medill to again travel west to Chicago in the early spring of 1855, with a letter of introduction to Charles H. Ray, a physician whose antislavery zeal was so great he left medical practice to launch a crusade through the Galena, Illinois, *Jeffersonian* before entering the political arena as a clerk to the Illinois state senate. A Chicago newspaper partnership of the two abolitionist editors was a definite possibility. A similar letter introducing Joseph had been sent to Dr. Ray, and they arranged to meet at Chicago's elegant 260-room Tremont House, where legendary hotelier John B. Drake formalized the introduction under the hotel's rotunda. Meanwhile, Medill had made preliminary arrangements for his brother James to buy his interest in the *Leader* and to succeed him as its editor.

On his second trip to the muddy outpost of Chicago, Joseph found a city that also had eighty-five thousand inhabitants supporting more than one hundred houses of ill repute and more than five hundred saloons. Its urban landscape and sociological makeup presented something like a Rorschach test in which a visitor might distinguish one of several Chicagos. There was the idyllic garden city of proper gentlefolk on the river's North Side, where early investors had tamed the district's dense forest and built leafy park-surrounded mansions, each set in the center of its own city block. To the east of this island of propriety and stretching uncontrollably along the lake was the Sands, a sordid no-man's-land of shacks and brothels, a breeding ground for depravity, crime and sudden death. But away from the high ground of nouveau privilege and the gutter of squalid poverty, there was a third Chicago, an exciting, dynamic—though rough and gritty—new metropolis on the move. What Joseph saw on his second trip was a vibrant, energetic city full of promise and potential, yet nothing had changed but his perception.

Medill's arrival was simultaneous with the beginning of the city's rise out of an overlay of recalcitrant mud. "Compared with Cleveland," he wrote, "Chicago is a quagmire on the lake, but it is clear this prairie metropolis will become a great city." Streets throughout the area were a grid of thick mire from which periodically a pole would rise, tacked with a sign announcing, "No Bottom Here." In 1855, the city council passed the first of two ordinances to raise the grade of major streets by four to seven feet, and workmen were beginning to drain the city's swampy base, install sewers and put down gas and water pipes before elevating the streets and paving them. The visionary in Joseph was able to focus beyond the marsh of black sludge and to view Chicago as an exhilarating, vigorous city bursting with opportunity. Potter Palmer was in the process of inventing the modern dry goods emporium on Lake Street, while an ambitious bookkeeper named Levi Leiter toiled a few doors away at a rival shop where he and another newcomer, Marshall Field, would jointly experience their first success. Across the river, Virginia transplant Cyrus McCormick was turning out reapers in his factory, next to a site where Joseph's grandsons would one day erect the magnificent Tribune Tower. The giants who were destined to build Chicago were gathering in the vital center, now on the cusp of greatness, attracting the men who would make it great, with the promise of magnificent times to follow. And Joseph Medill was on the verge of stepping into its midst, where he would remain for the rest of his life.

JOSEPH MEDILL
AND THE MAKING OF THE
PRESIDENT (1860)

URING the spring of 1855, when most Chicagoans were celebrating the end of a long climb out of one of the fiercest winters in memory, Medill and Dr. Ray found more compelling
cause to rejoice. They had decided to purchase a controlling interest in
an existing newspaper rather than establish a new one, and so joined
forces in taking possession of the *Chicago Daily Tribune*. Medill bought
one-third of the property and Ray one-quarter, with each receiving
an annual salary of twelve hundred dollars plus profits commensurate with his share of ownership. Joining them were Alfred Cowles
and John C. Vaughn, Medill colleagues from Cleveland, and a pair of
existing *Tribune* owners, Captain Webster and Timothy Wright. Dr.
Ray, well known in the state and with local contacts, received the title
editor in chief, and Medill became managing editor.

Joseph plunged into the venture with what was becoming his customary precision, approaching production of the *Tribune* with the same
energy he had invested in each of his newspapers. He began by dealing
with the existing Adams printing equipment, a pathetic relic powered
by a geriatric blind horse stumbling around a rotating shaft. Learning of the steam-operated single-cylinder press recently developed
by New York inventor Richard March Hoe, Medill borrowed money
to obtain the new device. The combination of the Hoe press with the
purchase of Chicago's first copper-faced type immediately gave the

paper a cleaner, smarter appearance, and the new editors' sophisticated outlook expanded the *Tribune*'s formerly narrow viewpoint. Editorials became more vigorous, with added importance given to hard news, especially Washington news, and, not insignificantly, they began making the paper financially viable. The New England Protestants who had settled the city were losing their majority, soon to be out-numbered by Irish immigrants they imported to build their canal and railroads. Added to these new citizens were masses of Germans who, having fled the upheavals of 1848, clustered in a large, hardworking, beer-consuming colony on the far reaches of the North Side. Medill was never comfortable with German-Americans—or with any non-Anglo-Saxon Protestants—but he was a pragmatist and regarded immigrants not only as newspaper readers but also as prospective Re-publicans. His newspaper made an effort to embrace them all.

The *Tribune* was quickly becoming a significant influence in Chi-cago, and Joseph with it, although at thirty-two he was no longer quite the radiant young man he had been in New Philadelphia. He retained the handsome clean-shaven face and steely clear blue eyes, but people meeting him now were beginning to perceive the stern, rheumatic editor he would become—increasingly rigid, forthright, sometimes undiplomatic and often imperious. His personal bearing and remark-able self-assurance, combined with a certainty about his principles, gave him the aura of a man of consequence. Fact and opinion were rarely separated in Medill's writing, which worked in his favor. It made him appear to be receiving divine guidance, or at least signifi-cant information that was eluding others. Almost immediately he and the other new editors were benefiting from the paper's increased pres-tige, a stature that motivated politicians and other dignitaries to call on them from the beginning of their ownership.

One day, during the first harsh spring, Medill heard a pair of boots mounting the stairway to his office and looked up to see the dark, sunken face of a craggy-featured stranger. "He was a very tall, remark-ably thin man," Medill remembered. "His legs were absurdly long and slender, and he had enormous hands and feet." When Joseph asked,

"Please tell me whom I have the pleasure of addressing," the visitor drawled, " 'Well, down on the Sangamon River they used to call me Abraham Lincoln. Now they generally call me Old Abe, though I ain't so very old, either. . . . I'm in a hurry, but I ran up to subscribe for your paper. . . . Now I want to pay for six months,' and he pulled from the cavernous pockets of his jeans a pocketbook, untied the strap and counted out four dollars. 'I like your paper; I didn't before you boys took hold of it; it was too much of a Know-Nothing sheet.' " Thus was Medill's first meeting with the former postmaster, deputy county surveyor, state legislator, circuit-riding lawyer and one-term congressman with whom he would make history. Before long Old Abe was a recurring fixture in the *Tribune* office, using it as his headquarters for meetings when political or legal affairs took him to Chicago. He was soon so at ease with Joseph, and Joseph with him, that one day Medill came in and found his new friend's lanky form comfortably slouched in his managing editor's chair with the absurdly long and slender legs propped up on his workspace. In a bellow colleagues would remember and relate for decades, Joseph's voice resounded throughout the building when he boomed, "Get your damn feet off my desk, Abe."

Propelling the *Tribune* to its new standing, in partnership with Dr. Ray and their fellow owners, was consuming all of Joseph's thought and energy; he missed Kitty and the warmth of his family but was single-minded in his quest to perfect the paper. This meant spending the cold, gray winter of 1856 alone in Chicago, totally absorbed in work. Despite the occasional diversion of watching young people skating on the ice-covered river, or observing the jingling sleighs and bustling bobsleds on the streets, it was a dark and bitterly icy stretch. When the first ship sailed in from the East that spring, even Joseph left his desk to walk down to the riverfront, joining the crowd of men, women and children who gathered to celebrate an event that annually signaled the end of Chicago's glacial season of isolation. Soon the river would again be a confusion of freight-hauling sailing ships, guided in from the lake by steam tugs to moor along its bleak docks and austere warehouses. The sleighs and bobsleds would become carriages, with families like his setting out for long drives together on Sunday afternoons, and he knew it would not be long until he joined them with Kitty and the girls.

IN APRIL JOSEPH moved his wife and their daughters—three-and-a-half-year-old Katherine, now known as Kate, and fifteen-month-old Elinor, or Nellie—from Cleveland and settled the family in a house at what was then 266 Washington Boulevard, south and west of the curving river. Chicago's business center and much of the residential area had moved south by 1856, leaving the North Side to real estate investors and others whose livelihood did not require a routine of venturing from home to work on a daily basis. As lovely as the garden-surrounded houses of the city's original neighborhood were, navigating the river— with its unreliable bridges—was a deterrent to living there. The Medill house at Washington and Morgan, near the newly created Union Park, was within an area removed from the din and congestion of the river's main stretch but close enough to the *Tribune* office to satisfy the hard-driving Medill; a reliable bridge spanned the south branch of the river at Van Buren and another was being constructed at Madison Street. It was a community evolving into a district of flower-surrounded white houses, shaded by elms and poplars like those to the north, and the participation of successful businessmen like Medill was making this a fashionable residential neighborhood.

Both Morgan Street and Washington Boulevard were peaceful thoroughfares and on the latter there was the steady, sure rhythm of horse hooves trotting by the Medills' new house. Tidy carriages of neighbors who would soon be friends swept gracefully along the boulevard, an important artery known for its solid brick Protestant churches, with soaring spires that dominated the area's skyline. Kitty soon learned to rely on the old town bell hanging in the Unitarian church to announce the official beginning of the workday, noon lunch break, workday's end at six o'clock and finally the nine o'clock curfew. Yet young Mrs. Medill's attitude toward her new city was not entirely positive. She had just written her father, "Tomorrow I hope to be housekeeping. Have a German girl who can't speak a word of English to help me. Chicago is certainly the oddest looking place to be called a city I ever saw. . . . It looks like fifty little wooden towns huddled all up together. There are few brick houses, all wood. People live over stores and groceries. Houses are scarce and rents are high." She would discover that neighbors throughout the area knew each other and, like people in cities everywhere, had their own routines and traditions. On Saturdays men gathered to talk business and politics at R. H. Countiss's general store on the corner of Clark and Van Buren streets. The neighborhood women shopped at a red brick market in the middle of the road on State between Lake and Washington, where the provisions were always fresh and plentiful; produce was carted in daily from the prairie by farmers, fish arrived directly from Lake Michigan and area purveyors gathered fruit from local trees. There was a pleasant formality among the people she encountered and a level of decorum that would permeate this part of the city for many decades in the future; businessmen on their way to work wore tall black hats, and shopping ladies wore proper long wide skirts, shawls and bonnets. She would soon feel as comfortable in Chicago as she had in the home she left behind.

Nevertheless, Kitty's initial apprehension regarding her new life had not been unfounded. She was a member of a category of women who replace an overbearing father with another demanding man. Just as Judge Patrick had depended upon Kitty's devotion to him, bemoaning the marriage that deprived him of an acquiescent unpaid servant, Joseph too counted on her competence as an ever-present assistant. Not only was she responsible for the mechanics of the household but she was also his emotional mainstay. Much of the persona he presented to the outside world was based on the unquestioning support of this extraordinarily attractive, intelligent woman and her steadfast loyalty to him. She had quickly fallen under his spell, becoming a captive of his moods and attitudes; and though they drained her and ultimately would undermine her health, the reciprocity of their relationship was as essential to her as it was to him. The long months alone in Cleveland had given her a respite from Joseph's domineering presence, but now, rested, she had returned to a role that may have satisfied a fundamental need within her. For the rest of their lives together his reliance on her—and her wish to justify that reliance—was the adhesive that held them closely together and provided, throughout their long marriage, the basis for a loving, harmonious and mutually satisfying relationship.

KITTY SOON LEARNED that her days and nights with only the girls for company had just begun. Almost immediately Joseph would leave for the capital, and over the next few years he would spend long stretches of time there as the *Tribune*'s Washington correspondent, writing under the pen name "Chicago."Although convinced that much of the credibility of the new *Tribune* was based on hard reporting from the nation's capital, Medill loathed living there. And it was not merely being away from his family. His Washington home consisted of sterile boardinghouse quarters and his office, he wrote Kitty, was in his hat. He would never become accustomed to the capital's climate, but most of all he missed Chicago, the city he had initially resisted. He managed to return frequently to visit Kitty and the girls, and to nurture the trio of endeavors in which he felt an ownership: the *Tribune*, the Republican Party and his growing involvement in the political future of Abraham Lincoln. Often he was able to combine the three.

On May 29, 1856, Medill attended the first Illinois State Republican Convention in downstate Bloomington, both as a delegate and a *Tribune* reporter; there he witnessed a stirring historical phenomenon known as Lincoln's "lost speech." It was an electrifying, even world-changing, event, which Joseph remembered beginning somewhat inauspiciously. "Lincoln sat in the back part of the meeting place. He got up as his name was called, and came forward with a giraffelike lope—he never walked straight like other men—and stood in front of the pulpit." The giraffe-like man began to speak—without text and initially in a shrill, high-pitched voice—but soon his voice normalized and his presence lit the room, igniting it in a way that no one there had ever before known. So spellbinding was Lincoln's oration that Medill neglected to take notes; when he recovered his senses, he realized that none of the other entranced reporters had recorded Lincoln's words, either. Every man present that day was so galvanized by the speech— repeatedly jumping to his feet, stomping on benches, shouting and waving his hat in the air—that none had come away with anything in writing. The customarily severe Medill remembered finding himself "on the top of the table shouting and yelling like one possessed." He would later tell Lincoln biographer Ida Tarbell that the experience "paralleled or exceeded that in the Revolutionary Virginia convention of 81 years before when Patrick Henry invoked death if liberty could not be preserved." And he added, "My belief is that after Mr. Lincoln had cooled down he was rather pleased that his speech had not been reported, as it was too radical on the slavery question . . . he preferred to let it stand as a remembrance in the minds of his audience."

For the next two years the passion Lincoln ignited at Bloomington traveled across the state like a prairie fire until, in 1858, he challenged incumbent United States senator from Illinois Stephen A. Douglas for his seat in Washington. During the late summer and autumn, the two politicians engaged in seven historic debates in as many small Illinois towns, chiefly on the burning issue of the day, slavery—with Medill in the midst of the contests, coaching his man. Joseph advised him to add sauciness to his delivery, to sprinkle in ugly questions; Lincoln began following Medill's instructions, becoming more aggressive and putting Douglas on the defensive. The debates, an immense success with eloquence on both sides, won Lincoln the popular vote in the November election, but not the Senate seat in an era in which state legislators rather than voters chose United States senators. Nevertheless, Lincoln had made a significant impact and his great achievement that fall was the national prominence he gained through the debates, giving him name recognition he was able to build on by giving speeches throughout New England in the months to come, and a national visibility that would lead to his election as president two years later.

WHILE MEDILL WAS dividing his energies between the party, Lincoln and the newspaper, there were changes occurring at the *Tribune* that would have critical consequences in the future. In 1857, a fervent young abolitionist named Horace White joined the staff, quietly at first, but his presence would later have significant impact on Joseph's life. And then, in July 1858, during one of the nation's periodic economic panics, the *Tribune* faced its only authentic financial peril and merged with the *Democratic Press*, a rival Chicago newspaper owned by William Bross, John Locke Scripps and Barton W. Spears. Bross was a Williams College graduate, a bookseller and a scientist who endeavored to reconcile religion and science. Known as "Deacon" for his firm Presbyterian beliefs, he was a Chicago figure of great stature as an alderman, a future lieutenant governor of Illinois and a man to whom others listened and followed. Spears bowed out of the merger early; however, Bross and Scripps remained and the Scripps surname would thrive in the newspaper business through John's cousins and the Scripps-Howard chain. Consolidation of the two papers lasted for twenty-eight months, during which time the resulting newspaper was known as the *Chicago Press & Tribune*. Its partners were able to repay a $65,000, three-year loan in twenty-one months, while also absorbing the city's earliest newspaper, the *Chicago Democrat*. The name would revert to *Chicago Daily Tribune*, then *Chicago Tribune*, and the paper would never again face ruin.

During 1859, Medill had second thoughts about Lincoln and his support wavered in favor of Ohio's Governor Salmon P. Chase, his old law associate, but that passed. Then, in late December, Medill and Norman Judd scored a coup that was possibly the most significant of their machinations in securing the Lincoln presidency. Wearing his Republican hat, Joseph was an influential participant at the party's National Committee meeting in New York's Astor House, where he and Judd fought vigorously for Chicago vis-à-vis Indianapolis as the May convention site. Because Indianapolis hotel space was judged inadequate and Lincoln had not yet emerged as a viable candidate, they were successful in persuading the committee to decide in Chicago's favor, a crucial move that would give the Illinois candidate a decisive edge.

After Lincoln's dramatic May nomination at the Wigwam convention, the *Tribune* wasted no time in beginning to hammer away on his behalf and continued to do so through the November election. Every day the paper was filled with editorials, columns and not so gently biased articles supporting its candidate. In reality, Lincoln's nomination had been the true hurdle, because the Democrats didn't have a prayer. Their party had split into two factions and, with the addition of a third party, there were three presidential candidates opposing the Republican when Election Day arrived on November 6. John C. Breckinridge represented the Southern Democratic Party, Stephen Douglas stood for the Northern Democratic Party and John Bell was the Constitutional Union Party candidate. After a final Lincoln rally at the still-standing Wigwam on election eve, the following morning's *Tribune* urged its readers to turn out: "The labor of six years centers in this day. Be sure to vote." And they did so in force. On November 7, the *Tribune* was triumphant. THE GREAT VICTORY, its headline blared. Lincoln had trounced them all, capturing 180 of the 303 electoral votes.

On learning of the overwhelming conquest of its candidate, Chicago again exploded; this time with a fireworks display, a two-hundred-gun salute over the river and a torchlight procession that wound through the streets of the business district. Residents of neighborhoods joined in the celebration and rejoiced by lighting great bonfires that blazed in all sections of the city.

TRIBUNE EDITORS, AS well as the men and women whose faces reflected the joyful glow of bonfire light that night, would soon know the long, dark days of a tragic time ahead, but at the newspaper there were pressing technicalities to attend to first. In February 1861, in the midst of rapidly developing national conflict, the paper was incorporated as the Tribune Company through an act of the Illinois legislature, with the corporation's two thousand shares of stock valued at one hundred dollars a share. The distribution was 430 shares each for Medill and Bross; Scripps and Ray received 420 shares apiece and Cowles collected the remaining 300.

Medill returned to Washington after the election to fulfill a *Tribune* promise that one of its editors would always be stationed there to report directly from the nation's capital in perilous times. And times could scarcely be more perilous, with potentially catastrophic events unfolding weekly, then daily. Five days before Christmas, a specially assembled South Carolina convention voted unanimously to secede from the Union, followed in early January by a similar Mississippi vote, and, in quick succession, Florida, Alabama, Georgia, Louisiana and Texas also seceded. On February 8, delegates from the seven states met in Montgomery, Alabama, and formed the Confederate States of America, electing Mississippi's Jefferson Davis their provisional president. Within a few weeks, the remaining states of the Deep South would join them. Although tempers were raging on both sides, President James Buchanan—the lame duck chief executive until Lincoln's March 4 inauguration—refused to fight the rebels, insisting that if action were to be taken it must be initiated by his successor.

On April 12, South Carolina militia fired on Fort Sumter, and its commander, Major Robert Anderson, surrendered two days later. The Civil War had begun. It would be a long and bloody four years, a time during which Medill would often disagree with Lincoln personally. "We made Abe," he wrote to a *Tribune* colleague soon after the election, "and by G— we can unmake him." But throughout the conflict, he supported the president publicly, and the *Tribune* backed Lincoln's effort consistently and wholeheartedly. At any given time over the duration, as many as twenty-seven correspondents would cover the war, with eyewitness reports rushed back from the field to Chicago. When the president asked for a half-million men in July 1861, twelve of the paper's staff were first-day volunteers, including two Medill brothers, William and James. Tragically, the war would claim the lives of both, as well as that of William Bross's brother, John Armstrong Bross, a heroic victim of the 1864 Battle of the Crater. Joseph, prevented from serving by his rheumatic spine and an increasing hearing loss, was nonetheless active in his unflagging championing of Lincoln and the

Union cause. Throughout years of northern defeats that ravaged the president's popularity, Medill was steadfast in his editorial support and, when the now-deathless Gettysburg Address was virtually ignored by eastern newspapers, the *Tribune* was the nation's only major paper to print Lincoln's words on page one.

In February 1865, Joseph's loyalty was pressed further when Secretary of War Edwin Stanton demanded that he produce six thousand more troops in addition to the twenty-two thousand already sent from Chicago. Medill traveled to Washington to see Lincoln in protest of the request, meeting with him in his working office at the White House, a large, disorderly room located upstairs in the East Wing near the family living quarters. This room was the heart of the Civil War White House; it was where the president held cabinet meetings, received official guests and dealt with paperwork. Stacks of maps and military history books were piled haphazardly on a large walnut table in the room's center, and scattered randomly around it were piles of papers and additional maps. A portrait of Andrew Jackson hung on the wall above a fireplace and Medill could see—through a window behind the president—a partially built Washington Monument and the gloomy encampments of Union soldiers under somber winter skies.

After nearly two hours of talk, the president slowly unfolded his long, angular body and rose from the chair across from Medill. "I cannot do it," he said, "but I will go with you to Stanton and hear the arguments on both sides." Lincoln's face was gaunt, his dark eyes hollow and drawn. The two old friends made their way through the morning drizzle, west of the White House to the War Department, where they would meet with War Secretary Edwin Stanton. It was a hostile yet familiar gathering of the three men: two former associates of a small Ohio law office—one now a powerful editor; the other a crucial cabinet member—and the president both knew intimately. While Medill and Stanton argued over the request for additional men, a silent Lincoln sat on a haircloth lounge in a dirge-black suit with his long legs crossed, his eyes downcast. He suddenly lifted his head, turning to Medill with a black, ominous face and spoke words that would be forever etched in Joseph's memory and frequently replayed in his mind throughout the rest of his long life.

> You called for war until we had it. You called for emancipation, and I have given it to you. . . . Now you come here begging to be let off from the call for men, which I have made to carry out the war you have demanded. . . . And you, Medill, you are acting like a coward. You and your *Tribune* have had more influence than any paper in the Northwest in making this war. You can influence great masses, and yet you cry to be spared at a moment when your cause is suffering. Go home and send us those men!

"I couldn't say anything," Medill remembered many years later. "It was the first time I ever was whipped, and I didn't have an answer." He went back to Chicago and he did raise the men—totaling at war's end more than any comparable city of the North.

APRIL 1865 WAS a soul-shattering month. The war's grim destruction continued until the ninth, when surrender of the South at Appomattox produced weary jubilation, followed in less than a week by the deep sorrow of Lincoln's assassination. The effect of the president's death was a powerful reality for Joseph on many levels; Old Abe had been a protégé, a collaborator, a hero and a friend, someone with whom there should have been a fruitful future enriched by a shared past. The war was over and they had won, but now Lincoln was gone, and so quickly. As a member of the committee of one hundred, a solemn Medill escorted the president's body on its mournful journey to Springfield, Illinois, during the first week of May in preparation for his funeral and burial there, the culmination of a sorrowful, prolonged pageant that brought scant closure to a splintered nation.

The black cloud of war had produced profound anguish for all Americans, but it also presented a colossal silver lining for many, particularly in Chicago. The postwar explosion of the city's prosperity and status was such that it prompted German chancellor Otto von Bismarck to say, "I wish I could go to America, if only to see that Chicago." The four years of devastating conflict had built great fortunes for the city's dry goods merchants, meatpackers, boot manufacturers, brewers, purveyors of grain and others, creating sudden dynasties that endure today, and not least among these beneficiaries was the *Tribune*. Throughout the Civil War era the newspaper had grown and seen its circulation boom, with the numbers for both subscriptions and single-copy sales soaring. The war had made money for Medill's paper, serious money, for the first time. The years of diligence, cutting back and merger were paying off and the *Tribune* was an indisputable success— at the very moment it was slipping from Joseph's grip.

· 4 ·

THE GREAT CHICAGO FIRE: MAYOR MEDILL'S PERSONAL PHOENIX

IT was the beginning of a rocky time for Joseph Medill, now forty-two—high middle age for a nineteenth-century man. He remained tall and slender, but his appearance had continued to evolve, with little remaining of the man once thought to be the handsomest in Chicago. A beard hid the firm jaw of his youth and, like the abundance of auburn hair still crowning his head, it was shot with gray. Rheumatism had further bent his lanky body, producing an old man's posture with a cane to support it. But the greatest change came from diminished hearing, necessitating a black ear trumpet and dramatically increasing the impression of age. However, Joseph's deafness was selective; it allowed him to screen out the chatter of bores and lightweights while enabling him to carry on one-sided exchanges consisting chiefly of questions and monologues. Accentuating his aged appearance was the vintage costume he affected throughout his adult life, always considered outmoded: black frock coat over a matching vest, stiff white shirt with a stand-up collar, and a narrow black bow tie. Summer and winter, he wore knee boots and a black fedora.

Ill winds were blowing strongly against Joseph. His Republican Party had prevailed, but Lincoln was no more, and a power shift at the *Tribune* was moving leadership away from his control. John Scripps resigned as the war was ending and Medill's early colleague Charles Ray, a widower and in poor health, left the paper in late 1863 when his abolitionist goals were in sight; both men sold their stock to other proprietors. These developments were ominous for Joseph, now at odds with the remaining owners, including Bross. And he quickly lost further positioning to the young Horace White. While other owners were pulling out, White had formed a unity with Cowles, and together they financed a handsome new four-story Tribune Building. This latest headquarters, on "Newspaper Row" at Dearborn and Madison streets, was built at substantial cost and, because the structure was guaranteed to be fireproof, the partners did not invest in fire insurance.

Yet, throughout the postwar years, Medill was a lion in wait. Despite his appearance, he retained the fervor of youth, and destiny continued to paw the earth at his feet. Retaining his 20 percent ownership in the *Tribune*, he took a hiatus from the paper in 1866, moving back into public service to become secretary of the Republican Central Committee. And in November 1869 he was elected to the Illinois Constitutional Committee. He also used his new autonomy to travel, both for recreation and to gather material for *Tribune* articles, usually signed "Protection," another pseudonym that fooled no one.

His fellow *Tribune* owners settled into their comfortable new fireproof quarters, spending the long, dry, warm-weather months of 1871 writing smugly about fire hazard as though they looked down at a parched city from Mount Olympus. Typical of their repeated warnings of an impending inferno were words published on September 10: "Chicago is a city of everlasting pine, shingles, sham veneers, stucco and putty. It has miles of fire-traps, pleasing to the eye, looking substantial, but all sham and shingles. Walls have been run up 100 feet high and only a single brick in thickness." There was substance to their self-righteous editorials; great sections of residential property were pyres waiting to be ignited, and fires were erupting throughout the dehydrated city, as they had been every day and night for weeks. Then, on October 8, an act of God struck Chicago, one that would transform the remainder of Joseph Medill's life, the lives of all those around him— and of the generations to follow.

*   *   *

IT WAS HOT and dry in Chicago that Sunday evening, desertlike, although according to the calendar it had been autumn for more than two weeks. With scarcely an inch and a half of rain since early July, people throughout the area were convinced they were experiencing the worst drought in history. High winds swept across the prairie, whipping the arid atmosphere and sending whirls of prematurely parched leaves scooting along cracked ground, but still there was no respite from the suffocating heat. A major conflagration on the West Side the previous day had leveled four square blocks and was so challenging it left the city's firemen exhausted.

At just after 9 P.M. a new blaze broke out in a neighborhood of pine shanties on the West Side, one of several simultaneous outbreaks that night, confusing and delaying the already fatigued firefighters. Public reaction to the fire was sluggish, with fire-weary citizens paying scant attention to clanging emergency equipment on its way to a barn behind 137 De Koven Street, arriving too late to prevent the inferno at its source. It was not until more than a half hour later that the rapid spread of flames and menacing tolling of the courthouse bell finally drove scores of men, women and children from their houses. By ten o'clock there were hundreds of them, clutching clothing and other belongings, running toward the south branch of the Chicago River as the fire rapidly devoured entire blocks of pine shacks and hovels. Fierce winds and convection whirls accelerated the blaze, propelling burning masses of material through the air—as high as five hundred feet—and at one point igniting a church steeple four blocks away, which in turn torched the tinderbox of a riverside lumberyard. Terrified shrieks and ghastly moans, always punctuated by the steady toll of the courthouse bell, intensified the sheer horror of the night. Eerily, the furious conflagration produced little smoke.

Around midnight, citizens watched in horror as flames jumped the river to the South Side at Van Buren Street, and within minutes Chicago's business district was ablaze. A distraught mayor, Roswell B. Mason, telegraphed St. Louis, Milwaukee and Cincinnati, requesting firefighting equipment to be rushed to Chicago on railway flatcars, and he arranged for clear right-of-way for speeding freight trains that would bring them. It wasn't long before a flying mass of fire landed on the courthouse cupola and flames began working their way down to the prison level where one hundred and fifty hysterical inmates were trapped—and then quickly released. Some prisoners joined a host of random looters who ran through the streets, smashing shop windows and stealing all the merchandise they could carry. And adding to the general chaos was an increasing drunkenness produced by widespread looting of saloons. The courthouse bell continued its funereal toll until its cupola crashed to the ground, with the building that supported it continuing its burn to a ghostly shell. The ill-omened silence of the bell heightened the terror, but street noise was everywhere, rumbling wagons carrying trunks of belongings, men's shouts, the cries and shrieks of women and children and, periodically, the crash of brick walls. Flames poured diagonally from "fireproof" buildings and continued to incinerate everything in their path, consuming wood, toppling marble columns and felling brick, concrete and iron. Roadways became more congested, with refugees sprinting through a rain of sparks, fire particles and falling embers; bridges were choked with humanity as people rushed north to escape the business district.

Early Monday morning the unthinkable occurred when fire again vaulted the river, this time across its main channel to the North Side, where wealthy residents of the tranquil flower-encircled houses in the garden district had hurriedly buried family silver and other valuables, including a few grand pianos. The conflagration now began spreading more rapidly than before, taking less than an hour to level eleven square blocks of lovely wooden houses, along with their ancient shade trees and pastoral gardens. Stately homes quickly crackled and then dissolved into smoldering beds of live coals. Only the eerily blackened skeletons of great trees were left. Entire families of North Side residents scurried east toward the lake and others fled north to Lincoln Park; the streets in both directions were clogged with wagons spilling over with household goods. Most families, however, left in such haste that they had with them only what they could carry. Those who had rushed to the park cowered in the newly opened graves or behind the piled-up gravestones of a cemetery that was in the process of relocating. Leveled by the tragedy, the city's rich and powerful spent the night huddled among some of Chicago's most wretched denizens— vagrants, thieves, panders and prostitutes—as they looked south and watched their city burn.

JOSEPH MEDILL, ASLEEP at home, had awakened around midnight, immediately aware of the presence of a great fire in the city. Confident that the flames would remain far to the east of his house at Washington and Morgan, he threw on a shirt, suit and boots, and rushed toward the *Tribune* offices. Pausing on the Randolph Street Bridge only long enough to watch the courthouse catch fire, he made his way toward the paper, where he knew staff would be at work on Monday's edition. It appeared to be business as usual. Although fire raged around them in districts throughout the city, *Tribune* employees firmly believed they were in a safe zone, working in a "fireproof" building, surrounded by other "fireproof" buildings—and as professional observers somehow immune. Medill's brother Samuel was carrying out his duties as city editor, printers were setting type and Horace White was in his office preparing the following day's editorials. Sometime after midnight, Elias Colbert, the paper's astronomer-in-residence, came in and went to the roof with his telescope, as he often did to scan the night sky. Watching the skyline from above the *Tribune*'s four stories, he saw the fire leap from building to building, sometimes shooting flying brands to where he stood. Joseph joined him, bringing several men along, and together they fought the sparks and flames skipping over from other roofs to theirs.

Relentlessly pushing himself and the men around him, Medill fought not only to save the Tribune Building but also to scoop every other newspaper in town. "Our faces were black," he remembered.

"Our clothes had been on fire scores of times. Our hair and beards were singed. . . . Even our shoes were burned from stamping on the spots of fire on the hot roof." The diehard newsmen downstairs continued to write, edit and print into the early morning hours, updating what they now knew was a story for the ages. When smoke and flames seeped into the basement, they fought them with fire extinguishers and returned to work. And even when buildings directly across the street burst into flame and melted into nothing, the journalists continued on. Then water and gas mains burst, shutting down the presses, and within minutes McVicker's Theatre collapsed onto the *Tribune* building. Soon their "fireproof" headquarters too was ablaze. Joseph gave orders to evacuate the building. When they rushed outside, the fire was closing in. The men all fled, with Joseph and Samuel running east on Madison Street. When the brothers found their way to safety, it was mid-morning and both collapsed in exhaustion.

After two hours of sleep, the Medills were up and back on the job— this time working at the daunting task of resurrecting their newspaper. Joseph quickly leased space in a small job-printing establishment on Canal Street and found a neighboring press he could buy. Reassembling the *Tribune* staff, he led his men in producing the semblance of a newspaper, while continuing to replace lost equipment. He telegraphed Baltimore to buy a four-cylinder press and arranged to have it expressed to Chicago; a font of type was sent by the *Cincinnati Commercial* and sixty-five bundles of paper arrived from the *St. Louis Democrat*. Back in the offices they had fled early Monday morning, a singed bit of copy written the night before was found in the rubble: " . . . and the wind raging, and the fire burning, and London and Paris and Portland outdone, and no Milton and no Dante on earth to put the words together . . ." These were the only legible lines to survive the *Tribune*'s eyewitness account of the greatest newspaper story in Chicago history.

William Bross rushed to New York ostensibly to scout equipment for the paper, but he was also there to boost Chicago as the new land of opportunity. "Go to Chicago now!" he cried out enthusiastically

to one and all. "Young men, hurry there! Old men, send your sons!
Women, send your husbands! You will never again have such a chance
to make money!"

Meanwhile, Medill was prevailing on the home front with an October 11 editorial that began:

Cheer Up

In the midst of a calamity without parallel in the world's history,
looking upon the ashes of thirty years' accumulations, the people of
this once beautiful city have resolved that CHICAGO SHALL RISE
AGAIN.

With woe on every hand, with death in many strange places, with
two or three hundred millions of our hard-earned property swept
away in a few hours, the hearts of our men and women are still brave,
and they look into the future with undaunted heart.

A second editorial appeared the following day:

Rebuild the City

All is not lost. Though four hundred million dollars' worth of property has been destroyed, Chicago still exists. She was not a mere
collection of stone, and bricks, and lumber. These were but the evidence of the power which produced these things; they were but the
external proof of the high courage, unconquerable energy, strong
faith, and restless perseverance which have built up here a commercial metropolis.

After continuing in this vein for several more paragraphs, the
second piece concluded with the words, "Let the watchword henceforth be: CHICAGO SHALL RISE AGAIN." These cheerleading articles have been reprinted—or at least cited—in virtually every history
of Chicago published since the fire, and lauded as the most famous
editorials in *Tribune* history. Medill's position as symbol of the Fire's

projected phoenix was so prominent that when diverse international figures such as Grand Duke Alexis of Russia and Prince Iwakura of Japan sent contributions to assist the refugees, they were addressed to him. Joseph put the five thousand dollars sent by each in the hands of his wife, who carefully distributed the funds to various hospitals and other institutions where she felt the money would be most helpful.

THE ACT OF God that had temporarily destroyed a city put Joseph Medill back at the top of his game. Election time was a month away and Chicago needed a new, forceful mayor, a leader who could reassure, inspire and direct his citizens in rebuilding their home. Within days a political slate was formed, the Union-Fireproof ticket, and Joseph was nominated to head it. At first he refused, but then he reconsidered at the behest of Carter Harrison Sr., a member of the nominating committee and a future Chicago mayor. Medill's acceptance was on the condition that powers of the mayor's office in relation to the city council be strengthened. He then campaigned on a platform of strict fire prevention codes and won by a more than ten-thousand-vote majority. In his inaugural address four weeks later, he urged that the city be rebuilt with brick rather than pine, a stand without controversy, and he went on to lead in its renaissance.

Chicago astonished the world with the rapidity of its rise from ashes under Medill's leadership; in addition, he founded the city's first public library, re-formed the police and fire departments and strengthened the office of mayor. But it was not a happy term. Just as Medill's management style and his editorial output were products of his own rigid views, so was his leadership of the city; he was every bit as forthright and undiplomatic in public office as he had been at any of his newspapers. His inflexible intolerance for anyone who did not conform to his views of appropriate taste and conduct would be his undoing. Medill's dislike of immigrants, particularly those from Germany, continued to be predominant among his personal characteristics, with his disdain for recreational consumption of alcohol a close second, and these twin biases combined to torpedo his tenure as mayor. After six days of work, members of Chicago's large German-American population wanted nothing more than to spend Sunday afternoons relaxing with their families in community saloons and beer gardens. The question of Sunday closings of public drinking facilities was a lively one and had been an issue since the mid-1850s when Levi Boone, grandnephew of Daniel Boone, was mayor. During the first portion of his term, Medill opposed the closings but he eventually reverted to his inner compass, and repelled by such non-Presbyterian behavior, he fought strongly to enforce an old Sunday temperance ordinance.

Joseph's ardent crusade to keep the Sabbath dry failed and, following twenty months in office, it had exhausted him. In early August 1873, he requested the city council to grant him a leave of absence for the balance of his term, leaving an alderman, Lester Legrand Bond, as acting mayor. It had been a harsh lesson for Medill, but he now knew his passion for politics should not extend to public service, that his true genius was in shaping government through his words and skillful manipulation from behind the scenes. He subsequently declined offers of cabinet positions from two presidents and, when approached to run for the United States Senate, refused, saying, "Politics and office seeking are pretty good things to let alone for a man who has intellect and individuality." On August 27, he sailed from New York for a year of travel with his family, which now included little Josephine, born in 1866. Together the five Medills visited museums and art galleries and were guests in stately homes and country houses throughout Europe. Over the next few months, while revitalizing, Joseph sent articles and opinions back to the *Tribune* from the British Isles and then the Continent.

In 1874, he returned refreshed and rejuvenated, eager to launch the next phase of his amazing career. He was now determined, at any cost, to control the *Tribune,* and the cost was great. Close to fourteen years had passed since the company's incorporation and *Tribune* stock had quintupled in value. Joseph had added twenty-three shares to his original 430, but to gain controlling interest in the company he needed to acquire another six hundred at five hundred dollars each. To do so he borrowed three hundred thousand dollars at 10 percent interest from the richest and most influential man in Chicago, Marshall Field. For the following nine years, until the note was paid in full, Field considered himself an editorial partner, with a gratuitous stream of suggestions about how the paper should be run. Further empowering the merchant prince was his role as the newspaper's heaviest advertiser. When the final payment was made, the fiery editor would glare at his well-compensated backer and declare, "Now we meet again as equals, Mr. Field."

But the deal had been struck, and on November 9, 1874, with his 453 *Tribune* shares added to the six hundred purchased through the Field loan, Joseph held undisputed control. Horace White was out. And Medill was in as he had never been in before. Philip Kinsley, in his three-volume history of the *Chicago Tribune*, completed in 1946, wrote, "This was probably the most important change in the paper since Medill had first assumed its leadership in 1855. His personality as one of the great journalists of the age was stamped on the paper from that time until his death and lived on in his successors." More than ever before, Medill was remarkable in reigning over the newspaper as if it were his exclusive conduit to the reader, without regard to whom it might annoy or outrage, ranting on in the most immoderate manner. Blunt and tenacious, with evangelical zeal, Joseph stormed against business monopolies, immigrants and anarchists alike. For good or for ill, it would be a quarter century of one man's views dominating the opinions of the citizens of one of the world's great cities.

THE WORST TWO SHE-DEVILS
IN ALL OF CHICAGO

JOSEPH and Kitty's two older daughters appeared destined for happy, productive lives. An abundance of beauty, intelligence and prestige would be theirs, material wealth, fashionable schools, luxury travel and introductions to the legendary figures of their time. And so their lives began to unfold, yet along the way there was a fundamental disconnect. By late adolescence Kate and Nellie were both well on their way to becoming intensely unhappy young women—petty, dissatisfied and envious—prompting the bewildered Joseph to ask, "Is it my fault that I'm the father of the worst two she-devils in all Chicago?" It was his fault. Alternately pampered and neglected by their indulgent father throughout childhood, the two women inherited his creative energies without the opportunities of his gender. It's also probable that Kitty was in the early stages of tuberculosis while the girls were young and, after caring for Joseph's insistent needs, she may not have had energy left to discipline her daughters or to drill them in the basic principles of courtesy, gratitude and noblesse oblige.

Photographs and portraits present the sisters as tall, stately Victorian women staring arrogantly at the artist from beneath masses of artfully piled auburn hair, bodies corseted and augmented to form the coveted hourglass silhouette. Through the years, Kate wore her hair pulled back from her face, with only a cluster of curls at her forehead, while Nellie's auburn tresses were swept up into a bouffant pompadour surrounding her beautiful brow. The metamorphosis of the sisters from happy little girls to notorious vixens was gradual. Joseph had carefully supervised the education of his daughters in journalism, literature and government, in addition to the expected feminine subjects, and during the early years they were quite docile. According to her great-grandniece Alice Arlen, Kate was "a truly awesome woman . . . shrewder, brighter, more elegant and even more ambitious" than Nellie. And, although she was her father's favorite, a clue to his true priorities is that when she graduated from an Indiana boarding school in 1869, he was too preoccupied with the Illinois statesman phase of his career to attend her commencement exercises. Musically gifted, she was then sent to study piano and voice in Munich, but her initially sunny disposition was beginning to erode.

Like so many women of their time and station in life, the girls were thwarted by the mores of the era; a few years later these handsome, gifted women might have channeled their talents toward brilliant careers. Instead both moved through life shooting off incendiary sparks that charged the surrounding atmosphere, periodically creating random explosions that wounded all those around them. The damage began with the gentle, sensitive men they married, and continued in the exceptional children each produced. Theirs was the bridge generation, the only one in four that did not publish with panache, yet in analyzing the family dynamics it appears that Kate and Nellie were essential to the evolution of the Medill dynasty. Because their extreme behavior skewed the development of their creative offspring, it nurtured demons of genius lurking within each. It's possible then that Joseph Medill's she-devils were the unintended agents of the dynasty's sustained greatness—however, in the process they provided decades of torment for their unfortunate families.

The girls were on the threshold of their twenties during the family's leisurely tour of the British Isles and the Continent after Joseph left the mayor's office. The expedition was a revelation for both, giving them a taste of the luxurious, sophisticated way of life conducted in the castles and great houses of Europe. While traveling from one foreign city to another with their distinguished father, they attended magnificent parties in fine houses and country estates, surrounded by elegant, refined Europeans who carried themselves with a self-confidence, even an arrogance, that the sisters admired and wished to emulate. To reproduce such a life in Chicago might be possible, but it would require at least one essential ingredient: a rich, cultivated, fine-looking husband. Such a consort would be a splendid personal accessory who could also provide a grand house, the appropriate setting for entertaining the social elite of the city and visiting dignitaries. Obsessed with images of grandeur, and ignoring parental cautions, the headstrong women rushed to unite with husbands they were certain would supply the means for such elegance and style in their lives.

NOT LONG AFTER the family's return to Chicago, Kate discovered the man who would be her vehicle to the future she envisioned. Robert Sanderson McCormick was perfect; he was the very personification of her dreams. The well-traveled University of Virginia graduate was handsome, suave, courtly and rich, or at least he appeared to be rich. His scholarly and equestrian pastimes were those of a patrician gentleman; he possessed an expert's knowledge of the Napoleonic tradition and was a proponent of a fine public library for Chicago. Even more impressive were the relatives surrounding him; they were astonishingly rich—among the richest in Chicago—not the least of whom was his father's brother, the reaper king, Cyrus Hall McCormick. Aside from an ambiguity about Robert's ability to provide the wealth she required, there were other factors that might have given Kate pause before entering into what would be a virtually irrevocable contract.

Robert's father, William Sanderson McCormick, was an uprooted southern aristocrat in fragile emotional health. The mighty Cyrus had insisted that William and their equally capable brother, Leander, move to Chicago to work with him at McCormick Reaper Works, even though he refused to compensate them fairly. It was a catastrophic move for William, a sweet spirit who had inherited the McCormicks'

Virginia estate Walnut Grove, and wanted nothing more than to live out his days in its pastoral beauty. He and Leander nevertheless triumphed, investing their reaper company earnings in Chicago real estate, amassing considerable wealth and becoming core members of the Chicago establishment. It was a distinction that meant little to the displaced southern gentleman in William, who more than anything missed his beloved Virginia. But he succeeded as a northern businessman and even came within a hairbreadth of owning a piece of what was to be Chicago's greatest fortune. In January 1864, Marshall Field, then a young employee of the dry goods firm Cooley, Farwell & Company, called on him to ask for an investment in a store of his own. William wrote Cyrus, "He would like a connection with us," and added that Field was "sharpe & capable." But Cyrus hesitated. When the young merchant applied again in the fall, William thought of risking funds of his own, but this time it was he who hesitated, and the opportunity passed.

The gentle, tragic William was woefully aware of his delicate mental health, which continued to decline, and after an unsuccessful series of electric shock treatments, followed by equally futile water cures in New York and Cleveland, he committed himself to Illinois' Jacksonville State Hospital in August 1865. Just when his emotional balance was returning, he contracted what his Jacksonville doctor diagnosed as "dysentery of a typhoid nature" and died. He was fifty years old.

But to Joseph Medill, Robert's possible inherited instability was only a minor drawback to the union. The McCormicks, a clan of former slave-owning Virginians, had committed the greatest sin of all: they had been unrepentant, staunch southerners—Copperheads, in the parlance of the day—even after the great Cyrus moved his manufacturing operation northwest to the wheat harvest belt. In addition, there was a personal grudge between the two patriarchs. In an effort to counter the abolitionist influence of Medill's "dirty sheet," Cyrus had encroached on Joseph's professional turf to become publisher of the *Chicago Times*. Although he soon lost interest in the newspaper and sold it, this action forever tarnished all members of the reaping dynasty in Medill's eyes.

In addition, it developed that the prospective bridegroom, once a "poor" McCormick, had returned to that status. Amazingly, after William's death, his widow relinquished all claims to reaper rights on her children's behalf in exchange for a $400,000 lump sum, leaving three heirs to one of the nation's most affluent families without a claim to its riches. In addition, the considerable property William had accumulated would soon vanish with his son Robert, who foundered in McCormick, Adams & Company, the grain business he and a cousin, Cyrus Adams, operated in Chicago and St. Louis. But marry her handsome cavalier the willful Kate did in June 1876, exchanging her options as an eligible single woman to become Mrs. Robert Sanderson McCormick. Soon she was the wife of a man who was dependent upon her father not only for his job as *Tribune* literary critic but also for cash that would total $90,000 in loans he was never able to repay.

TWO YEARS LATER, Nellie followed her sister's matrimonial path. A haughty young woman of astonishing beauty, she had recently completed Miss Porter's School in Farmington, Connecticut, followed by Mademoiselle Vallett's in Paris for finishing. During the debutante season that followed, she met twenty-eight-year-old *Chicago Tribune* journalist Robert Wilson Patterson Jr., an employee of her father's paper who was her social peer. Patterson's father had established the Second Presbyterian Church, where much of fashionable Chicago worshipped, and it would be difficult to find, this side of the Medici popes, a man who matched the six-foot, six-inch Reverend Patterson in personifying the ultimate in both spiritual and social cachet. Late-nineteenth-century Chicago was said to be America's Presbyterian Rome, and Second Presbyterian to be Chicago's St. Peter's, but the unique blend of ecclesiastical and social prestige held by the Reverend Patterson did not end at city limits. He was also a founder of Lake

Forest, the Chicago suburb that continues today to be the city's seat of wealth and distinction. In 1855, when public disorder and foreign influences, as well as smoke, grime, noise and other urban by-products convinced his congregation to seek a bucolic refuge, Reverend Patterson and a small group of Presbyterians set out along a new rail line to find such a spot. Thirty miles north of the city, high on bluffs overlooking Lake Michigan, was unspoiled rolling terrain of leafy oak forests and romantically picturesque ravines. Floating through it all was the pure, cool lake breeze. The Presbyterians promptly acquired two thousand acres and commissioned a skilled landscape architect to lay out the exquisite, parklike village of Lake Forest.

Again both families were opposed to the union. Reverend Patterson, a southern moderate, detested Medill's political position and, although the Pattersons were close to the *Tribune*'s William Bross and his family, Joseph considered them another clan of Copperheads. Nevertheless, Nellie defied her father and married the man who had fleetingly caught her fancy, and like her sister she would soon regret the hasty action. Because of the times, both disasters were destined to last till death, and their effect would reverberate noisily in the next generation. Each was a fateful union; Kate and Robert's marriage was described by McCormick biographer John Tebbel as a merger of "the stubborn, aggressive, eccentric McCormicks" with "the willful, aristocratic, domineering Medills." And novelist and social historian Arthur Meeker added, "The Robert Sanderson McCormicks, whose blood was mixed with the brilliant journalistic Medills, were imperious with a dash of genius." Throw in the "religiously dogmatic Pattersons" and you have a genetic mix capable of producing not only four of America's most successful newspapers but also a level of uncontrolled behavior that would compete with a pair of world wars for battle headlines.

Although displeased with his daughters' choices, the indulgent Joseph did not stay angry long, ensuring that Robert Patterson's future at the *Tribune* was transformed by the marriage. Ironically, the talented young journalist's first newspaper job had been with Cyrus

McCormick's hated *Chicago Times*. Following that stint and a short one as managing editor of the religious monthly *Interior*, another publication despised by Medill, he had spent several years in various capacities at the *Tribune*. A Williams College graduate with a degree in classical literature, he was a gentle, honorable, almost poetic man, and like Medill tall, handsome and square-jawed. That Robert Patterson didn't join Nellie in relentless social games annoyed his wife, who considered him weak. But except in his dealings with his overbearing spouse, he was anything but ineffectual. He was the only man at the *Tribune*—or possibly anywhere—who would contradict Medill when he believed he was right. In one confrontation, Patterson resigned from the paper, after which Medill immediately reconsidered his position and insisted that Robert remain. He would become *Tribune* managing editor in 1882 and, within three years, begin to replace his often-traveling father-in-law as the power at the newspaper; from 1890 his title would be general manager. Patterson was a man of immense editorial integrity, a trait that impressed both his children and to which they would point repeatedly when they became editors of their own papers. His interest was more in producing a fine newspaper than in engaging in stormy politics, and under his direction the *Tribune* would be far more objective than in the Medill heyday.

WITH THE PROGRESSION of the century and increased consequence of the *Tribune*, Joseph and Kitty became entrenched in the city's establishment. Their lifestyle had continued to grow at an appropriate pace and by 1870 there were three servants: twenty-four-year-old Lizzie from Ireland; Julia Buck, a twenty-one-year-old German; and an Irish coachman, Frederick Buckley. Kitty, slightly less polished than her extraordinary husband but nearly as mobile, was a respected society matron and privileged to be selected one of twenty-four charter members of Fortnightly, organized in 1873 as Chicago's first woman's association. After leaving Washington Boulevard and living at a series of fashionable South Side addresses on Michigan Avenue, Calumet

Avenue and Lake Park Place, the Medills moved to the city's Near North Side in 1881.

Joseph paid one hundred thousand dollars to build a thirty-six-room brownstone at 101 Cass, on the northeast corner of what is now Ontario and Wabash. The dense façade of the solid French Renaissance–style mansion was significantly lightened by incorporating soaring windows, atypical of the era. Sunlight streamed into high-ceilinged rooms, illuminating the polished woods of the interior; two rooms on the ground floor were finished in mahogany, another in ebony, and the dining room was paneled in fine white oak. The final stroke of elegance was a ballroom that stretched across the full span of the mansion's third floor. Because crossing the river's reliable bridges now made Medill's trips to the *Tribune* a pleasure rather than a hazardous uncertainty, he enjoyed traveling down to the paper in a handsome carriage drawn by a pair of matched bays. But he did so infrequently; his home was so agreeable that it became his daytime base. The library, furnished with comfortable sofas and rocking chairs, held one of Chicago's finest private collections of books, predominantly history and science, no fiction, and next to the library was Joseph's study, where he spent most of his time. He wrote editorials at an old-style rolltop desk between two of the room's towering windows, and each morning met with Robert Patterson next to the study's welcoming fireplace. Afterward he returned to a routine of reading and writing.

Chicago of the early 1880s was as splendid as the new Medill house, providing Joseph and Kitty's daughters a fresh, glittering environment in which to raise their young families. Well into its post-Fire renaissance, the city had been rebuilt in red brick and creamy stone and, thanks to Medill's tenure as mayor, the central portion was without wood construction. Furthermore, the destruction of the business district had produced a vacuum for a dazzling new concept in commercial buildings, attracting skilled engineers who became the celebrated architects of the renowned Chicago School. Laying a foundation for further civic beauty was the massive debris left by the conflagration, moved to the edge of the lake and eventually transformed into the grassy stretch of Grant Park, and later Millennium Park. With its heightened fame as an American metropolis, Chicago was on the agenda for fashionable visiting foreigners, who invariably marveled at the city's revival. Lady Duffus Hardy, a well-traveled Englishwoman, wrote of the chic stores on State and Clark streets, with dry goods and millinery shops displaying window dressings "that might stand side by side with our fashionable establishments at home." Residential neighborhoods had their own new flair; the young Pattersons lived in a substantial Near North Side house on Superior Street a few doors east of today's Wabash Avenue, but the Robert McCormicks had to make do with undistinguished rentals nearby: first, a narrow, vertical house and then an apartment, both on Ontario Street. Ironically this put them at the edge of a posh section of the city known as "McCormickville," a cluster of almost a dozen luxurious mansions owned by McCormicks who had retained capital, or at least their stake in the reaper company.

If Kate and Nellie had chosen gentle, docile men whom they could dominate and would grow to despise, Joseph Medill, perhaps unknowingly, facilitated this advantage, giving each of the young women a degree of affluence and reflected power exceeding that of her husband. Both sisters had married into what was considered Chicago aristocracy, but there was a discrepancy in the professional status of the two husbands. One was destined for editorship of the city's most prestigious newspaper, and the other was merely a failed grain merchant and literary critic without further prospects. The intense rivalry between the sisters increased, with Nellie preceding Kate as a social power in an arena that mattered greatly to both. "Getting ahead" became the key phase in an ongoing contest between the two and, for once, Kate got ahead when she gave birth in May 1877 to the first Medill grandchild, Joseph Medill McCormick, forever to be known both formally and casually as Medill.

Less than two years later, in January 1879, both women delivered babies, and each was ecstatic. Nellie Patterson was catching up with her sister by giving birth to a son, also named for his grandfather, but this Joseph Medill would always be Joseph or, more often, Joe. Kate, who had yearned for a little girl to pamper and clothe in frilly dresses, received exactly that in little Katrina McCormick. When the baby died six months later, Kate was distraught but soon became pregnant with another child, whom, according to gossip at the time, she vowed she would name Katrina II, whether the baby was a boy or girl. The birth brought Kate two disturbing pieces of news: first, the child was a boy—the future Colonel Robert R. McCormick—but, even more upsetting, the doctor informed Kate she would never again give birth, depriving her of ever having the darling little girl of whom she dreamed. After much convincing by her family, Kate agreed to give her baby boy a masculine name, Robert Sanderson McCormick Jr.—which he didn't keep long. Recalling her Medill grandmother's connection with Anne Rutherford, mother of Sir Walter Scott, she switched the middle name to Rutherford, but addressed the boy as Roberta, and sometimes even Katrina. Though she dressed little Roberta in girls' clothing, this was not as bizarre a custom in the Victorian era as it would be today. And eventually the name was shortened to Bertie, a family nickname that continued throughout his life. As a pre-Freudian woman, it probably never occurred to Kate that raising a boy as a girl was anything but wholesome; however, it really didn't matter. Her ambitions—and full attention—were pinned on her first son, Medill; she was intensely aware that her greatest asset was her position as mother of the generation's oldest male.

The last of Joseph's grandchildren, a daughter born to Nellie and Robert Patterson in November 1881, completed the generation of formidable twentieth-century media figures. The baby was christened Elinor for her mother, but because Joe called her Sissy, soon family members, including Grandfather Medill, were doing the same. She would change the spelling of both names, but to the world she would be known as Cissy Patterson. The family was now whole; however, its complex interactions had only begun.

As the marriage of Robert and Nellie became increasingly icy, they addressed each other as Mr. and Mrs. Patterson, and Robert retreated to his stable to drink among his horses or to the Chicago Club, where the genial male companionship was more forgiving than what he was experiencing at home. It is unclear whether there was basic instability in his character or if it was a result of his tragic marriage and increased alcohol consumption, but Patterson would soon experience periods of profound emotional disturbance. Not unsurprisingly, this weakness became a weapon in his wife's hands, an ominous example she held up for her children. In addition, there was the strong suggestion, veiled in Victorian euphemism, of serious sexual disappointment on the part of Mrs. Patterson, though its nature was never clear.

The relationships swirling about the spoiled, headstrong sisters became increasingly troubled; as years passed, they would refuse to speak to each other and begin communicating only through Joe and Bert. In the younger generation, Cissy openly adored her brother and became infatuated with her unstable cousin Medill. Soon Joe was flirting with socialism, and throughout it all Bert was entirely disregarded. The ticket Kate held to *Tribune* regency through Medill's seniority in his generation was a precious permit and the only advantage she had over her sister, giving him an importance eclipsing that of her younger son, whom she virtually ignored. Although Medill had the edge, there was always a chance that Joe—second in line of succession—might outmaneuver him, transferring to Nellie the position of *Tribune* queen mother, with the means and influence to rule Chicago society. Thus, unable to carve out careers of their own, the sisters' roles were to manipulate behind the scenes through husbands and sons, with each becoming territorial, and fearful that the other's son would "get ahead" of her own.

AS YOUNGSTERS, THE McCormick boys lived alone on the top floor of their parents' rented house, accompanied only by an autocratic Scottish nanny who terrified the children while providing their earliest tutoring. The boys probably saw less of their parents than did other Victorian children of their station and, when they did, the maternal ambition surrounding Medill substituted for a mother's love, but his brother had not even that. To Bert's credit, there was an acceptance of his lot in the family, and he always exhibited fondness toward his favored sibling, without resentment toward a brother who more or less ignored him. Despite slights from Kate, Bert treated her with affection and respect; it wasn't until he was well into maturity that he commented, "My mother hated me," and then added, "My mother and aunt were real bitches."

Lost in the drama of inheritance rights and almost completely overlooked, Bert's life was a solitary one, causing him early to adopt a lifelong attitude of aloofness. When his great-aunt Nettie McCormick, the reaper king's saintly widow, recognized how alone the little boy was, she invited him to her house to spend the night, which he refused. "She tried to adopt me," he complained. But Bert was not the only twentieth-century press lord whom Nettie McCormick wished to "adopt." In 1905, an American missionary to China accompanied by his seven-year-old son called on her to ask for funds for his Christian mission. Nettie was so captivated by the child that she offered to raise him in her household. After praying over the matter, the youngster's parents declined her offer, but Nettie nevertheless paid for much of the boy's education and remained his angel and confidante for the rest of her life. The beneficiary of her largesse was Henry R. Luce, who matured to cofound *Time* magazine and preside over its sister publications, which included *Life, Fortune, Sports Illustrated* and eventually *People*. The two media giants would become rivals of titanic proportions, with Harry Luce ridiculing McCormick through decades of witty gibes in *Time* magazine. During the newsmagazine's irreverent 1930s, '40s and '50s, as its influence grew to become among the most powerful voices in the nation, there was not a family it pummeled with more frequency than the McCormick-Patterson clan.

There were no winners in the dynasty's third generation. Even Medill, who exhibited the least damage as a child, would limp through adulthood on the arm of a strong wife. And because the fundamental elements of civility and consideration for others were not practiced by the sisters, their offspring, particularly the Pattersons, did not receive the usual foundation for good manners conveyed to children. Bert, whose superficial etiquette as he matured would be impeccable, benefited from exposure to an exceedingly courteous father. Later his aunt Nellie wrote, "He is self-contained and a dutiful son. . . . He and Medill are both too well-bred to make scenes—they are like their father & *my* father." Joe's basic gift for empathy led him to exhibit thoughtful—although sometimes uneven—manners as an adult, unlike his sister. Cissy learned a few surface skills, perfect posture perhaps, and surely graceful carriage, through Nellie's insistence that she practice walking with a book on her head. "I am a snob," Nellie told her daughter, "and what's more I intend to be a snob. . . . I'd like to know where you'd be today if your mother and father hadn't been snobs." Born with a journalist's memory for the language, her mother's words were so imbedded in Cissy's mind that she would use them in her autobiographical novel *Fall Flight*.

Cissy's analyst—also a sympathetic friend—wrote many years later, "To understand Cissy you must understand her childhood, because that is when the pattern is shaped, and the pattern sticks." She reacted to her upbringing by vacillating between a need for the luxurious life of a European aristocrat and a desire to hobnob with cowboys and kitchen help. As a child she often reacted with episodes of minor rebellion, once climbing the steeple of St. James Church, now Chicago's venerated Episcopal cathedral, at age ten, or on another occasion—to her mother's horror—operating a lemonade stand in front of the Patterson house. She would recall these symbols of freedom in *Fall Flight*, written in midlife when comparing an upheaval created by her book's heroine to rebellious incidents in her own girlhood. "It was like ringing doorbells in the old days in Chicago; like climbing church steeples, and walking down Clark Street in the dark. It was like all the forbidden excitements of her childhood."

As soon as Joe could select his own companions, the future founder of the *New York Daily News* would consort with socialists, derelicts and barflies. And both junior Pattersons would seek to dominate their own children as their mother dominated them—but with less success. Joe might have withered under the weight of the overbearing Nellie;

instead he aggressively rebelled against her conformity and relentless social climbing, and, with the Mcdill sisters routinely suggesting genetic imperfection in their spouses, there was always the lingering hint that it had taken hold in the heirs. In adulthood, Joe wrote in a letter to his wife, "I *don't* come of good blood—and I can never never be much good. But I'll try, I promise you, and never quit trying to be at least a little better than blood." As they matured, Cissy would harden, like their mother, with Joe adopting the sensitivity of their father.

It cannot be emphasized too greatly that Joe was Cissy's rock, her anchor, throughout childhood and for the remainder of his life. In the early years, her father and grandfather joined him as a trio of men she loved beyond all others, and each reciprocated. With her father, it wasn't merely that she adored him and he was devoted to her; there was an element of vengeance in their relationship. When she climbed onto his lap and snuggled in close to him, it demonstrated to Nellie that both father and daughter preferred each other to her. Another lap Cissy loved climbing onto was her grandfather's. Joseph Medill saw extraordinary qualities in his granddaughter, without the negative traits of his daughters. He talked with Cissy seriously, and she listened. His conversation with her was often very grown-up, laced with his views on nineteenth-century American history and journalism—subjects he knew and had experienced with an intimacy that few others had or ever would. He sensed in Cissy a capacity that surpassed that of his grandsons and he fed that intellect. When she was away at school or traveling with Nellie, he wrote to her regularly, giving her advice, love and understanding.

But while her relationships with these men were important, they could not compensate for the love and support her mother withheld. Cissy would never recover from the sense of her beautiful mother's disapproval and the feeling that Nellie thought her awkward and unlovely. It was by no means paranoia; Nellie made no secret of her disappointment that Cissy had not inherited her extraordinary beauty. "Your teeth aren't as good as mine," she would say, "but they're even and white." Or "your mouth is a little full. Try sucking it in at the corners." Then there was the thoughtless reminiscing: "I was so handsome, Mama wouldn't let me walk down Main Street alone, men stared so. My bust was developed like I was twenty-five. . . . You're very underdeveloped." More words from her beautiful mother that would remain etched in Cissy's memory to be mirrored years later in *Fall Flight*. Only once did Cissy remember her mother uttering a positive remark: "Your shoulders have a pretty line to them." Scant compensation, if teeth, mouth, breasts and general appearance are lacking.

THE TALL, DIGNIFIED Mrs. Joseph Medill had stepped willingly into the lady bountiful role expected of the wives of successful men, and throughout her years in Chicago she served on a spectrum of charitable boards, societies and committees, always in the spirit of genuine concern for those she was aiding. It was an example that seems to have made little impression on her daughters, whereas, Louise de Koven Bowen, a contemporary of the girls, wrote, "I had been brought up with the idea that some day [*sic*] I would inherit a fortune, and I was always taught that the responsibility of money was great, and that God would hold me accountable for the manner in which I used my talents." Although Louise Bowen was one of the city's most persistent do-gooders, eventually serving as president of the Hull House Association, she was more typical of her generation than Kate and Nellie, whom the spirit of noblesse oblige eluded. One striking exception occurred two days after the Fire, when the girls, then eighteen and sixteen and still on agreeable terms, joined their mother in distributing clothing and household goods that had been sent from other cities. Their cooperation in post-Fire benevolence continued through the following year. From then on the altruistic choices of the sisters were governed more by pragmatism than compassion.

Organizations promoting charitable activities and women's rights had been in place since the late 1860s, but even without a schedule of meetings for improving the world around her, there were many ways a woman of social position could occupy herself. There were Plato clubs, Browning societies and groups for studying such subjects as pre-Raphaelite art, the history of fiction, or pre-Shakespearean dramatists. Socialites gathered regularly to practice speaking French and German or to raise funds in support of excavations in Greece. The Medill sisters, including the much younger Josie, were frequent participants in these activities. Josie, who trailed the others by more than a decade, never married and managed to live decorously with her parents without the turmoil generated by their other daughters. In 1887, she and Kate became charter members of the Friday Club, organized "to encourage every literary and artistic inspiration."

Similarly important to the four Medill women and their peers was wardrobe maintenance; fashion was vital to nineteenth-century Chicago, with its ladies keenly aware of what their contemporaries in New York and Paris were wearing. A Chicago woman's spirit of competition with her sisters in New York and Paris was not unrealistic; *Godey's Lady's Book*, *Dressmakers' and Milliners' Guide* and *Report on Fashion* were publications meticulous in providing detailed illustrations and descriptions of the season's fashion trends. These books were scrupulously studied by the city's milliners and dressmakers, who copied their models to create the wardrobes of the Medill women and their well-dressed peers. And the dry goods firm Field & Leiter, succeeded by Marshall Field's, carried the finest imported fabrics and trimmings available anywhere, with shipments arriving weekly.

The busy lives of fashionable ladies were also filled with lists of visits to be made, letters and notes to be written, menus to be planned, and lunches, teas and dinner parties to attend and give, each with its own protocol. An essential ritual for gentlewomen was that of visiting, or making formal calls on one's peers—a custom the Medill women practiced with regularity. By 1876 Chicago had a complex visiting procedure to follow, documented in *The Chicago Society Directory and Ladies' Visiting and Shopping Guide*, which also carried a list of Chicago's elite women with their addresses. Ladies living on the North Side received callers on Monday afternoons between two and five, South Siders were "at home" during the same hours on Tuesdays and a rigid etiquette governed how the calls were to be made.

By the late 1880s, Kate and Nellie were moving through their gaslit parlors with gallant style. There was never quite enough money to satisfy their lofty ambitions but the two women were admirable in stretching the resources their husbands provided, and whatever additional funds they might coax from their father. On Monday afternoons, each sat at her respective tea table receiving callers by the fire. Between visitors, she might stitch on a piece of fabric in an embroidery hoop while listening for the tinkle of the bell at the front door. When it wasn't a footman with a visiting card followed by a guest, it might be the postman with another packet of letters, one of several such deliveries each day. The children, when the sisters saw them at all, served as accessories. The well-barbered McCormick and Patterson sons wore sailor suits with high laced shoes and Cissy was always beautifully clad in a becoming dress; in the winter she might wear a fur tippet and matching muff over a tailored wool coat. The outfits were selected by their mothers, and nineteenth-century children wore what they were told to wear. Joe was about eight when Nellie managed to persuade him into a blue velvet Lord Fauntleroy suit with knee breeches and an immense white lace collar and matching cuffs; he wore it, but that experience alone might have propelled him toward his adult penchant for extreme down-dressing.

There was an easing up in the summer, a time for resort travel. Although exhausting for their mothers, the children adored these holidays and were left with marvelous memories of long, aimless interludes of warm, sunny days. While separately making the rounds of Newport, Bar Harbor and other fashionable summer communities, Kate and Nellie each stretched her limited budget to lease a large house, staff it properly and contrive to join the "right" clubs and entertain the "best" people. It was never satisfactory for either, because their peers were always richer women who the sisters invariably felt were of inferior stock, but both sustained the effort.

THE MEDILL SISTERS'
UPWARD SCRAMBLE

AFTER years of frustration, the Robert McCormicks' future expanded in late 1888 when President-elect Benjamin Harrison appointed Robert Todd Lincoln his minister to England. At Kate's behest, Joseph appealed to Harrison to throw a minor British diplomatic post in his son-in-law's direction and, as expected, the junior Lincoln was delighted to accommodate his father's loyal supporter. To complete the package, Medill augmented the post's scant compensation with sufficient cash for the couple to live and entertain in a manner suitable for American diplomats. Thus in April 1889, Robert Sanderson McCormick became second secretary of the American legation, launching the diplomatic career of a man who more than anything else was genial, polite and diplomatic.

Now on even social ground with her sister, a triumphant Kate was at last on her way to fulfilling the destiny to which she had so long aspired. In his memoirs, Bert presented an assessment of the couple's qualifications, "My parents were splendid diplomats because they had no inferiority complex. My father, one of the last of the pre–Civil War school, looked upon himself as of the Virginia aristocracy, the equal of any aristocracy in Europe. My mother reached her viewpoint by another route. Her father had been an intimate . . . of President Lincoln, and also a supporter and intimate friend of General Grant." What Bert didn't mention is that Kate's memory of an intimacy both she and her father shared with Grant had grown with the years. Although Medill and Grant knew each other well over a period of time, it was not the intense relationship the *Tribune* editor had with Lincoln. And as she stepped onto the international stage, Kate was moved to tinker with her name and genealogy, slipping in her maternal grandmother's maiden name, Van Etten, as her middle name and altering another ancestral surname, Westfall, to the more aristocratic and Dutch sounding West Vael. She also saw that Bert was known by his middle name, Rutherford, at his schools in England and later in the United States.

The new second secretary and his wife established themselves in a rented house in Mayfair's Brook Street, between Hyde Park and Grosvenor Square, where Medill and Bert shared a room facing the square. The boys, formerly students at the University School in Chicago, were sent away for the first time. Dispatched to Harrow, Medill became a schoolmate of the young Winston Churchill, and Bert entered Ludgrove in Middlesex, attended by Churchill's cousin Shane Leslie. Young Leslie, whose mother was the American Jennie Churchill's sister, warmed to Bert as a countryman and became one of his few boyhood friends. Theirs was a casual relationship, but one that would continue throughout their lives. Of Ludgrove, Sir Shane wrote, "The school was gentlemanly and happy—it collected Norfolk squires, Queen Mother's four brothers, the Bowes-Lyons. . . . It has the finest reputation of any Prep School in England." The English years were critical in Bert's development because they formed his negative attitudes concerning that nation—views ultimately to be foisted upon *Chicago Tribune* readers and traditionally thought to have been formed by his English public school education. Sir Shane's theory instead was that Bert's attitude stemmed from the fact that Prime Minister Lord Salisbury snubbed his father. "One cup of tea at Hatfield in the last century," Churchill's cousin posited, "could have changed the status of Britain in Chicago journalism in the present century."

There were frequent trips to the Continent during the English years, with childhood adventures the adult Bert delighted in recounting, and possibly embellishing. During a visit to an elegant German spa with his parents, he remembered being out for a stroll on the grounds one day when the family encountered the future King Edward VII and his nephew Kaiser Wilhelm II. Bert, who was dressed in a child's sailor suit with the name of a British ship on its cap, was infuriated when the guttural Wilhelm sputtered, "Ah, a nice little English boy." The anti-British Bert blurted out, "I am an American," which amused the Kaiser and produced the boy's demand for a new ribbon for his cap, one with an *American* insignia. He was accompanied by both parents on this occasion, but there seems to have been loose supervision during many of his escapades. On one of these, the eleven-year-old was visiting the south of France with his mother and became acquainted with another boy his age. Somehow the two acquired a small boat, which they used to sail toward the horizon with Africa as their naïve destination. Happily, before they were out of sight of land a larger boat caught up with their little vessel and escorted them back to shore, putting an end to a possibly perilous caper, which the adult Bert recalled only with fondness and amusement. A year later, he and Medill spent the summer living in Versailles at the household of a French widow with the purpose of becoming fluent in French. In addition to perfecting their language skills, the boys' education was broadened through exposure to their hostess's unusual habit of taking arsenic as a recreational drug.

BERT WAS ELEVEN and Medill fourteen in the summer of 1891, when their mother's twenty-five-year-old sister Josie joined the family for the London social season. A highlight of the visit was her presentation to the queen, after which she and Kate left for a three-month tour of Touraine. The two sisters traveled back to Paris at the end of the year, and in early January Josie caught a cold, which quickly developed into "grave pulmonary congestion in both lungs" accompanied by a high fever. Diagnosed with influenza complicated by bronchitis, she seemed to be recovering, but on January 8, she relapsed and pneumonia set in. She lived only until the next night.

The following morning, January 10, 1892, Kate, exhausted and heartbroken, sent the following cable to her parents at their winter home in Pasadena, California. Because periods and commas could not be transmitted by wire, it read:

DEAREST MOTHER AND FATHER YOU MUST BEAR THE GREATEST SORROW OF YOUR LIVES NOW OUR DARLING JOSIE DIED LAST NIGHT TEN THIRTY PAINLESSLY AT LAST BUT HAVING SUFFERED MUCH FROM SUFFOCATION TWO PREVIOUS DAYS BORE SUFFER-ING WITH MOST PATIENT COURAGE AND DID NOT APPREHEND AT ANY TIME THAT SHE WAS IN DANGER DOCTOR HAD NO ANXIETY TILL FRIDAY MORNING

She ended by cautioning them not to leave the warmth of California:

WE WILL BRING OUR DARLING HOME AND GO AT ONCE OUT TO YOU HAVE BEAUTIFUL LIFE SIZE PORTRAIT WHICH SHE HAD TAKEN AS SURPRISE FOR YOU YOUR DEVOTED DAUGHTER

The *New York Herald European Edition* published an account of the choral service held for Josie a few days later at the American Church in the Avenue de l'Alma. Although Robert McCormick was seated in the front pew with the two boys, "Mrs. McCormick herself was forbidden by her physician to attend, she having totally broken down under the strain of the last few days." The *Herald* went on to report, "the coffin was almost hidden under masses of flowers, principally camellias and white roses," and the service closed with the " 'Dead March in Soul' played on the organ with powerful effect." Josie's body was returned to Chicago for a funeral in the third-floor ballroom of her parents' Cass Street house; after the service, the room's doors were closed and the vast space never used again. Her casket was transported by slow horse-drawn hearse to a vault at Graceland Cemetery to await inter-ment following the return of Joseph and Kitty in the spring.

The young woman's sudden death was a shock to all the Medills, none more than Joseph and Kitty, in whose house she had continued to live. Both would feel the loss of their youngest daughter profoundly on a daily basis, particularly Joseph; she had been his companion whenever his wife retreated to the family's country house in Elmhurst, as she often did. He most missed their frequent carriage drives through the city together, so similar to trips with his young family during their early days in Chicago. Outwardly his grief was expressed through the endowment in her memory of a unit of beds in a Paris hospital. Kitty never recovered from the loss, which further weakened her frail constitution. And Kate was devastated; the trauma of losing her sister so suddenly and unexpectedly, intensified by an inability to prevent the death, sent her descending into a spiral of depression. She had witnessed how quickly a young person can be swept away and became obsessed by possibilities of mortality for either herself or her elder son—upon whose future career at the *Tribune* her ambitions were founded—extending the despondency for many months.

THE FOLLOWING YEAR, 1893, was the most spectacular in Chicago history. Sixty years after the remote frontier outpost was incorporated as a town, it had become the second-largest city in the country, a milestone celebrated with extravagance. The opportunity first presented itself in 1889 when city fathers learned that New York's leadership was scheming to host a great international fair to mark the four hundredth anniversary of Christopher Columbus's arrival on the North American continent. The celebration, the World's Columbian Exposition, promised to be a magnificent occasion and feisty Chicago dared to compete for the honor of hosting it. But the prize would not come easily; the pledge of a vast amount of money was required and it took the mighty force of Joseph Medill to move his fellow citizens to actually raise the cash. "Chicagoans must not expect that such a fat morsel as the World's Fair will come to the city without an effort," he wrote in one of a torrent of *Tribune* editorials. "Such a golden apple will not fall into their laps unless they shake the tree. They must work for the prize, and must understand that it will cost money to get it." And Joseph was specific about the sort of tree to be shaken. "It takes too many . . . ten dollar subscriptions to raise a million," he continued, calling upon a single Chicago millionaire to volunteer to "break the ice today with a hundred thousand dollar subscription. . . . Who will speak first?" This was a challenge the ostentatious goat-whiskered George Pullman could not resist; the palace car prince stepped forward with the requested pledge and his Prairie Avenue neighbors fought to line up behind him. Their response was so wholehearted that only Chicago among American cities was capable of committing to the $20 million cash expense for the fair. The resulting extravaganza, which missed the official quadricentennial date by but a year, was extraordinary. At nearly ten times the size of the 1889 Paris world's fair, the World's Columbian Exposition of 1893 was the greatest such exhibition ever to have been mounted.

Within months, and as if by magic, the glistening city, created by Chicago architect Daniel Burnham and his team of leading national architectural firms, emerged along the lake on the South Side. It was a new realm, a neoclassic fairyland that managed to combine the exotic, the ultramodern and the dreamily fantastic with the classically beautiful; it was a phenomenon like none before. The enchanted metropolis, surrounding a glistening artificial basin, was completely white and bathed in the new miracle of electric light—stupefying to even the most jaded 1893 eye. Ordinary people from throughout the country mortgaged their houses or cashed in burial savings to come to Chicago that summer, along with Spanish nobility, Buffalo Bill Cody, Florenz Ziegfeld Jr., Diamond Jim Brady and an exotic dancer known as Little Egypt, the sensation of the fair. After urging the endeavor upon the city, Joseph had stepped up as one of forty-five guarantors who pledged support of the awesome event; Nellie became a member of the prestigious Board of Lady Managers for Bertha Palmer's pioneering Woman's Building; and Robert McCormick served as the exposition's official American commissioner in London, a position for which he took a leave of absence from his post there. He and Kate returned with their boys to Chicago for the fair's launch and remained through its duration.

The year was also the beginning of a link between the Medills and another prominent Chicago family. Throughout the decade of the fair, newspaper society writers focused on stories about Florence and Alice Higinbotham, daughters of exposition president Harlow Higinbotham, a Chicago leader who was also a partner of Joseph's bête noir, Marshall Field. The comings and goings of the pretty girls, including such incidentals as their return from an early autumn holiday in the Adirondacks, were duly reported. Writers were especially interested in Alice's December 1898 debut at the family's house on fashionable Michigan Avenue, where, of the eight hundred coveted invitations issued for the reception, only a select twenty were also for the dinner that followed. Previously, during the year of the fair, the *Tribune* society page had reported on the equestrian expertise of Florence and noted that her younger sibling, Alice, "is as good a horsewoman as her sister and handles the ribbons as well as any experienced jehu. Her two pretty ponies are at present enjoying a vacation in the country while Miss Alice is at school at Farmington." What the article did not mention was that during her term at Miss Porter's in Farmington, Miss Alice was becoming very friendly with another Chicago student at school in the East, Joseph Medill Patterson.

The fair gave a boost to Chicago's economic development as well as its image, with the construction of stylish new hotels and other amenities to accommodate visitors. Residents and tourists alike marveled at the steam-powered elevated train, which sped them along a scenic route from business district to fairgrounds for a five-cent fare. It seemed that both the city and its inhabitants presented their best for visitors who swarmed Chicago to see the White City. Julian Ralph, a visiting American journalist, wrote, "Their stylishness is the first striking characteristic of the women of Chicago. It is a Parisian quality, apparent in New York first and Chicago next, among our cities. The number of women who dress well in Chicago is very remarkable and only there and in New York do the shop-girls and working women closely follow the prevailing modes. Chicago leads New York in the employment of women in business. It is not easy to find an office or a store in which they are not at work as secretaries, accountants, cashiers, type-writers, saleswomen, or clerks." The fair also marked Chicago's leap into the modern world. Soon the wealthy in homes throughout the city were turning on lights equipped with electric bulbs in place of the old gas jets. Gas had moved to their fireplaces, and certain of the rich had telephones. The world of the Medills had changed, improved perhaps, but it would never be quite the same.

AFTER THE SEMINAL year of the fair, Kate and Robert returned to London, leaving Bert in the United States with his brother to attend Groton, the Massachusetts preparatory school where Medill and Joe Patterson were already students. If Joseph Medill, who engineered the admission of his grandsons to the most Brahmin of American educational institutions, had set out to find a patch of New England turf in which to nurture the boys' insecurities and biases, he could not have found more fertile ground. Groton was founded in 1884 by the Reverend Endicott Peabody with the financial backing of J. P. Morgan and modeled on the Eton/Harrow–style English public school. Designed to produce "Christian gentlemen," Groton and its headmaster, Reverend Peabody, provided the model for the late Louis Auchincloss's peerless 1964 novel, *The Rector of Justin*. During the Peabody era, virtually all his students were males from insular, privileged backgrounds; therefore the rector believed it essential to refrain from coddling his boys.

Groton students were not coddled. They spent frigid Massachusetts winters shivering in drafty classrooms and hallways, sleeping in unheated cubicles and showering in icy water pumped up from the Nashua River; they attended chapel twice a day, competed in myriad athletics and participated in nonstop activity of every sort. Months of perpetual bone-piercing cold affected Bert so severely that he was routinely pulled from school during the winter months to nurse bouts of what was characterized as pneumonia, and sent to the warmer climes his grandfather seasonally sought for himself and Kitty. A primary aim of Reverend Peabody was to keep the boys pure for their God through the vulnerable years of hormonal turbulence. To offset any possibility of carnal temptation, students were strongly discouraged from forming close friendships, forbidden to walk, sit or stand in pairs, and nowhere was there privacy. Bathroom facilities and sleeping cubicles were without doors, and hooks on cubicle walls took the place of closets. If, heaven forbid, two boys should form a "close friendship," it would require colossal diligence and imagination to consummate such a relationship anywhere within the Peabody orbit.

Joe, already resisting Nellie's social-climbing pretentions, detested anything that smacked of snobbery or elitism, and he loathed regimentation of any sort. It is difficult therefore to know whether he objected more to Groton's excessive scheduling or to being surrounded by the rich kids he despised. If he was the chronic revolutionary that one of his instructors portrayed, the hypergentility of the Groton atmosphere did nothing to temper his views. Unfortunately, Nellie sent him off to school in an English blazer with gold buttons, which the school's old boys found comical in contrast with his obviously midwestern American enunciation. The prevailing accent, St. Grottlesex lockjaw incorporating a broad-*a*, dropped-*r* pronunciation, was not far from the diction the McCormick boys had acquired in England, but Joe went out of his way to preserve an Illinois twang. There was nothing young Patterson had in common with Groton and he was very lonely there, fervently wishing to drop out and return to Chicago. His daily letters home are heartbreaking: "I will die if you don't take me away. I do wish I was ded [*sic*] only I know I will soon see you. If you don't I will die. I think it cruel to keep me here. In the name of mercy take me away. Please, please, please take me away. I will die." When his father convinced him that leaving would be unmanly, he forced himself to overcome his natural disinterest in athletics to build up his body and compete in sports. But because he read what interested him rather than the assigned books, his grades were never more than average.

When Bert complained to his father about the snobbery of his classmates, he was instructed, "You tell them that they are descended from Boston tradesmen while you are descended from Virginia gentlemen." This audacious reversal was so effective that Reverend Peabody called the boy in for a lecture about how Groton frowned upon "sectional arguments." Even so, Bert's American boarding school scars would last a lifetime. If his English upbringing infected him with Anglophobia, the Groton years gave him an equally fervent dislike for American easterners—but revenge was on the way. The New Yorkers and Bostonians who dismissed the three Chicago boys as backwoods primitives would—like the English—live to suffer decades of editorial retribution from the future Colonel McCormick.

A more personal animosity was brewing during the Groton years. Among Bert's aristocratic schoolmates was one who like him had a famously domineering mother; the difference was that, while Kate virtually ignored Bert, Sara Delano Roosevelt deluged her precious only son with attention. The contrast was most startling when the two boys were patients in the Groton infirmary during a scarlet fever quarantine. Although visitors were not allowed to enter sick rooms, Mrs. Roosevelt traveled to Groton, climbed a ladder outside Franklin's window and read aloud to him through it, while nary a word was heard from Mrs. McCormick, who remained an ocean away. This was merely the first brush the grandchildren of Joseph Medill would have with the future president and his extended family over the next half century in a pair of volatile, and extremely public, scenarios.

School vacations were in vivid contrast to the eastern academic year. The McCormick boys spent classic American summers riding and hunting at ranches in Montana and Idaho, shooting polar bear in Hudson Bay, joining an Arizona cattle drive and camping out in the woods of Michigan with a supply of firecrackers to ward off wild animals. During one school hiatus Great-Aunt Nettie McCormick hired a man to instruct Bert in the practical application of the new marvel, electricity. With a natural aptitude for mechanical activities, he quickly became so adept at installing doorbells that he turned it into a small business in the neighborhood around Ontario Street. But the carefree seasonal respite always ended too soon, and waiting for the boys at the end of each summer was Groton, where Reverend Peabody's entire student body prepared for university acceptance in either the school's Yale Division or its Harvard counterpart.

The three Medill grandsons were headed for Yale, which each found much less restricting than Groton. After the tight control and continuous activity of the structured boarding school, Joe and the Mc-Cormicks discovered an amazing degree of freedom in college. They could eat what and where they wanted to eat, study or not study, go out at night if they wished, drink, smoke, hang out at Mory's or Tontine's, participate in the long-standing traditions of Bottle Night, Washington's Birthday and Dewey Day, or just spend time in general foolishness. Medill, the first to graduate, went straight through four years of Yale and directly to a job at the *Tribune*, acquiring a serious drinking habit in the process. Joe, on the other hand, graduated in a not-so-gentlemanly six years, spending what should have been his Yale freshman year herding cattle in Wyoming and northern Mexico, and taking a leave of absence following his junior year to dabble in foreign corresponding for William Randolph Hearst's *New York Journal*. Later he was uncharacteristically sentimental about his alma mater in telling the *New York Times* that its students' "love for Yale is like the love of a knight for his King or a lady." But he eventually reversed himself by writing to his daughter Alicia when she was school age, "Groton was very strict and made me step around and do what I didn't want to do. . . . Yale was very easy and I got away with murder. The consequence is that I look back at Groton with great affection and I am glad I went there, whereas I look back at Yale without any affection." But he did glean material for one of the most successful of the novels he would write, *A Little Brother of the Rich*, in which its hero Paul Potter is a poor midwestern boy who attends Yale only to be corrupted by his classmates' worldliness.

Bert blossomed and became far more gregarious at New Haven than he had been in previous schools, and he didn't object when Rutherford, his middle name and official school designation, was twisted into the fond nickname Rubberfoot. He was accepted by Alpha Delta

Phi fraternity and, like Joe and Medill, was tapped his senior year by Scroll and Key. He also embraced polo, a decision that would give him satisfaction for many years. But he did not become involved with the opposite sex. Kate's recurring advice to her sons, who were suddenly beyond the reach of her own or anyone else's close supervision, was "Don't dally with a poor girl; you may have to marry her." She needn't have worried.

THE LAST DECADE of the nineteenth century brought the inevitable twilight years of the dynasty founders. Both Joseph and Kitty were from good stock, with long-lived forebears, and each seemed destined for an extended old age despite infirmities. Joseph's mother had lived until late 1889, when she died of "dropsy" at her home in Canton, Ohio, at eighty-nine. And an Ohio newspaper published an article in 1883 praising Kitty's father, ninety-year-old Judge Patrick, commenting that he was "still able to walk uptown every day and attended the Pioneer Picnic on August 10." Even so, Kitty had been consumptive for much of her adulthood, possibly infecting Josie and making her vulnerable to the illness that took her life so suddenly. As early as May 1863 Joseph had written his brother William that his wife's health was so poor he "must take steps to improve" it. But her frailty continued and two months after the 1871 fire, when she was the wife of the new mayor, Chicago matron Annie Hitchcock wrote a friend that "Mrs. M. worked for weeks on the Special Relief Committee but her health threatening to give way she resigned." The resilient Kitty lived for more than another two decades, continuing as Joseph's close and devoted companion, with every appearance of living well into old age.

During their later years, the couple retreated each October to the warmth of their house in Altadena, California, just north of Pasadena and near the winter home of Chicago mapmaker Andrew McNally. There they remained throughout the bitter midwestern winters, not returning home until June. Despite the warmer climate, Kitty suffered an acute attack of grippe in 1891, followed by a spell of bronchitis that was unresponsive to either medicine or weather change. In June she drafted a will, handwritten on her personal notepaper. "I desire," she wrote, "that my diamonds shall be evenly divided between my two daughters Mrs. Katherine Medill McCormick and Mrs. Elinor Medill Patterson with the exception of a three stone diamond ring I wear— that ring I wish given to Sissy Patterson." She was confined to the Cass Street house during much of 1893 and 1894 while Joseph traveled alone, faithfully communicating in a devoted stream of letters, touchingly addressing her as "My beloved."

The crisis came in the summer of 1894, when the misplaced paternalism of George Pullman brought bitter strikes from his employees and the notorious Pullman riots. Joseph was infuriated by the inflexibility of the brilliant but arrogant tycoon—as well as his own inability to produce peace in the labor dispute—and he suffered a heart attack. Nursing her husband back to health was more than Kitty's delicate constitution could bear. On October 1, 1894, she died—possibly of aggravated tuberculosis—at the Medills' suburban retreat in Elmhurst. She was sixty-three.

Two years later, Joseph built another country estate, on a five-hundred-acre tract west of Chicago, near Wheaton, Illinois. He commissioned Boston architect Charles A. Coolidge to design the new house and christened the property Red Oaks. Now near the end of his life, he was drawn back to the rural landscape of his boyhood and Red Oaks reflected his frame of mind. On its grounds was a working farm, where corn grew high under summer sun and cattle grazed in its pastures, providing a carefree, rustic atmosphere for his grandchildren. The young Pattersons and McCormicks spent summer days there, riding, shooting, playing cowboy and sitting at the feet of the patriarch. Medill also commissioned a statue of his idol Benjamin Franklin to be erected in Chicago's Lincoln Park in 1896. The nine-foot bronze figure by Chicago sculptor R. H. Park was dedicated on June 6 to the printers of Chicago in a ceremony attended by three thousand. Although something of a visual non sequitur in the intensely Illinois setting, the image today commands attention similar to that of a neighboring statue of Abraham Lincoln by Augustus Saint-Gaudens.

With his health beginning to decline, Joseph was considering how best to wrap up and secure his estate when Victor Lawson, owner of the *Chicago Record-Herald,* approached him with an offer to buy the *Tribune.* It was an option he considered, though Kate was bitterly opposed; the prestige and political influence of the paper was her only leverage in sustaining a diplomatic career for her husband. Even more against the sale was Robert Patterson, who would find himself without employment. The opportunity passed and Joseph went on with his routine. With the loss of Kitty and his own increasing frailty, in the fall of 1898 he moved his cold weather headquarters from Pasadena to San Antonio, where he kept a suite at the Menger Hotel. Although not officially ill, he rarely left the suite, where he was surrounded by the books he loved.

The McCormicks withdrew eighteen-year-old Bert from his last year at Groton that winter so he might be with his grandfather throughout the season. In addition to providing companionship for the old man, Bert was able to avoid his annual Groton "pneumonia" and at the same time prepare for his first year at Yale. His greatest joy came from experiencing another stretch of long sessions with his grandfather, who had lived through so much of American history. While listening to Joseph's stories, Bert gained a continuing love for the subject. His grandfather's suggestion that he read the *Personal Memoirs of Ulysses S. Grant,* rather than a Conan Doyle historical adventure during their season together, pointed him in the direction of becoming a Grant authority and writing the books *Ulysses S. Grant: The Great Soldier of America* and *The War Without Grant.* It was a precious—and poignant—winter for grandfather and grandson, and the last for Joseph. Serious problems with both his heart and prostate were wearing him down and he had developed a kidney infection but was too exhausted to travel for treatment. On the morning of March 16, 1899, three weeks short of his seventy-sixth birthday, Joseph Medill was dead.

*   *   *

FLAGS WERE FLOWN at half-mast in Chicago and all city offices and public schools closed on the day of Joseph's funeral. His body was buried next to Kitty's in the family plot at Graceland Cemetery, a lovely green park punctuated by great shade trees and the marble monuments and mausoleums of the men who built the city. Joseph's daughter Kate, in her custom of making audible remarks at funerals, announced during his burial ceremony, "That's where we'll all be someday." With few exceptions, she was correct.

Joseph left a $4.5 million estate. His majority ownership of the *Tribune*—worth $2.5 million—went into a trust with two thousand closely held shares to be supervised by three trustees: his lawyer, William Gerrish Beale, and his two sons-in-law. In addition to generous cash bequests, each Medill daughter would receive a sizable income from her portion of *Tribune* stock. Joseph had assured that the carefully drawn document protected the property from the whims of the quixotic women, giving them neither the right to individually sell shares nor the privilege of dictating newspaper policy. "The *Tribune*," he wrote in a warning that accompanied the document, "cannot help continuing indefinitely to be a lucrative property; our family is really founded on it. Therefore, if you regard and respect my wishes, you will all stick together in retaining control of this great organ of popular opinion. . . . This is important for the family." It was a statement that would resonate mightily with two of his grandsons. Typically the sisters paid little note to their father's words while focusing on his personal estate. Performing as usual, they squabbled because Nellie was given a scant three hundred dollars more than Kate, reimbursement for state inheritance taxes she had prepaid.

Both women were now focused on seeking new levels to which they might aspire. Though Joseph's legacy provided equal means for scrambling toward these goals, Nellie was already well "ahead" in elegant housing. Several years before his death, Joseph's extravagant gift to the Pattersons had been an Italian Renaissance palazzo on Astor Street, one of the finest houses in Chicago and among the few designed

by New York society favorite Stanford White. The handsome four-
story mansion, rivaling the awesome Potter Palmer Castle for sheer
jaw-dropping extravagance, boasted doorknobs of agate and marble
bathrooms with silver fixtures. While the Palmer Castle was razed
many years ago, the Patterson house stands today as one of the city's
most stately. Its plentiful rooms, once home to a family of four, now accommodate several households in apartments ranging from quite chic
to among the grandest in Chicago.

Joseph balanced this largesse by leaving both his Cass Street town
house and Red Oaks farm to Kate. She cared little for the Wheaton
estate and turned it over to Bert, but lived at 101 Cass with her husband
until 1902, when a more intriguing European future beckoned. With
Joseph's legacy transforming the sisters' prospects, both had quickly
identified new realms to conquer.

CISSY COMES OF AGE

THE fluidity of nineteenth-century Washington created a magnet for social climbers with mountainous ambitions. When a city's establishment is reshuffled every four or eight years, yesterday's parvenu can become today's aristocrat in a twinkling. Adding to its luster, the city attracted titled foreigners to reign over its legations and embassies, providing a tenuous link with the nobility of Europe and a powerful pull for ambitious women with marriageable daughters. The city's most remarkable model for success was Mary Theresa Leiter, a Chicagoan within the Medill social circle. Mrs. Leiter's fabulously wealthy husband amassed a considerable amount of downtown Chicago property before selling his half interest in the city's premier department store to Marshall Field, providing Mrs. Leiter with almost unlimited funds for launching her three daughters in society. But Chicago did not have the scope to properly display the girls, for whom Mary Theresa held the implausible goal of marrying to members of the English aristocracy.

The Leiters moved to Washington in 1881 and within a dozen years were living in a spectacular house built for them on New Hampshire Avenue at Dupont Circle, the city's then epicenter of wealth and fashion. The fifty-five-room, classically inspired mansion was considered the finest in the city. And, astonishingly, within another five years Mrs. Leiter had exceeded even her own expectations. In 1898 the Leiters' eldest daughter, Mary, who had married the English Lord Curzon, became vicereine of India, placing her second only to Queen Victoria as the loftiest lady in the British Empire, and she would forever remain Britain's highest-ranking American, male or female. Both of Mary's sisters soon followed in marrying English aristocrats, assuring that Leiter blood would flow eternally in the veins of the British nobility. Mrs. Leiter's extraordinary example did nothing to diminish the ambitions of other rich Americans wishing to better their position—and certainly not the daughters of Joseph Medill.

While the patriarch's death raised Robert Patterson to official head of the *Tribune*, it also made Nellie a rich woman in her own right. Typically ignoring her husband and inspired by Mrs. Leiter's triumph, she extended her influence to the nation's capital, where she established a personal base in 1901. She was followed by other midwestern women seeking to create seats of social power in Washington's welcoming climate, among them the widowed Mrs. Marshall Field, who built an immense pink Italianate confection for her final thirty years. Nellie's own capital climb began when she paid $83,000 for a prime parcel of land at 15 Dupont Circle and hired New York's Stanford White to design their second collaboration. A notorious womanizer, White would soon be murdered by Harry K. Thaw for "debauching" Thaw's beautiful wife, Evelyn Nesbit, but he was also a brilliant domestic architect. His design for Nellie was a four-story, thirty-room white stone and marble mansion; the interior of the $200,000 house contained a ballroom in Louis XVI taste, a fruitwood-paneled drawing room and jeweled doorknobs similar to those White had specified for the Pattersons' Chicago palazzo.

Turn-of-the-century Washington was architecturally mixed, with grand houses next to the humble, but it was nonetheless a monumental city, spacious and well laid out. The paved streets were romantically lined with sixty thousand transplanted trees, and, because its sole industry was government, the city was not defaced by factories or commercial office buildings. Instead there were art galleries and libraries, creating a cultural draw for intellectually pretentious arrivistes.

Washington's continuous round of formal social events was augmented by smaller dinner parties where guests discussed the arts and literature—an ideal environment in which the determined and newly rich Mrs. Patterson might operate with success. And for the present there was no wily sister to worry about. Following Robert McCormick's posting in London, he and Kate had eked out a courageous existence in Chicago, living on her annual allowance of six thousand dollars, while Robert kept face by occupying himself as a member of the public library board. Then everything changed. If the quality of Nellie's life had soared forward with her inheritance, Kate—now as rich as her sister—would soon bound ahead as never before, irking Nellie considerably. However, Kate's maneuvering would have resounding social implications for the Patterson family, particularly their daughter.

THE FIRST OF Joseph Medill's grandchildren to emerge a star was Cissy, who by late adolescence would become an international socialite. Her face and features were a condensed mirror of her mother's patrician beauty, shorter, rounder and punctuated by the surprise of a pug nose. Though not classically beautiful, from adolescence onward she was astonishingly fascinating to men. Dramatic coloring—shiny auburn hair, pale white skin and lively brown eyes—complemented her tall, slender body and tiny, supple waist. Cissy's magnetism came not from her looks but from a sensuality she projected. Her voice was soft, deep and seductive, and her graceful, sinuous carriage so notable that President Theodore Roosevelt would remark, "Watch the way that girl moves. She moves as no one has ever moved before!" But first there was "finishing" to be accomplished. At fifteen, Cissy was dispatched to Boston and Miss Hersey's School, where she breezed through scant academic work while acquiring some amount of the required polish and her first beau, a nineteen-year-old Harvard man. She then moved on to Farmington, her mother's alma mater. Fashionable and formidable, the fifty-four-year-old school subscribed to the belief of founder Sarah Porter that young women were as deserving of a fine education as their male counterparts. But Cissy was not there long enough to benefit from its more serious curriculum; she developed an undiagnosed malady and retired to the warmer clime of Thomasville, Georgia, to recover, accompanied by the entourage of a nurse, cook and a French companion-tutor. Her condition improved upon arrival and she was able to enjoy the resort's plentiful equestrian sports, enhanced by her distance from both school and mother.

Cissy was blooming and Nellie Patterson, after years of neglect and ridicule, had become solicitous, fluttering about her daughter and managing her social career. Her own beauty diminished by time and her body swollen from immoderation, Nellie was living vicariously through her child, while also anticipating the reflected glory of Cissy's growing social success and potential for a splendid marriage. She lavished Worth gowns upon her, and jewels from Cartier, but she also monitored the girl's every move, reading mail, rummaging through drawers and critiquing beaux. Now it was Cissy's turn for cruelty; she defied her mother at every opportunity, consistently lied to her and began ridiculing Nellie as she herself had been ridiculed. Her imitations of her mother and exaggerations of her characteristics were so devastating that the formerly impervious woman often fell into tears. But determined as always, she kept on in her campaign to showcase her daughter, and a formal debut was a crucial component in her plan. The Pattersons' Astor Street mansion provided a superb setting for Cissy's presentation to Chicago society. She dazzled her parents' friends and the young men of her generation at her coming-out party, the first of several debuts over the next few years. Among her admirers a favorite was Frederic McLaughlin, whose entrepreneur father had built a prosperous coffee empire, and for that reason Nellie objected to the romance, remembering the imposing W. F. McLaughlin as a mere delivery boy. Nevertheless, it was a great young passion on both sides, and Freddy, future owner of the Chicago Blackhawks hockey team, would reappear in Cissy's life through the years before—and after—ultimately marrying international dancing star Irene Castle.

Cissy's social success in Chicago was merely the beginning. It was on to Vienna, where she was presented at the Austro-Hungarian court,

Europe's most exclusive enclave. After that it would be the Imperial Court of Russia and then Washington, D.C., where she became a darling of society writers. And she owed her success at least in part to the audacity of her aunt Kate. Shortly before the assassination of William McKinley, Kate McCormick asked the president to award her husband with an ambassadorial appointment, falsely representing herself as the *Tribune*'s major stockholder. The newspaper, through no doing on Kate's part, had supported McKinley in his 1896 election and the implication was that she was calling in a personal chit. This enraged the Pattersons, who would later exact appropriate revenge.

Nevertheless, on March 7, 1901, Robert McCormick was sworn in to represent the United States as minister to the glittering Court of Franz Josef, Emperor of Austria and King of Hungary. His position was soon elevated to ambassador. This long-awaited McCormick triumph was further enhanced by the provenance of the official residence. A previous owner had been Baron Albin von Vetsera, whose eighteen-year-old daughter, Maria, was the ill-fated mistress of the Archduke Rudolf in the shocking murder-suicide at Mayerling. The new American ambassador's wife responded by dipping deeply into her personal reserves to redecorate the house, where she was hostess to a succession of luxurious dinners and parties.

Kate was genuinely fond of Cissy, a substitute for the daughter she had lost, and invited her for an extended visit at the embassy. Although ambivalent about the offer, Nellie recognized a remarkable opportunity for Cissy. The Austrian Imperial Court, with its social season of grand balls occurring almost nightly, provided a glamorous new theater in which Cissy might perform, reflecting well on the ambassador and his wife. In addition to formal balls, she found Vienna a heady milieu of race meets, grouse shoots, elegant teas, opera parties and carefree picnics in the Vienna Woods. The season in the turn-of-the-century capital coincided with Lent, beginning with the first court ball six weeks before Easter. Court balls, the most prestigious events of the season, were exclusive in the strictest sense, attended only by the imperial family, a formal diplomatic corps, members of the Austrian nobility and other European aristocrats, including scores of handsome young men in elaborate military dress. Among the Austrians, only aristocrats with sixteen quarterings—four previous generations in which all ancestors were of noble birth—were permitted to attend the grand occasions.

ON THE NIGHT of the first court ball, a line of sleek carriages moved slowly toward the great doors of the Hofburg Palace, one transporting the Honorable Robert S. McCormick with his wife and niece. When the vehicle reached the palace entrance, a footman in silk knee breeches opened its door to allow the ambassador to descend; another handed Kate and then Cissy down the high carriage steps. After entering a large marble foyer, the three Americans joined a stream of other guests ascending a high marble stairway, carpeted in maroon and flanked by two rows of footmen in traditional eighteenth-century livery. At the top of the stairs, the ladies were each given a *Damenspende,* a favor to take home; inside was a dance card.

When they entered the first ballroom, the scale of its regal grandeur impressed even Cissy and the blasé McCormicks. The creamy gilded walls were embedded with immense gold-framed mirrors, reflecting and multiplying the flickering light of thousands of candles from gleaming chandeliers and shining crystal wall sconces. Swirling counterclockwise to the strains of Strauss waltzes were magnificently jeweled ladies in elaborate ball gowns and diamond tiaras, led by tall, lean men in uniform. Even Ambassador McCormick wore a uniform crafted for him by an Austrian tailor, a deep blue jacket, with epaulettes, gold braid and brass buttons, paired with matching trousers tucked into shiny black boots. Although in America McCormick's attire would appear ludicrous, the costume for a character in a comic operetta, it seemed appropriate here, where the only men in civilian formal dress were musicians. Cissy's lush red hair was piled high on her head in a fashionable upsweep and, because pink was a dramatic foil for her hair color and flattered her delicate ivory skin tones, she often wore it for formal occasions. On this night her gown was of pale pink silk with a becoming décolletage and a full skirt that emphasized her narrow waist.

The ball appeared to extend in all directions; there were another six ballrooms, with a total of ten orchestras playing during the evening. Walls and ceilings of the grand salons were predominantly creamy-white with gold leaf detailing, and the floors, rich, gleaming parquet. Some rooms displayed seventeenth- and eighteenth-century tapestries from Brussels; in others the walls were covered in silk. French furniture, added during the nineteenth century, ranged from red-upholstered Louis XV chairs and sofas to massive Empire pieces. The McCormicks had previously met some of the guests and were aware of the identities of others. There was the Archduke Otto, who had already consumed more champagne than others would all evening; the witty Princess Metternich, wearing a yellow gown, one of only two colors she ever wore; and the Duchess of Cumberland, whose father was King of Denmark; one sister was Alexandra, the English princess of Wales, and another was Dowager Empress Marie Feodorovna of Russia, mother of the czar. Uniformed men, young and old, approached the Americans and bowed, asking to sign Cissy's and Kate's dance cards. Surrounded by a growing entourage of young men, the McCormicks and their niece sipped champagne, chatted with old friends and new acquaintances and enthusiastically joined in the dancing.

Abruptly the music stopped. Three sharp raps on the floor announced the arrival of the emperor, and the gay, animated room fell silent. Franz Josef began his slow walk through the room, stopping to speak briefly with some of his guests. He was a dignified figure whose life had been filled with tragedy, including the death in infancy of his oldest daughter, Sophie; the execution of his brother, Maximilian, Emperor of Mexico; the murder-suicide of his son, Archduke Rudolf and Rudolf's mistress, Baroness Maria Vetsera, in the scandalous Mayerling affair; and, finally, the stabbing assassination of his wife, Empress Elisabeth, the beautiful Sisi, by a mad Italian anarchist. The seventy-two-year-old Franz Josef was slender, erect and bald, with rosy cheeks, a full white mustache and side-whiskers. As he approached each party,

the ladies prepared to curtsy, the men to bow, and all guests were expected to reply to the emperor in the language he chose to use. Recog-
nizing the McCormick trio, each of whom had been formally presented
to him, the emperor spoke pleasantly to all three in English before continuing to move through the room. It was a night Cissy would always
remember, and the prelude to an extraordinary season.

After the first ball, she plunged enthusiastically into Vienna's social
whirl, attending balls and parties virtually every night. While waltzing
through an evening at one of these galas, she glimpsed a dashing, but
somewhat older, man standing in a group across the dance floor and
in a split second she knew her future had been forever transformed.
For the present she simply felt a little weak, but was soon aware the
impact had been mutual. The man who had caught her notice was staring from the other side of the room. He broke away from the crowd
of young women surrounding him, and without waiting for formali-
ties began striding over to Cissy to introduce himself. She watched
him move across the long space toward her, crossing the dance floor
in what seemed to be slow motion, and, as he neared, she later recalled
that she "felt her fingertips turn icy cold" while her heart began to beat
in "heavy, sickening thuds."

The man who would revolutionize Cissy's life was Count Josef
Gizycki, a thirty-five-year-old Polish aristocrat. He was the requisite
tall, dark and handsome, as well as literate, intelligent, fluent in many
languages and with a title that stretched back to the ninth century.
Although he had been brought up in Austria, where his mother was
lady-in-waiting to Franz Josef's mother, he reportedly owned estates
scattered throughout Poland. As Cissy would discover, the count was
an extremely complicated being. His Polish father, who had squan-
dered much of the family fortune, was at his death insane, while Josef's
unhappily married Austrian mother had lavished affection perhaps too
abundantly upon her son. The lovely countess was a gifted pianist,
who had been a pupil of Franz Liszt, and Josef's devotion to her was
as excessive as hers was to him. His idealization of her virtues was so
intense that when she died six years earlier there had seemed to be a

deadening of any warmth that may have been within him. "I don't believe he has cared in his heart for any other woman," a mutual friend confided to Cissy.

Underlying Gizycki's charm and magnetism was a dark side. He was a serious drinker, compulsive gambler and his womanizing was so flagrant that, not unlike Cissy's great-grandfather Judge Patrick, an overwhelming number of the children in the region of his castle resembled him. In Josef's case his brood of illicit offspring was enlarged because he routinely exercised droit du seigneur in bedding a vassal's bride on the first night of the marriage. But not all his progeny were peasants; one aristocratic love child was the international socialite Etti Plesch, who died at age ninety-nine in 2003. The *Times* of London quoted a description of the count from Etti's mother, Countess May Wurmbrand. "I think it was the main interest of his life—the pleasuring of women in a physical way. . . . He was amoral and cynical, but he was a marvellous lover." When the Pattersons received news of the romance, they were as divided on this development as they were on most matters. Robert Patterson, already in tenuous mental health, was furious and determined that the relationship be halted immediately. But Nellie was rather pleased and her influence trumped his.

EVENTS WERE MOVING swiftly across the Atlantic and in September 1902, while the Pattersons were disagreeing over Cissy's new love, Robert McCormick was transferred to St. Petersburg, an exotic shift from inbred Vienna. The ambassador's new assignment afforded the American family with a glimpse of imperial Russia's rich tapestry of dramatic contrasts, but it was only a narrow sliver of the nation's considerable scope. The court balls at the Winter Palace, where the czar entertained three thousand seated guests, were considered the most extravagant and dazzling in the world. Yet the disparity between those living within the palace walls—or in its nearby mansions and embassies—and the multitude existing in poverty beyond was horrific. Russia at the turn of the last century was an immense land with a greatly diverse populace; its varied mix of bloodlines and dispositions produced individuals ranging from the unimaginably cruel to the deeply spiritual, an assortment vivified by the exotic extremes of thundering Cossacks and a tradition of Siberian mystics. More prosaic, and plentiful, were the peasants who scratched the unyielding soil for an existence in the vast, bleak landscape. These pitiable souls were invisible to the American visitors; it was only the aristocracy and fellow diplomats the McCormicks would see.

Soon Cissy found herself in the czar's brilliant court and a succession of events, which included the magnificent court ball of January. As in Vienna, she accompanied her aunt and uncle through the night to a brilliant spectacle in a historic palace. Sleighs and carriages swept over snow-covered streets toward the bank of the frozen Neva, reducing speed as their ranks began swelling. Before long the McCormick carriage was at a near standstill in a long, slow line inching its way toward an entrance to the great Winter Palace. Everything that night happened with precision and every guest followed his or her role in a traditional plan. Each couple or group of guests entered the palace through one of four designated entrances. When the carriage carrying the American ambassador drew up opposite Their Majesties' entrance, the trio was handed out into the penetrating cold of the night, joining other dignitaries as they moved into the palace. Military dress uniform was again proper attire for men, and for ladies there were special overgarments to which they attached visitors' cards. Etiquette required married women to wear diadems on their heads and young ladies to attach flowers to their hair. Although not mandatory, virtually all women guests displayed jewels—usually diamonds—at their throats, ears, wrists and possibly also at the bosom and waist.

Once inside the palace, Ambassador McCormick with his wife and niece mounted a velvet-carpeted staircase to a splendid mirror-lined corridor, where one of several masters of ceremonies advanced toward the McCormicks and led them to their positions in a formation of diplomats in the grand ballroom. At precisely eight-thirty, the grand master standing at the door announced, "Their Imperial Majesties." As the doors swung open, a hush swept over the ballroom and, in unison, the many distinguished heads dropped in a communal bow. When they raised their heads, standing before them within the golden doors were Nicholas II, Czar of all the Russias, and Empress Alexandra. The crowd divided its ranks along the middle of the room, stepping back to form an avenue down its center. Ambassador McCormick stood on one side with his diplomatic counterparts; Kate and Cissy were on the other. Once the formation was accomplished—with a neat allée bisecting the human forest—the orchestra began to play in a slow, regal tempo, signaling the start of a procession led by Nicholas and his empress. As the imperial couple passed, each spoke briefly to the ambassadorial corps lining their pathway, Nicholas to the men, Alexandra to their ladies.

Cissy remembered the empress as "a vision in flashing jewels, swathed in white and silver," taller than her husband, with "a face from which every vestige of human expression had been stricken . . . pale beneath the weight of its glittering diamond crown." Cissy sank to the floor in a curtsy, and as she rose the czarina spoke to her in slow, stilted, unaccented English, "And do you like St. Petersburg?" Cissy mouthed a silent assent, observing the empress, who was "like a crystal statue carved in one piece." The regal lips uttered in the same deliberate, measured cadence, "And is this your first visit here?" Almost before Cissy could answer, the czarina was moving on to the next ambassadress in line with "her immense silver, sable-bordered train dragging slowly by."

After the procession passed, each gentleman at the edge of the allée, as his turn arrived, offered a hand to the lady opposite and joined the promenade. Once the polonaise reached the end of the ballroom, the ball began, with quadrilles, waltzes and mazurkas. Guests then proceeded into a great candlelit room where dinner was served amid palm trees surrounded by beds of roses and hyacinths, the ultimate luxury in a night that registered thirty degrees below zero beyond the soaring palace windows. Cissy was seated at a round table with a party that included several unmarried grand dukes of her generation. After they had been sitting at dinner for almost an hour, everyone at her table suddenly rose to their feet. The czar, who had been moving about the room from one table to another escorted by a pair of equerries, was coming toward them. He sat at the table for a few moments, sipped from a glass that was handed to him and spoke briefly with each. He soon departed, on his way to another table, and then another, working his way through the rooms in a pleasant repetition of the ritual of ostensible intimacy. Following the banquet, dancing resumed, with Cissy whirling from the arms of one tall, uniformed Russian to another in a heady series of classic dances. Too soon there was the cotillion finale and the remarkable evening was at an end.

The exotic glamour of St. Petersburg's social season continued during the extreme Russian winter, featuring banquets, balls and grand galas, with the American ambassador's niece at its center. A tradition she especially enjoyed was the carousel, a quadrille performed on horseback by regiments of the Russian Guard, an event with such cachet the czar was often a spectator. Cissy's equestrian skills, enhanced by her graceful form smartly attired in a scarlet hunt jacket and tricorn on her shiny copper hair, put her in demand as a carousel participant. The St. Petersburg of the late Romanov reign was a vivid, exciting arena for a young girl, and its winter festivities supplied all the ingredients of Cissy's time in Vienna, except one, Josef Gizycki.

ONE DAY, SUDDENLY, he was there. That Josef should appear in St. Petersburg seemed a miracle, and yet it was perfectly reasonable. Although an Austrian nobleman through his mother, with close ties to the court of the Austrian emperor, Josef was also a Polish aristocrat, therefore a subject of the czar. From the moment he arrived in St. Petersburg the two were inseparable, skimming over the snow in troikas to supper dances in splendid palaces and gala dinner parties, attending the ballet, musical presentations and fancy dress balls, always together. She was his "filly," his "little girl"—belittling terms of affection, which in a few years the future newspaper publisher would never tolerate, but were treasured by the young infatuated Cissy; everything Josef said or did, no matter how demeaning, captured her heart and increased her love for him. He was there with her for a few weeks and then, just as suddenly, he was gone, leaving Russia as abruptly as he had arrived.

The next appearance of Count Gizycki occurred almost immediately, not of his physical presence but in a formal letter addressed to Mr. and Mrs. Patterson in Washington, asking for their daughter's hand. Robert Patterson demanded the count provide documents proving his estate was not burdened with liens or mortgages. But Nellie took charge and replied that Gizycki's request was premature, in what she claimed was a gesture "to show these foreigners that some American girls were not available for the mere asking." Instead she sent Cissy traveling with a cousin-chaperone from one European resort to another—Gizycki in ardent pursuit—while she supervised the restoration of her Dupont Circle house following a fire. When the house was ready, Nellie decided Cissy should come out in Washington, although, at twenty-two, she was past debutante age. To smooth matters over, the invitation from the Pattersons was worded to state that the party was "in honor" of their daughter who "made her debut last winter at St. Petersburg."

THE MALE COUSINS:
HEIRS, PAWNS, VICTIMS,
SURVIVORS

Fʀᴏᴍ the age of four Medill McCormick had known he was the anointed dauphin, the grandchild who would one day ascend to the throne as publisher of the *Chicago Tribune*. Kate's elder son was a handsome boy in a long-faced, almost soulful way, an appealing façade that masked a high-strung, erratic personality. It was a contradiction that would entrance Cissy, as well as many of the adults he encountered, and certainly his mother, whose own future as *Tribune* dowager queen was entwined with his. Until his seventeenth year, the *Tribune* birthright with its promise of an illustrious future as a baron of journalism governed all Medill did and everything surrounding him. However, destiny intervened that winter when his parents sent him with Bert—who was convalescing from his annual bout with respiratory problems—to join their vacationing grandfather in Thomasville, Georgia.

Then in its heyday as a fashionable winter resort, Thomasville was an antebellum relic resurrected as a late Victorian haven in the green rolling hills and wine-colored clay of southern Georgia. Among other notable Americans wintering there that year were Chicago publisher and bakery tycoon Herman Kohlsaat and Ohio industrialist Marcus Alonzo Hanna, one of the nation's most powerful late nineteenth-century political figures. Mark Hanna, a future United States senator, Republican National Committee chairman, and presidential "kingmaker," would shepherd William McKinley into the White House in 1896, and campaign strategy was under way. McKinley, with his wife who suffered from epilepsy, had joined the Hanna family for a Thomasville holiday, bringing unexpected diversion to Bert. At fourteen the boy was young enough to be amused by Mrs. McKinley, who frequently "threw a fit" at dinner, during which her husband discreetly placed a napkin over her face. But to his dismay, Bert had to watch from the little table, where he was seated with children, including his cousin Cissy and the Kohlsaats' daughter, Pauline.

In the party, but initially confined to her room, was Mark Hanna's lively fourteen-year-old daughter, Ruth, convalescing from whooping cough. Within days, the tall, slender Ruth was well enough to spend leisurely afternoons strolling the resort's grounds with young Medill, and soon they were riding on horseback under the Spanish moss of live oak trees, participating in picnics and dances together, sharing secrets and dreams. The early spring of Thomasville provided an intensely romantic atmosphere, combining a temperate climate and pine-scented air with a profusion of dogwood, rosebushes and magnolia. Although not conventionally pretty, Ruth possessed soft brown eyes, a wide, ready smile and the gregarious personality of a natural politician. Medill fell in love with the warm, outgoing girl almost immediately and never wavered in his affection for her. A strong, loyal and forceful woman, she would be his staunch supporter and closest friend throughout the rest of his life.

But there were years of formal education ahead for both. Ruth, who had been at the Masters School in Dobbs Ferry, New York, would soon transfer to Farmington, and Medill would return to Groton to prepare for Yale and a career at the *Tribune*—a very different young man. It was more than meeting Ruth and falling in love; a window had opened through which he glimpsed political life at its very pinnacle. Just as exposure to Kitty and her father had turned Joseph from law to journalism, observing the world of the Hannas revealed the possibility of politics as an alternative career for Medill. Nothing in his life would be quite the same after that winter in Thomasville.

*   *   *

FOLLOWING HIS 1900 Yale graduation, Medill plunged into a hectic schedule at the *Tribune*. The long-awaited entry of its McCormick heir into the family newspaper coincided with the birth of a new century and the dawn of the post–Joseph Medill era. Now employing three hundred men, the paper was anticipating a move to a greatly enlarged, seventeen-story headquarters at the Madison and Dearborn location in May 1902, and, although commercially surpassed by Hearst's *Evening Journal* and Victor Lawson's *Daily News* and *Morning Record*, the prestigious *Tribune* had a dignity and substance lacking in the mass appeal papers. Medill served for three months in his grandfather's former post as Washington correspondent before traveling to the Philippines and then China as a foreign correspondent. While in the Philippines, he determined that, although a career in politics was a definite goal, it would be prudent to first establish himself as a Chicago personage— and the *Tribune* was the likely vehicle to do so. It would be a long wait for a man who was often filled with unusual energy and enthusiasm, followed by doubts and misgivings.

Medill's return to the Chicago office was met with an unanticipated level of distraction, his diligence compromised by constant interruptions from Kate, too self-centered to realize they were counterproductive to her ambitions for him. In desperation, he went to his father, pleading with him to keep her from interfering for "ten or twelve unbroken weeks," but Robert McCormick had no more influence than he. So Medill simply did his best to maintain focus while his mother continued to press her persistent needs upon him with petty interruptions, including the periodic insistence that he leave his work to join her wherever in the world she happened to be. His one move in the political direction was to begin a long association with Theodore Roosevelt by accepting presidency of Chicago's Roosevelt Club.

Medill and Ruth had become secretly engaged during the Thomasville winter but could not marry for almost a decade. When they did it was over the objections of both Mark Hanna, who thought Ruth too young, and Kate, who was just being Kate. "Mother must not only be civil to her—she is that," insisted Medill in again asking his father to intervene, "but she must bridle her tongue when she discusses Ruth in the family or out of it." Their wedding, on June 10, 1903, in Cleveland, was a near state occasion. The twelve hundred ticketed guests included John D. Rockefeller and the uninvited Theodore Roosevelt, who was eager to better his relationship with political kingmaker Mark Hanna. The president traveled by special train from Washington, speeding through the night from Washington with his reluctant daughter, Alice, brought along as a ploy to further strengthen the bond. Alice, complaining that she scarcely knew the bride, was cheered by Ruth's warm welcome and further pleased to discover that a mutual friend, the Russian ambassador's daughter, Marguerite Cassini, was there at her own father's behest.

The scale of the wedding fully justified journeys made by many of the guests. Upon entering Cleveland's St. Paul's Episcopal Church they found themselves in an arched grove of palms, ferns and vines, twined with bittersweet and more than ten thousand peonies, to commemorate the bridal couple's Thomasville meeting. The matron of honor was Ruth's only sister, Mabel Parsons; much older than Ruth and "feebleminded," she had been married a year earlier to a guardian, with a generous settlement on the condition that there would be no children. According to her grandniece Kristie Miller, Mabel "spent hours sitting in a swing, rolling her eyes and simpering when spoken to," and was so invisible within the family that, when Mabel died in the early 1930s, Ruth's twelve-year-old daughter was unaware that she had an aunt.

Following the ceremony, a wedding breakfast was served under tents on the smooth green lawn of the Hanna estate, Glenmere. Throughout the meal there was the requisite ado over the corned beef hash—a specialty of the Hannas' cook, Maggie Maloney—accompanied by champagne served from crystal pitchers. The festivities featured only minor family drama, with Cissy pouting publicly because her beloved Medill was now married, and Alice Roosevelt conducting a brazen flirtation with the groom's brother, Bert. However, all twelve hundred present—including the president—were upstaged by the conspicuous absence of the mother of the groom, Kate McCormick.

Despite the many obstacles they would face in marriage, theirs was a great love affair. Their personalities complemented each other. Medill was spiritual and intellectual; Ruth was organized and disciplined, bringing energy and order to his vague impracticality. Together they were idealistic political animals who truly enjoyed each other's company and always found interesting projects to pursue and engaging subjects to discuss. For the most part, they had fun together. But the year following their wedding was a difficult one for Ruth. Her adored father, by then Senator Hanna, contracted typhoid in late December and died on February 25, 1904. It was also during the honeymoon months that she began to grasp that Medill's emotional roller coaster was beyond mere eccentricity, and possibly as powerful as the depression suffered by his grandfather. The specter of William Sanderson McCormick was an abiding presence, and one that Kate periodically brought out to hold up as a dire warning for both her sons and now her daughter-in-law. Even without his mother's malicious counsel, Ruth was forced to admit to herself that Medill was fighting serious mental illness, and in a time before the recognition and chemical management of bipolar disorder, she felt helpless. Furthermore, there was Kate's chronic interference in their everyday life, coupled with Medill's use of alcohol to counteract his increasing depression. Even for a woman with Ruth's inner resources and fundamental optimism, the situation was daunting.

The inheritance her father left her meant that Ruth had become— with Louise de Koven Bowen and Edith Rockefeller McCormick— one of the three richest women in Chicago, giving her an income far greater than that of her husband. Yet the social life into which they settled was to Kate's eyes Bohemian; it included friends who were writers and political activists whom the young McCormicks entertained at Sunday-night suppers, which Kate considered avant-garde. The implication was that, by consorting with socially nonpedigreed intellectuals, Medill was jeopardizing his emotional well-being. "Don't forget the horrid possibility which unfortunately all the McCormicks have to face," she cautioned. "Hereditary tendencies are *hereditary tendencies*. . . . For God's sake stop going to the theatre and giving these late supper parties!" The continuing negative interference produced a growing temptation in the young McCormicks to find a respite.

With his grandparents' strong Ohio roots reinforced by marriage to Ruth, it seemed natural for Medill to think of acquiring the *Cleveland Leader*. Kate, sensing this might further her journalistic ambitions on his behalf, agreed to invest a quarter of a million dollars of her capital in the paper her father had established, as well as its afternoon companion, the *News*. Medill and Ruth moved to Cleveland, where he spent much of his time concentrating on his new acquisition, and it was encouraging that while copublisher of both Cleveland papers, he was made treasurer of the *Tribune*. But the *Leader* was losing money under his ownership and when he approached Kate for additional cash, she refused. The knowledge of having dissipated a portion of his mother's fortune, compounded with the stress of handling both jobs, plunged him into an emotional breakdown. When he was advised by professionals to take a three-month hiatus to recover in California, Kate countered with a twenty-thousand-dollar bribe for him to take a rest cure with her in Paris instead. He did neither.

In 1907, Medill sold the Cleveland papers to his brother-in-law Daniel Hanna and returned full-time to the *Tribune*. But soon after moving back to Chicago, his life with Ruth took another turn when—along with much of literate America—they read *The Jungle*, Upton Sinclair's bestselling book exposing the city's meatpacking industry. Unlike their contemporaries, the young McCormicks didn't merely cluck at the deplorable conditions supporting the lavish lifestyles of some of their friends. Instead, to experience these conditions themselves, they moved down to Packingtown, the wretchedly deprived neighborhood where stockyard workers lived. Maintaining their Lake Shore Drive residence, they assumed aliases during their Back of the

Yards tenancy, and Ruth went so far as to take a job, joining the wives of eastern European immigrants in manning a meat chopper. When she was terminated by a supervisor who suspected her motives, they left Packingtown, but kept their social conscience.

During this time Medill was finding his niche at the paper—on the business rather than the editorial side. The *Tribune* had always been passive in seeking advertising, but he changed that by hiring aggressive young salesmen who brought in a sizable increase in revenue. Encouraged, he engaged Yale classmate William H. Field, whom he insisted be paid eighteen thousand dollars a year. After a skirmish with the directors, Medill won, to the great advantage of everyone involved. Bill Field, who would become one of the most valuable executives in Tribune Company history, launched market research in the five-state circulation area and produced sound statistics, which increased and upgraded advertising. The *Tribune* soon became the largest carrier of national newspaper advertising in the country and second only to the *Saturday Evening Post* in American publishing. Medill was rewarded with titles of vice president and secretary in addition to treasurer, and a salary of twenty thousand dollars a year, five thousand more than his editor-in-chief uncle.

THE EARLY TWENTIETH century was a curious time for *Tribune* leadership. Robert Patterson's uncertain mental health and copious alcohol consumption often kept him away from the paper for long stretches of time, and the unpredictable Medill, increasingly dependent upon alcohol himself, was still far from a seasoned newspaperman. The true hands-on professional who kept the *Tribune* afloat during this period was a talented nonfamily member, managing editor James Keeley; he was ably supported by another skilled journalist, city editor Edward Scott "Ted" Beck, a civilized, erudite product of the University of Michigan. Although Keeley was poorly educated and lacked finesse in dealing with people, he was one of the most gifted, and dedicated, men ever to edit a newspaper in any city. A self-proclaimed orphan from the slums of London, he was the child of parents, who—although possibly alive—had abandoned him in this country. During adolescence he had supported himself by selling newspapers on American trains, where he discovered his innate news sense. While peddling papers he listened to passenger conversations, and soon the cash he received from selling overheard tidbits to newspapers was greater than the money he made from selling the papers themselves. This early experience was probably the root of his enduring motto: "News is a commodity and for sale like any other commodity." Keeley employed this talent while working for papers in Memphis and Louisville before Robert Patterson hired him as a twenty-one-year-old police reporter in 1889, and by 1898 he was managing editor. Not only did Keeley possess an inherent aptitude that made him a brilliant newsman, but he was also a compulsive workaholic who sat with the paper at night until it was "put to bed" around midnight, after which he stayed to begin preparations for the following day's edition.

Under Keeley's leadership, the *Tribune* gained recognition for community service and pioneered self-help features. He hired the famed actress Lillian Russell to write a beauty column and added advice to the lovelorn, as well as columns on cooking, gardening and parenting. But it was his instinctual sense of breaking news that gave the editor his greatest distinction; his gift for knowing what was happening— and where—led to a staggering number of "scoops" in his career. This talent was augmented by a fleet of informants, men who received generous compensation from the *Tribune* treasury for reliable news tips. But Keeley was also a pompous newsroom tyrant who would not speak directly to reporters; orders were given through an intermediary. And although he terrorized the men who worked for him, he commanded respect, a combination of emotions that prompted underlings to refer to him as J. God Keeley. But to get to that point, new reporters had to survive an initiation ritual.

In what appeared to the neophyte to be an inconsistent quirk in Keeley's character, he loosened up on Saturday night when the final edition was completed. After rounding up unwary reporters and guiding them to a backroom poker game, he proceeded to win every hand.

New recruits quickly learned that the boss's card-playing instincts were as keen as his sixth sense for news, and knew to vanish from the city room as Saturday drew to an end. But Keeley didn't seem to mind that he was universally disliked. "A good newspaperman has no friends" was his slogan. When his wife complained that with a dearth of close friends she wouldn't know whom to ask to be his pallbearers, he immediately shot back, "There are 10,000 men who would give their right eye to be my pallbearers."

Not the least of Keeley's contributions to the *Tribune* was his hiring of the adventure-loving but courtly political cartoonist John T. Mc-Cutcheon, who would become one of the towering legends of Chicago journalism. The young artist was hired first by the *Daily News* and had become a successful cartoonist for the *Record-Herald* by 1903, when Keeley offered to double his $65 weekly salary. The *Record-Herald*, aware of their cartoonist's value, raised his compensation to $110. A short time later, Keeley countered with a colossal $250 offer, which Mc-Cutcheon accepted, beginning a mutually agreeable employment with the *Tribune* that would last nearly a half century.

After moving to the *Tribune*, McCutcheon spent fourteen years as a popular Chicago bachelor and fixture in the city's literati and social establishment, combining world travel with artistic work, which he carried out in his animal-trophy-studded Michigan Avenue studio. Although he kept a Gold Coast pied-à-terre, much of his time was spent in a cottage at Ragdale, the Lake Forest estate of architect Howard Van Doren Shaw. When McCutcheon returned from one of his frequent exotic travels, he would sit by the fire at Ragdale, regaling the Shaws and their three little girls with tales of his adventures in Samarkand or Kashgar; one of the daughters, Evelyn, was so entranced that she swore from the age of seven that she would marry none other than her father's friend Mr. McCutcheon. And in January 1917, she did. A few months before, McCutcheon had satisfied a lifelong ambition by purchasing, sight unseen, Salt Cay, an island in the Bahamas, a few miles from Nassau, complete with main house, outbuildings, furnishings, lagoon, sandy beaches, a yacht and staff. This was his wedding gift to

Evelyn and would be their family retreat for decades to come. The cartoonist's unique personal qualities as well as his professional contributions to the *Tribune* endeared him to members of the extended Medill clan, who would not only repeatedly count on McCutcheon's skills and sound judgment, but also embrace him within their inner circle for the rest of his life.

WHEN ROBERT PATTERSON's health was seriously failing in 1907, the family decided to make his nephew Medill the paper's titular leader, with Keeley in control of editorial matters. This was not a successful move; by 1908 Medill was drinking more heavily and Kate, scarcely a teetotaler herself, was nagging him—as well as Ruth—about his alcohol consumption. She said to Ruth, "my dear child he drinks all the time! He drinks at nine, at ten, at eleven, at twelve . . . he never stops the whole day." She begged Ruth to take him out of the country for professional help and threatened that she would have him removed from his job "unless you and Medill are off for Europe within the next 10 days . . . as he is not now competent to do any work of any kind." For once Kate was right. Pressure from work, along with her constant meddling, had sent him into an emotional tailspin. In November Medill requested, and the *Tribune* board granted, a two-month leave of absence while he and Ruth traveled to Zurich to consult legendary psychiatrist Carl Jung, who blamed Medill's "demon" on "infantile relations with the mother." Away from both the newspaper and Kate, Medill's condition improved and he appeared to be normal when he returned in early 1909.

Greeting Medill on his homecoming was Keeley's new slogan, "World's Greatest Newspaper," soon to undergo trademark registration and appear daily at the top of the front page. This self-proclaimed assessment was both a goal to strive toward and a target for ridicule—but there it was, and there it would remain for several decades. With a family member firmly in the publisher's office and others possibly on the way, the long-term future of James Keeley seemed uncertain. Abruptly he left Chicago in September 1909, announcing that he was off for a long holiday in Japan. His only instructions to the editorial staff before leaving were that they were to follow Medill McCormick's orders, which led to the curious incident of the red book.

During Keeley's absence, Medill interfered little with the paper's editorial content except to insert noticeably laudatory comments about his friends. Annoyed by what *Tribune* chronicler Lloyd Wendt referred to as "Keeley's somewhat amused coverage of the city's red-light district," Medill also requested a list of names of "respectable villains," seemingly decent, churchgoing individuals who received income from illicit activities, typically ownership of houses of ill repute. These names, and they were legion, were for eventual publication and included those of some of Chicago's leading citizens. City editor Ted Beck feared that publication of such a list would be disastrous for the *Tribune*, but remembering Keeley's words, he ordered staff to compile the list and place it in a red leather book, where it stayed.

In February 1910, Tribune Company directors voted against a hefty salary increase Medill had requested, a rejection that sent him again spiraling downward. This rebuff coincided with the reappearance of Keeley, who then very quickly heard about the red book. When Beck fetched the book and handed it to him, Keeley only said, "Lock it up." That night at midnight, Medill McCormick—dressed in white tie, tails and opera cape—appeared in the *Tribune*'s composing room. Presumably on his way home from a gala social event, he placed his ebony walking stick and silk opera hat on a table, put his arm around his editor and laughed. He did not say goodbye and didn't mention the red book. He simply turned away from Keeley, then walked out of both the composing room and the *Tribune*. The next day he and Ruth were on a ship bound for Europe and another trip to Carl Jung's sanitarium. This third nervous breakdown was official and nothing more was ever said about the red book.

WHEN BERT GRADUATED from Yale in 1903 he presented a striking silhouette. His height, a shade over six foot four, was unusual for the time, and his long, full, youthful face, pleasing as it was, would soon prompt him to grow a mustache to add maturity to its lingering boy-ishness. It was not only Bert's appearance that was lagging in development. At almost twenty-three he was still a virgin. He had never been to bed with a woman—or a man; he had participated remarkably little in the spectrum of courtship activities expected of a man in his early twenties, just as he had engaged in almost no competitive sports aside from polo and the other equestrian activities for which he was developing a lifelong passion. Although socially poised, the solitude he had experienced almost all of his life had made him shy, which manifested in an attitude of aloofness. Yet in some ways he was exceptionally sound and mature.

Kept away from a career at the *Tribune* by his mother, Bert decided to pursue the legal profession. After a short holiday in Central America he enrolled in law school with the goal of someday becoming a judge or possibly governor of Illinois. Although he would have preferred to remain at Yale, his father convinced him that Northwestern would provide more appropriate preparation for a Chicago practice. In fact, in an era when few lawyers were university trained, any institutional instruction would have given him an advantage over those who merely "read law." Additionally he apprenticed at Isham, Lincoln & Beale, the firm established in 1873 by the late president's son Robert Todd Lincoln in association with Edward Swift Isham, a member of one of Chicago's most distinguished pioneering families. In 1884, the partners brought William Gerrish Beale into the firm, and until it was dissolved in 1988, Isham, Lincoln & Beale remained one of the city's most prestigious white-shoe law firms. Beale, a brilliant trusts and estates lawyer, was author of the famous will that kept Marshall Field's estate intact until the fifth generation, and he also designed the Joseph Medill will that managed to keep the two warring sisters from destroying their *Tribune* legacy. However, William Beale's greatest contribution to the Tribune Company was perhaps the strong guidance he provided as one of its three trustees during years when the other two, Robert Patterson and Robert McCormick, wavered for varying reasons.

Robert McCormick's advice to Bert proved correct; his Chicago

legal background—even in its developing stage—positioned him ideally for embarking upon an almost immediate political career. In 1904
the first-year law student was approached by Republican boss Fred
Busse to run for alderman of what is now Chicago's Forty-Second
Ward. A more heterogeneous area could scarcely be imagined than
this district, encompassing as it did the fashionable Gold Coast and
a squalid territory of bars and slums. Nor could there be a more surprising candidate to represent it than the aloof, fastidiously turned out
Bert, who in his bespoke London suits, shoes and linens resembled an
English aristocrat. He nonetheless accepted the proposal and promptly
swung into a classic Chicago-style competition. He launched his campaign on St. Patrick's Day, announcing he would meet every man in
the ward by election time, which entailed a good deal of hand shaking
with strangers on the street and marching into saloons with the announcement that his name was McCormick and he was buying drinks
for the house. Soon the standoffish patrician was a rousing success as a
man of the people and his would-be constituents were addressing him
as "Mac." Although the Democrats swept Chicago in the next election, Bert captured a seat in the city council, where he managed to fit
in with fellow aldermen who were authentic men of the people. Only
once, when he hurried into the council chamber in jodhpurs and polo
helmet after a late-running match, did it occur to his council colleagues
that perhaps "Mac" might not be one of the boys after all.

Within a few months, Bert was again visited by Fred Busse and a
pair of fellow Republican bosses, who offered to back him as candidate
for presidency of the notoriously corrupt Sanitary District of Chicago.
In a city with a history of dangerously contaminated drinking water,
this department was—and still is—a crucial local government agency.
Various cutting-edge engineering solutions had been explored to protect the purity of the water supply. One involved tunneling six hundred
feet beneath Lake Michigan and far out to a water source away from the
pollution of the Chicago River; this strategy had sufficed for a time, but
eventually failed to keep up with the needs of a growing population.
The most recent remedy, embarked upon in 1889, was to reverse the

river's flow with a system of locks. When Bert ran for district president in 1905, the construction was in its final stages, with the river soon to flow away from the lake and toward the Mississippi River.

As a candidate for the second time in two years, Bert was again out among the people and—because this was Chicago—frequenting the city's many watering holes. He wrote his Yale class secretary, "If you were to say that I have felt obliged to spend 90 percent of my time in saloons, and the remaining 10 percent in barrooms, you have it about correct." In this citywide campaign Bert had to work to dispel confusion with the "rich" McCormicks, especially his cousin Harold—a son of McCormick Reaper founder Cyrus, who had recently married John D. Rockefeller's daughter Edith. This time he benefited from a Republican sweep and as the new Sanitary District president he filled the position with seriousness and a high degree of accomplishment. The Republican bosses who selected him may not have been aware of the precision of their choice in Bert for the job, but he could not have been more perfect. Most conspicuously, he was honest, traditionally an uncertain quality in many holding Chicago elective offices. Rather than having the hunger for money customary in the area's political hacks, he possessed only a gnawing need to prove his ability, and with the presidency of the Sanitary District he achieved that. Second only to his exceptional integrity was Bert's extraordinary aptitude for mathematics and engineering. He was a visionary and the district provided a fruitful environment for a man who would later become an inventor with seven patents in his name and anticipate such innovations as ethanol from cornstalks, automobile seat belts and elevated highways, sometimes by decades. The political years provided an important chapter in Bert's life, during which he performed with expertise, demonstrating again and again that he was a highly intelligent, competent man, thus establishing to himself and others for the first time that he was more than the disregarded younger brother.

Plunging into the challenge of leading the Sanitary District, Bert became an expert in the relationship between Great Lakes and Mississippi water and exhibited the considerable skill with which he was able to study a problem, envision its solution and then accomplish it. He replaced unqualified but politically connected workers with university-trained engineers, cut legal costs by establishing in-house counsel, brought financial viability to the district and consistently saved money for taxpayers. In one instance he discovered that rushing water, dropping thirty-four feet through the Sanitary Canal toward the Mississippi at nearby Lockport, was generating power at one-third the expense of commercial plants. He proposed selling the electricity to the city at cost, which brought him into a public dispute with energy tycoon Samuel Insull. Bert won, garnering widespread favorable regard. When his tenure was over in 1910, Chicago streets were illuminated by electricity from Lockport.

While leading the Sanitary District, Bert also found time to complete his law study at Northwestern, pass the state bar exam and found a law firm. When his career in politics disappeared after the Democratic landslide, he was already successfully practicing law with partners Stuart Gore Shepard and Samuel Emory Thomason in an office on the Tribune Building's thirteenth floor. However, Shepard, McCormick & Thomason was more than merely "a law office"; it was antecedent of one of the great firms in the nation's history, today's Kirkland & Ellis. Bert approached practice in the future colossus with great seriousness, despite an income from a $150,000 trust fund and a $20,000 yearly allowance from his mother.

DURING THE YEARS the future Colonel McCormick was substituting local politics and the study of law for a journalism career, his cousin Joe Patterson worked for the *Tribune*. The family iconoclast had finally graduated from Yale, despite interruptions for cattle herding out west and foreign corresponding for Hearst. The early Hearst experience was an invaluable detour for Joe. Although he almost died of fever during the process, it gave him his first thorough concept of journalism for "the people" and brought stirrings of what would become the unerring Joe Patterson radar for news the masses wanted to read. He began as a *Tribune* reporter in 1901 and soon graduated to serve as assistant

Sunday editor. His salary, fifteen dollars a week, was in contrast to the two-hundred-dollar weekly allowance he received from his mother, a discrepancy that didn't seem to disturb his socialistic conscience.

Like his sister and the McCormick boys, Joe was complex and eccentric, a product of atrocious parenting. The collective childhood of the cousins had created demons that would mature with time, leaving each with an insistent—and ultimately fatal—need for alcohol. Tall, rangy and craggily handsome with brown eyes and a disarming grin, Joe was capable of great charm when he wished. However, his disdain for the mores of his peers—or even basic middle-class values—was reflected in his dress, which was at best tweedy. Throughout his life he affected shabbiness and made a point of not looking rich, although he was supplied with a valet from age fourteen. His taste ran to workmen's shirts and rumpled trousers, and when the occasion required a dark suit, white shirt and well-knotted tie, he would conform—stopping short of footwear, which was invariably unpolished and dusty. This was an eccentricity he took to the maximum by wearing muddy shoes to the opera on one well-documented night. The description of Joe's opera attire that evening may have been overstated, or even apocryphal, but the fact that it has been frequently reported supports its repetition. Allegedly his shoes were not only mud-caked, they were tan; his custom-tailored tail coat and trousers were unpressed and the shirt he wore with them was a work shirt open at the throat. A rival account printed much later in H. L. Mencken's *American Mercury* referred to Joe as "wearing two pairs of trousers to the opening of the opera and doffing one pair in the lobby to a chorus of gasps from first-nighters." Perhaps nothing sums up Patterson's grooming style more than the fact that in the army, where it is virtually impossible to deviate from the prescribed look, his nickname was Sloppy Joe.

Long before he began frequenting drugstore counters and workingman's lunchrooms to keep in touch with the tastes of the common people, he did so out of preference. A favorite pastime of Patterson's throughout his adult life was to prowl the city's roughneck saloons, and the Chicago First Ward of his youth provided some of the most perilous watering holes anywhere. Journalist George Seldes wrote that Joe "does not go slumming, like his sister Eleanor. He goes because of that old Socialistic urge." But there was more to it than that. To assure himself, and others, that his comfortable, luxurious life was not making him soft or sissified, he periodically visited such local dives as Hinky Dink's. Formally known as Workingman's Place, the saloon was run by Alderman Michael "Hinky Dink" Kenna and patronized by the derelicts and panhandlers whom the disreputable politician counted among his core supporters. Joe, who appeared to be one of them, would walk up to the roughest-looking brute in the place and engage him in a fight. Once the slugging began, there were usually other drifters who joined in the skirmish, with Joe invariably finding himself thrown through the saloon's swinging doors and out to the street. The resulting bruises and battle wounds were visible proof that he was not just another cosseted rich kid.

Joe's conduct was consistently inconsistent; he spouted the outsider line but ended up marrying pampered department store heiress Alice Higinbotham. The well-traveled Alice was known within their set primarily as an expert horsewoman and an accomplished linguist, a skill she would continue to hone through frequent travel away from her husband in future decades. The two became engaged in June 1902, when she was twenty-one and he was twenty-three, and their marriage the following November took place in an afternoon service at Chicago's Grace Episcopal Church. In its coverage of the wedding, the *Chicago American* focused on its floral abundance, first marveling at the immense number of arrangements massed throughout the church and then describing the even greater profusion of flowers at the reception that followed in the Higinbotham's Michigan Avenue house. The bride, whose long veil was held by a coronet of orange blossoms in her hair, carried a large bouquet of showering white orchids. Medill McCormick was Joe's best man, and the wedding party included Bert, Cissy and Medill's then-fiancée, Ruth. Alice's maid of honor was her sister, Florence, who would soon become wife of Chicago plumbing magnate Richard Teller Crane Jr.

*   *   *

LIKE BERT, JOE served time in politics. When his father secretly arranged a Republican seat for him in the Illinois legislature in 1903, he commuted to Springfield and promptly made news. While engaged in a debate involving streetcar lines, he launched a demonstration that sent the Speaker of the House to the cloakroom to avoid being hit by flying inkstands and books. He gained further public attention in March 1905 when he supported Democratic reform candidate Judge Edward F. Dunne in his run for mayor on a platform of "municipal ownership," and announced at a Dunne rally, "Capitalism has seen the end of its days as we have known it." This outburst was devastating to Joe's immediate journalistic career. His father, who was in Washington at the Theodore Roosevelt inauguration, rushed back to Chicago and presented Joe's resignation to a specially convened meeting of the *Tribune* board. Nellie was enraged that her son had so cavalierly obliterated his prospects at the *Tribune* and destroyed her trump card in the game against her sister. In a heartbreaking letter to her written a few days later, a sheepish Joe wrote he had "always wanted to be in politics. I did not particularly like my position on the *Tribune*. . . . Neither should I care to be an English duke nor a great artist." He concluded with "I hope you won't dislike me personally. Don't be too hard on me. I am not especially happy. Affectionately, Joe."

The McCormicks were understandably ecstatic with this unexpected boost for their son. Even the courteous, reserved ambassador jumped into the controversy, writing William Beale from his post in Paris, "It seems to me that this extreme step of Joe's should settle once and for all who shall be the one man to assume the management of the Tribune . . . when Robert Patterson retires from that position." But Joe had won—for the present; Dunne's campaign was successful, rewarding his Patterson supporter with a position as commissioner of public works. In this capacity Joe discovered that State Street department stores were extending their basements under city streets, leading him to further enrage his family—and Alice's—by fining each of the stores a half-million dollars, including

his father-in-law's Marshall Field & Company. He followed in pushing family relationships even further by launching an effort to raise
taxes paid by Chicago newspapers.

A year later, he once again pressed the self-destruct button by giving
up his job as commissioner and writing a much-publicized open letter
of resignation to Mayor Dunne, which read in part, "Money is power
and dominion. It is wine and women and song. It is art and poetry and
music. It is idleness or activity. . . . No one possesses it, but it possesses
everybody." He went on to announce, "In other words, as I understand it, I am a socialist." By that time Joe's quirkiness had caught the
attention of the national press. Three days after the announcement of
his defection to socialism, young Patterson was in New York. On his
way to a Socialist convention in Connecticut, he had passed the night
in a suite at the Holland House, a rich man's hotel at Fifth Avenue and
30th Street. After sleeping until 11 A.M., Joe received a reporter from
the *New York Times*, whom he told in classic traitor-to-one's-class
fashion, "It isn't fair that because my grandfather worked hard and left
money I should have everything and many people should have nothing. All sources of production should be vested in the people. Rockefeller has no earthly right to control the God-given oil springs. Alfred
Vanderbilt and others like him are not entitled to the share they receive
of other people's earnings." He finished by telling the reporter, "I am
really undecided as to my future. . . . For the present I shall probably
rest. I have been working very hard for quite a long time and I think I
have a rest coming to me."

FOLLOWING ABRUPTLY TRUNCATED careers in both journalism and
politics, Joe retreated to an estate he had bought in the Libertyville
horse country north of Chicago, where he began writing novels and
plays, always with a left-wing thrust. On the surface Westwood
Farm appeared to be an idyllic setting for writing and raising the
three daughters he and Alice would have: Elinor in 1903, Alicia three
years later and Josephine in 1913. A tree-lined allée led to a handsome
garden-surrounded brick house, designed by architect Howard Van

Doren Shaw, best friend—and future father-in-law—of the *Tribune*'s John T. McCutcheon. Alice thought of Westwood as a stately country estate, but Joe regarded it as an experimental farm, a place to raise new crop varieties. When she planted a stand of trees, he tore them out because they threw a shadow on his crops. She ordered fertilizer taken from the organic compost mound to nourish her decorative plants; he wanted it used only to fertilize his crops. Friction between husband and wife intensified when, after putting one hundred thousand dollars into the property, Joe had to mortgage it to pay his lavish-spending wife's debts.

Westwood Farm would be their only home for the first dozen years of their marriage. When they were in town for the winter season, they would stay at the Virginia, a fashionable residential hotel at Ohio and Rush streets, built by Leander McCormick on the pre-Fire site of his house. Alice enjoyed the social life in which they had both been raised; Joe loathed it. Years later, one of their daughters, Alicia, reminisced about this conflict: "He hated parties with grim determination and it was only by coaxing and scolding that mother ever got him to Lake Forest. She won 75% of the time, but I am sorry to relate that father, when he found himself trapped, never took his defeats with good grace. Mother often came home weeping because father had been rude to one of the guests. Home was father's castle and he was quite happy there with his family, his books and his black loam soil." Although Alice loved order and disliked noise and controversy, she was courageous in daring to be the second woman to fly with the Wright brothers. "She would have preferred a more conventional life," her daughter remembered. "In fact, she took everything gallantly, from riding to hounds to going up in an old 'box car' plane, circa 1911. Father always said she was the bravest woman in the world. . . . To be a Socialist in those days was about equal to being a Communist now. Mother, who found the life perplexing, was once asked by a reporter how she felt about it all. 'I don't know what being a Socialist is,' she said, 'but if that is what my husband is, I'm for it.' " Joe would eventually become disillusioned with the party, but not before serving as national campaign manager for Eugene V. Debs in his run for president on the 1908 Socialist ticket.

Living at the farm allowed Joe to focus on his writing, and he became markedly productive, but there were agreeable distractions. His property adjoined the estate of utilities baron Samuel Insull, who raised pheasants as a hobby. Before long Joe was bagging pheasants by lying behind a fence with a shotgun and watching for birds flying over his property. Distractions aside, it did not take long for Joe Patterson the newspaper heir and erstwhile politician to become Joe Patterson the writer. His article "Confessions of a Drone," published in the August 30, 1906, issue of the *Independent*, combined them all. In an era when scions of wealthy families did not publicly thumb their noses at the class into which they were born, the piece created a sensation. "The work of the working people, and nothing else," he wrote, "produces the wealth, which, by some hocus-pocus arrangement, is transferred to me, leaving them bare. While they support me in splendid style, what do I do for them? Let the candid upholder of the present order answer, for I am not aware of doing anything for them."

Burton Rascoe, a venerable Chicago journalist who worked for many years at the *Tribune* and was a great admirer of Joe, believed that his professed socialism rose from a reaction to his mother's dominance. Nellie held an increasingly tight grasp on his income and, according to Rascoe, the great heir was feeling a "money pinch." This assessment was seconded by Alicia, who, when in her fifties and married to a man of immense wealth, wrote, "People who do not know me very well assume I grew up rich from the start. In fact, father was nearly broke when I was born, in 1906, and we were living on a basic income of thirty-five dollars a week. . . . His family had cut him off."

The breakthrough for Joe came with his writing. His well-publicized novel *A Little Brother of the Rich* was published in 1908 and almost immediately a stage version was enjoying a successful run on Broadway. The novel's women, who mirrored the mischief-making daughters of Joseph Medill, spent their energies conniving, usually in manipulation of the men around them. Meanwhile, on life's stage,

Nellie was attempting to conspire woman-to-woman with Alice. In June 1908, she wrote to her daughter-in-law, from the Hotel de Castiglione in Paris, "Wish Joe would go back to the *Tribune* . . . in any capacity. He could be on the editorial staff and write one article a week on farming or education. There is *prestige* for him in being on his Grandfather's paper. Don't say I said this as he is so obstinate—you could talk with his father about it. Tell him it is *your wish* too."

BUT ALICE WAS having her own problems with Joe. In 1908, wearing his author hat, he was on his way to Vienna to research a project. While crossing the Atlantic on the USMS *St. Louis,* he wrote a letter to her that is perhaps the most revealing existing glimpse into the soul of Joe Patterson and the inner workings of their marriage.

"Dear Aluss," he began, launching into a chatty description of his fellow passengers, before abruptly switching into the highly personal.

> Do you know Al, that no matter how well I might ever write no matter if I got off a big, big play—still I'd be unhappy & wretched. I'd like to be kind and simple and *good*, a successful husband & father more than anything else in the world. But I *can't*—Do you know I have tried (I don't believe you know it—but it is true) tried again and again and over again to make you happy—and failed. Oh, how horribly I've failed. . . . Sometimes I say 'A—why did I ever marry you?' But the question were better 'why did I ever marry anyone?' I was unfit for it—born unfit—For as I look back on the different girls that I might possibly have married there does not appear one whom in the light of my present knowledge I would rather have married. That at least is true.
>
>   . . . now just when wisdom begins at last to visit us, it is almost too late. Oh, honey, we must do the best we can— such as it is. Be brave, Alice, and be big—big all the way through. Don't be pettish or peevish or small—don't give way to yourself. Don't be like most every *lady* you know—inert

or futilely maliciously harmfully active in the business of immaterialities.

Remember if you haven't much of a husband—and I concede it, you haven't. As a husband I am distinctly in the Z class—you have two pretty fine kids, whose lives will be more made or marred by your influence than any other one influence in the world. Your life is in your own hands—and you can make it useful and radiant, in spite of me.

If we could only get on together everything else would solve itself—But its knowing we can't, that I grate on you, that my point of view, my way of doing & seeing things, my way of running the farm, my way of arranging the books, my way of wanting a window in the study, my way of filling in, my way about roads, that all these ways of mine are not your ways—To go deeper, all these ways would be your ways if I were your sort of a fellow—But I am not—and I can't say I blame you.

All I can promise—and I do promise it—is that I will do the best I can on my return—and I hope we shan't quarrel & jangle & jar.

Joe

Their marriage of less than six years may have been having problems, but Joe's new career was in full flower. The following year, 1909, he collaborated with James Keeley and another writer, Harriet Ford, on a play, *The Fourth Estate*, which also enjoyed a successful Broadway run. There were additional novels and plays, including *Rebellion*, which was both, and *Dope*, a playlet implying that a slum environment caused narcotic abuse and could be remedied through socialism. For years *Dope* survived as a vaudeville staple, in which Joe's message was often lost on the audience. Along the way he produced a 1907 *Saturday Evening Post* article, "The Nickelodeons," probably the earliest serious piece of film criticism ever written, foreshadowing his enduring devotion to motion pictures, as both editorial pioneer covering the subject and an avid movie fan. Another *Post* piece criticized management of female employees by Chicago dry goods companies, including Marshall Field & Company—another slap at his father-in-law's store. Although his writing was almost uniformly antiestablishment, Joe's core attitudes sometimes fluctuated. In 1913, when Yale's sophomore class was moving to abolish the university's secret societies, his defense of the august clubs verged on the antediluvian. He told a *New York Times* reporter that the underclassmen were "deliberately trying to abolish all the romance and glamour of Tap Day." The onetime socialist then announced that these objections were "right in line with the leveling tendencies of the age." This was not a new Joe, but merely the same conflicted, inconsistent Joe Patterson.

CISSY:

DEBUTANTE COUNTESS

C ISSY'S 1903 presentation to the society of a fourth city was a brilliant success, immediately providing her in Washington with the social standing she held in Chicago, Vienna and St. Petersburg. After settling into a lively but proper post-debutante routine—ranging from formal dinner dances to foxhunting in Chevy Chase, Maryland—she attracted the restless eye of Alice Roosevelt. The high-spirited daughter of the president recognized a kindred soul in Cissy and included her in the "Cabinet Circle," made up of only a few young women—one of whom was the young actress Ethel Barrymore—and every desirable bachelor in town. In addition, she brought her into an even more exclusive group, a threesome of only herself, Cissy and the Russian countess Marguerite Cassini, currently the city's most glamorous young woman. Marguerite's father, Count Arthur Cassini, had been appointed the czar's first ambassador to the United States during the William McKinley administration and continued to serve into the Roosevelt years, with Marguerite his hostess. Washington's society press dubbed the trio "the Three Graces," to the delight of naïve readers, but to the cognoscenti, Cissy was in dubious company.

Alice Roosevelt, innocently lovely in appearance, was one of the most outrageous young women of the time. As soon as her father became president, she emerged an instant celebrity and fashion icon, the era's Princess Di. National newspapers elevated her to royalty, christening her "Princess Alice," and when it was noted that she often dressed in a particular shade of blue, the color was dubbed "Alice Blue," copied by women throughout America. But Washington insiders knew of the First Daughter's shocking behavior, with escapades that included late-night partying, betting on racehorses and a flagrant lack of chaperonage. When her father banned her from smoking under his roof, Alice climbed onto the White House roof and smoked there. She so exasperated the affable Roosevelt that he once commented to author Owen Wister, "I can be President of the United States, or I can control Alice. I cannot possibly do both." She managed to further test his patience by practicing a form of black magic, using it on the last night of his term when she buried a voodoo idol on the White House grounds along with a hex on William Howard Taft and family, who would be moving in the following day.

Marguerite, the seductive, dark-eyed Countess Cassini, was even more appalling. Never completely accepted by Washington society, she was considered "fast," even by the president who unsuccessfully forbade Alice to see her. When she arrived in the capital amid great press fanfare in 1898, the Russian ambassador's daughter was an ultra-sophisticated sixteen-year-old, carefully groomed for a life in diplomacy. She spoke six languages, understood the intricacies of protocol and possessed a comprehensive knowledge of such subjects as Russian history, international politics, vintages of fine wines and the lineage of European titles. But it was her offense of using "too much physical charm" that shocked conservative Washington, particularly the flirtatious mannerism of powdering her nose with a swansdown puff she kept stashed in her décolletage. She smoked long Russian cigarettes and drove her red touring car around town at the law-defying speed of thirty miles per hour, but most disquieting of all was an ambiguity surrounding her origins.

Marguerite was rumored to be the ambassador's illegitimate child by his housekeeper; however, the truth was more complex. Ambassador Cassini, a distinguished diplomat with close Romanov ties, was also a thrice-married gambling roué, who had left a number of angry, highly placed women in his wake. Therefore, his third marriage to Stefanie Van Betz, a European vaudeville performer—which produced Marguerite—was kept secret from the czar and everyone else. Stefanie lived in the shadows of the Cassini household, introduced only as her daughter's governess, while Marguerite was presented as the child of the count's late brother. With such mystery and intrigue, it is little wonder that proper Washington kept the young countess at a distance. The ambassador's daughter simply ignored the controversy; she was having a marvelous time. "Could there be a better place or a happier time to have been a young girl than Washington at the turn of the century?" she wrote in middle age, recalling a succession of social seasons. There were cotillions, receptions, lawn parties, balls, coaching parades, summer yachting trips and winter sleigh rides, punctuated by house parties in New York, Boston and Newport—all of which she attended with Alice and Cissy beside her.

Into this mix of Washington "Graces" sauntered a young Ohio congressman, Nicholas Longworth, dashing, witty and, like the count, an enticing hazard to women. Congressman Longworth was also a cultivated man, a skilled violinist and a superb chef. Marguerite was the first of the three to meet him at a Washington dinner party. When their hostess introduced them, she warned the countess, "Be careful; he's dangerous." She then turned to the congressman, "And you be careful because she's *very* dangerous." A thirty-four-year-old bachelor of means, Nick's former loves had included such contemporary beauties as Mary Leiter, before her reign as vicereine of India, and Irene Langhorne, the original Gibson Girl. Nick Longworth adored the Graces, flirted with all three and escorted them as a trio. The Graces reciprocated. Although Marguerite would return to Europe at the end of her father's posting, Nick remained a fixture in Washington and in the lives of Cissy and Alice for many years after.

Joe Patterson became one of the many American men to come under Marguerite's spell, during a curious episode that occurred in early 1904, when he had been married to Alice for more than a year and was father of the infant Elinor. Ambassador Cassini had learned Joe was visiting the Patterson women in Washington and saw a rare opportunity to influence the pro-Japanese *Chicago Tribune* on behalf of Russian interests in the Far East. After receiving intensive briefings from her father on the czar's position in the Russo-Japanese War, Marguerite asked Cissy to seat her next to Joe at a Dupont Circle dinner dance. The plan was a success; Patterson was charmed by the countess in spite of her single-minded lobbying of the Russian position regarding Port Arthur, the nation's only ice-free port on the Pacific, which was currently under Japanese attack. She continued her mission after dinner, sitting with him on the mansion's marble staircase and ignoring others who danced nearby in the ballroom. While hypnotizing her quarry with her practiced enchantment, she continued the campaign, interrupted only by Joe's periodic departure to fetch more champagne. "Never did I work so hard to charm," she said later. At one point her companion disappeared and returned with pockets full of silver favors, which he dropped into her lap. At four in the morning, he suddenly said, "All right, you win. I agree. Now will you marry me?" When the stunned Marguerite pointed out that he was already married, he replied, "I won't be if you wish." She insisted it was not her wish, but he pressed, and she laughed him off. That was the end of it, almost. Aside from a brief encounter at Cissy's wedding she would not see Joe again for thirty years. And when he did reappear in her life, it would be with the amazing revelation of the antagonism she had created that night.

THE WASHINGTON SOCIAL whirl provided all Cissy could desire— apart from the Polish count. She longed to marry him and he was still in her fervent pursuit. Fearing elopement, Nellie gave consent to the marriage by cable to Count Josef Gizycki, in care of the Vienna Jockey Club. The wedding would be small, not more than forty guests, and its date was set for April 14, 1904, at noon, with Ruth McCormick as Cissy's only attendant. When Josef arrived in Washington for the ceremony, he charmed Cissy's friends, particularly Alice, whom he addressed as "Princess" and presented with a silver cigarette case. But he was not invited to stay at 15 Dupont Circle and, thoroughly offended, checked into a local hotel.

Rather than the usual mood of jubilation surrounding the approach of a wedding, there was a developing sense of foreboding, and as the day of the ceremony grew closer, negative vibrations dominated. Robert Patterson fumed, Nellie became increasingly concerned and, throughout the prenuptial night, Ruth begged Cissy not to marry the count. But the bride-to-be insisted she knew of Josef's many mistresses, repeatedly stating, "Suppose he is marrying me for my money and virginity. I love him." Her mother, predicting disaster, kept reminding her, "Darling, remember you can always come back to Chicago." Then, late that night, a desperate Nellie knocked on her daughter's door with the frantic last-minute barter of her own pearls if Cissy would only change her mind.

Nellie retained her pearls and Cissy's wedding took place as scheduled in the formal rooms of 15 Dupont Circle. Banks of white flowers lined the fruitwood-paneled drawing room, where the Russian and Austrian ambassadors and other guests sat in anticipation of Cissy's arrival on her father's arm. Slender and luminous, she descended the stairway and prepared to enter, wearing a bridal gown of white Liberty gauze over silk and chiffon. A veil of white tulle framed her eager face and she carried a bouquet of white roses. Waiting at the altar were the bridegroom, his best man, Count Ivan Rubido-Zichy, and a priest who, because Josef was Catholic, had been engaged to perform the ceremony. Nearby, round tables set for six or eight were centered with lavish floral displays for guests who would enjoy a formal wedding breakfast following the ceremony. And outside, ready to carry the newlyweds to the railroad station for the first lap of their honeymoon, was the nuptial carriage, its wheel spokes decorated with orange blossoms and celebratory white ribbons tied there by Marguerite. The environment was flawless, but the union was doomed.

When Cissy left to change to a traveling costume after breakfast, her groom also disappeared. According to a buzz of rumors, the Pattersons had reneged on the dowry. Best man Ivan, dispatched to find Josef, reappeared to explain that the count was at his hotel and would meet Cissy at the train station, but Marguerite learned from him that the million-dollar dowry had not been deposited. Furthermore, the groom was incensed because Robert Patterson had refused to shake hands with him following the ceremony. Now firmly positioned for exquisite vengeance, Gizycki remained absent throughout a flurry of protracted negotiations while the accounting error was corrected and deposit of the dowry verified. Following a long delay, Cissy reappeared, looking wan but elegant in a fashionable tan traveling ensemble, the long plume of her large picture hat trembling. Stepping into the blossom- and ribbon-decorated bridal carriage, she began the trip toward her honeymoon train, accompanied not by her bridegroom but with a severely shaken Nellie. As the two women arrived at the station, Nellie said again, "Darling, remember, you can always come home." A half century later, Marguerite recalled, "I always felt that Cissy, who was proud, held it against me that I had been a witness to this humiliating page of her life. Of course, from Gizycki's point of view, a bargain was a bargain: his chateaux needed repair; in return, he was offering an illustrious and ancient name and an enviable social position. It was a fifty-fifty affair. But he had to be sure there was no slip."

Cissy's humiliation had only begun. The newlyweds arrived at their New York hotel and, after a late supper, the count announced, "Now go to bed, little filly; perhaps I will see you later," and vanished. Some hours after, he reappeared to rape her, but not before staring at her unclothed body and exclaiming, "Ugh!" This was only the beginning of a pattern in which Cissy was alternately ignored and humiliated by her husband. Despite his treatment, or possibly because of it, she would insist for the rest of her life that he had been her greatest love and, when regaling friends with the tale of her wedding night in later years, she always finished with "But he was a *man*, every inch of him!"

* * *

HAVING ACCOMPLISHED PERFECT revenge against the Pattersons, while establishing supremacy in his marriage, Count Gizycki concentrated on employing the finely honed talents for which he was best known. During their two-month honeymoon in Paris and Vienna, Josef made expert love to his bride, an enthusiastic pupil who responded with a sexuality that matched his own. And he schooled her in food and wine; however, aside from bed, the table and a mutual love of horses, the two had little in common. As he had cautioned her, the count had nothing to discuss with "little girls, little snowfields like you." One night in Vienna, he disappeared after dinner and did not return until dawn, when he pounded on her bedroom door in their Sacher Hotel suite until she allowed him to enter. He had lost money gambling and needed eleven thousand dollars "for a few days," but he needed it immediately. Cissy produced the money and, as she must have known, it would not be for a few days.

When the extended honeymoon reached its inevitable conclusion, the count and his young bride traveled by train from Vienna, where they embarked on a daylong carriage journey to Narvosielica, the ancestral seat of the Gizycki family. Halfway between Odessa and Warsaw within the Russian border, it was one of several villages to which the count might travel only once a year to collect rents. As the site of the magnificent Gizycki castle, this village was unique among Josef's holdings. Cissy had long anticipated this day, and she was growing impatient to see the property her husband had so frequently described and of which she would be chatelaine. She watched excitedly while their carriage crossed miles of rural land where only peasants working in fields were visible; not unlike the American Old South, this was a region in which inherited estates were owned by a few and worked on by many. Cissy's eagerness was increasing; soon they would be crossing the drawbridge to the castle where she and Josef would build their future together, love, entertain, give balls, host hunts and house parties, where she would bear children and they would raise a family.

As the carriage approached a break in the monotonous landscape, Josef gestured toward it, proudly announcing, "Our village." Cissy's eyes followed the direction of his hand toward a huddle of mud huts with thatch roofs. A straggle of peasants stood beside the road, gaping at them, and she began to notice how many children's faces bore the Gizycki imprint. When they came to a gate where more tenants were gathered, Josef said, "This is the beginning of my estate." Peasants standing there had dressed to welcome the couple and wore brightly colored clothes; some girls, although barefoot, had twined flowers and ribbons in their hair. The carriage stopped and the oldest two men within the welcoming party produced ceremonial black bread and salt, traditional tributes presented to newlyweds. When the carriage passed through the gate and was headed along a road lined with poplars and blooming lilac, Josef waved broadly, saying, "This is our private park."

Then, in a bewildering moment she would never forget, Cissy saw her new home. There were no turrets or flags flying, there was no drawbridge, nor was there a moat; the building she saw bore no resemblance to any castle, chateau or stately home she ever seen or imaged. Rather the Gizycki castle of which Josef had so often spoken was a bleak, unembellished, two-story white frame building, wide and spare, with uncurtained windows staring vacantly out at a desolate park. "My father never finished this place" was Josef's inadequate explanation. "He had several big estates and didn't come here very often. But you and I, little filly, we will work here together."A pleasant image returned to Cissy, a vision of the two of them joyfully "working together" to restore the property, making it a warm and lovely showplace. They entered a hall where there was some decoration, generations of portraits of Josef's ancestors, but the drawing room that followed was as spare as the exterior of the building, with blank walls and bare floors. Aside from a large fireplace, a few mammoth tables, a pair of chairs with cracked leather upholstery and a scattering of further chairs, the shabby room was empty. The staff of seventy Josef had promised consisted of perhaps a dozen untrained peasants, who worked not for pay but for food and a negligible gift at Christmas;

among them were an ancient, ill-clad butler and four barefoot house-boys. Fortunately, Cissy had brought a personal maid.

There were more ominous surprises to come. Josef's bedroom was adorned with photographs of women—many women—aristocratic women, women in court dress, and women in riding costume, all with fond inscriptions. There was particularly one woman, a woman with a child, obviously his; Cissy would discover that he had lived with this mistress for five years. Moving on to her own room, connected to his by a spiral staircase, she found hairpins and other feminine items left by a previous occupant. When she objected to a boudoir that had obviously been inhabited by a paramour, he calmly told her there were "quite a lot of other rooms in the house" from which she could choose. He soon made it clear there would always be other women and his sole interest in her was money. Equally humiliating was the announcement that his lovemaking, which had become rough and brutal, was only to produce children. The count's rages began to terrify her, frightening her as only her mother's had, but she couldn't run to her father or grandfather as she had then. With Josef it was only money and heirs. He was furious that she was not pregnant with his son and, although there had been as much as a million dollars in Cissy's dowry—with the couple also receiving between twenty and thirty thousand dollars in annual income from the Pattersons—he continually badgered her to go to her father for more. "A man marries to get something he has not got" was his continuing theme. "Otherwise, why would he marry? And besides children, I want to improve my property, buy more land, pay off more mortgages."

Cissy's only companions were Josef's female cousins, who felt he had married down and were displeased that his children with Cissy would not possess the "sixteen quarterings" necessary for inclusion in the European aristocratic milieu. Her greatest diversion and a godsend for her sanity were house parties at assorted manors throughout the region. As many as fifty aristocrats would travel great distances to gather for weeks at an estate where they might ride and hunt or engage in polo, tennis or croquet. Often, entertainment and masked balls were arranged during these gatherings and guests assembled for elaborate meals, each of which required specific clothing. They also amused themselves with gossip, flirting and sometimes carrying on affairs. It was a pleasant distraction for Cissy, who might otherwise be alone in Josef's castle with a few unkempt servants and nothing to do but exercise her horses or read novels. As winter neared she became ill, so ill a Viennese physician was consulted. The diagnosis was that Cissy was at last pregnant. Josef, expecting a male heir and showers of money from the Pattersons, was delighted. Cissy was not. Her pregnancy was a harrowing stretch of months during which she was so weak and sickly that she several times collapsed, one breakdown necessitating a traumatic journey by sleigh to a Vienna hospital twenty-four hours away. Josef found her feminine frailties displeasing and after her return to the castle he disappeared, initiating events that would produce a watershed in their marriage.

Following Josef's abrupt departure, a furious Cissy retaliated by breaking into his desk, where she found a diary, essentially a catalog of his many sexual exploits, listing names, places and dates, with detailed physical descriptions and evaluations of his pleasure with each. When he returned to find his diary missing, he was as violently angered as she was in finding the book, creating an irreconcilable breach between them. Although her due date was near, he again vanished without providing a doctor to deliver the child who would be born in his absence. Nellie arrived from America and moved Cissy to a friend's Moravian estate, Blansko Castle, hoping for adequate medical care. Even so, there was no doctor. Presiding over Cissy's labor and the baby's birth was only a peasant midwife, who terrified Cissy by greeting her anguished cries with incomprehensible Gypsy utterances. The final blow for all was that the child was a girl. Josef was furious to be without the son he had anticipated, and Cissy was shattered to think she had failed in her one opportunity to win his esteem. Amid all the unhappiness leading up to her birth and surrounding her presence, amazingly the child was christened Felicia.

Cissy's life did not improve, and her existence as Countess

Gizycka—the feminine version of the name—continued as it had before the birth of her child. For another two years the brutal treatment and condescending attitude from the man she adored was accompanied by his drinking, gambling and womanizing. Finally Cissy rebelled. In December 1907, during one of Josef's frequent trips away, she enlisted the help of three servants who hated her husband and escaped by sleigh on a bitterly cold night. Soon she and Felicia were speeding across the frozen, snow-covered ground toward the border and a train to Paris. She was free!

Seeing his fortune slipping away, Josef followed and charmed her into spending time with him in the French resort of Pau, a reconciliation that did not go well. His nights out alone, gambling and with other women, continued. One evening when she objected, he beat her and dragged her across the floor by her hair. When he left to go out that night, so did she, bound for London with Felicia. He would never again persuade her to return.

ROBERT PATTERSON, IN London at the time, located an inconspicuous house for Cissy and the child in Hampden, Middlesex. Small and unpretentious by Patterson standards, the hiding place was not sufficiently modest to elude detectives Josef had hired to trail Felicia, now his greatest hope for Patterson riches. On a balmy afternoon in early May, the count arrived at the little house in an automobile and, finding Felicia in the care of her nurse, announced he had come to take the child for a drive. Soon newspaper front pages throughout the world screamed headlines of the kidnapping, conferring upon Cissy and Felicia a notoriety that would haunt them for the rest of their lives. In the midst of the unwelcome hoopla, Joe Patterson gave an interview, in which he referred to the count not merely as a kidnapper, but also a drunk, adulterer and blackmailer; Josef countered with a million-dollar demand in damages from his brother-in-law, creating further sensational coverage. Gizycki held a valuable trophy, which he guarded carefully; he installed his daughter in an isolated Austrian convent and kept her hostage in return for a cash settlement. But the count, in his arrogance, underestimated the international reach of the Medill clan.

Mrs. Potter Palmer's niece, Princess Cantacuzene, had married a member of the Imperial Court and was Cissy's good friend during her stay in St. Petersburg. Although the princess was unable to intervene herself, she arranged a private audience for Cissy with the czar's mother. The formidable widow of Alexander III astonished the young American by offering to arrange for Josef to be imprisoned until his attitude improved. When Cissy suggested it was an extreme measure, the old dowager empress smiled back and said, "Child, I have had people beheaded for absolutely nothing." Next Aunt Kate stepped in with her own self-promoting barter. Ambassador McCormick had been transferred from his Russian post to France in 1905, but was now in need of a new ambassadorship. He and Kate had maintained a connection with the Russian court and she, seeing an opportunity to further her husband's career as a diplomat, offered his services to intercede in St. Petersburg on behalf of the Pattersons—if the *Tribune* would support their cause. Kate's audacity enraged Cissy's father, who, although recovering from a nervous breakdown, flew into action.

Patterson contacted President-elect Taft and explained that the McCormicks had earlier misrepresented their position with the *Tribune*, and followed by asking for the new president's assistance in retrieving his grandchild. Taft quickly grasped where true power resided at the newspaper and facilitated the return of the little girl by enlisting the intervention of Nicholas II, to whom the Polish count's allegiance lay. It was only after the czar issued an imperial decree ordering Felicia returned to her mother that Cissy was able to recover the child, but even that would take time. An added outcome of this chain of events—much to the delight of the Pattersons and the chagrin of the McCormicks—was that there would not be another ambassadorship in the McCormicks' future. With the loss of his diplomatic career, Robert McCormick's health failed rapidly. And Kate, also without a role that had defined her for a half-dozen years, refused to return to Chicago, visiting only infrequently. She commissioned John Russell

Pope to design a mansion at 3000 Massachusetts Avenue, later the Brazilian embassy, where she also spent little time, preferring a suite at the Ritz in Paris.

Still, Cissy was without her child. It wasn't until the summer of 1909 that Josef returned to his estate to collect rents. He was arrested on arrival and served with the czar's order, which he was forced to obey. While Cissy waited in a Vienna hotel suite with Medill and Ruth McCormick, Felicia was released from her convent and promptly delivered to her mother by an emissary. Cissy and Felicia were then able to travel with Ruth and Medill to Germany, where they boarded the *Kaiser Wilhelm der Grosse*, the first ocean liner bound for New York, arriving on August 18, 1909, to a clamor of press attention.

In September 1910, Cissy received a decree of separation from courts in Austria in preparation for filing for divorce in Chicago. It would be a long wait for Cissy before she was thoroughly rid of Count Gizycki.

· 10 ·

DYNASTY IN JEOPARDY

As the first decade of the twentieth century drew to a close, the future of the Medill dynasty at the *Tribune* was in grave danger, with the crisis rapidly escalating. Deep depression and heroic bouts of drinking had kept Robert Patterson away from the paper for much of the previous five years, and like Medill McCormick he was an intermittent patient of Carl Jung at his Zurich clinic. Ambassador McCormick, whose health had been destroyed with his departure from the Foreign Service, was declared incompetent by his wife. Moreover, after checking him into a Boston sanitarium in late 1909, she assumed his seat in the company's ruling triumvirate with William Beale and the elusive Robert Patterson. The extreme chaos of the situation, with its potential for collapse of dynastic leadership, prompted Joe to suggest to Bert that they enlist the support of their mothers in staging a coup against his father, but Bert demurred. "Aside from the fact that we had no voting powers," he later explained, "I felt Mr. Patterson's long service in the paper entitled him to great consideration and that he should not be removed." Bert's conviction that the family should stand together had developed through years of observing the severe hostilities that had torn it—and possibly the newspaper—apart. Joe did not yet share this view.

When in a balanced state Robert Patterson was genuinely concerned with keeping the family in top management, and in February

1910 he took steps to secure the future of the Medill family's presence at the paper by making Joe secretary and Bert treasurer—to outsiders, an amazing action since, as the *Chicago Evening Post* said in a front-page story, Bert had "never before identified with the company." The hidden story behind the surprise developments was that the appointment of the uncompensated Bert to replace his well-paid brother in the treasurer's office occurred following a bizarre incident. In Bert's words, "I was accustomed to box at the Chicago Athletic Club and afterwards take a plunge in the swimming tank. One day a friend told me there was a man in the hot room, evidently intoxicated, signing *Tribune* checks. I found this to be so and told Mr. R. W. Patterson. He said, 'We will correct that by making you treasurer and you can sign the checks.' " Although unpaid, the position brought Bert ten shares of precious *Tribune* stock, which his uncle—severely discouraged by what he perceived as the disintegrating condition of the paper—sold him for three thousand dollars each. With the stock came a modicum of voting clout Bert had previously been without.

During the same month, the stalwart William Beale announced that he could no longer serve as a company trustee unless Medill Mc-Cormick was officially removed; he was joined in his despair by Robert Patterson, who now wanted nothing more than to be rid of the *Tribune* and his responsibility there. Then on March 1, the directors gave Keeley "absolute authority in all departments." It was in this atmosphere of acute emergency that Bert—while visiting Washington later in the month—stopped in to see his aunt Nellie at her Dupont Circle mansion. Also there, on a rare visit to his wife, was her husband, who was in the East to be with his dying mother in Atlantic City. During a brief discussion between the two, Patterson puzzled Bert by enigmatically stating that the younger man should succeed him at the *Tribune*.

A FEW DAYS later, Bert was in his law office in the Tribune Building when he received an urgent message from Anna Garrow, the *Tribune*'s head telephone operator. Her first shocking announcement was of the sudden death of Robert Patterson in Philadelphia. She then added that the company's directors were at that moment holding an unscheduled meeting in Mr. Patterson's office. When Bert went down to learn what was happening, he found Tribune Company principal stockholders gathered on a matter completely unrelated to his uncle's death. In fact, Robert Patterson had called the meeting himself to carry out the sale of the *Tribune* to Victor Lawson, owner of the competing *Record-Herald*. The Lawson offer, almost certainly motivated by a desire to merge the *Tribune* with his paper to strengthen its morning position, was not a sudden proposal. Rather it was the extension of a series of discussions the *Record-Herald* owner had begun with Joseph Medill a decade earlier and which he, Lawson, continued with trustees Patterson and Beale throughout 1909. According to Robert R. McCormick biographer Joseph Gies, "Had Patterson lived a couple of days longer, McCormick was certain the sale would have gone through and the *Chicago Tribune* would have had a different history." Lawson, who had long coveted the *Tribune,* was now going for the jugular, threatening that without a deal he would launch a price war against the Medill paper.

Although the official cause of Robert Patterson's death was an apoplectic stroke following a cold, he had been a suicide, alone in a room in Philadelphia's Bellevue-Stratford Hotel. The means, according to a letter to Bert from his mother, was "an overdose of Veronal," but no one has ever been able to determine what took Robert Patterson to Philadelphia, a city completely out of his usual orbit, on that April Fool's Day in 1910. Because his passing occurred within hours of that of his mother, the beautiful Julia Quigley Patterson, a double funeral was held a few days later in Chicago's Second Presbyterian Church, where Reverend Patterson had earlier reigned in the pulpit. It was reported in the local papers as one of the most notable funerals the city had ever witnessed, but not everyone was mourning. The departure of her husband was a relief to Nellie, who did not feign grief. And it created a new source of envy on the part of her sister, who audibly remarked at the funeral, "Nellie sure got ahead of me that time!"

The official removal of Medill McCormick, at least for the duration of his health problems, had finally occurred. On March 24, a week before Patterson's death, William Beale—continuing his threat to resign as trustee if Medill remained—had engaged Bert and Joe in a long meeting during which all three agreed it was a necessary move. This was followed by an April 6 board decision to grant Medill an extended leave without salary. Then, two weeks after Patterson's sudden death and the stockholders meeting, Bert ran into Alfred Cowles Jr., son of Joseph Medill's longtime partner and a *Tribune* stockholder. Cowles declared he was in favor of a sale because, according to Bert, without "someone vitally interested" at the helm, the paper would decline. Furthermore, he conveyed that this was the opinion of other minority stockholders, including seventy-six-year-old Horace White and Azariah T. Galt, trustee for the Henry Demarest Lloyd family. White's stake was 100 shares, Cowles held 305 and Lloyd's children had inherited a whopping 510 shares from their grandfather William Bross. When Bert asked, "Would it make any difference in your feeling if I should take an active part in the property?" Cowles answered, "It certainly would." Bert made calls on shareholders in Chicago, Boston and elsewhere, convincing them to hold out. The crisis was deferred, but in the middle of June Victor Lawson announced to *Tribune* directors that beginning July 1 he would slash the price of the *Record-Herald* to one cent. The three trustees, William Beale, Kate and now Nellie, who had replaced her late husband, were scattered around on summer travels, mostly in Europe; therefore Bert secured the board's promise not to cave in to Lawson while he traveled to visit each of them. His mission was successful. The trustees refused to sell and Lawson went ahead with his threat, cutting the price of the *Record-Herald* to one cent, with the *Tribune* promising to follow with a similar cut. What ensued was an era of legendary violence, one that would bring a century of international notoriety to the city of Chicago.

IN 1885, WHILE the patrician Joseph Medill, hero of the Great Fire, former mayor of Chicago and owner of the city's leading newspaper, was presiding over his empire from a stately Near North Side mansion, a shadow dynasty was emerging across town in a West Side tenement. Tobias Annenberg, recently arrived from the village of Kalvishken in East Prussia, was scratching out a living and producing a family that would soon collide with Joseph's. Rough, scruffy and dancing precariously close to the dark side of the law, it was a line that in its own destructive way would be no less influential than that of Medill. Tobias had fled his nation's bloody pogroms with his wife, Sheva, and their eleven children to seek the fresh air, peace and freedom of America. But within two decades of arrival, the name Annenberg—through two sons, Max and Moses—would strike terror in the soul of anyone associated with the newspaper business. And no two men would be more influential in their impact on the history of Chicago. Although the name Annenberg would forever remain synonymous with Chicago's bloody circulation wars, it wouldn't stop there. The systematic newspaper beatings and murders the brothers engineered set a climate of lawlessness that would escalate and permeate Chicago for decades. Out of the circulation wars would rise racketeering, bootlegging and the universal lawlessness of the gangster era.

After working variously as newsboys, messengers, bartenders, scrap iron salesmen and partners in a grocery business, Max and Moe became newspaper subscription canvassers and then circulation chiefs. In July 1900 William Randolph Hearst's paper the *Evening American* had arrived in a city already glutted with nine newspapers, and the word *circulation* quickly became a euphemism for activities to ensure that a publisher's papers, and not those of the competition, were sold to readers—*through any means necessary*. In 1902 Hearst added the *Morning American*—later titled the *Examiner*—putting an even more urgent squeeze on the *Tribune*. According to *Tribune* writer Burton Rascoe, who witnessed the process, "Those who were accustomed to purchase their morning *Tribune* at the corner newsstand on their way to work suddenly found that, morning after morning, the *Tribune* was 'sold out.' There would, however, be plentiful stacks of the *Examiner*.

Grumbling, they would take an *Examiner* in lieu of a *Tribune*." In his memoir, *Before I Forget,* Rascoe wrote, "the Annenbergs . . . hired a crew of sluggers and gunmen. The gunmen would waylay *Tribune* delivery trucks, confiscate the newspapers and dump them into the river. The sluggers would visit the newsstands and intimidate dealers into refusing to take an adequate supply of *Tribune*s and, by way of making their requests clear, would beat up those who protested, wreck the stands and destroy the *Tribune*s. This was the beginning of gangsterism and racketeering in Chicago."

But the *Tribune* was far from innocent. Quickly transforming its role from victim to combatant, the *Tribune* countered by hiring Max and his hoodlums away from the *Examiner*, prompting Hearst to sue for violation of its exclusive contract with Max—a suit dismissed on grounds that the activities described in the contract were illegal. Undeterred, the *Examiner* engaged a replacement crew of hired killers to operate against the *Tribune*, and the wars began with the goal of each side to persuade newsdealers to sell only its paper. Or in Max Annenberg's words, "to give them to understand that they were not only through with the newspaper business but that they were through on this earth." Weapons—sometimes revolvers—were issued, and the hoodlums socked, knocked, kicked and shot their way to circulation highs. Soon they were setting fire to newsstands and blowing up delivery trucks. Max was entirely visible at various incidents and described by the *Daily Socialist* at one as a "wild man . . . dressed as a typical tenderloin representative. He wore a flaming red sweater and over his low brow was pulled a soft cap. With a malicious leer upon his countenance, he swaggered around the elevated station . . . using foul language in the presence of women . . . flourishing and brandishing his revolver like a maniac." It was a dangerous business even for those on the side of the thugs; one Annenberg hood tried to leave the business, and he found himself first beaten, then shoved down a *Tribune* elevator shaft. When he reached the bottom, he was picked up and taken to a sink to be cleaned up by *Tribune* employees, but his assailant followed and began shooting at him and his rescuers. The murder toll climbed, with additional victims crippled and otherwise injured. Eventually the wars subsided and peace returned to Chicago's newspaper scene, but only for a few years.

When the *Tribune* cut its price to one cent on October 3, 1910, matching the *Record-Herald* in its attempt to drive the Medill paper under, it was a declaration of war. And war meant reengaging the Annenberg army—this time in a fight for the life of the *Tribune*. James Keeley was able to hire Max and his team away from Hearst within a week, in spite of the fact that his brother Moe remained Hearst's circulation manager. Soon Max was working his bloody magic from a menacing black limousine truck that circled the Loop on behalf of the *Tribune*. The vehicle would park close to a newsstand until a competing delivery truck arrived and Max's *Tribune* thugs opened fire on the truck. The war almost immediately became reciprocal, resulting in dozens of casualties, including newsdealers, gangsters and innocent passersby. The *Tribune* won the war with sales numbers that soared over both the *Record-Herald* and a current Hearst paper, the *Examiner*. Some of the thugs who worked for the Annenbergs soon graduated to the gangster hall of fame, including Red Connors, Walter Stevens, Dutch Gentleman—with his brothers, Pete, Mike and Gus—and Mossy Enright. In May 1911 Mossy murdered Dutch in Pat O'Malley's saloon and blithely justified his action by saying, "I had to get him before he got me."

Amazing as it seems, aside from the *Daily Socialist*, never was a word of the Chicago circulation wars reported in the city's newspapers, nor did the principals ever express shame or embarrassment about them. Max Annenberg in fact forged a loyalty to the *Tribune*—and to the family itself, understandable on his part because Bert's law firm had defended him in a murder case during the circulation wars. But it was mutual. He followed with legitimate circulation work for the dynasty, most notably for Joe in New York during the 1920s. His déclassé background fascinated Joe, who even consulted him on editorial matters such as headlines. While keeping the dubious glamour of his unsavory past alive with tough talk and the attire of a ruffian,

Max crossed over to mainstream behavior by playing golf and riding horseback in Lincoln Park. As time passed both Bert and Joe appeared to forget that the gangsters recruited and trained by the Annenberg brothers went on to activities other than newspaper wars, leading to the citywide bloodshed of the Al Capone era that followed. In a 1952 radio broadcast reminiscing about the good old days, Bert told his radio audience, "Max Annenberg . . . proved to be much the best circulation manager in town."

Moe became hugely successful in his stranglehold on American horseracing information as owner of both the *Daily Racing Form* and his racing wire, *General News Bureau*. When he purchased the *Racing Form* from founder Frank Brunell in 1922, it was for cash—literally— four hundred thousand dollars wrapped in newspapers and delivered to the seller in New York. From that questionable nucleus Moe formed the company that went on to produce such mainstream publications as the *Philadelphia Inquirer, Seventeen,* and *TV Guide* in a package that was eventually sold to Rupert Murdoch for $3.2 billion. But Moe Annenberg did not survive to enjoy the playboy and art-collecting pleasures of a multibillionaire. He spent twenty-three of the last months of his life in the federal penitentiary at Lewisburg, Pennsylvania. After being admitted on July 23, 1940, he became so frail that by the spring of 1942 prison officials feared that he would die there. He was released for treatment on June 3 and died at the age of sixty-five less than seven weeks later. The irony is that Moses Annenberg's imprisonment was not for murdering or crippling innocent newsboys, or even for laying the foundation of gangsterism in America, but for massive criminal federal income tax evasion—the largest such case to date in the nation's history.

Perhaps the dynasty's greatest similarity to Joseph Medill's was that Moe Annenberg also spawned she-devils—seven of them. He also produced one son, Walter, who threw his energies into enlarging the empire and attempting to gain a positive image for the dynasty. The man spent his adult life in earnestly attempting to bring a modicum of dignity to the wretched family through becoming one of the major philanthropists of the twentieth century, amassing a great art collection, to be given at his death to the Metropolitan Museum of Art in New York, and wangling his way to the prestigious position of American ambassador to the Court of St. James's.

THROUGHOUT MOST OF the century's first decade, while the *Tribune*'s emotionally frail titular heads, Robert Patterson and Medill McCormick, sporadically ran the paper with the able professional guidance of James Keeley and Teddy Beck, both Joe and Bert were remarkably successful in substituting other activities for journalistic ambitions—and each had vigorously demonstrated that he could thrive outside the *Tribune*. Bert had been content in politics and was aware that his prospects for a successful political career were excellent. After demonstrating that he was indeed that rare animal, an honest Illinois politician, a bright future in Congress or the governor's mansion was a definite possibility. Joe was a flourishing novelist and playwright, well recognized in the national world of letters, and neither man had reason to abandon the successful career he had established on his own and without direct assistance from the family or its newspaper.

Yet with the paper in crisis, Joe and Bert both left the careers they were nurturing and joined forces to save the family business. The fiery Medill blood that had created the *Chicago Tribune* flowed in their veins and remained at their core. To Bert the *Tribune* had "always been much more to me than either a newspaper or a source of revenue." As for Joe, working at the paper would be an extension of his political philosophy, the opportunity to become the "drone" of his writing. "I shall go to work," he announced, "and try to produce hereafter at least a portion of the wealth which I consume." There had been many years to contemplate this eventuality and the two cousins earlier agreed that, if circumstances made it necessary, they would shed other concerns and share in *Tribune* management; furthermore, they secured Keeley's willingness to work for them—in his own peculiar recalcitrant style. Editor Burton Rascoe remembered Keeley treating Joe "as a minor irritation in his job as editor. Whatever Patterson would suggest to him, no matter how bright the suggestion was, Keeley would dismiss it with the impatience of a tetchy roughneck dealing with a moron. There was on Keeley's part jealousy there, and a deeply felt intimation that this clear-eyed, well-mannered, intelligent, unaggressive, eager-to-learn young man would one day supplant him if he gave him half a chance. . . . But Patterson bided his time."

He wouldn't bide it long. On March 1, 1911, exactly eleven months after the death of Robert Patterson, there was a resurgence of the Medill dynasty. With proxies from minority shareholders, the directors approved a management shuffle in which Joe became chairman of the Tribune Company, and Bert, president and chief executive officer. The plan was for Joe to focus on editorial concerns, especially features, and for Bert to devote himself to the business end, with the immediate concern of stabilizing the newsprint supply, and surprisingly Keeley agreed to continue his excellent management of the daily paper. The cousins would be equal in their leadership, but not quite. Bert once explained why he held an almost imperceptible edge. "The family knew I didn't know anything about the newspaper business," he said, "but also they knew I wasn't a Socialist."

As would become evident in the decades that followed, Robert R. McCormick's journalistic gift was not editorial brilliance; his true genius was in building a comprehensive media business and in anticipating allied developments, often years before the competition. During the summer and autumn of 1911, he made four decisive moves. The first was minor, but difficult: he called a halt to the puff pieces Keeley was running about Commonwealth Edison, the utility giant created by his friend Samuel Insull.

Second, the new chief executive gave autonomy to business manager Bill Field in his efforts to reorganize the advertising department, a move that developed into a major strength of the *Tribune*. Medill McCormick had brought his Yale classmate into the paper but Bert boosted him further, saying Field "invented the science of newspaper advertising as we know it." Bill Field continued in the development

of his groundbreaking market research, set up a staff of copywriters
to assist advertisers in creating their ads, organized classes in window
display and advertising budgeting and taught advertisers to target their
campaigns. At the same time Bert directed the marketing of the paper
itself through promotions, contests, giveaways, parades and patriotic
festivities.

Bert's third move—the job he gave himself—was to tighten the
company's business procedures, in which he found a surprising amount
of chaos, prompting him to bring in a crack auditor from the Sanitary
District. By the July board meeting he was urging construction of a
paper mill in Canada; his ammunition was a demographic borrowed
from the Sanitary District projecting a Cook County population
growth to 4.5 million by 1950. The *Tribune*'s newsprint needs would
soar; paper prices were without government regulation and their newspaper did not possess the chain buying power of Hearst, which was
paying five dollars less a ton than the *Tribune*. To cinch his proposal
was a clause within the 1861 *Tribune* charter allowing the company to
manufacture paper. The board was sufficiently impressed to approve
preliminary plans to develop a Canadian operation convenient to raw
materials, power supplies and transportation. They voted an expenditure of $1 million. This move was the beginning of decades in which
Bert would spend weeks at a time in the spruce forests of Canada,
buying great tracts of land, establishing colonies of workers, enlarging the Tribune Company presence there and periodically negotiating
with local governments while building what would become one of the
country's major industries.

FINALLY, BERT DIRECTED Joe's full energies to the Sunday edition.
By coincidence, the *Tribune*'s current Sunday editor left abruptly for
South America to escape paying alimony, providing an instant opening. For Joe it was a miracle and the beginning of a ride that would
last for the rest of his life—in more than one way. In virtually any
newspaper, the Sunday edition is the flagship that leads the week in

circulation and advertising, producing approximately three-quarters of its profits, and the *Tribune*'s flagship was losing dynamism. Joe had proven himself as a novelist and dramatist, but now the Medill DNA was surfacing with urgency. He had a challenging new goal to accomplish and his self-designated assignment was to develop material that would completely engage readers throughout the circulation area. He was determined to design a Sunday edition that would bring families into their living rooms after church on Sunday mornings, with the *Tribune* spread out, children on the floor with the funnies he would create and their parents engrossed in features. Soon his vision would begin to take hold and Joe—along with the newspaper industry—would discover he had the knack for conceiving material the masses craved. But not before he found the perfect partner to join him in realizing his vision.

Already installed in the Sunday department was Mary King, the attractive, blond Roman Catholic daughter of a New York physician. Mary had been secretary to Medill McCormick before being transferred to a job as secretary/assistant to a succession of Sunday editors. Originally she had begun working at the *Tribune* merely to have something to do until she became someone's wife, but then she met Ruth McCormick, who "gave me a new attitude toward my work." By the time Joe arrived as Sunday editor Mary had become a seasoned professional in the department, and because Joe's management style—sometimes gruff, impatient and dictatorial—could be counterproductive, she was invaluable as a buffer between Patterson and his staff.

Mary was highly inventive, with a knack for providing material that engaged the reader. She and Joe began publishing fiction from writers such as H. L. Mencken, George Bernard Shaw, H. G. Wells and G. K. Chesterton. Mary initiated the idea of soliciting movie listings in the form of paid ads from motion picture companies, a newspaper first. For Joe, one of America's earliest and most avid film buffs, this was a natural; she and Joe also collaborated with motion picture studios in printing chapters of serials that would be shown in theaters the following week along with still photography. They added the enticement of cash

prizes, ranging from fifty dollars to five thousand, to readers who cor-
rectly solved a serial's mystery, and they moved further into the genre
by beginning to print early fan coverage of film stars.

Within the next four years, the Sunday edition grew to seventy-
two pages, eight of which were usually lucrative department store ads,
with sixteen more carrying the even more profitable classified advertising, and four of comics. In addition to news, the Sunday edition
was bursting with a wide spectrum of information, including sports,
beauty, clubs, household hints, society and education. And maps.
Burton Rascoe commented that Joe was "mildly insane on the subject
of maps and never let an edition of the Sunday paper appear without a
map made according to one of his own suggestions." His goal was to
provide such a range of material that his Sunday paper would make
magazines obsolete. By 1914 more than half a million families would
be paying five cents each for the Sunday *Tribune* with Joe and Mary's
features. Together the pair added such audience builders as "Isn't It
Odd?," a section that told of mind-boggling natural and scientific
oddities that would never have otherwise come to the reader's notice,
but that sparked animated conversations in living rooms and at Sunday
dinner tables throughout the circulation area.

But the most important change for Joe was that he had found a soul
mate. He was married to a woman with whom he shared few interests.
Although Alice Patterson was a fine, substantial woman, her pursuits
were those of her era and social level: clothes, jewelry, parties, society
and participating in leading what Joe considered an empty life of the
idle rich. As lovely as she was, Alice represented almost everything
her husband was against. Mary, on the other hand, was central to what
was rapidly becoming the core of his life, the creation of editorial material to captivate the newspaper-reading public. They were involved
in an intense, highly creative undertaking, inventing something new
together, creating a genre that had not existed before. It was a heady,
seductive environment for a man in a troubled marriage and a pretty
young virgin of exceptional intelligence, with an aptitude for the innovative communications form they were crafting together. It was not

the family's first life-changing newsroom romance—Joe's grandparents had fallen in love while setting type together—and it would by no means be the last.

Theoretically Joe and Bert were running the *Tribune*, but compensation was not commensurate with their positions. Bert was not married, but Joe had a wife and family to support. There had been lean years for the Joseph Pattersons, and although Joe's circumstances had improved, raising a family would be expensive even if Alice were not extravagant or his mother's grasp on the purse strings firm. From her Washington mansion, Nellie would dole out money according to her whim; as late as October 7, 1912, Joe wrote his mother from Berlin, "Thank you very much for the check. I tell you we needed it." But the *Tribune* itself was making money for its owners and an unexpected twist of circumstances for Bert was that the paper's profitability was bringing his mother to realize her younger son had value after all. She began calling him "Dearest Lamb" and using such phrases as "a dear sweet boy" in referring to him.

IN 1912 MEDILL McCormick had recovered sufficiently to wish a return to the *Tribune*, but he was discouraged by Joe. "Make good elsewhere for a period," his cousin advised, possibly in a spirit of self-interest. "Demonstrate that you are strong enough to do continuous, steady and difficult work." Kate, also aware that it was not the time for him to return to the *Tribune*, was nevertheless against his remaining in D.C.; she told him to "show yourself" in Chicago and "take off that horrible beard which gives you such a wild look." But Medill and Ruth were becoming established in the capital, where the Hanna name continued to carry weight, and during a shipboard crossing following their most recent visit to Dr. Jung they encountered Theodore Roosevelt, who was returning from a fourteen-month safari in Africa. The former president encouraged Medill toward a career in politics, the life Ruth had known and loved through her father. Soon Medill—along with much of the nation—became caught up in the Progressive movement and he attached himself to Senator Robert La Follette, a Wisconsin liberal with designs on the presidency. He even appeared to be prepared to back La Follette in a move against Roosevelt, but then switched allegiance and joined TR's team, infuriating the Wisconsin senator, who condemned Medill as a traitor. Roosevelt, still a relatively young man, wanted a return to the White House but William Howard Taft, the successor he had picked, was equally eager to remain there, creating a falling-out between the two former friends. Taft won the Republican nomination for president and Roosevelt was slated to head the new Progressive—or Bull Moose—Party ticket with Medill as national campaign committee vice chairman. It was a perfect fit for Medill, who backed TR while running as a Progressive Party candidate for the Illinois General Assembly.

Allegiance was more difficult for Cissy. As grateful as she was to Taft for his role in securing her daughter's release from Josef, she continued to be devoted to her cousin Medill, and Roosevelt was the father of one of her closest friends. She threw her energies into the campaigns of both Medill and TR, writing releases and working on their public relations. In doing so she became friendly with Medill's close friend Elmer Schlesinger, who would later be a key player in her life. She found the tall, rangy lawyer attractive, but married. Nevertheless, they became platonically connected within the excited, exhausting atmosphere of a political campaign. She responded to the interest he had in her not merely as a woman—she was accustomed to that—but also as an intelligent, interesting human being. The campaign was successful for Medill, gaining him a seat in the Illinois assembly; however, it was less so for Roosevelt. TR finished with nearly a million more votes than Taft, but both lost to the Democratic candidate, New Jersey governor and former Princeton University president Woodrow Wilson.

Fortunately, Medill's immediate political ambitions survived both the national Democratic victory and his jailing for public intoxication in August 1913 after inexplicably climbing off a train as it moved through northern New York State. His election to the Illinois House of Representatives in 1912 was followed by a second term in 1914; however, his drinking during these years had become serious enough for Ruth to move out. She stayed either in a Chicago apartment or with her brother Daniel in Ohio, although Dan Hanna was also battling alcoholism. But when Medill's problem became so severe that Bert, long his brother's champion, felt he should be institutionalized, Ruth refused to cooperate. Kristie Miller, in her 1992 biography of Ruth, wrote, "Finally, Medill appeared one day and announced to his wife, 'I'm not telling you this time, I'm telling myself in your presence, I'm never going to touch another drink.' " Kristie, who is Ruth and Medill's granddaughter, believes "he may have stopped drinking, but he probably continued to experiment with drugs to control his depression."

Medill carried on with his political career and, raising his political sights even higher, ran for a seat in the U.S. House of Representatives in 1916 and was elected. Following that, he won a seat in the United States Senate in 1918. Also flourishing was his domestic life; he and Ruth began producing children. Katherine Augusta, born in 1913, would legally change her name to Katrina as an adult, but was known informally as Triny. She was followed in 1916 by Joseph Medill McCormick, called John, and in 1921, Medill and Ruth would have little Ruth, known as Bazy. While campaigning around Illinois in 1912, the McCormicks found and purchased a lovely stretch of land near Byron, a hundred miles west of Chicago. Their Rock River Farm eventually became a 2,200-acre dairy farm with a fine herd of Holstein cattle that supplied milk to the Borden Company. It seemed that their life had at last become stable.

ALL APPEARED TO be going smoothly at the Tribune in the spring of 1914, smoothly enough for both Joe and Bert to be out of the country at the same time. Joe left for Veracruz in April to cover the marines' occupation there, and Bert's quest for a Canadian operation took him to a remote region some two hundred miles north of Quebec City. While there he came upon a French language newspaper with a Chicago item announcing that—abruptly and after nearly two decades at the *Tribune*—James Keeley had left the paper to lead the *Record-Herald*. Deeply concerned that the editor had taken key men with him, and knowing Joe was in Mexico, a panicked Bert rushed back to Chicago to discover his worries unfounded and that, aside for a couple of expendable men, staff was intact. However, the new Keeley operation appeared to be a definite threat; bakery tycoon Herman H. Kohlsaat was the paper's principal owner, Victor Lawson was still involved and additional backers included Samuel Insull, Sears' tycoon Julius Rosenwald, meatpacking heir Ogden Armour and several other prominent and wealthy investors. With Keeley at the helm, the paper, renamed the *Herald*, could be devastating competition for the *Tribune*— especially now that the latter was without the editorial leadership of the city's finest newspaperman.

Keeley's exit had been without warning or notice, yet a page-one announcement of his departure, cosigned by Bert and Joe, was remarkably magnanimous. After commending their former employee on his work at the *Tribune* and wishing him "Godspeed," they assured readers that the family of Joseph Medill would continue to carry out management of the *Tribune* in the tradition of its founder, guided by his ideals. Bert and Joe then knuckled under, dividing editorial responsibility between them, each determined to end the intrusion of family differences in the operation of their grandfather's newspaper. Joseph Medill had believed a newspaper should have one voice, expressing the thoughts of a strong editor, and the cousins knew that for his empire to survive it would require the two of them to merge their wills and talents to cooperate completely. United they would prevail.

Privately they drew up an informal contract, ripping off a piece of newsprint and tearing it in two. On each portion they drafted in Bert's handwriting an "iron-bound agreement," which pledged their shared responsibility for the paper's management and policies. They promised to lead the *Tribune* as a team and never to disagree, but if they should conflict, to bring in an independent arbiter. There was also the pledge that if a third party were to be summoned both would follow his decision. The two copies ended with "The ironbound agreement lasts until we both are dead." They signed the fragments and each took one and stashed it away. It was never necessary to consult the agreement again, and the two men's versions were not found until both had died. For more than three years Bert and Joe had successfully governed separate areas of the paper and now they would share editorial policy; this seemed an impossible feat for two men who could scarcely have been further apart politically or philosophically; however, to their everlasting credit they made it work. One month, the ultraconservative McCormick produced the editorial page and the next Patterson, with his leftist persuasion, wrote it, and so forth—with the paper seesawing up and down in an odd sort of balance in viewpoint. Strangely there was little comment about this unique policy, which continued until Joe left for New York to focus entirely on the *Daily News* in 1925.

Concern about the effects of Keeley's departure had been unwarranted. Core *Tribune* staff members, who numbered some of the most competent in the city, remained with Bert and Joe, among them, managing editor Teddy Beck and the brilliant city editor Walter Howey. During the first post-Keeley year, *Tribune* circulation increased by forty thousand, with a steady climb in the following years. As their paper strengthened, Keeley's *Herald* declined. What had initially appeared to be ominously threatening competition first stumbled, then merged with Hearst's *Examiner*, creating the *Herald-Examiner*, and the formidable editor James Keeley became a public relations executive.

The McCormick-Patterson team had succeeded; they had saved their grandfather's newspaper from sale to the enemy, and won further battles the same enemy had waged to crush the paper. With the war over, Bert and Joe now had to deal with the tedium of peace. After working diligently every day to produce a successful product, Joe went home at night to a difficult marriage and possibly another round of the social circus he so despised. But Bert had no home to return to, beyond an apartment in the chic Pullman Building at Michigan and Adams. He spent the early portion of the evening exercising at the Chicago Athletic Club, followed by dinner and possibly the theater, which he often left early to return to the *Tribune*, where he oversaw production of the suburban edition. It was a largely solitary existence and an extension of his aloneness as a boy—creating an environment for the dramatic next phase in his personal life.

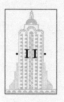

THE COUNTESS AND
HER ADMIRERS

FTER the heady years in European courts and disappointments of an aristocratic marriage, Cissy returned to the understated elegance of Lake Forest, Illinois, "the most glamorous place in the world," wrote F. Scott Fitzgerald, who believed it was "in the same league as Newport, Southampton and Palm Beach." The elite Chicago suburb founded by Cissy's Patterson grandfather stands above Lake Michigan on bluffs some thirty miles north of the city. Lush vegetation and deep ravines give surprise and mystery to an abundant natural landscape; tree-shaded streets curve around manicured grounds, edged with hedges and fences that shield from public view a sampling of the nation's finest nineteenth- and twentieth-century country houses. Successive generations of Chicago's great dry goods, meatpacking, banking and real estate families have danced on the lawns and terraces of these estates, frolicked in their swimming pools, competed on the tennis courts and spent languid summer hours on wide porches surrounding well-appointed houses. Always permeating the communal memory is the dreamy Fitzgerald legend of gala summer evenings under the stars, with canvas stretched out over the perfect green grass, Chinese lanterns strung on wires above and an orchestra playing from the terrace. Presiding over it all from 1895 has been Onwentsia, the area's premier country club.

The Cissy who returned to bucolic Lake Forest was not the

debutante who left turn-of-the-century Chicago. She had been well known then within her set and was a member of one of the city's most prominent families, but on her return both she and Felicia were international celebrities. Marriage to an exotic count, followed by the infamous kidnapping of her child and intervention of two heads of state, had given both mother and daughter a fame bordering on notoriety. On January 28, 1911, Cissy sued Count Gizycki for divorce in Chicago Circuit Court, naming three Viennese women as corespondents. Once again an international press detailed the drama of her marriage, Josef's abuse, the kidnapping and the czar's imperial command for the child's return. But added to the pictures and headlines were new details of their life together, now public for the first time, from abandonment on her wedding day to the physical violence in Pau. Even the staid *New York Times* detailed the 1907 Pau incident in which "the count struck his wife, knocking her down," and some accounts erroneously insisted that a half-million-dollar ransom had been paid to Gizycki for Felicia's return. But the legal process was excruciatingly slow, and it would be another six and a half years before a divorce was granted, giving Cissy official custody of her daughter. Count Gizycki, who never remarried, resided in a Riviera hotel for a time and then lived at the Vienna estate of Count Charles Rudolf Andreas Kinsky, Gizycki's good friend and fellow Casanova. The Austrian Kinsky is best remembered as a lover of Winston Churchill's mother, the übersophisticated Jennie, for whom he was said to have been "like opium."

Cissy continued to be a magnet for men. Her supple body and the amazing carriage that had caused comment from President Theodore Roosevelt still mesmerized all those who observed her. Years later, Felicia would describe her mother "as the most graceful human being I have ever seen. She ambled across the room; she melted into a chair. She commanded everyone's attention. She was made for tea gowns and dresses with long trains." Among the admirers—new and old—drawn to the older, more sophisticated Cissy was Freddy McLaughlin, an ardent suitor from her debutante days, now recovering from the collapse of his first marriage. The coffee company heir and consummate horseman continued to be a well-matched companion for Cissy; stag hunting in Poland and foxhunting in France had polished her skills as an equestrienne and intrepid jumper.

A rival suitor, competing for Cissy's attention in both Washington and Chicago, was Germany's handsome ambassador to the United States, Count Johann Heinrich von Bernstorff. One night, the rival McLaughlin quietly followed Cissy and the German count as they drove along a back road near Lake Forest. When Bernstorff parked his automobile and began to embrace Cissy, Freddy jumped from his car and attacked him with a whip. Because she had made a wise exit with Freddy's arrival, the amorous ambassador raced off without his lady, and it was the last either would see of him for some time. It was just as well; Bernstorff—greatly in demand by hostesses when all things German were fashionable—was suffering a backlash created by the war atmosphere, and the romance was beginning to reflect poorly on Cissy.

The Lake Forest house Cissy chose to lease had been commissioned by meatpacking heir Louis Swift for his daughter, Bessie Fernald. Designed by Howard Van Doren Shaw, the white Colonial featured the screened porches so welcoming on indolent summer afternoons before the marvel of air-conditioning. When Felicia and her mother were not in Lake Forest or at her grandmother's Washington mansion, they would spend time in the fashionable Rhode Island resort of Newport, often with Ruth and Medill, as they did during the summer of 1914. Newport was an enchanting location to experience the final great season "before the lamps went out" and war ruptured the serenity of Europe and upper-class America, forever. Life would never be the same for those who remembered the civility of those last glittering, unhurried prewar days.

For Cissy, one of the happiest aspects of her return to Chicago was the presence of her brother Joe; he had not yet left for New York, and his Libertyville farm was not far from her house in Lake Forest. The two great, untarnished loves of Cissy's life had been her father and brother, and now she and Joe were able to be together frequently. He talked with her about his ideas of inequality and she sympathized with him and his troubled marriage. When he spoke to her of his theories about journalism, she listened with interest and later used almost everything he told her. She began reading the *Tribune* as never before, watching the kernels Joe described to her take root and grow in print. The Lake Forest years also coincided with Cissy's acting phase, during which she appeared in a succession of amateur community plays, including benefit productions at Jane Addams's Hull House. Her dramatic flair made her a natural actress, and she was thrilled when her adored brother pronounced her the best amateur he had seen. Although critics from Chicago newspapers gave her performances raves, it was merely a diversion during a phase of her life when she was searching for direction and self-expression.

The negative of those years was that the disaster of Cissy's marriage gave Nellie the opportunity to step in again as a debilitating presence, eroding her daughter's vitality. During the interminable period in which she waited for her divorce to become final, Cissy became weak and sickly from her mother's smothering. Nellie, in turn, fed on this frailty, which only made it worse. She wrote her daughter-in-law Alice in February 1912 describing Cissy as "nervous" and "high strung," which had become true. Felicia's memory of her mother in those years was that of "a delicate woman who went to doctor after doctor, spent a lot of time in bed, took rest cures and went on different diets." Ultimately Cissy was informed by doctors that she was teetering at the edge of nervous collapse. Ironically it was the greatest gift Nellie could have given her, because it forced Cissy to flee to an environment to which her mother was physically incapable of following. And the escape transformed her life.

IN 1916, WITH eleven-year-old Felicia, a French maid and seven wardrobe trunks, Cissy spent six days traveling to the Bar BC dude ranch in Jackson Hole, Wyoming, a dusty ten-hour wagon ride from the nearest rail station. During the long last day, the wagon driver periodically told the women to get out and walk while they mounted a steep grade. Felicia remembered watching her mother hike ahead in her long-skirted Paris tweeds and bespoke leather boots from London. "She looked like a big wildcat," she wrote in a 1965 *Vogue* magazine article, "and her red hair flamed in the mountain sunlight." The remote colony they found was a brutal shock to three women who were expecting a vacation spot similar in comfort and civility to the Newport of previous summers. The sniveling maid and six of the trunks were immediately sent home, but mother and daughter remained, Felicia exuberant, because—for the first time in her life—she was free of a nanny. Initially Cissy stayed in Jackson Hole to prove she had the stuff to rough it in a rudimentary cabin without plumbing or electricity, but slowly she felt the transcendent power of the valley's natural beauty, with the majesty of the Tetons looming above. Her strength returned within days, and she embarked on a rigorous elk hunt in the mountains with Felicia, ranch guide Cal Carrington and a boy to cook and look after the horses. In her *Vogue* piece, Felicia recorded an evening during the last part of the elk hunt. They were high in the hills, running out of food and enduring a late August snowfall, when "my mother enchanted Cal and myself by reading Tolstoy aloud to us, as we huddled around the stove in her tent while the snow hissed on the warm canvas." After three arduous weeks of stalking her bull elk all day, followed by nights in a leaking tent, Cissy shot the creature on the twenty-second day. She had hunted many times before, but in overly civilized, social situations and certainly never under these conditions. It was a new kind of achievement.

During those three weeks she bonded with Cal, a former cattle rustler, beginning a relationship that would last for more than two decades. Carrington, then in his early forties, was a tall, handsome, barely literate cowboy—a tan, rugged precursor of the Marlboro Man, but completely authentic. He had been born Enoch Julin in Sweden, abandoned in this country by his mother and raised partially by Mormons but primarily by himself. He named himself California, for another cowboy, and Carrington for an Englishman who had shown him kindness. Soon Cissy's feelings for Cal and Jackson Hole began to run so deeply that both would become a permanent part of her life. The following summer, she saw Cal's spread, Flat Creek Ranch, and fell in love with it at once. The beautiful valley, under Sheep Mountain, was an arduous fifteen-mile ride from Jackson, up and down hills, through a small river and finally up a narrow climb over a high hill. His valley was carpeted with a meadow that sprouted wildflowers and was bisected by Flat Creek, a trout stream that furnished clear, cold drinking water to the ranch. Moose, elk, bear and other animals came to drink from the sparkling creek, along with varieties of birds. Back in his rustling days, Cal had found the ranch perfect for secreting the horses he stole with his gang. There was ample pasture for the horses and should the law appear, he reminisced, "I could see the sheriff a'comin' either way." All he had to do to shut off the canyon was to "put up two pair of boards."

Cissy insisted on buying the property from Cal, a project that took persuasion, a bit of trickery and time. After at last acquiring the ranch, she moved into the main cabin, with Cal living in another nearby. Her cook and maid shared a third cabin, and a chore boy stayed in a fourth near the barn. Once it was officially hers, she had an immense dressing room added to her own quarters and a large lodge built nearby. Three distinctive features dominating the hospitable lodge were a living room—with a dance floor and a colossal fireplace—a glass-walled dining room overlooking the surrounding scenery, and a spacious porch with a heart-stopping view of the mountains. Soon furniture began arriving: an immense Persian carpet, Navajo rugs, tables, chairs, chests, cabinets—some new, some antique—and a grand piano. It was a tricky balance, but while maintaining the integrity of its rugged Wyoming locale, Cissy managed to imbue Flat Creek Ranch with her own opulent style. She also bought a cow pony, which Cal helped select; she named him Ranger and he became her favorite mount. Not only was Ranger "born with nineteen legs" and surefooted on the mountain trails, but he also could point and flush like a hunting dog. Cissy returned summer after summer to ride, shoot and become immersed in the peace and unspoiled beauty of the meadows and mountains. She felt comfortable with the people there; they accepted her as an individual and were warm and friendly but complied with her need for privacy.

Periodically, Cissy and Cal, with a cook and a store of rations, would set out for weeks at a time on hunting expeditions. Together they rode on horseback throughout the territory and into the Canadian Rockies, shooting goats, sheep, bear and other prey. All urban pretension fell away; Cissy hunted wearing a fringed buckskin vest over a man's shirt and Levi's or sheepskin chaps, with a five-gallon hat covering her copper hair. She and Cal drank gin together on these trips and, according to Cissy's chore boy, "Cal was a quiet drunk. You wouldn't know he was drunk until he talked. But Cissy could be a mean drunk. The way she talked you thought she came right out of the alley." Always, she was equal to any challenge presenting itself, and she succeeded in being the first woman to navigate the rapids of the Salmon River of Idaho—the River of No Return—in a canoe. To Native Americans it was the Forbidden River. During Cissy and Cal's 163-mile white-water excursion, they came across the empty boat of a man who had preceded them alone, and their captain knew of two men who had drowned earlier in the season, as well as another he had buried the year before.

The relationship between the countess and the cowboy intensified; they fascinated each other, neither had been in a relationship with anyone like this before and Cal, who had always been on the receiving end in his liaisons with women, amazed Jacksonites by buying Cissy a pair of black angora chaps. He respected her courage but also felt protective of her, a bond Cissy would mirror in *Glass Houses*, a novel that was percolating in her mind. In it she would describe the tender rapport between the Washington, D.C., sophisticate Mary Moore and Ben Furruseth, the rough but gentle cowboy who had cared for the urbane Mary intermittently since childhood. Her Wyoming experiences made for good novel material but she also contributed to such periodicals as *Field & Stream*, where the reader was her hunting and fishing peer. In addition, her renown as a big-game hunter had become so widespread that she was known as one to the ordinary reader, prompting the *Chicago Herald-Examiner* to commission her to write a series for its Sunday edition in late 1920.

Cissy made another lifelong Wyoming friend in Rose Crabtree, a Jackson Town Council member and proprietor of Jackson's Crabtree Hotel. Throughout the nation women were agitating for voting rights, but in Wyoming they had been voting since 1896, and Jackson was the only town in America administered by women. Rose had run against her husband and "beat him two-to-one," according to a piece Cissy wrote for the *Omaha World Journal*, her first newspaper article. She loved the homey ambiance of Rose's kitchen. "She'd like to sit among the help and pretend she was one," said Rose. For Cissy, it was a return to her childhood, where she spent time in the kitchen with the servants, preferring their downstairs world to the upstairs environment of her mother. She rapidly came to consider Cal and Rose her social equals and would repeatedly bring both to Washington and entertain them with her society friends. She took Cal with her to Paris, where they visited the tourist sites, rode horseback in the Bois de Boulogne, sat together at sidewalk cafés and took in the ebony magnificence of Josephine Baker dancing nude. She sent him to Italy when he wanted to go and she didn't, and to Africa when he decided he would like to hunt the continent's big game.

She adored Rose, explaining they were both tough, shanty-Irish bitches, and wrote her, "I've laughed with you and cried with you more than any other person in the world." Rose was the only woman friend with whom Cissy never quarreled and Felicia believed she was "the greatest influence" in her mother's life. It was through her that Cissy learned "she could do anything, that there was nothing she *couldn't* be. Mother . . . was used to being waited on hand and foot by servants—but Rose told her she couldn't be that way out West." Felicia believed the Jackson Hole years were her mother's happiest. "Her curiosity about people came awake. She loved to get their stories. The first writing she ever did was about the West, and this in turn led her into the newspaper business."

*   *   *

CISSY WAS SPENDING enough time in Washington to have a residence there, but living with her mother in Dupont Circle was not feasible. Felicia remembered Nellie and Cissy quarreling "fiercely when they were together. Grams was striving vainly, and too late, to mold her character. Grams did not approve of her beaux . . . and tried to control her by spying on her." The solution was for Cissy to buy a house on R Street, which she kept as a Washington base. Ruth and Medill had acquired a house nearby, which delighted her, and Medill, then in an emotional upswing, was conveying an excitement about plans he had to run for the U.S. Senate—possibly even higher office eventually. Ruth, a friend since their Farmington days, joined Cissy's set of women friends, along with Mrs. Eugene Meyer, the overbearing mother of Katharine Graham, who would achieve renown in her own right at the *Washington Post*. Agnes Meyer was an intellectual and a connoisseur of art, particularly Chinese painting, and, although headstrong and egocentric, she was without the vices of many of Cissy's friends. The two enjoyed each other immensely and spent hours together lunching, attending theater, gallery-hopping and engaging in high-level gossip.

Another close friend was Evalyn Walsh McLean, pampered daughter of an Irish miner who had become fabulously rich though a colossal Colorado gold strike. In 1905 Evalyn was critically injured in an automobile accident that required massive quantities of morphine, sending her spiraling into intermittent but lifelong addiction. Following her physical recovery, she eloped on a whim with Edward Beale "Ned" McLean, the handsome, equally pampered offspring of John R. McLean, owner of the *Cincinnati Enquirer* and *Washington Post*. In the years that followed, Ned inherited the *Washington Post*, along with a half-million-dollar annual income, but the two fortunes simply melted away. Ned, increasingly alcoholic, carried on a ruinously expensive affair with Marion Davies's sister Rose, while the morphine-dependent Evalyn splurged on the world's most famous gem, the Hope diamond. Ultimately Ned suffered a nervous breakdown that sent him into an institution, and throughout all of the long drama, Evalyn remained within Cissy's circle of intimates.

Alice Roosevelt had fallen away, and for good reason. Cissy's men friends were often Cissy's lovers and frequently they were married to others. The most notable among them was Nicholas Longworth, Alice's husband in a blatantly open marriage. Nick, who would become Speaker of the House in 1925, was thought to be a potential presidential candidate, thus the pull keeping the Longworths together was a possible return to the White House for Alice, as attractive a prospect for her as a presidential term was for Nick. Another conflict between the two old friends involved Senator William Edgar Borah of Idaho, a stirring orator and thoroughly masculine man, who—without being handsome—held irresistible appeal for women. The powerful senator, known for a sexual appetite so insatiable that his nickname was the "Stallion of Idaho," was married to a mousey, childless woman, who was conveniently away from Washington for long stretches of time. Borah was one of Cissy's prime men friends and, to complicate matters, he and Alice were also engaged in a dalliance so flagrant that she was known around town as "Aurora Borah Alice." In 1925, when Mrs. Longworth surprised friends by producing a child following eighteen years of a barren marriage, the baby resembled neither the Roosevelts nor the Longworths but was strikingly similar in appearance to Senator Borah. Nick put his foot down when Alice suggested naming the child Deborah; instead she was christened Paulina, either in honor of the Apostle Paul or after a street in Chicago where she was born—the source of the name was as enigmatic as that of the baby herself.

If the two old friends' crisscross romances complicated their relationship, Cissy continually aggravated the situation. Even so, years later Alice was quoted with "I said a lot of things, but Cissy *did* them." She also reminisced, "If any man ever caused trouble between Cissy and me, it was my husband Nick. He adored her." But at the time, Cissy's shenanigans were too outrageous even for a free spirit like Alice. In an often-reported incident, both Cissy and Nick became noticeably drunk at one of Alice's parties and disappeared. When someone opened an unlocked bathroom door and turned on the light, there lying on the tile floor was an extremely disheveled Cissy in carnal embrace with her hostess's husband. In a similar story that circulated around Washington for decades, Cissy and Borah each arrived separately for another Longworth party but vanished together after a couple of drinks. The next day a maid found Cissy's distinctive hairpins in the library and Alice returned them with a note reading, "I believe they are yours." Cissy retorted with a note of her own, "And if you look up in the chandelier, you might find my panties." The anecdote grew and was transformed into several versions, all starring Cissy and Alice. By 1933, the story would be so well known that during a Women's National Press Club skit, Cissy, cast as a female editor modeled on herself, threw in an ad lib: "Stop the presses! Stop the presses! My drawers are caught in the presses"—a line that succeeded in stopping the show as well.

While she was engaged in other activities, printers ink had been simmering in Cissy's veins, and the first of three men to recognize her incipient talent was the great Walter Howey. Unlike the actors who played him in *The Front Page*, Howey was not a handsome man; in fact, he was quite ordinary-looking except that his left eye was made of glass, which led Ben Hecht to insist that it was the warmer of the two. He was not Cissy's usual type, but she was fascinated by Howey's energy, originality and flamboyance. In many ways he was her masculine mirror, feral, unconventional and devoted to good whiskey and great literature. He would take her to Schlogl's Restaurant and quote Shakespeare or instruct her on his journalistic prescription: 10 percent information, 90 percent entertainment. Howey also believed—as did virtually all newspapermen of the period—that local news towered over national stories and was far more urgent than foreign news. Cissy respected his publishing theories, as she did those of her brother, carefully listening to and remembering everything he told her.

After Howey left the *Tribune* to edit Hearst's *Herald-Examiner*, he offered thirty-eight-year-old Cissy an assignment to cover the 1920

Republican National Convention in Chicago. Cissy jumped at the opportunity to be a newspaperwoman and even allowed Howey to publicize the fact that his reporter, Eleanor Gizycka, was the sister of *Chicago Tribune* co-editor Joseph Medill Patterson. None of this was lost on her aunt Kate McCormick, who, over otherwise sedate chatter at a Lake Forest luncheon, was heard to loudly predict that Hearst would soon lament hiring Cissy, an error the *Tribune* would *never* make. The 1920 convention's leading candidates for nomination were former army chief of staff Leonard Wood; Illinois governor Frank O. Lowden, who was George Pullman's son-in-law; and California progressive Republican senator Hiram Johnson. Mr. Hearst was backing Senator Johnson, for whom Cissy had campaigned during primaries in the spring. Senator Borah, also a Johnson supporter, was a possible candidate for nomination himself, which would have pleased Cissy immensely. She was greatly enjoying the national political experience in her hometown and gave a dinner for the Hiram Johnsons in one of the Drake Hotel's private dining rooms; among her guests were Joe and Alice Patterson, Ruth McCormick, the William Wrigleys and her co-worker in the 1912 Progressive campaign, Elmer Schlesinger, who had separated from his wife.

While Cissy and her guests were dining at the North Side Drake, downtown at the Blackstone Hotel, Republican political bosses were secreted in the soon-to-become-historic "smoke-filled room," engaged in selecting the controllable Warren G. Harding as their candidate. "We've got a lot of second-raters," concluded one of the frustrated kingmakers, "and Warren Harding of Ohio is the best of the second-raters." The same logic was followed in choosing Calvin Coolidge as his running mate. Even Harding's campaign manager announced, "The day of giants in the Presidential chair is past." As it developed, Harding may have been controllable but his young mistress Nan Britton was not. Her book, detailing the conception of their love child "on a couch in his Senate office"—accompanied by a description of the five-feet-square White House closet where they rendezvoused on other occasions—was soon the buzz of the capital. When Harding died suddenly, catapulting Coolidge to the presidency, the plausible rumor circulated that he had been poisoned by his wife.

The Harding-Coolidge decision taking place at the Blackstone was unknown to Cissy, who wrote an adoring *Herald-Examiner* piece on Borah, referring to him as "a lion—a good-natured and experienced lion." So fawning was the article that Howey slapped on the headline, BORAH IS COUNTESS GIZYCKA'S HERO, angering the married senator, who felt the piece hinted at their affair. Consequently Cissy's initial venture into political journalism not only ended their romance but also—temporarily—stopped her newspaper career in its tracks.

WORLD WAR I AND
THE CREATION OF COLONEL
ROBERT R. McCORMICK

Bert's belated loss of virginity occurred in his midthirties at the Wheaton, Illinois, house of a married mainstay of that very Christian community. Like her pupil, the lady was a member of the elite Chicago Golf Club, where more than the greens were said to be fast. Following his tardy awakening, McCormick never lacked for female companionship, although future liaisons almost invariably satisfied a fundamental need for the cozy family ambiance he had never experienced as a boy. Following the Wheaton incident, much of his romantic life would be spent in a series of ménages-à-trois, in which—as the ever-present bachelor in a warm, well-ordered household—he provided cash to an overextended husband and willing cuckold. This state of affairs occurred repeatedly, twice leading to divorce, at considerable financial cost to Bert, who suddenly found himself with a wife.

The first of these situations erupted during the deep winter months of 1914, when all of fashionable Chicago was suddenly abuzz over Bert's affair with the wife of his alcoholic cousin Edward S. Adams. Amy Irwin Adams, eight years older than McCormick and thus an adequate mother substitute, was the daughter of Bernard J. D. Irwin, a distinguished Indian fighter, Civil War surgeon, Union Army general, and winner of the nation's first Medal of Honor. The senior Irwins had moved to Chicago in the early 1890s and had been embraced by the city's Old Guard. By the time their daughter came into Bert's personal orbit, she was a handsome, socially adept young matron, highly regarded within the Chicago establishment. Originally known as Amie, the childless Mrs. Adams was a skilled amateur painter, French linguist and, like McCormick, an accomplished equestrian. The arrangement had begun innocently enough after Bert's first year at Northwestern. Without close family of his own in Chicago that summer, he spent much of the season with his cousin and his cousin's wife at their apartment in town. When autumn arrived, it seemed natural for him to move into the couple's Lake Forest country house, where Amy kept a stable of fine horses and Blue Ribbon dogs. It wasn't long before she and Bert became inseparable, competing in Onwentsia Club horse shows, riding together on the area's abundant wooded trails, joining in local fox hunts, and eventually years later becoming lovers. Meanwhile Ed Adams drank.

Kate McCormick, who had wished for harvester heiress Marion Deering as a daughter-in-law, was fueling the gossip. "Poor poor Bertie!" she wailed. "I can't get over his moral deterioration caused by a bad woman." Nellie, pleased with her sister's discomfort, increased it by proclaiming the affair would never have occurred if Kate had remained in Chicago and maintained a proper home for her bachelor son. "It is his Mother's fault that he lived at the Adams' for 10 years," she wrote Alice Patterson from Washington in early 1914. "He had no home from the time he was 21." A few months later she continued from New York's Ritz-Carlton, "Poor Bertie—Amy seized him when he was barely 23 & very immature for his age & she has fascinated him ever since." At the same time, Kate kept up her end with such statements as "That old tart shall never have a cent of mine, or a *stick*, nor a *shred, living or dead*." The phrase "old tart" formed her ongoing theme, while Nellie was more forgiving of her nephew's lover: "Who could live with Ed Adams without trying to get away?"

The divorce for which Amy filed in February 1914 was received on March 6, resolving the matter and allowing talk to die down. But in September Ed Adams appealed to reopen the case with a $300,000 countersuit for alienation of affection. Inexplicably Bert brought greater attention to the situation by filing his own suit asking for payment of $38,000 in loans to Adams. Once again gossip picked up and new speculation made the social rounds. The affair, with its various complications, was common knowledge in clubs and drawing rooms throughout the fashionable environs of the city, but—like the newspaper circulation wars—it was never mentioned in the Chicago papers. Only the *Day Book*, a gossip sheet that was not part of "the publishers' trust," printed facts and their accompanying rumors. New York and Milwaukee papers, also full of the news, were valued trophies to be passed around among members of the smart set. Not only did "everyone" know of the cozy triadic living arrangements, but they were also aware of Adams's alcoholic needs and his alleged physical abuse of his gentle wife. Bert's mother continued to make matters worse; never one to disappoint when it came to mischief making, Kate announced that the "old strumpet" had snared her son by faking pregnancy. It all made for delicious scandal. And the lovers needed to get away.

WHILE CHICAGO WAS whispering about the McCormick-Adams affair, with the she-devils churning up further trouble, legitimate turmoil erupted abroad. On June 28, 1914, Austrian Archduke Franz Ferdinand was assassinated in Sarajevo and, within less than a month, the nations of Europe were at war. The very notion of war with Germany was a distant specter especially for Americans of means, who had long included the country in their recreational travel, and many—including the Joseph Pattersons—had hired German governesses to ensure their children gained fluency in the language. But war is always news and the *Tribune*, along with other major American newspapers, sent correspondents to cover it. By August Joe Patterson was in Belgium reporting on activities of the German army there, but virtually no one in the American press was covering the Russian army.

Few journalists anywhere were as well connected within Russia's top circles as Bert's family. It was natural for him to call on his mother for assistance in arranging for access at the highest levels, and happily she cooperated with her own version of the Grand Tour ploy. Like so many mothers before and since, Kate believed if Bert traveled far enough away for a sufficient length of time he would forget his beloved. She also threw in a fifty-thousand-dollar enticement for him to leave both Amy and the country, and immediately contacted the Russian ambassador to the United States George Bakhmeteff. The Russian diplomat replied that Commander in Chief Grand Duke Nicholas, who "preserved the best remembrance of the late ambassador, Mr. McCormick . . . consents, as a unique exception, to admit your Mr. McCormick on the field of active fighting." It was also stipulated that Bert would be admitted as "a distinguished foreigner personally known to the Grand Duke" rather than as a war correspondent; however, it was implied that he would not be prevented from filing dispatches to his paper.

McCormick now had the necessary entrée but he also required an aura of military pomp and credentials that would serve him at the uppermost czarist echelons. He called on Governor Edward F. Dunne, whom Joe Patterson had supported in the politician's earlier bid for mayor of Chicago, to ask for an Illinois National Guard commission. Dunne was most obliging, providing Bert with the rank of colonel on his personal staff. After outfitting himself in appropriately impressive military attire, McCormick traveled to New York to confer with the dashing foreign correspondent Richard Harding Davis, who counseled him to file a report every day no matter how insignificant the news might seem. Preparations thus accomplished, the new "colonel" left for England on February 10, 1915, aboard the S.S. *Adriatic*. Among his pleasant distractions during the crossing was dinner with glamorous soprano Mary Garden, who was active not only in the Chicago Opera Company but also in the amorous life of Chicago meatpacker Ogden Armour. Amy followed a few days later and, on March 10, they were married in London at the registry office of St. George's Church, Hanover Square. Although Bert's age was recorded as thirty-four, his bride, "Amie de Houle Adams formerly Irwin," was gallantly registered as being "of full age." Bert presented his bride with two pearl necklaces purchased with Kate's fifty-thousand-dollar bribe, a precious gift Amy wore every day for the rest of her life. While in England, McCormick interviewed Prime Minister Herbert H. Asquith, First Lord of the Admiralty Winston Churchill and other British leaders for stories he filed to the *Tribune*. He also lunched with the fabulously successful British newspaper tycoon Lord Northcliffe, whose journalistic prescience would later figure importantly in Tribune Company fortunes. Continuing on to France, he developed further newspaper dispatches in that country before sailing with Amy for Malta and then Greece, from where they traveled by train through Serbia, Bulgaria and Romania into Russia.

IN ST. PETERSBURG McCormick received instructions for a meeting with the czar at Tsarskoe Selo, or Czar's Village, seventeen miles south of St. Petersburg. Originally a summer home for the imperial family, the eight-hundred-acre Tsarskoe Selo embraced the ornate Catherine Palace and smaller Alexander Palace, a farm, kennels, an arsenal, numerous follies and a variety of other structures and embellishments added during the eighteenth and nineteenth centuries. Red-uniformed Cossacks in great black fur caps patrolled a tall iron fence surrounding Tsarskoe Selo's grassy park, separating it from a summer colony of St. Petersburg aristocracy, eager to be near the imperial presence. Nicholas II, whose personal style was in his own royal way nearly as offhand as that of Joe Patterson, was born in the Alexander Palace; he had lived much of his life there and felt most comfortable in its well-worn surroundings. The smaller residence had become the family's St. Petersburg home following a 1905 gunfire incident at the Winter Palace, and it was here, in his working office, that the czar conducted day-to-day business and met with visitors such as the newspaper publishing son of the former American ambassador. He and the czarina, who was even less interested in pomp and social contact than he, now ventured into the Winter Palace in St. Petersburg only for court balls and other state occasions.

McCormick's train arrived at the Tsarskoe Selo station at one-thirty that April afternoon. Despite the two o'clock scheduling of his meeting with Nicholas, he was instructed to wear the diplomatic white tie and tails, making identification effortless for the imperial coachman when a tall American wearing a silk top hat stepped off the train. Ten minutes later the carriage was entering through open palace gates to the Alexander Palace, where Bert was shown in and led to a dark oak-paneled reception room. While waiting, he memorized his surroundings: the tall, double-glazed French windows overlooking the park, walls hung with a variety of oils and watercolors, a Turkish carpet covering the room's floor, and the fireplace where flames had recently died down to embers. He walked over to a large table piled with books, noting a volume about Reims and others concerning military vehicles and hydraulic engineering. At precisely two o'clock, two officers in red appeared and, simultaneously, the door to the czar's working study opened.

Bert entered a room very much like the one he was leaving, except that standing in front of him, wearing a simple olive uniform with one medal, and knee boots wanting polish, was the Czar of all the Russias. The emperor extended his hand to Bert and said, "I am very pleased to meet you, Mr. McCormick." In appearance, Nicholas II was a near duplicate of his first cousin George V of England, and Bert remembered him as having "the largest eyes I have ever seen in a living mortal." He later reported that the czar spoke English with "less of an accent than Britain's Edward VII." The room had the passé look of the 1880s, dark and very masculine; it was furnished with old pieces Nicholas had found in other rooms of the palace, an L-shaped desk with a French lamp swinging above it, and square-shaped chairs upholstered in green leather. Walls were either paneled in dark, hand-waxed walnut or painted a deep imperial red. Along one wall, at a corner of the office, was an extended built-in divan, covered in Oriental carpets; this was where the czar sometimes slept after working late. Near it were a child's chair and table for his son Alexis to use during visits with his father.

The short audience was ended when a door opened and a young

girl, one of the ill-fated grand duchesses, appeared briefly to inform her father that lunch was waiting. McCormick was returned by carriage to the station and, because he had not eaten, he ordered a picnic meal from a Russian menu he couldn't decipher. What arrived was a cheese sandwich, two varieties of caviar and a bottle of kvass, a Russian beer. He then returned to St. Petersburg on the 3:17 train.

BERT'S NEXT APPOINTMENT with a member of the imperial family occurred only a few days later. Amy remained in St. Petersburg while he traveled to Poland and Imperial Russian Headquarters at Stavka, the rural post of the Russian commander in chief, Grand Duke Nicholas. Then fifty-eight years old, the six-foot, six-inch Nikolai Nikolaievich was a grandson of Czar Nicholas I and cousin to Nicholas II. An awesome figure, he was physically fit, highly disciplined and God-fearing, with astonishing blue eyes and a trim gray beard. Not only was the charismatic grand duke a great warrior and a near god to his men, but he was also a legend throughout the land, a giant who was expected by some either to succeed the weak-willed current czar as Nicholas III or to act as regent to the next. The field post, located off a railway junction between the Austrian and German fronts, was composed of a group of army trains, which as the war continued were covered with roofs and connected by a system of wooden walkways. The Grand Duke presided from a private car, personalized with an abundance of icons, Oriental carpets and bearskins. McCormick's National Guard commission proved an asset among the Russians, to whom the word "guard" carried special prestige, and he communicated easily with those in the field, conversing in French, the diplomatic language.

The information Bert gathered not only provided for exclusive dispatches the *Tribune* carried at the time, but also for a book he would write on his return to Chicago. And, according to reports received by the czar, he had made a favorable impression on the commander in chief, whom he would meet again after the Russian Revolution. Seven years later, Bert encountered the grand duke and his wife, the Grand Duchess Anastasia, at Cap d'Antibes, where Anastasia asked his assistance in selling her jewelry. "There was one very large yellow diamond, a gift from the Sultan of Turkey, which I was able to dispose of," he remembered, "but a pink diamond, the size of a man's thumbnail, was valued at a half million dollars, which, of course, I could not obtain." The grand duchess had perhaps had a hand in her own fate. She and her sister the Grand Duchess Militza, daughters of King Nicholas I of Montenegro, had introduced the menacing monk Rasputin to Empress Alexandra in 1905, creating an association that contributed to the downfall of the Romanovs. The two dark-haired, dark-eyed women, jointly known within court circles as "the black peril," had entirely fulfilled the long-held conviction of Russian aristocrats that they were a dangerous presence.

After his successful visit at the front, McCormick returned to St. Petersburg and to Amy, with whom he thoroughly explored the city before making a side trip to Moscow. Among the entertainments they enjoyed was the ballet, which they attended twice, and where Bert was surprised at the ovation received by a dancer he did not think exceptional. He was correct, although unacquainted with the backstory that lifted this ballerina, Mathilde Kschessinska, from the ordinary. She was from a family of famous dancers with aristocratic roots, and in 1889 Nicholas II's father, Czar Alexander III, with members of the imperial family, had attended her ballet school graduation performance, creating an enduring Russian legend. At a supper that followed, the czar demanded to be seated next to Mathilde, with his son, Nicholas, on the other side. It was a charmed evening during which the future Nicholas II was bewitched by the seventeen-year-old dancer, beginning a celebrated love affair. The ballet graduation party was followed by many romantic meetings at Kschessinska's house and lavish gifts of diamonds and sapphires, but the two could never marry. Their relationship lasted until Nicholas's engagement to Princess Alix of Hesse, his greatest love and the future Empress Alexandra, and Kschessinska went on to continue a splendid career as both a prima ballerina and a grand horizontal. She would survive the revolution and many lovers, eventually marrying Grand Duke Andrei Vladimirovich, a cousin of the czar, and living contentedly in France until her death at age ninety-nine in 1971.

Having achieved his double objective of leaving the heat of scandal in Chicago and successfully covering the coveted Russian front, Mc-Cormick took Amy home by way of Stockholm, London and Paris, where they spent two months at the Ritz. Kate's damaging behavior continued with rumors she circulated about the couple in Paris, where she claimed Bert spent his stay at the Ritz sobbing without stop in regret over his marriage to Amy. This bit of gossip prompted the scandal sheet *Town Topics* to print the falsehood that the notorious couple would make Paris their home to avoid ostracism in America.

JOE PATTERSON WAS having domestic troubles of his own. In 1914 he and Alice had rented a furnished house in Chicago's Gold Coast, which they would keep in addition to Westwood Farm for the next six years. But the Pattersons' life was far from settled; among Alice's exasperating characteristics was a financial casualness that could drive a husband mad. She had no concept of money and, in addition to being chronically overdrawn in her own bank account, she neglected to pass bills on to Joe so that money matters would simply drift. She was neglectful about such matters as routine family correspondence and began a pattern of frequent travel without Joe. A favorite destination was the Greenbrier in White Sulphur Springs, West Virginia, a resort of choice for America's rich since 1878, especially during its late fall and spring seasons. Alice usually took the older two girls with her but there were times when all three children were left at home with their father. Joe's letters and wires to her during these excursions are touching, but evidence of her communication with him is minimal. While she was there with Elinor and Alicia for several weeks during March and April 1915, for example, he wired a series of sweet messages addressed TO ALICE ELINOR AND ALICIA . . . FROM JOE AND JOSEPHINE, but heard nothing back throughout the first month. Then on March 31 a mutual friend who had also been at the Greenbrier telephoned to say that Alice was suffering from anemia and would not return for another two or three weeks. He wired, I SHALL BE VERY LONELY BABY IS WELL. He kept writing and wiring sympathetic wishes, hearing nothing back. Finally on April 9, he wired, FOR THE LOVE OF MIKE WHAT ARE YOUR PLANS WHEN ARE YOU RETURNING. The following season she left the three girls with him, along with domestic problems. The cook's departure immediately followed Alice's, and although it is unclear who was providing their meals, Joe wrote that he was eating with the children every night. Eventually she returned, but less than four months later she was back at the Greenbrier and the girls were again with him.

Domestic problems were insignificant compared to the black cloud of war continuing to envelope Europe. International events took a sinister turn on May 7 when the *Lusitania* was torpedoed and sunk by the Germans, with almost twelve hundred lives lost. Suddenly the war "over there" had become a grim reality for Americans, whose countrymen accounted for 128 of the *Lusitania* casualties. When Bert and Amy arrived back in America in midsummer 1915, it was to a decidedly pro-Allied nation. Closer to home, Kate's own war against Amy had not abated; she had peppered Bert with nasty letters while he was away and now she was in Newport fanning the fires of gossip, referring to her son as a "poor wrongheaded goat." Ed Adams, she said, had received eighty thousand dollars "for a worthless antique already pawed over and cast aside by half a dozen very inferior men." On Bert's birthday a year later, her comment was, "Poor baby boy 36 with an old tart of 48 on his back. I suppose he is bored to death!" She was mistaken on both counts. Amy was forty-four and Bert was anything but bored.

Aside from enjoying time with his bride, co-editing the *Tribune* and working on a book about his experiences with the grand duke, McCormick was involved in an exhilarating new project, a ground-breaking form of communicating war news to the American public, the newsreel. Separately he and Joe had each developed a startling war documentary, which shown jointly would galvanize viewers. While

Joe was covering the expanding European war in Germany, Belgium and France for the *Tribune*, his photographer Edwin Weigel recorded a visual account of the action. Knowing this, Bert had taken freelance photographer Donald F. Thompson with him to the eastern front. The footage of both men, "With the Russian Army" and "The German Side of the War," began showing at Chicago's Studebaker Theater on Michigan Avenue in the autumn of 1915; lines at the box office ran a block long. The public had never seen anything like the realism in this new documentary form and was fascinated by it as the actuality of the Great War came closer to home. Bert's next project was collaboration on a serialized novel, *1917*, which explored the premise that Germans might invade the United States and drive as far west as the Mississippi River before being halted. The success of the serial coincided with a move on the part of Under Secretary of the Navy Franklin Delano Roosevelt to strengthen the navy. It was an opportunity for a short period of cordiality between the two old boys who had not been close at Groton.

The nation was not yet in the fighting, but the war was now on the minds of most Americans, and the future Colonel McCormick was already becoming exaggerated in his military conduct. Burton Rascoe, a military historian as well as a longtime *Tribune* journalist, told of his employer seeking him out at the newspaper for serious discussions on the subject. "He would come in, attired in whipcord breeches, English officer's jacket boots, spurs, Sam Browne belt and officer's cap, a polo stick in one hand and three yelping German police dogs on a leash. He would go up to the roof of the Tribune building, mount a mechanical horse and practice polo shots from the contraption, and . . . discuss with me, as one man to another who knew a thing or two about military affairs, the plans of the German army. To me this was comical."

War was in the air, everywhere. An immediate, and terrifying, threat to the United States occurred in March 1916, when a band of Mexicans led by the bandit/revolutionary Pancho Villa killed seventeen Americans in Columbus, New Mexico. President Woodrow Wilson ordered a sealing of the border, and 150,000 National Guardsmen were called to duty, including the First Illinois Cavalry. Bert, having relinquished his temporary commission as colonel on Governor Dunne's staff, carried the rank of major, and by this time Joe had joined the First Illinois Artillery as a private, declining the governor's offer of a commission. The two cousins, the private and the major, reported to the border, leaving the *Tribune* in the competent hands of Ted Beck and Bill Field. The Pancho Villa incident's most significant impact on the paper was that it triggered a well-known court case, one that would mark the beginning of Bert's lengthy fixation with First Amendment issues. Off in Detroit and not as patriotic as *Tribune* leadership was automaker Henry Ford, who declared that his company would not pay wages or benefits to National Guardsmen called into service during the crisis. On June 23, 1916, the *Tribune* printed an editorial labeling Mr. Ford "an anarchistic enemy of the nation which protects him in his wealth." The furious Ford filed a $1 million libel suit against the paper; the jury returned a verdict in Ford's favor but awarded him only six cents in damages.

THE QUESTION OF American participation in World War I had been hotly debated for almost three years when the United States finally declared war on Germany in April 1917. Shortly afterward, President Wilson appointed General John J. "Black Jack" Pershing to command the American forces in France, despite the tragic recent loss of the general's wife and three of their four children in a fire that swept the family's quarters in San Francisco's Presidio. The *Tribune* had maintained a strong isolationist position regarding the war, but once declaration was made Bert and Joe joined the effort without hesitation. Joe, a lieutenant in the artillery, would see three months of action in the Lorraine sector. Eventually promoted to the rank of captain, he was commanding officer of Battery B, 149th Field Artillery of the Rainbow Division, with which he participated in the Second Battle of the Marne.

In typical fashion, Bert shot straight to the top of the Pershing hierarchy. Soon after the general's appointment, McCormick received a notice to report to his headquarters in France, and he prepared for the assignment by adding a monocle and walking stick to his military attire. The glass in his eye, he said, was to correct poor eyesight that had been with him since childhood, and the stick was for a knee injured in football, disabilities that had not been previous issues. Before leaving, McCormick was again in touch with Franklin Roosevelt, in a "Frank" and "Bert" correspondence, through which the latter promised editorial support of the navy as well as the contribution of his own yacht, a seventy-five-foot vessel. Roosevelt accepted. On the eve of his June 30, 1917, departure, Bert lunched with Franklin's adventurous cousin Theodore at the Harvard Club. As he left, the former president in his usual boisterous enthusiasm exclaimed, "Lord, how I wish I were going with you!" With that send-off, Bert was on his way to Pershing's headquarters in France, again accompanied by Amy, whose presence—because of her strong family military background—would prove beneficial.

In reality, McCormick was a valuable asset for Pershing. The general was dealing with leaders of the depleted French and English forces who wished to absorb American soldiers into their own armies; hence one of the challenges Pershing faced was that of maintaining autonomy for his command. Bert, with his fluency in French, his personal friendships with Allied leaders and his unique familiarity with both the eastern and western fronts, would provide a significant service to the general in this difficult predicament. On their arrival in Paris, Major and Mrs. McCormick were greeted by General Pershing with a copy of the *Chicago Tribune*'s army edition from the paper's new office in the Rue Royale; among the correspondents based there were a trio of journalistic legends, bureau chief Floyd Gibbons, Charles MacArthur and Ring Lardner, who professed he had been assigned to report on "the funny side of the war."

The Great War had been under way for almost three years and the blood-soaked trenches zigzagging their way through the picturesque farmyards of pastoral France were already the scene of a slaughter that was extinguishing the lives of more young men than historians have been able to count. In addition to cannons, rifles, grenades, machine guns, bayonets and other means of delivering sudden death, there was now the dreaded specter of poison gas. Moreover, with the arrival of 1918, a lethal epidemic of influenza—the infamous Spanish flu— began sweeping the globe, killing as many as 100 million men, women and children worldwide, and by spring the plague had arrived on the European continent. Spring 1918 also found Major Robert R. McCormick in the battlegrounds of France, as an early member of the celebrated First Division. Variously known as the Big Red One and the Fighting First, it is the United States Army's oldest continuously serving division and has fought in the nation's conflicts from May 24, 1917, through the present.

A CHINESE PROVERB defines a crisis as "an opportunity riding the dangerous wind." If so, the wild and turbulent wind raging toward the major that spring was carrying the supreme opportunity of his life. He would soon be poised at a juncture that would establish both his personal signature and a controversy that would surround him for the remainder of his days. In late May, he was in rural France in command of the First Battalion, Fifth Field Artillery. When the virulent influenza epidemic struck in the area of his command, along with nearby explosions of gas shells, he was positioned with his men some seventy-five miles north of Paris near the village of Cantigny, site of the first sustained American offensive of World War I. McCormick suffered an attack of the dreaded flu, accentuated by a small inhalation of gas, but because of a dearth of experienced officers, he had to remain with his unit and operate from his bed by field telephone. This was his condition when the order came to initiate the historic American offensive against the German-held Cantigny. By May 26, doctors insisted on his hospitalization, but the major stood firm and remained with his men.

Shortly before the attack, which was scheduled for the morning of the twenty-eighth, conditions began moving toward McCormick's advantage. During the night of the twenty-seventh, German soldiers holding the village were replaced by troops having less experience, and with several other factors playing in the Americans' favor, the attack was over by 7:30 A.M. The taking of Cantigny accomplished, the major collapsed and was evacuated to a Paris hospital, where he slept for forty-eight hours. He had survived poison gas and the influenza of 1918. But more than that, he had been a hero in the victory of Cantigny, the central highlight of a life that would continue to be extraordinarily eventful.

The above account is basically what McCormick would be reporting for the next thirty-seven years. Although his veracity regarding his role in the victorious battle of Cantigny has been questioned, there is nothing in the official records to challenge his version of what occurred during those dangerous days in May 1918. In August, three months short of the war's end, Robert R. McCormick was promoted to the rank of full colonel, and he returned with Amy to Chicago, where he was assigned to Fort Sheridan, north of the city. He was offered a commission as brigadier general, which he declined, and awarded the Distinguished Service Medal. A War Department citation stated that he displayed "rare leadership and organizing ability, unusual executive ability and sound technical judgment." He was discharged a colonel on December 31, 1918, and remained a colonel—and more significantly the Colonel—for the rest of his life.

·13·

THE JAZZ AGE
COLLIDES WITH THE
CHICAGO TRIBUNE

WITH the chaos of war resounding in their ears, American doughboys returned from the trenches of France to the certainty of home. But home was no longer a certainty; the tempo of American life was accelerating, and returning troops were soon hearing a new sound to replace the staccato rhythm of gunfire. The new sound was jazz, and it was everywhere, blasting from phonographs and radios, surrounding them in movie houses and night clubs—pulsing out from objects and places they had never known before. And accompanying the new sound was a new kind of dancing, performed by a new breed of woman, a frenetically gyrating creature in sequins and fringe, bobbed hair, rolled stockings and rouged knees. She was free and independent, smoking cigarettes, drinking whiskey and behaving with wild abandon. Automobiles—now called flivvers—were no longer a novelty; they were everywhere. They were cheap, fast and brought even greater independence. And there was money to spend, along with more leisure time in which to spend it. Energizing it all and throbbing throughout the nation was Prohibition.

The Eighteenth Amendment to the Constitution, followed by the enforcing Volstead Act, came into effect at midnight on January 16, 1920, turning the country dry. The resulting chaos produced speakeasies, bathtub gin, hip flasks, bootlegging and organized crime. Lawbreaking by law-abiding citizens was rampant; respectable Americans now thought it daring, new and exciting to shiver in a cold, dark speakeasy, especially when everyone they knew was doing the same. The Nineteenth Amendment, giving women the right to vote, quickly followed and the world would never be the same.

The epicenter of the new America was Chicago. Annenberg-trained hoodlums found fresh need for their services and quickly organized in "gangs" to provide thirsty citizens with the alcohol now denied them through legal channels. There was an excitement, with a peculiar sort of glamour, to the gangster phenomenon, and it didn't take long for the city's newspapers to discover this added circulation builder. Stars could be created from disadvantaged young men who were able to make quantities of money through crime, and before long the charismatic Al Capone was boosting circulation in the way film stars and rock musicians would later. Immigrant readers who had come to the land of opportunity only to find continuing poverty lived vicariously in coverage of rags-to-riches gangsters. Soon Hollywood discovered the appeal of the phenomenon and a new film genre was shooting its way to popularity.

The newspaper business to which Bert and Joe returned was entering a near-mythical period during which the talent of Chicago editors, columnists and reporters was thrusting the city's journalistic world into a legendary era. Ring Lardner and Charlie MacArthur returned home to join Walter Howey, Ben Hecht and other newspaper superstars, each of whom at one time or another worked for Bert and Joe. Their antics at the *Tribune* and Hearst's *Examiner* would soon be immortalized in Hecht and MacArthur's play *The Front Page,* first on Broadway, and then Hollywood, where its film versions slipped neatly into the gangster movie craze. Just as Hearst's 1900 arrival in Chicago had triggered the beginning of the circulation wars, the chain's continuing presence was fueling the intense rivalry of the Front Page era. But the battlefield had been transformed; the combat for circulation had shifted from the bloody "persuasion" of newsdealers to a contest for scoops that legitimately sold papers, with editors and reporters moving from one paper to another in cutthroat competition to create the city's most compelling editorial content. Newspaper reporting had become a seductive calling, and as serious writers were drawn to the Chicago literary renaissance, some dabbled in journalism, including Carl Sandburg, who worked for the *Chicago Daily News*. None the least of the era's reporters was a woman who joined the Front Page men's club with resounding success. Crime reporter Maurine Dallas Watkins captured the mood of the era in a *Tribune* series that was continuing to entertain audiences almost eight decades later. Watkins spun her coverage of two sensational 1924 booze- and jazz-influenced murders into a recurring stage and film property that eventually evolved into the 2002 Oscar-winning hit film *Chicago,* starring Catherine Zeta-Jones and Renée Zellweger.

THE TOWERING LEGEND who personified the epoch was *Tribune* city editor Walter Howey, Hecht and MacArthur's model for Walter Burns, in *The Front Page*. Central to the image of the freewheeling Howey was his disdain for marriage, with threats to fire—or at least slash the salaries of—reporters who married. What none of his colleagues seemed to know was that Howey had an intriguing wife at home; her name was Liberty and she was as independent as he. Born Elizabeth Kelly, "Liberty" rechristened herself because she wanted admirers to say, "Give me Liberty or give me death." Howey, who was making eight thousand dollars a year as city editor of the *Tribune*, was offered a gigantic thirty-five thousand to defect to the *Examiner* to become managing editor. He declined. Coincidentally, he met filmmaker D. W. Griffith, who was able to facilitate the Hollywood career of Liberty Howey's niece Colleen Moore. According to legend, Howey wrote a favorable article about Griffith, which Joe Patterson felt was a puff piece—and he felt it so strongly he wrote an editorial apologizing for the article—causing the furious Howey to leave for the Hearst camp after all, where he stayed. The *Tribune* lost a celebrated editor, but Colleen Moore gained a spectacular career, becoming one of Hollywood's great silent-screen stars. Joe paid for his cavalier treatment of the brilliant city editor not only by losing him to the *Examiner* but also in creating a bloodthirsty adversary who would go to any length to even the score editorially. He said as much to Patterson, but then added, "And what's more, I'm going to seduce your sister!" He would do so eventually, but in the meantime a figurative seduction sufficed when he enticed Cissy over to the *Examiner* to cover the 1920 Republican National Convention.

Howey also attempted to steal Ring Lardner away from Patterson and McCormick but was unsuccessful in spite of valiant efforts. Their prized sportswriter went to extraordinary lengths to avoid becoming Howey's kidnap victim. By switching hangouts, cronies and even his residence, he eluded the new *Examiner* managing editor and remained with the *Tribune*. He was not overreacting. Howey, who was equally determined to recruit Frank Carson, his protégé and successor as *Tribune* city editor, gave a party at the newspaper hangout Schlogl's to celebrate Carson's promotion to Howey's former job. After Carson had consumed a sufficient number of boilermakers, Howey handed him a piece of paper, requesting an autograph. When he returned to sobriety, Carson learned he had signed an employment contract with the *Examiner*, at a sizable salary increase. Howey needed Carson with him at the *Examiner*, because Frank was a paragon of the Front Page–style, an editor who knew every policeman in Chicago and also the mistress of every policeman. While Frank was still under the influence of boilermakers, he also signed a stinging Howey-drafted letter of resignation to Joe. "I address you as 'Mister Patterson,' " it began, "because your phony pretensions to democracy, urging the help to 'Just call me Joe,' turn my stomach as they do all who must lick your boots for pay." Although the letter continued in similar language and was successful in severing Carson's connection with the *Tribune*, it would not be the end of his relationship with Joe, who recognized talent.

PRESIDING OVER CHICAGO'S Prohibition years was William Hale "Big Bill" Thompson, who became mayor in 1915 and, with a four-year interruption, served five two-year terms during the heyday of the gangster era. He was an oafish, boisterous and thoroughly repugnant demagogue, to whom the city is forever indebted for facilitating its image as headquarters of the Roaring Twenties. Only Big Bill's lax oversight made possible the Hollywood prototype of a city wide open to the spectacle of rampant gangland warfare, nightclub machine-gun battles, political payoffs in bulging suitcases and thrilling car chases climaxing in massive explosions. Under his regime, Chicago was a town that rolled out a money-green carpet for bootleggers and gangsters, with Thompson receiving substantial financial gain that included generous campaign contributions from Al Capone. It is hardly surprising that police were virtually powerless in preventing wholesale crime or making arrests in the bloody gangland warfare.

Bill Thompson was the mortal enemy of the McCormicks. Because Medill defeated him in the 1918 primary for United States Senate and Ruth united Chicago women against him for mayor, both were political rivals, and his hatred of Bert resulted from the *Tribune*'s continued exposure of his administration's corruption. Big Bill sued the paper for $10 million in damages when it printed the redundant accusation that the city under his leadership was "bankrupt, insolvent, broke, in a bad financial condition, and so improperly and corruptly administered by its officers that its streets were not properly cleaned and its laws not efficiently enforced." He lost the case, appealed and lost again. Next the *Tribune* discovered that Michigan Avenue's new double-decker bridge had run a million dollars over projections because of fees paid to "expert consultants," whose only expertise lay in producing voters on Election Day. This prompted the *Tribune*, filing as a taxpayer, to bring a $1,732,000 taxpayer's suit against Big Bill, temporarily vanquishing him—until 1927, when his return to office was facilitated by a half-million-dollar contribution from the grateful Mr. Capone. It is not surprising that gangsters eventually infiltrated law enforcement in Chicago. When machine-gun barrels emerged "from a curtained automobile" to assassinate young assistant state's attorney William McSwiggin, the newspapers were outraged. Then slowly details of McSwiggin's involvement with saloon owners in the Capone territory of Cicero came to light. Professing innocence, Capone was quoted as saying, "I liked the kid," followed by the even more incriminating "I paid him plenty."

The *Tribune* became the subject of a sensational murder story in 1930 when one of its reporters was gunned down early on the afternoon of June 9 in a pedestrian underground passage at Michigan Avenue and Randolph Street. *Tribune* executives—particularly Bert, who had begun evolving into the increasingly starchy Robert R. McCormick—were outraged to learn that the victim of a gangland-style killing was Alfred "Jake" Lingle, a *Tribune* veteran of eighteen years, valued for his "connections." A $25,000 reward for bringing in the killer was announced, with the paper mourning Lingle as a martyr, a hero who possibly had died just as he was nearing an exposé of notorious mobsters. Yet when McCormick spoke to a hastily assembled meeting of the Chicago Publishers Association, his peers were slow to act. Bert's growing distance from his reporting staff had kept him from being conscious of what most others in the business suspected was more than a possibility, and they were correct. At the morgue it was discovered that Lingle, salaried at sixty-five dollars a week, was carrying fourteen hundred dollars in his pocket. He was also wearing one of the diamond-decorated belts dispensed by Capone to special friends.

IT WASN'T ALL gangsters and crime reporting at the *Tribune* after World War I. The McCormick-Patterson team was elevating its newspaper circulation, which had been in third place locally when they inherited it, to the nation's most widely read daily. Under their leadership the *Tribune* had remained Chicago's newspaper of record, while also returning to the position it held under Joseph Medill as the preferred newspaper for a large swath of the country. By 1922, the company was free of debt, had $1.4 million in cash reserves, and was expanding to include thousands of acres of Canadian forest, power dams, paper mills and a small navy of ships. But Bert and Joe also kept tweaking various aspects of the publication itself; immediately after the war they imported the city's first rotogravure press from Germany to print a Sunday supplement with four-color photographs in a sepia format, providing one more enticement for Sunday readers. An appreciative board rewarded them with salaries of fifty thousand dollars each. If the nation's prosperity had dipped with the recession of 1921–22, it quickly rebounded in a period of opulence that would last until the end of the decade. Bill Field and his advertising manager, Eugene Parsons, were so successful in selling space they were becoming rich men from their bonuses and Bert felt it was only fair to extend the advertising bonus system to other top executives. Max Annenberg, now a cozy member of the *Tribune* staff; Teddy Beck; and business manager Emory Thomason, each of whom Bert felt shared in the paper's prosperity, received rewards. He convinced Joe of the wisdom of the system by saying, "The greatness of Marshall Field and Carnegie lay in their willingness to let their associates become rich while they became billionaires." As son-in-law of a man whose wealth had sprung from Field's formula, Joe understood well.

With its postwar success, the *Tribune* was outgrowing its seventeen-story headquarters, and Bert, as a former alderman, was privy to a plan to shift much of the city's business district north and east. Pine Street, a largely residential road, would be widened and linked by a double-decked bridge with Michigan Avenue, which then ran only from the river south. The resulting thoroughfare would be today's Michigan Avenue. Sensing imminent implementation of the project, McCormick proposed an incremental move of the company's headquarters and received a green light from the board. The first step was to acquire a parcel of land near the river's north bank, facing the anticipated connected stretch. In 1920, a six-story *Tribune* printing plant was unveiled on the new site almost simultaneously with the opening of the Michigan Avenue bridge, and two years later, accompanied by great hoopla, *Tribune* directors announced an international competition for the design of "the world's most beautiful office building" to be built next to the plant. Although the competition was open to all qualified architects, a list of ten had been formally invited to submit designs, and among these was New York's John Mead Howells, son of famed novelist William Dean Howells. News of the project with its fifty-thousand-dollar first prize elicited an overwhelming worldwide response; there were more than five hundred queries and 285 designs were submitted.

Forty-one-year-old New York architect Raymond M. Hood, a modernist with a slight résumé, was in the Concourse at Grand Central Terminal one day that summer when he ran into former École des Beaux-Arts classmate John Howells. The well-connected Howells told him about the competition, which he himself could not enter because of his workload. The two men said goodbye and had walked a few steps in opposite directions when Howells spun around with an amazingly generous offer for the underemployed Hood: he could use Howells's office to design an entry under their joint name—and keep the fee if they won. The "collaboration" resulted in a design that was neo-Gothic in style at a time when there was a passion for pared-down commercial architecture.

The popular competition choice—and the design overwhelmingly preferred by other architects—was submitted by second-prize winner, Finnish architect Eliel Saarinen. His highly influential model heralded the Art Deco skyscraper with modernist, forward-thinking lines, which were radical for the time; the Saarinen design was so fresh and new that it widely influenced other architects over the next decade, most notably John A. Holabird and John Wellborn Root Jr., for their 333 North Michigan Avenue building, directly across the river from the Tribune. It is not surprising that the Hood and Howells Gothic revival proposal, based on the Button Tower of the Rouen Cathedral in France and decorated with such flourishes as gargoyles and flying buttresses, would capture the vote of a committee selected by *Tribune* management. However, the ensuing uproar prompted Hood to borrow money for a new coat in order to travel west to convince McCormick and Patterson that he could successfully supervise the construction of the controversial design. It was not a difficult position to sell.

When the award became official, with a first prize of fifty thousand dollars, Hood's life was transformed, and just in time; his wife took the check and traveled around Manhattan in a taxi to show it to the couple's creditors. It was the beginning of a productive career for Hood and the launch of a long and fruitful relationship between the architect and Joe Patterson.

The new Tribune Tower, constructed from the Hood and Howells design, opened in June 1925 and remains the company's iconic symbol. What most people have never seen is the twenty-fourth floor. The original plan was that offices for Bert and Joe would occupy the entire floor, which was anything but Joe's style. Therefore, he ordered a small personal office for himself, designating the balance of his space to be made into a squash court, with the back adjoining Bert's office. He would rescind his request eventually but enjoyed the tease for a number of months. Characteristically, Bert had immediately laid plans to use every inch of his half floor for a palatial office suite, which would become central to the image of the daunting Colonel McCormick through the following three decades.

JUST AS BERT and Joe were securing their careers, Medill McCormick, who served successfully in the United States Senate from 1919 until 1925, lost in the primary for reelection by less than six thousand votes to former Illinois governor Charles S. Deneen. It was a devastating setback for a forty-seven-year-old man who had finally found a role for himself. There were feelers for his talents here and there. Hearst publisher Arthur Brisbane suggested that with his strong newspaper background Medill might take over leadership of the *Washington Herald;* there was also speculation that he would join Calvin Coolidge's cabinet, and he received well-placed support to be named British ambassador. But nothing gelled.

In late February Medill went to Washington to wrap up his Senate business, leaving Ruth in Chicago to be with new mother Alice Longworth, who had traveled out to give birth to Paulina. Because childbirth at forty-one was then considered risky, Ruth convinced Alice to have the baby delivered by her own obstetrician, Dr. Joseph De Lee, whose practice was in Chicago. With no warning of imminent crisis,

Ruth was unconcerned about allowing her husband to go alone, but on the morning of February 24 he was found dead in bed in his suite at the Hotel Hamilton. According to the hotel doctor, Medill—who suffered from ulcers—had died of a gastric hemorrhage, and the coroner's report cited myocarditis. However, in a replay of his uncle Robert Patterson's suicide fifteen years earlier, Medill had poisoned himself. Congress adjourned the following day while a funeral was held at the Patterson house on Dupont Circle. Washington's purple arrived for the service, including the Calvin Coolidges and Herbert Hoover. Although a productive life remained ahead for Ruth and she would go on to a trail-blazing political career of feminine "firsts," the loss of the man she had loved so completely was devastating.

But Medill's remarkable widow was a survivor whose life would continue for another two decades, while she raised the three McCormick children, married a former Republican New Mexico congressman, Albert G. Simms—whom she met in 1929 while serving one term as representative at large from Illinois—and moved with him to Albuquerque. Publicly she prevailed as a politician and formidable political strategist. She would become the first woman elected to a national statewide office and the first nominated for the United States Senate by a major party, for which Joe Patterson's congratulation was "Attaboy, girl!" And she would be Thomas Dewey's campaign manager in his 1944 pursuit of the nomination for president—another feminine first. She also continued the dynasty's newspaper tradition by acquiring the Rockford, Illinois, *Daily Republic*, consolidating it with another area paper, the *Register-Gazette and Morning Star*, and adding a local radio station to her mini-conglomerate. But her own Senate campaign was a rough one for Ruth. After what she had lived through in her marriage, she was understandably "dry" and did not receive unqualified support from the family newspaper. The *Tribune* was increasingly blaming Prohibition for the gangs and corruption tarnishing the quality of Chicago life; thus when she ran for Medill's former Senate seat in 1930, the paper endorsed her, but with reservations. She lost by 720,000 votes to

Democratic candidate James Hamilton Lewis, who had campaigned to repeal Prohibition.

IT SOON BECAME apparent that Joe's transformation of the *Tribune* Sunday edition was merely the first in a spectacular series of achievements he would experience in delivering newspaper content craved by the populace. The next would be his development of the modern comic strip. For decades during the twentieth century, the circulation muscle of almost any American newspaper would be the section devoted to "comics." And because papers with the most appealing strips were the papers subscribers wanted, battles were fought over the rights to prime properties. Once the tradition was established, some comics gained an enormous following, others were flops and nobody knew why—with the exception of the man who invented the genre, Joe Patterson.

Before leaving for duty in World War I, Joe had begun applying his particular gift to developing the form, which had risen from a venerable tradition. Its earliest roots were page-one cartoon commentaries on a specific current event. Long a newspaper staple, the news-related drawing was a prephotography solution for providing visual content to a solid wall of print. By August 1895, the *Tribune* was periodically carrying four pages of unrelated caricatures commenting on various incidents in the news. The random appearance of these omnibus pages created little note, but the same year an innovation exploded in the city room of Joseph Pulitzer's *New York Sunday World*, shaking Park Row and creating a sensation throughout New York. The simple but phenomenal breakthrough was the spectacularly popular Yellow Kid, a single-frame cartoon in which a grinning urchin ridiculed a different establishment trend each Sunday. When Hearst lured Yellow Kid artist Richard F. Outcault away for the chain's Sunday *New York Journal*, Pulitzer quickly replaced Outcault's sassy yellow drawing with a rival Yellow Kid by cartoonist George Luks. New York readers were now treated to a pair of Yellow Kids every Sunday, provoking the term "yellow journalism." Two years later, Rudolph Dirks pushed the cartoon concept a giant step further by creating a strip with a continuing story line in his hugely successful *Katzenjammer Kids* for the *New York Journal*, and this is where the tradition remained for another two decades.

It took Joe to successfully tinker with Dirks's strip concept and, when he did, he began producing a new generation of "funnies" incorporating plot and continuity, with the Patterson fingerprint on each. There would be other editors who might recognize a potentially popular comic when it was presented by an artist, but Joe ruthlessly vetted the proposals, skillfully massaged those he chose and became cocreator of strips that grew to be American institutions. His phenomenal run began in February 1917 with *The Gumps*, a depiction of the everyday lives of very ordinary people, and he could credit his mother for its name; it was a term the snobbish Nellie used in referring to members of the uneducated masses. Joe worked closely with *Gumps* artist Sidney Smith—sometimes plotting the story line himself—in creating a strip that enthralled readers. *The Gumps* was followed in November 1918 by another extraordinarily popular strip, *Gasoline Alley*, inspired by men Joe saw tinkering with their automobiles in the alleys of Chicago neighborhoods, and drawn by Frank King. Another of Joe's ideas was to create a strip for the new working woman, which appeared two years later as Martin Branner's *Winnie Winkle*, the ongoing story of a plucky young lady who worked to support her parents and adopted brother. Comics were a serious undertaking for Patterson, and his package of *Tribune* strips quickly captivated an audience with the loyalty that would later be commanded by a network's slate of hit television programs. The recipe he gave each of his artists specified his ingredients for a successful strip: "Youngsters for kid appeal, a handsome guy for muscle work and love interest, a succession of pretty girls, a mysterious locale or a familiar one." With his funnies, Joe created not only the most significant reader attraction for most of the nation's newspapers but also a source of millions of dollars for the Tribune Company through its newspapers and syndicate.

In contrast to his career, Joe's home life was more unsettled than ever; in April 1919, Alice's eighty-year-old father, Harlow N.

Higinbotham, was in Manhattan for a military event when he was struck by an army ambulance on Madison Avenue. He died later in the day at Doctors' Hospital with Alice's sister, Florence Crane, and her husband, Richard, at his bedside. For a short time, all Joe's newspaper work came second to consoling his wife while he participated in making funeral arrangements and selecting pallbearers. Before that interlude and after, Alice was rarely nearby; her frequent travels had evolved into tours of Europe with their daughters, leaving Joe alone for long stretches of time either at the Chicago Club or Westwood Farm, where renovations to the Shaw-designed house were being made under the supervision of Chicago's fashionable young architect David Adler.

Communication between the Pattersons was chiefly about the girls, often consisting of Joe's complaints that neither Elinor nor "the baby" Josephine ever wrote to him. But he also conveyed pleasure when he learned Alice would allow Elinor to attend Miss Spence's School in New York rather than having her spend another winter in Europe. His increasing concern that his eldest daughter would become "expatriated" reflected prejudices more expected of his grandfather and cousin. "I certainly think it would be terrible if she married a Dago of any variety and that includes the English," he wrote Alice in mid-1921. By August he had selected a potential candidate for Elinor's hand, Samuel Insull Jr., son of the utilities magnate who owned the neighboring estate. He wrote Alice, "I had lunch with Insull yesterday and also called on him the day before after dinner to smoke a cigar. . . . His son graduated from Yale this year and was voted the brightest boy in his class. . . . He will probably be exceedingly rich and besides that he's a neighbor. . . . I told him Elinor was pretty and appeared sweet on the surface, but inwardly was a ravaging wolf."

It is odd that Joe's relationship with his neighbor would be so cordial. Not only was Insull a notably difficult man but he had also invested in a rival newspaper and probably knew Joe was picking off his pheasants when they flew over Westwood grounds. The two men did, however, share an interest in experimental farming. Insull's Hawthorn

Farms, although dominated by an ornate Benjamin Marshall–designed Italian villa and considered one of the most sumptuous country estates of the grand era, was dedicated to experimental farming. Joe was correct about the future of the junior Insull. His personal worth would rise to more than $13 million, although a mere pittance compared to his father's $3 billion empire of more than 140 companies.

Occasionally Alice left Josephine with Joe, as she did in October 1922 while she stayed at New York's Ritz-Carlton with the older two girls. He wrote he was paying the eight-year-old "five cents a day for fixing her bed and she likes it. I bought her two tiny gold fish." He added that her coat "appears to me both short and too light. I notice the other kids of her age going to school wearing something like polo coats. I mention this because perhaps you would like to get her something of the sort in New York." Two days later he followed with the announcement that he had just learned Josephine and another little girl "make a practice of smoking cigarettes in your bathroom behind locked doors every rainy afternoon."

JOE WAS ALREADY moving on to the next phase of his phenomenal career with the creation of a new kind of newspaper for the fast-moving America of the post–World War I era. His innovation, a publication as dynamic as the times it reflected, would become the most successful newspaper in the nation's history.

The venture had begun on July 20, 1918, during one of the most pivotal nights of both of their lives, when Joe and Bert were stars in an unlikely but true drama. The scenario has all the elements of a 1930s Great War film. A pair of rich and famous first cousins suddenly together for one evening during a pause in battle: a picturesque farm in France, artillery fire in the background, a shared bottle of Scotch and seats made of straw—with a cameo played by the future World War II Supreme Allied Commander of the southwest Pacific theater. Bert, on his way home to organize troops for a new offensive, had detoured to visit Joe, who was stationed at the French village of Mareuil-en-Dôle—first stopping to borrow a helmet and gas mask from an American officer named Douglas MacArthur. The cousins met in a farmhouse near the Ourcq River where they began conversing, but because of noise within the field headquarters, they exited through a French window and continued their conversation seated on what Bert would later theatrically claim was a manure pile. They passed a bottle of Scotch back and forth, watching the flashing of distant gunfire, while Joe disclosed his dream of starting a New York picture paper within the *Tribune* empire.

He had been in Paris in 1914 with John T. McCutcheon, who had shown him a revolutionary new form of journalism, a half-size, highly pictorial daily newspaper. "In Paris we stayed together at the Crillon for several months," remembered McCutcheon. "This was before the air raids, and before Big Bertha, the seventy-five-mile gun. Every day I used to bring back to our room a copy of the *London Mirror,* in which lively tabloid [William] Haselden's cartoons were then appearing." Joe became caught up in the innovative British newspaper and the concept stayed with him as a journalistic format that might be successful in New York; he even traveled to England on furlough to visit *London Daily Mirror* founder Lord Northcliffe, who agreed that New York was ripe for a paper similar to his 800,000-circulation tabloid. He told Joe, "New York's got to have a tabloid. If the rest of you don't see the light soon, I'll start one myself." Northcliffe also advised him to keep the paper "simple and bright enough for the masses to understand and enjoy," words Joe never forgot.

The paper Joe envisioned would combine the characteristics of a newspaper with those of a magazine; he saw its content as one-half photographs, one-quarter features and the rest authentic breaking news—but news conveyed in a manner that every subway rider and day laborer could easily digest. The language would be simple and sentences short, but lively and sprinkled with humor. The cousins had discussed acquiring a New York paper in the past, and four years earlier McCormick had traveled to Newport to meet with *New York Herald* owner James Gordon Bennett Jr. to discuss the purchase of his paper, but the war had intervened. Although Bert and Joe continued to have mutual respect, their political philosophies were creating increasing divisiveness, and an added paper would allow the cousins to operate separately. The clincher was the excess cash available in the *Tribune* coffers, money otherwise destined to go for taxes. Bert agreed to the investment on the spot. Thus, seated together on the apocryphal dung heap in rural France, the future owners of the phenomenally lucrative *New York Daily News* raised their shared Scotch bottle and drank to the venture's success.

·14·

THE RISE OF
THE *NEW YORK DAILY NEWS*:
LOVE, SEX, MONEY AND MURDER

WAITING for Bert and Joe in Chicago at war's end was an exhausted Bill Field, who had spent the duration of the war at the *Tribune* with added burdens, including editorial. Not a greedy man, he had been made rich by the *Tribune,* rich enough to retire to Vermont for the rest of his days, which was exactly what he proposed to do. Evidence of Field's reluctance to muscle into McCormick-Patterson territory was the sign behind his desk throughout the war: "This is Joe Patterson's office. He is fighting in France. I am sitting in his chair for a little while until he comes back." But Bill Field was one of the most valuable men ever to work for the *Tribune,* and after considerable urging he was persuaded to remain with the company as its eastern vice president, based in New York. He would be relieved of his heavy workload, yet accessible for company challenges as they arose. In the meantime, the war ended in November and the situation was perfect for the next step in the company's growth.

Bert began work on the tabloid venture almost immediately. Approaching the board for seed money, he asked for installments in twenty-thousand-dollar increments not to be repaid until the paper was profitable, possibly in three to four years. At the February meeting, the directors authorized Field to begin preparations for the new publication, either with the purchase of an existing New York paper or through the off-hours use of an evening newspaper's plant. Field, who had sold his lakefront estate north of Chicago to future Carson Pirie Scott department store chairman Bruce MacLeish, was now ensconced in the University Club on Fifth Avenue at 54th Street. Rested and ripe for challenge, he dove into the project at once. The following month, his choice of Arthur L. Clarke as the projected tabloid's managing editor was approved. Clarke, then city editor of the *New York Evening World,* was a seasoned newspaperman who had worked with papers in San Francisco and Chicago, including serving as *Tribune* day editor under Robert Patterson. The fit was perfect; Clarke was also convinced of the possibilities for a New York tabloid, so much so that he had been seeking backing from J. P. Morgan to launch one himself.

At the May meeting the directors adopted the resolution, "That the officers of the company be empowered to take the steps necessary in their discretion to institute a subsidiary pictorial newspaper enterprise in New York City." Field quickly determined that no New York paper was available for acquisition but the *Evening Mail* might lease its presses and composing facilities at 25 City Hall Place, as well as provide personnel to operate them. The *Mail* had been a successful mass-market evening paper while managed by Joseph Pulitzer but had weakened under his Harvard graduate son, who had attempted to raise it to a paper that would interest his friends. Not only would Pulitzer rent his presses for printing the new tabloid but he cleared out a floor of his building for its editorial and business use.

Arthur Clarke and an editorial staff of three began developing a mockup in the *Tribune*'s Park Avenue advertising office. With the enterprise of journalism students designing a new college weekly, they annexed an old leather sofa as a work table and—using Northcliffe's *Daily Mirror* as a guide—created a dummy from Underwood & Underwood news bureau photography, wire service stories, and cartoons, comics and articles borrowed from the *Tribune.* Always hovering over the New Yorkers was the unseen presence of Joe Patterson, who remained in Chicago but devoted half his time and energy to the *News.* Patterson's instructions were to concentrate on the three subjects he considered of most interest to readers: Love/Sex, Money and Murder—in that order. A fourth was Health, which he felt was connected with the first. It was Joe's basic recipe for success and, along with provocative photography and catchy copy, it would be the enduring Patterson formula.

After several weeks of tweaking, Joe and his New York staff came up with a format in which page one would be dominated by a single scrollwork-framed photo surrounded with further flourishes. The design for the premiere issue, planned for publication during the last week of June, would be the prototype they would follow. Its focus was Edward, Prince of Wales, scheduled to visit New York later in the summer, with his royal presence dominating the first page. The glamorous pre–Wallis Simpson prince, a favorite of New York shop girls, was shown on horseback in a stock photo, and the only other pictorial element on the first page was an inset of Edward lighting a cigarette. The headline GERMANS BLOCK SIGNING OF TREATY, running across the top of the page under the logo, was followed by the subhead "Newport to Entertain Prince of Wales in August." A small photo caption in the lower right corner completed the page. It is a layout that today looks hopelessly dated, but nevertheless intriguing.

DURING THE NIGHT of June 25, 1919, 150,000 copies of the inaugural issue of the *Illustrated Daily News* rolled off the *Mail* presses and early in the morning of the twenty-sixth they were delivered to newsstands throughout the city. The paper was a curiosity; it was peculiar-looking but had the appeal of novelty, and the run sold out within hours. On the third day, only 100,000 sold, then fewer than 50,000, sinking by August to under 27,000, and on one August day, to only 11,000. The *News* was doing so poorly that press lords who had been considering a New York tabloid—including William Randolph Hearst and Bernarr Macfadden—dropped the thought, and the enterprise was such a disaster the reportorial staff of four was slashed to two. It was a wretched disappointment for Joe and even he was ready to abandon the project, but Arthur Clarke was still optimistic. "Remember," he wrote Patterson, "we are new in a hostile field, that we are trampling on all the newspaper traditions and that we have got to educate the public." Joe bounced back, responding to Arthur's confidence by ordering the paper increased in size from the original sixteen pages to twenty. Clarke followed by introducing a new format in which the back page was dedicated to sports photos and news.

From the beginning, both Patterson and Clarke conveyed a sense of adventure to their tiny staff, which took it up with vigor. It was uncharted territory they were traveling, venturing in new directions, and using innovative, often audacious schemes. If their colleagues didn't see it then, they did in retrospect. Two decades later the *New Yorker* reported, "In its early days the staff worked with a rip-roaring spirit and a pride of banditry that gave the tabloid's columns a gutsy flavor pleasing to the mass appetite. Reckless, rakehell lads the star staff men were . . . backed by an office policy of getting exclusive stories and pictures regardless of the cost of the finer ethical distinctions." Meanwhile, that evil genius of circulation Max Annenberg went to work, this time through aggressive, but legal, means. Max deposited the new publication on foreign-language newsstands—a brilliant stroke, because immigrants didn't need to read English to understand its saucy pictures. And he focused on distribution to subway riders who appreciated crime and sex stories.

By September, sales were up to thirty thousand and they began rising by ten thousand a month. Perhaps it was the annual New York swing into the pace of autumn, or possibly readers sensed the paper was capturing the new postwar rhythm beginning to pulsate throughout the nation. In any case, the *News* was moving. Joe was now certain the paper would survive, and in October the Tribune board agreed to continue to support the project financially—an immense relief to a jittery New York staff. Intrigued, the newspaper trade journal *Editor & Publisher* interviewed Arthur Clarke and printed an article about the groundbreaking new daily.

The crisis seemed to be over but, always, the unseen spirit of Joe Patterson was pushing further development, urging, commenting, criticizing and cheering in missives from Chicago. More news pictures, he insisted, more crime photos, more action images—although candid photography of any sort was primitive, problematic at best and beset with technical difficulties. Yet photography was the life's blood of the *News*—its logo was a winged camera—and Clarke was carefully putting together a staff of photographers, as well as seeking that staple of the Chicago Front Page genre—picture chasers—quasi-thieves or sometimes just hungry kids willing to risk anything to obtain a shot. Five dollars was awarded to anyone who submitted a usable image; telephone tipsters were paid at least a dollar for any bit of inside information, and far more if the tip led to a story.

From Chicago, Joe was urging departments and features he thought essential. "For goodness sake," he wrote, "remember to publish knocks, and vicious ones, every day." Knocks were letters to the editors containing criticisms or complaints; in the *Tribune* it was "People's Voice" and in the *News*, "Vox Pop." Initially the editors made up their own knocks; typical of these was an anonymous comment sent by Joe that read, "I hear people say the trouble with the *News* is the bad paper it's printed on. I tell them it isn't the paper, it is what you put on it." A similar department was "Beg Your Pardon," in which editors confessed to making an error; this was a device for avoiding libel. Continuing features included society coverage from other New York papers, reworked and published under the byline "Van Rensselaer," as well as health advice from Dr. Evans and other columns from the *Tribune*.

TOWARD THE END of the year, there was a genuine breakthrough when editors created what became a citywide phenomenon, a contest in which four lines of a limerick were printed and a hundred-dollar prize offered to the reader submitting the winning fifth line. The first limerick, published during the last week in November, began,

A princess from far off Cathay
Found a dressmaking pattern one day.
Said she 'If I could
Get the dress goods I would....

"Have Cal-cutta dress right away" was the triumphant punch line to the first segment of this new sensation. Not only did the limerick contest become a fad that swept the subway crowd, but it also traveled up Park Avenue during December and throughout the winter, with hostesses using the contest to enliven dinner parties. This may be when the alibi "the cook brings it in" began, but, increasingly, affluent New Yorkers seemed to be thoroughly acquainted with the paper, though they professed not to buy it themselves. The limerick contest created a turning point for the *News,* and Joe celebrated with a generous Christmas gift to Alice, one-half interest in Westwood Farm. Although she cared little for the farming aspect of the estate, the property continued to be more than a pretty parkland and was marginally profitable. During the twenties, the cattle census reached more than forty, in addition to a pair of bulls, a half-dozen pigs, four horses and more than two hundred chickens, with an estate manager to supervise their care.

Slowly but unquestionably, Joe's vision was proving valid; the paper's tabloid format, with its pioneering editorial content—pictorial and somewhat salacious—was catching on. Readers were becoming involved in its coverage of the questionable activities of the era's figures. As the twenties progressed, Fatty Arbuckle, Peaches Browning and Arnold Rothstein would make juicy headlines with their sex felonies, love nests and criminal activities. The public would learn the euphemisms: "dilettante" meant philanderer, "exotic" was erotic, "showered with gifts" stood for kept and "bizarre friendship" meant lesbianism. *News* editors were becoming adept at creating provocative headlines that sizzled, and in producing compelling pictures to accompany their stories. The journalist in Joe had decreed that important news stories be reported, but concisely and with verve. The rest of the material was chosen for its titillating subject matter.

Much of Joe's inner life, facets that had been simmering within him through the decades—including his disdain for elitism, his kinship with the masses and his appreciation for the Hearst style of journalism—burst forth in the *News*. The paper was his continuing passion, and it repaid him with immense personal satisfaction and, eventually, financial reward. With increasing success came solvable problems; the familiar difficulty of circulation disruption became an issue, but without the violence of the Chicago wars. As sales soured for rival New York publishers, they encouraged their shared delivery service to neglect dropping off bundles of the *News* to dealers. Joe approached the issue by purchasing his own fleet of delivery trucks and forty-two horse-drawn wagons. And when staff began to outgrow Pulitzer-shared facilities, Bill Field found a five-story building on Park Place. In September 1920 the fifteen-month-old *News* earned a profit, two to three years before schedule. The next step was to add a Sunday edition, which began with a circulation of 187,000 in its initial issue in May 1921 and grew from there.

Patterson's dream, first divulged in a war-shattered farmyard north of Paris, had become a New York fixture, with much of its success a product of the hands-on research of its originator. Joe was still based in Chicago, but during frequent trips to New York he became an even greater man of the people, delving further into what it was readers wanted in a newspaper. His always casual appearance grew seedier as he roamed New York at night, going into bars, subway stations and sleazy movie houses. With the passage of years and copious consumption of alcohol, his face had become gnarled, and flecks of gray now stippled the preppy haircut. He appeared to be just another Joe in the crowd while conducting informal polls, casually asking strangers their opinions of the *News* and its content. He haunted newsstands and subway cars, observing the sort of person who bought his paper and what part of it he or she read: was it photo captions? editorials? comics? news stories?

He took his editors with him on early-morning excursions to Queens and Brooklyn for firsthand inspection of readers there, "to make you fellows realize that every line you put in the paper ought to be aimed directly at these people." He also convinced potential advertisers to accompany him to survey newsstands and to prove that men who appeared to be vagrants were buying the *Times*, while affluent executives often bought the *News*—yet a Wall Street type buying the *News* might also buy the *Times*, but to hide the *News*, which he read inside it. To convey the same message to advertisers who couldn't accompany him, he assigned a motion picture cameraman to document the purchase of his paper by well-dressed executives. An important trend he observed in his subway excursions was that when a passenger left a copy of the *News* on a seat, it was quickly picked up by another rider, which led to his printing the suggestion that passengers should leave their papers on the seat when departing a car. This proposal was followed by a letter to Vox Pop recommending that free copies of the *News* be sent to nonreaders. The writer was certain that, once seeing the paper, they would become loyal *News* fans. Sensing a promotional idea, editors offered to send a free copy to each name on a list of five new prospects submitted by a current reader.

IT IS ALMOST impossible today to imagine a world without photojournalism. If newspaper cartoons, and then comic strips, had mesmerized readers, actual photography—particularly action photography—captured public imagination in a way never before achieved with visual imagery. The motion picture was still in its infancy, *Life* magazine wouldn't appear until the end of 1936 and the widespread viewing of television trailed by another fifteen or so years. The public to which Joe presented his *Daily News* was one that was completely visually naïve.

Therefore, photography was the soul of the *News*, and dependence upon picture chasers as a source of eye-catching visuals had its limits. One solution was to buy an existing photo agency, but negotiations always broke down when the deep pockets of the Tribune Company were discovered to be behind the purchase. Consequently, at the end of 1921, the *News* and the *Tribune* formed their own agency, Pacific & Atlantic Photos, beginning with eight American branches and others to be formed later in European countries. In the days before Wirephoto, the Associated Press service for transmitting pictures by telephone wire, photography traveled by plane, boat, train or automobile, and obtaining the image was merely a first step in the challenge of providing the eye-catching pictures on which the success of the paper depended. Planes were rented, deals were made with Pullman porters and tugboats were hired. In one instance, exposed film was handed to a steamship passenger who looked "like a regular fellow" and turned out to be British prime minister Stanley Baldwin, but he cheerfully delivered the package. When Wirephoto was established later in the decade, the *News* would use it before the competition. If the potential picture story was big, Joe was ready to spend money to get it. "Remember one thing and don't forget it," he told an editor. "I want results in this paper and I don't care what it costs to get those results." During a New York visit by the British monarchs he hired twenty-five freelance photographers in addition to an equal number of *News* men "to have a picture if any nut took a pot shot" at the king. Joe's philosophy was "to anticipate where things will happen—and get them when they do. Many unusual pictures have resulted from this successful policy."

The most sensational photograph of the decade was the electrocution picture of husband-murderess Ruth Snyder, "a chilly-looking blonde with frosty eyes," in the inimitable language of Damon Runyon. Ruth's frosty eyes and blond hair were hidden under a macabre black hood in the scandalous photograph snapped illicitly by Tom Howard, a wartime buddy of Joe's. Howard, a private in a Rainbow Division company under Joe's command, had formed a close friendship with Captain Patterson in the trenches of France and after the war Tom joined the *Tribune*, where he learned to be a photographer. This was an instance of Joe's egalitarianism paying off for the world to see. The Sing Sing death chamber, where photography was strictly forbidden, was crowded with reporters who would each concoct a prose description of the horrifying scene. But Howard, based in Washington and unknown to the others, managed to survive the prison's entrance frisk with a miniature camera of his own design, fastened by adhesive tape to his ankle. A cable, attached to the camera's shutter at one end, was fed up his trouser leg and through a hole in his pocket, into a bulb that when squeezed would trigger the shutter. Howard sat in the front row, crossed a leg with the cuff raised and, at the moment of the fatal electric charge, squeezed the bulb for a six-second exposure. The effect was galvanizing: the picture of the hooded woman strapped to the electric chair was sufficiently grainy and out of focus to simulate movement and create a sense of electric charge surging through her body. The caption: DEAD! Further language would be superfluous. Four hundred thousand extras sold; some advertisers were scandalized and backed out, but those who canceled their contracts later renewed.

When *News* daily circulation neared a half million, William Randolph Hearst panicked. Betting against the tabloid format was one of the few mistakes the Chief ever made as a publisher. The *News* had surpassed his *American* in circulation and was nearing the *Journal*. He reacted in typical Charles Foster Kane fashion by throwing cash at the problem. A big money lottery was announced by the *American*, offering a top prize of one thousand dollars. Patterson countered with a competing lottery; his grand prize was twenty-five hundred. Hearst upped his bribe to readers with five thousand; Joe went to ten. Trucks filled with coupons streamed out of delivery garages to Times Square, the Battery, Columbus Circle and other familiar New York hubs, where the numbered coupons were distributed to excited crowds, who scooped up the *News* and the *American* to see if they held the lucky numbers. The lottery was not popular with employees of either newspaper and they finally called a truce, with circulations falling back to prepromotion numbers.

While Joe was successful in gaining the attention of the man in the street, he needed to assure potential advertisers that the appeal of the *News* went beyond the common man. Retailers of low-priced women's shoes had been the first to find Joe's paper a powerful medium. Slowly department stores came in—first Macy's and later Wanamaker's, Bloomingdale's and Franklin Simon. Next his advertising department added divisions designated to handle automobile, financial and real estate accounts. But the challenge remained; it was essential for the paper to convince advertisers they could rise above the low end. The breakthrough came with Joe's good fortune in enlisting the services of Leo E. McGivena, a promotional wizard who was, in his way, as successful at marketing the *News* to advertisers as Bill Field had been with the *Tribune* years earlier. One of McGivena's tactics in addressing the challenge was to engage the services of a market researcher, a young woman named Sinclair Dakin, who made a study of New York's Lower East Side, where the *News* enjoyed great popularity. Sinclair discovered that residents of this area, widely recognized for both its ethnic mix and its poverty, had the highest margin of disposable income in New York. These were the upwardly mobile children of immigrants, who combined high wages with low cost of living; furthermore, their level of brand recognition was sophisticated, and they would pay top prices for first-rate goods. Dakin's research revealed a heretofore untapped trove of potential purchasers: Lower East Siders who were ripe for Park Avenue style, and they were avid *News* readers. McGivena eagerly seized the research and coined a phrase to maximize its concept, "Tell it to Sweeney! The Stuyvesants will understand." His slogan was magic in gaining advertising from those wishing to reach the Stuyvesants (the educated elite) as well as the Sweeneys (the ethnic audience), and continued to be effective in *News* ads as well as its rate cards for years to follow.

JOE HAD ENTERED an exhilarating yet disturbing time in his life. While the increasing success of the *News* was bringing fulfillment, extreme personal complications were pulling him in divergent directions, with attention divided between two women, two newspapers, two cities and soon two families. When it seemed as though his existence could not become more challenging, it would. Although he and Bert had been eager to establish separate domains, both agreed it was premature for him to leave Chicago permanently before the *News* was firmly established; therefore he would remain at Tribune Tower into 1925 and his loyal secretary, Kitty Higgins, even longer, continuing her daily writing of a dutiful letter to Nellie over Joe's signature. He was, in effect, separated from Alice, but there were recurring problems. Following an informal financial arrangement made in October 1922, he was sending her two thousand dollars a month "until further notice." Nevertheless, her casual regard for money continued and created unexpected concerns. In August 1923 he found it necessary to write the following letter to Cartier in New York: "Gentlemen: It has recently come to my knowledge that my wife, Mrs. Alice H. Patterson, purchased, or purchased conditionally, three pearls from you last April, at a price of about $70,000.00. This is to make it clear to you that this purchase on her part was a personal one by her and that I am not responsible for any payment thereon."

The productive Patterson-King partnership had progressed to a passionate affair, but Mary King and Joe could not form a legal union because Alice would not give him a divorce; furthermore, they were now based in different cities. Mary had moved to New York as soon as the *News* stabilized and was working out of the Park Place office, while also remaining Sunday editor of the *Tribune*. She lived first at the Vanderbilt, a then-fashionable residential hotel at 34th Street and Park Avenue, and later at the Gotham (now the Peninsula) Hotel on Fifth Avenue at 55th Street. During the first few years of the *News*, when he was juggling duties at both papers and physically present in New York only sporadically, Joe usually stayed at the University Club, but by 1923 he had signed a twenty-four-month lease, at eighty-five dollars a month, for two rooms and a bath on the fourth floor of 28 West 51st Street. His Chicago quarters during this period consisted of a three-room suite on the sixth floor of the Drake Hotel. He would keep both residences through the end of September 1925.

Joe's prolific association with Mary reached its zenith in 1923 when the couple brought forth their greatest collaboration, James Joseph Patterson, the son for whom Joe had so long yearned and been unable to produce within his marriage to Alice. To the world, Jimmy was Joe's "adopted son" and would remain so throughout much of his life. The logistics were complicated; Mary took a leave of absence from the two papers and traveled to England for the birth of their child, returning when Jimmy was a few weeks old. She and the baby moved into Riverdale quarters they would share with two King sisters and a succession of nurses and governesses, but she quickly resumed her work schedule at the Park Place office.

Into all of this personal chaos, another new venture emerged to absorb Joe's attention. He and Bert founded *Liberty,* a general-interest weekly magazine to compete with the phenomenally successful *Saturday Evening Post.* They would sink some $15 million into this venture, which carried first-rate fiction by such authors as F. Scott Fitzgerald and Theodore Dreiser and articles with the bylines of famous personalities of the day, among them Clark Gable and Babe Ruth. Paced for the modern reader, *Liberty* featured short stories of one page in length and features with a clock logo indicating how long the piece would take to read. The advent of *Liberty,* with editorial offices in New York, created another compelling reason for Joe to move to Manhattan permanently.

The success of the *News* had not been lost on Park Row; in June 1924, exactly five years after the launch of Joe's paper, Hearst countered with the *New York Daily Mirror.* By then, *News* circulation was well over 800,000 daily and the paper was firmly entrenched. Rather than offering serious competition, the *Mirror* drew circulation from Hearst's other New York morning paper, the *American.* Three months later, Bernarr Macfadden jumped into the game with the *Evening Graphic,* which crossed the fragile line into journalistic bad taste, offering such ersatz substitutes as photomontages when it could not obtain the real thing. During its eight years of existence, the Macfadden paper was invariably referred to by *Time* magazine as the "pornoGraphic." But it wasn't merely tabloid copycats that were influenced by the *News.* Joseph Gies, in his biography of Robert R. McCormick, wrote that other publications were "influenced by the glib and grabby style. *Time* magazine was a . . . glossy, intellectualized version, and newspapers everywhere, after seeing a few copies of the *News,* brightened up their head and caption writing." Many years later, *Time* itself wrote, "The *News's* headlines crackled; its pictures were good, and masterfully played; its news stories were models of clarity, conciseness and coarse wit. Joe Patterson's journalism owed more to P. T. Barnum than to Adolph Ochs. No story in the *News* was 'important but dull'; if the news was important, there was no need for it to be dull. In world affairs, the *News* could tell in two columns most of what the *New York Times* took eight to tell. But the *News* did best on what the *Times* aloofly did not consider Fit to Print."

SIX YEARS AFTER the debut of the *News,* both the paper and Joe's personal finances were firmly established, and he marked the passage by moving to New York permanently. He prepared by first providing generous lodgings for the family he was leaving in Chicago. In October 1925, he bought a handsome 6,500-square-foot apartment in what continues to be one of Chicago's finest cooperatives, the new eighteen-story Benjamin Marshall building at 209 East Lake Shore Drive. The units, each with stunning views of Lake Michigan and the sweep of Lake Shore Drive, are two to a floor, and the Patterson apartment stretched across the east side of the building's thirteenth story. The building, long a Wasp enclave, has since become home to some of the city's most substantial and visible Jewish families. The Hyatt Hotels' Pritzker family, two branches of the Toni hair products' Harris family—including the late Irving Harris, grandfather of New York restaurateur Danny Meyer—and Eppie Lederer, aka Ann Landers, have all lived in luxury at 209. The Patterson unit was basically for Alice and twelve-year-old Josephine—but also when they wished, the two older girls. His home, when he was in Chicago, would now be the library of the East Lake Shore Drive apartment, a cozy room with a fireplace, which overlooked the lake and the graceful curve of the drive. A bathroom was added and the space organized so that he could walk directly into his personal quarters from the unit's entryway without intruding on Alice's privacy.

Celebrity visited the Patterson family in a new form in 1925, when theatrical producer Morris Gest discovered twenty-two-year-old Elinor and decided she had the perfect face for portraying the nun in the American production of *The Miracle*. Elinor, who had inherited her grandmother Nellie's beauty, was eager to play the role and agreed to make a formal social debut on the condition her parents would allow her to accept Gest's offer. *The Miracle*, a Max Reinhardt mime play, was first a 1912 silent film starring the celebrated English beauty Lady Diana Manners. By the mid-1920s the stage version, a hit in England, was on a twelve-year world tour. Following a roaring success in New York and Boston, the production opened in Chicago on February 3, 1926, starring the English actress Iris Tree and Lady Diana alternating with Elinor as the nun. In reporting on the opening, *Time* magazine—in one more installment of its almost constant coverage of the Patterson-McCormick clan—wrote, "Folk who went night after night fell to comparing the performances of the three actresses who appeared in turn as the nun. They thought that Miss Patterson and Lady Diana brought the greatest spirituality to the part, that Miss Tree had not quite their ethereal innocence together with the sense of warm, alert youth that is required."

ALTHOUGH ALICE CONTINUED to refuse a divorce, by 1928 the Pattersons had become officially separated. But Joe, now a rich man in his own right, was nevertheless living like a clerk in a rented New York apartment furnished with indifferent pieces. The time had come for more permanent Manhattan lodgings and fortunately Joe knew the perfect man to provide not merely permanent living quarters but an immense leap in lifestyle. During the construction of Raymond Hood's controversial design for the Tribune Tower, Joe had cemented a firm friendship with the architect, a quirky visionary like himself, who had also fallen in love at the office; in Hood's case it was with his secretary, whom he was able to marry without the impediments hampering Joe.

The commission was for a ten-story limestone building at 3 East 84th Street, with one apartment to a floor and an elegant penthouse at its top for Joe. Specifications for the stylish Art Deco structure included a private entrance on the ground floor leading to a separate elevator speeding directly to the penthouse. Alicia, now twenty-one, would live in one of the eight other apartments, with a further floor occupied by James A. Farley, Franklin Roosevelt's gregarious and highly visible postmaster general.

Located just off Fifth Avenue and steps away from the Metropolitan Museum of Art, the building was designed to give an American twist to some of the finest elements of the decade's Paris apartments. Today it is one of the city's Art Deco landmarks and remains among the Upper East Side's few examples of that distinctive sleek jazz-modern style applied to apartment living. The centerpiece of Joe's penthouse was a double-size living room with ten-foot ceilings and a wood-burning fireplace; next to it was a library, paneled in fine dark wood, with a hidden bar and an adjacent powder room. His living room and a large dining room each featured French windows opening out to Juliet balconies, and in addition to the master bedroom suite, there were two other large bedrooms with baths. Before the plaster was dry, Joe suddenly notified Hood that he wanted to move into the apartment—furnished—the same evening at eight o'clock. A night watchman was dispatched to a furniture store on Third Avenue, where he selected what in his taste were the most elegant floor samples, among them matched sets of ornate furniture, plush club chairs and sofas, and a bed with a canopy. Joe had no complaints except that he spent the night in the reception hall on an iron cot because he couldn't sleep in "that damned covered wagon."

The New York architectural alliance of Patterson and Hood had just begun; the following year they collaborated on a midtown office building. The *News* had clearly outgrown its Park Place quarters and it was now appropriate for the paper to have a building designed for its specific needs. Daily circulation had grown to more than a million by 1926, with a million and a quarter on Sunday, and, although a second printing plant had been added in Brooklyn two years earlier, it was no longer adequate. The site they selected was 220 East 42nd Street at Second Avenue, where the headquarters would extend along Second to 41st Street. Initially Joe had envisioned a structure to house only the offices and printing plant of the *Daily News*, but Hood presented him with plans for a thirty-six-story skyscraper, which included income-producing office space he insisted would greatly increase the paper's profits. Joe was unconvinced, but Hood's obvious devastation at being denied his soaring dream tugged at Joe's sensitive soul. While they were discussing it one day, he walked over to Hood, put his arm around him and said, "Listen, Ray, if you want to build your god damn tower, go ahead and do it."

The skyscraper Hood produced in 1929 was so far from the retro look of the Tribune Tower that it became the model for Superman's *Daily Planet* building. There were also inimitable Patterson touches; above the 42nd Street entrance were carved Lincoln's words about God's love for the common people, "He made so many of them." And, following Joe's fascination with maps, the theme for the lobby integrated the design of a compass, meteorological charts and maps, and an immense revolving globe within a large depression in the middle of its floor. Patterson's ninth-floor office reflected the owner's offhand style: cork walls littered with thumbtacked papers, utilitarian green carpeting and an old mahogany desk that traveled with him from Park Place. The room's chief embellishment was a globe, which Patterson twirled frequently when checking or confirming foreign locations.

Joe continued to excel at collaborating with artists on their comic strips. *The Gumps, Gasoline Alley, Winnie Winkle* and *Harold Teen* now appeared in both the *Tribune* and the *News*. Among strips that followed were Milton Caniff's *Terry and the Pirates*, and *Smilin' Jack* by Zack Mosley. In 1924 Harold Lincoln Gray, who had spent six years submitting ideas to Joe while working in the *Tribune* art department, finally hit a bonanza with *Little Orphan Annie*. In Gray's quest to find the perfect cartoon to suit the Captain, he consulted Sidney Smith, who had struck gold with *The Gumps*. He showed Smith an idea with an orphan boy as the central character. "Sid said the child must be clean and cute and sweet to appeal to women readers," Gray remembered thirty years later. "So the kid was cute and had golden curls." He showed his proposal, Little Orphan Ottor, to Patterson, who growled, "The kid looks like a pansy to me. Put a skirt on him and we'll call it Little Orphan Annie." The immediate and overwhelming appeal of an entirely humorless, politically reactionary strip is baffling; its central character was a solemn waif with vacant lozenge-shaped eyeballs and only one red dress, but what a sensation she created. Although the comic was madly popular and extremely lucrative, Joe turned violently against Annie a little more than a year after her debut. The addition of a rich guardian, the war-profiteering Daddy Warbucks, was becoming increasingly annoying to Patterson. He had watched Annie's improbable evolution from orphanage inmate to life in a mansion surrounded by servants, limousines and European aristocracy, and he blew up. "Who ever heard of a rich orphan?" he stormed. "Kill the strip." After a day of readers flooding the paper with telephone complaints, Annie was back in action. The following morning, two days' strips appeared in the *Tribune* with a page-one apology promising that such an omission would never again occur. But it was not merely the ordinary newspaper reader who was addicted to the strange little orphan. When her dog Sandy vanished in 1933, the Tribune Syndicate received an urgent wire from Detroit, PLEASE DO ALL YOU CAN TO HELP ANNIE FIND SANDY. WE ARE ALL INTERESTED. HENRY FORD. Such was the power of Annie that the crotchety automaker would overlook the milliondollar libel suit he had filed scarcely a decade and a half earlier against the very company from whom he was soliciting help. But Annie was not entirely without detractors; the national communist newspaper, the *Daily Worker,* was so annoyed by the antilabor orphan that it published a rival strip, dubbed *Little Lefty*.

Patterson's coaching and pampering of his artists continued, accompanied by generous salaries of between twenty-five and eighty-five thousand dollars a year. The creation of another household name occurred in 1931, when he worked closely with Chester Gould, who submitted a strip he had titled *Plainclothes Tracy*. Joe's modifications included changing the name of the hero—and hence the title of the strip—to Dick Tracy. In 1944, *American Mercury* commented on Joe's hand-drawn gold mine. "Collectively the comics under his control reach some 50,000,000 people, and it would be a very casual observer indeed who did not credit the comics which he inspired or guides with at least some of the *News*' overwhelming popularity."

JOE WAS IN his early forties during the founding of the *News*, and in many ways he had changed very little since his postcollegiate days. His passion for motion pictures had not abated; if anything, the growing sophistication of film had made it more appealing to him, and the increased prevalence of movie houses made cinemagoing an almost daily activity. Although his mind was continuously working, researching, creating and reworking a newspaper, he always had the relaxed look of a man ambling along on his way to the old fishing hole. There were numerous reports from friends and associates who ran into him strolling along a busy Manhattan street, jacket over a shoulder and either a Popsicle or Eskimo Pie in his hand. There was only one fixed appointment in his daily schedule, an eleven o'clock meeting for the following day's editorial page with Reuben Maury, who wrote editorials in words that were indistinguishable from Joe's own, and cartoonist C. D. Batchelor. The meeting ended by noon and Joe would saunter off to lunch, probably at the sandwich counter in a nearby drugstore, followed by a trip to a movie house to catch a recent release. He didn't return to the office until late afternoon, when he would look over the men's work and possibly make a few changes in Maury's editorial.

His appearance was still so unkempt that he was once denied entry to the lobby of the Daily News Building by a new guard, and there remained that duality in his nature. His casual appearance belied a formality in his dealings with employees, and to all but a few he was either Mr. or Captain Patterson. Bill Field called him Joe, as did another old-timer, Burns Mantle, but his editorial writer and thus alter ego, Reuben Maury, called him Chief. Out of his presence he was affectionately known as the Old Man and, in writing, J.M.P. If Joe distanced himself from those who worked for him, he treated them with dignity, and *News* employees quickly learned that the Old Man rarely gave orders, or at least not in the language most employers do. They understood that when Captain Patterson said, "Let's try this" or "What do you think about" he was conveying the only way that would be acceptable. His movie critic Paul Gallico discovered this when Joe, possibly the most enthusiastic motion picture fan of his generation, commented, "Don't you think you are being a little hard on movies?" Gallico said, "I kept on calling the bad ones bad. All of a sudden I wasn't the movie critic any more, and this was the first time I realized that when Patterson said 'Don't you think' it was an order."

His slumming excursions continued, though no longer for the purpose of testing his manhood as they had been in his youth. And although they functioned as *Daily News* research trips, there would always be something within Joe that truly enjoyed being among working-class men and derelicts. When a cabdriver seeking change entered a New York restaurant, he spotted Joe dining with friends. After greeting Patterson with a slap on the back, he was apprehended by a waiter who began pulling him toward the door. "Don't give me that," said the driver. "Joe's an old friend of mine. We bummed on the Bowery together, didn't we, Joe?" Joe rose, put his arm around the cabby and asked him to join the group for dinner, which he did, saying, "Joe, you always could go out panhandling and come back with half a dollar and a pack of cigarettes, but what's your racket now?" After dinner and the departure of the cabdriver, Joe took his skeptical companions to the Bowery, where the reception he received from old buddies convinced his uptown friends that the district had indeed featured in Patterson's biography.

Perhaps the strangest constant in Joe's life was the presence of Max Annenberg. When Annenberg died, Joe, who always refrained from printing anything resembling an obituary on his editorial page, wrote a brief note at the top of a column that otherwise dealt with current issues, "Memo to Max Annenberg: Good-by, I am going to miss you a lot. Hope to be seeing you someday. J.M. Patterson." Another curious facet in Joe's makeup was his capacity for hero worship. His idols ranged from lion tamer Clyde Beatty to socialist and writer Jack London. Film and stage stars fascinated him. Among those whose photos appeared regularly in the *News* and about whom he wrote in his sacrosanct editorial page were Greta Garbo, Helen Hayes, Grace Moore, Katharine Cornell and opera diva Lily Pons. On the other hand, he was furious when Edward VIII abdicated to marry Wallis Simpson. He viewed the former prince as a moral coward who had weakened the stature of the monarchy, an amazing position for a one-time socialist. It was a stand he maintained, despite the romantic sentiment of his readers, and he used his editorial page to periodically criticize Edward during his years as Duke of Windsor.

WHEN THE JOY ride of the twenties came to a halt in 1929, Joe—with his uncanny journalistic sixth sense—instructed *Daily News* staff that the big story now was the Depression and its effect on all Americans. It was one he experienced firsthand when he lost $5 million in bank stocks in one day, but a $5 million loss to Joe Patterson was negligible compared to what others, both rich and poor throughout the country, were being subjected to from the economic collapse. In a speech to the *News* editorial department, he said, "We're off on the wrong foot. The people's major interest is no longer in the playboy, Broadway and divorces, but in how they're going to eat, and from this time forward we'll pay attention to the struggle for existence that's just beginning. All signs point to the prospect of a great economic upheaval and we'll pay attention to the news of things being done to assure the well-being of the average man and his family." Joe's adjusted focus was to lead the *News* in avid support of the New Deal, and he would back Franklin Roosevelt throughout his first two terms. Although sex and crime were still essential ingredients in the newspaper, it was with the knowledge that readers depended on the *News* to bring an escape from their drab existence. This philosophy paid off in revenues from Depression-era advertisers who tended to restrict their budgets to two New York papers, the solid *Times* and the flamboyant *News*, pulling away from anything in between. Formerly successful businessmen may have been selling apples on the street, but *New York Daily News* employees continued to receive their annual bonuses throughout the Depression years.

No business can sail forward without a periodic reversal and Joe and Bert didn't have many, but any time they might feel smug about the success of the *Tribune* and the *News*, there was always *Liberty* magazine to consider. Although *Liberty*'s 2.5 million circulation surpassed that of *Collier's*, it was never able to summon adequate advertising. They finally made an exchange with Bernarr Macfadden in 1931, receiving in return his failing *Detroit Daily Mirror*, which they killed after two years. However, the collapse of these publications can be considered mere hiccups in the overall scope of Bert and Joe's accomplishments.

In June 1939, when the *New York Daily News* celebrated its twentieth anniversary, its circulation was the nation's largest, and third strongest of any newspaper in the world; the other two were London tabloids. The publishing bible *Editor & Publisher* used the occasion to devote a large section of the weekly trade paper to the unparalleled American tabloid, praising the amazing success of the *News* but referring to Joe as "the kindly tyrant who is a czar one moment and asks in his next breath how a hireling's children are." Joe, who would not be interviewed for the piece, did agree to submit a statement. It was eighty-seven words in length.

The *New York Daily News* was to be Joe's continuing passion, his great love; it was a living, breathing organism that would repay him with immense personal satisfaction. In his 1909 play, *The Fourth Estate,* he had written, "Newspapers start when their owners are poor and take the side of the people, and so they build up a large circulation, and presently, as a result, advertising. That makes them rich, and they begin, most naturally, to associate with other rich men—they play golf with one and drink whisky with another, and their son marries the daughter of a third. They forget all about the people, and then, their circulation dries up, then their advertising—and their paper becomes decadent and feeble." Never did Joe Patterson "forget all about the people."

Thirty-two-year-old Joseph Medill was thought to be "the handsomest man in Chicago" when he arrived in 1855 to buy a stake in the *Chicago Daily Tribune*. (*Col. McCormick Research Center*)

Joseph Medill's appearance had already begun to change dramatically by 1860, the year he participated in engineering the Republican nomination of Abraham Lincoln for president. (*Col. McCormick Research Center*)

Kate Medill McCormick, the elder of Joseph Medill's "she-devils," was the mother of United States senator Medill McCormick and the *Chicago Tribune*'s Colonel Robert R. McCormick. (*Col. McCormick Research Center*)

Nellie Medill Patterson, a great Victorian beauty, provided decades of torment for her husband, her children, and all those around her. (*J. M. Patterson Papers, Lake Forest College Library Special Collections*)

Although an effective *Chicago Tribune* editor, Robert W. Patterson Jr. was belittled at home by his wife, Nellie. He often retreated to his stable to drink with his horses or to the Chicago Club, where the company was more forgiving. (*J. M. Patterson Papers, Lake Forest College Library Special Collections*)

Four generations of Pattersons posed for this studio portrait toward the end of 1904. The alcoholic Robert W. Patterson Jr., then fifty-four and editor in chief of the *Tribune*, was also suffering from severe depression and periodic nervous breakdowns. With him are his mother, Julia Quigley Patterson; his son, Joseph Medill Patterson; and Joe's eldest daughter, Elinor. (*J. M. Patterson Papers, Lake Forest College Library Special Collections*)

An unhappy Colonel McCormick—
dressed as a girl and dubbed Roberta
by his mother, who was heartbroken
over the death of her baby daughter.
(*Col. McCormick Research Center*)

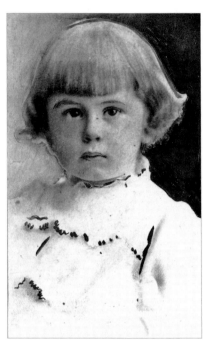

When this photograph was taken,
Medill McCormick (*right*) was
considered the dauphin who would
one day reign as publisher of the
Chicago Tribune. However, it was his
younger brother, Robert (*left*), who
would personify the newspaper as
the fearsome Colonel McCormick
throughout much of the twentieth
century. (*Col. McCormick Research Center*)

Joseph Medill was a loving
grandfather to his Patterson
grandchildren, Cissy and Joe. Joe
would remain the most important man
in Cissy's life as long as he lived. (*Col.
McCormick Research Center*)

His life was drawing to a close in 1898 when this picture was taken of the patriarch, Joseph Medill, surrounded by his grandchildren. Clockwise from lower left are Robert R. McCormick, who would inherit his grandfather's role at the *Chicago Tribune*; Cissy Patterson, future owner and publisher of the *Washington Times-Herald*; Medill McCormick, soon to leave publishing for politics; and Joseph Patterson, future founder of the *New York Daily News.* (*Col. McCormick Research Center*)

Ambassador Robert Sanderson McCormick and Mrs. McCormick represented the United States at embassies in Vienna, St. Petersburg, and Paris during the early twentieth century. (*Col. McCormick Research Center*)

Robert R. McCormick
Candidate for
ALDERMAN
21st WARD

Robert R. McCormick was in his first year at law school in 1904 when he was approached by a Republican boss to run for alderman of what is now Chicago's Forty-Second Ward. The campaign required the aloof McCormick to shake hands with strangers on the street and march into saloons announcing he was buying drinks for the house. (*Col. McCormick Research Center*)

Alice Higinbotham Patterson posed with the eldest of her three daughters, Elinor, later an actress and a renowned beauty. (*Mrs. Michael Arlen Collection, Lake Forest College Library Special Collections*)

Cissy and her five-year-old daughter, Countess Felicia Gizycka, sat for this picture on Valentine's Day, 1910. (*Col. McCormick Research Center*)

Cissy and Felicia Gizycka, age seven, enjoyed a summer spectator event in Lake Forest during a pleasant interlude in their stormy relationship. (*Col. McCormick Research Center*)

Count Johann Heinrich von Bernstorff was Germany's ambassador to the United States as World War I was nearing, only one of the strikes against him as a serious suitor for Cissy's attentions.
(*Col. McCormick Research Center*)

Medill McCormick was embarking on a successful political career in 1914. After serving in the Illinois House of Representatives he would be elected to the United States House of Representatives in 1916 and to the United States Senate in 1918.
(*Col. McCormick Research Center*)

Lt. Joseph Medill Patterson in Domjevin, France, March 11, 1918. Eventually promoted to the rank of captain, he was commanding officer of Battery B, 149th Field Artillery of the Rainbow Division, with which he participated in the Second Battle of the Marne.
(*Col. McCormick Research Center*)

Robert McCormick's affair with his cousin's wife Amy Irwin Adams, eight years his senior, scandalized Chicago. They defied the gossip, married, and lived happily together—for a while. (*Col. McCormick Research Center*)

Joe Patterson took time to relax in 1919, the year he launched the *New York Daily News*, the most successful newspaper in the nation's history. (*Col. McCormick Research Center*)

When Joe Patterson (*left*) and Robert McCormick (*in the light suit*) laid the cornerstone for the *Chicago Tribune*'s new printing plant in 1920, it was the first step in creating the immense Michigan Avenue complex known as the Tribune Tower. (*Col. McCormick Research Center*)

Cissy was in her late thirties
when she stood for this
1920 studio photograph in
Washington. She would soon
sample the expatriate life in
Paris, where she consorted
with the Hemingways and
the Fitzgeralds while writing
a bestselling novel. (*Col.
McCormick Research Center*)

Joe and Mary Patterson's son, James,
was sixteen when his parents were
finally able to marry. He followed
a lifelong passion for the military,
eventually attending West Point.
(*J. M. Patterson Papers, Lake Forest
College Library Special Collections*)

For many years Joe Patterson's daughter Alicia shaped herself to please her father. She shared his early love of aviation and his passion for journalism. (*J. M. Patterson Papers, Lake Forest College Library Special Collections*)

Robert McCormick's sports all involved horses. His country estate featured a polo field, and he and his wife, Amy, rode to the hounds during an annual hunt season that lasted from the end of September into December.
(*Col. McCormick Research Center*)

On December 21, 1944, Robert McCormick married former Baltimore belle Maryland Mathison Hooper in a ceremony at the Chicago apartment of his cousin Chauncey McCormick. In the wedding party were (*left to right*) best man Joe Patterson; matron of honor Marion Deering McCormick; the bridal couple; host Chauncey McCormick, who gave the bride away; and Mary King Patterson. (*Col. McCormick Research Center*)

In 1948 Robert McCormick bought a B-17 bomber, which he transformed into a luxurious private plane for the series of seven "around the world" trips he made with his second wife, Maryland. (*Col. McCormick Research Center*)

English bulldog Buster Boo was the Colonel's closest companion toward the end of his life. Buster celebrated McCormick's seventieth birthday with a serving of ice cream, to the amusement of McCormick and Mrs. John Knight. (*Col. McCormick Research Center*)

Newsday, founded by Alicia Patterson, was America's most successful post–World War II newspaper. (*J. M. Patterson Papers, Lake Forest College Library Special Collections*)

· 15 ·

THE CARTIER LIFE

A FEW months after he founded the *Daily News,* Joe's mother suffered a heart attack that left her "fuzzy-minded." It wasn't long before she became convinced that the area around Dupont Circle was excessively noisy and, within three years, she abandoned her imposing Washington establishment in favor of a quiet suite in Chicago's Drake Hotel. More significantly for Joe and Cissy, Nellie also reversed two parsimonious decades by opening her purse in 1923 and dividing much of her property and income between them. Suddenly, both were rich.

Cissy, after years of living on an allowance of ten thousand dollars a year, was now a wealthy woman and mistress of a Washington showplace. She sold the house on R Street and took over her mother's mansion, with its thirty rooms, ten bathrooms and staff of eighteen. Books filling the two libraries were now read, and fireplaces throughout the house lit. Also to be lit were one hundred candles in the ballroom's crystal chandeliers; their reflected flickers in mirrors at each end of the room threw a flattering glow both on the faces of guests and against full-length portraits of Cissy and her mother. Now that it was hers, the house received her singular high-low stamp. The heavy furnishings and Nellie's Victorian taste were banished, replaced by Cissy's lively style. Heads of caribou, deer, elk and mountain lions she had shot in the West now lined the marble stairway and a Gobelin tapestry hunting scene decorated the foyer. With Cissy, the house was bright and modern but still so majestic that, while the White House was being repaired after a fire in 1927, the government rented it as a temporary executive mansion for President and Mrs. Coolidge. Cissy reveled in the place now that it was hers, entertaining with zeal, imagination and magnums of champagne. She threw dinner parties in a dining room that held sixty, followed by dancing to a live orchestra in the ballroom and wee-hour poker games where the pot might run as high as ten thousand dollars. Like her friend Alice Longworth, she stoked the fires of her parties by inviting enemies and seating them together.

But Cissy's freewheeling life didn't stop there. While walking along Fifth Avenue in New York one afternoon, she passed Cartier, where she was drawn to a fabulous string of black pearls in one of its windows. Each of the twenty-two pearls was separated from the next by a diamond, and matching the necklace was an exquisite pair of earrings. She inquired and learned the set had been consigned to the jeweler by the Russian Prince Yusupov, Rasputin's assassin, and two of the pearls had belonged to Catherine the Great. Cissy wanted them; she wanted them now, and at any cost. When Pierre Cartier informed her that Prince Yusupov had not yet put a price on the jewels, she simply signed a blank check and handed it to the jeweler.

She also acquired a private railroad car, the era's answer to a private jet, and hers was pure luxe, with a permanent staff of three and gold-plated bathroom fixtures—although she and her guests still managed with an outdoor privy in Jackson Hole. The cost of maintaining the car, which she named *Ranger* after her favorite mount, was fifty thousand dollars a year, but Cissy would use it often and she frequently lent it to friends. With all this grandeur, she needed a place to retreat. At the top of 15 Dupont Circle, down the hall from the servant's quarters, she carved out a little apartment for herself, with a sitting room, a bedroom and a bath in between. Hidden in her robin's-egg-blue bedroom, she could look out through windows curtained in yellow chintz to green leaves on the surrounding treetops.

It was like Jackson Hole: simple, natural and away from opulence, artifice—and anyone she didn't want to see.

CISSY, WHO HAD had such a difficult relationship with her mother, was repeating the pattern with Felicia. "When I reached my teens, Mother wanted me around all the time," Felicia recalled of the eerie duplication of Nellie's sudden attention to Cissy when she blossomed. The seventeen-year-old, soon to graduate from Farmington, was maturing into a blond beauty, with a pinup figure and no physical similarity to Cissy, aside from a throaty voice. But she did resemble Josef Gizycki, so every time Cissy looked at her daughter the worst memories returned. One night shortly before a Dupont Circle dinner party, a female guest canceled and Felicia was enlisted as substitute. The man seated next to her was a twenty-four-year-old writer and teacher of writing named Drew Pearson. Not yet the iconic journalist he would become, Pearson was only seven years Felicia's senior, but "older than God," she thought. Drew was instantly smitten with the young countess and after dinner took her to her first nightclub, where he had the dubious distinction of buying the future Alcoholics Anonymous poster child her first drink, a planter's punch.

The following summer, Cissy, concerned that Jackson Hole was not providing appropriate male companionship for Felicia, invited the young writer to join them for a stay at Flat Creek Ranch. Drew, barely eking out an existence as an author of syndicated features, was tempted by the opportunity to know both Cissy and Felicia better and borrowed money to travel out to the ranch, where he found an accelerating battle raging between the two. Felicia later reported, "I was always afraid of the next moment, the next sentence! She wasn't reasonable; she had no emotional self-control. . . . And I always fought back . . . after it was all over, Ma always laughed at her anger and her fights, but I hated it." Drew's presence didn't help matters and he got nowhere with Felicia, who found him a dreary old codger. But while he was there, conflict between the two women escalated close to the point of explosion, until one day, Felicia recalled, "She and I had a knock-down, drag-out fight, which included hair-pulling and having my shirt half-ripped off."

While Cissy was napping that afternoon, Felicia vanished, leaving a trail of evidence indicating she had run away from home. Dispatched to intercept Cissy's unruly child and bring her back, Drew accompanied Felicia on the train as far as Salt Lake City but was unable to dissuade her. It was she who discouraged him by declaring, "You bore me, and the more I see of you, the more bored I get." He left and returned to Jackson Hole. Later, detectives traced Felicia to the San Diego area, where the new Farmington graduate adapted well to the situation. She took an alias and managed to find a job as a waitress in a short-order restaurant near the naval base. One of her employers was a female bootlegger, and her lodging was in the apartment of another waitress and her sailor husband. Felicia was justifiably proud of her ability to cope in the alien situation and always insisted she was a good waitress. Cissy continued to have her watched but did not otherwise interfere.

ALTHOUGH JACKSON HOLE remained an important part of her life and she considered both Cal and Rose among her closest friends, the restless, aimless Cissy soon moved on to Europe. Paris of the 1920s was a magnet for free spirits, including Cissy, and she joined the expatriate set that gravitated to the glamorous city. Among those she befriended were Ernest Hemingway, at the time writing *The Sun Also Rises,* and his first wife, Hadley; Zelda and Scott Fitzgerald; James Joyce; Man Ray; James Thurber; and Helena Rubinstein, who had left Poland at about the same time Cissy had. But the expatriate psychology was not for Cissy, nor did she starve in a Left Bank garret; her Paris home was a suite at the Ritz, and without apology. Nevertheless, she was as authentic as any, producing work that many of the American writers could envy. She sold the concept for a novel, written in French, to both a book publisher and the venerable French literary magazine *Revue de Paris,* where it was published as *André en Amérique.* In 1926 after English translation, the novel was retitled *Glass Houses* and published in book form by the American house Minton, Balch & Company.

While diligent about her writing schedule, Cissy did break away to spend time with other writers and was particularly close to the Hemingways. She and Ernest enjoyed talking about guns and hunting and, in their early friendship, she listened to the couple's descriptions of an inn where they had skied in Austria and commiserated with them about their loss of luggage containing Ernest's entire output of manuscripts for the year. Then, as the Hemingway world darkened, she became a necessary rock for the lovely Hadley, distraught when her husband discarded her for the predatory Pauline Pfeiffer, who worked her way into the marriage to become his second wife. Cissy appreciated the vivid Scott Fitzgerald and his wife, Zelda, then teetering on the brink of her first depression, and marveled at Scott's ability to abruptly embrace sobriety to focus on writing, always a transitory state but nevertheless amazing to her.

Gertrude Stein's studio in the sixth arrondissement was still the place to visit for anyone wishing to be immersed in the art of the moment and the artists who were creating it, although there were not as many painters in the assemblage as there had been earlier in the century. Guests who gathered at 27, rue de Fleurus for the famous Stein Saturday evenings at home now included rich and not-so-rich visitors to the city, along with a lingering scattering of painters and some emerging writers from America and the British Isles. The studio was part of a rambling space Gertrude shared with her brother Leo and her lesbian partner, Alice B. Toklas, a dark little birdlike woman, with bangs above her eyebrows and the shadow of a mustache powdering her upper lip. The legendary studio was packed with outsized furniture and its walls lined top to bottom with paintings that now hang in the world's great museums. Among them were canvases by Matisse, Renoir and Bonnard, a multitude of Picassos and a long row of Cézanne watercolors.

Saturday evenings at the Steins' began at nine o'clock and continued into the early-morning hours, with Gertrude holding forth in one of her almost nonstop monologues about other English language writers. She admired the work of Fitzgerald but not that of Sherwood

Anderson. She disliked Ezra Pound because he had abused her hospitality by sitting down too firmly on a chair and breaking it, and she especially disliked James Joyce, whom she had never met, because his work represented a threat to her own. Hemingway remembered, "If you brought up Joyce twice, you would not be invited back." She even stopped patronizing the Shakespeare & Company library and bookstore at 12, rue de l'Odéon when its owner, Sylvia Beach, published Joyce's *Ulysses*.

After Paris, Cissy wandered on to the French Riviera, where she hobnobbed with Somerset Maugham at Cap Ferrat and launched an intense affair with the upwardly aspiring William Christian Bullitt Jr. The future ambassador to Russia and later France possessed a family tree with members ranging from the *Bounty*'s Fletcher Christian to Pocahontas. Bill Bullitt was ten years Cissy's junior and had been married to two beauties, fellow Philadelphian Aimee Ernesta Drinker and Louise Bryant. The latter, whom playwright Eugene O'Neill had also loved, was best known as the young widow of communist activist John Reed (portrayed by Diane Keaton in Warren Beatty's film *Reds*). Bullitt was rich, charming, impeccably groomed, supremely self-confident and voted "most brilliant" in his 1913 class at Yale. He captivated Cissy, whose attraction for him may have been that her concentrated sexuality helped him overcome his chronic impotence. She was quite serious about their romance before deciding she did not want to grow old in Bullitt's arms, and probably would not have the opportunity to do so.

When she returned to America, Cissy—intent on becoming a successful novelist—established a New York base to be at the hub of the publishing industry. In addition to a large Carlton House suite, she kept a bare-bones studio at 6 East 61st Street, a fourth-floor walk-up with a Murphy bed she could pull down for naps or when she worked through most of the night. It was a hideout unknown even to her closest friends, with old brocade at the windows, the simplest of furniture and no clocks. An added attraction to New York was the presence of Joe, whom she accompanied on his newsstand rounds to study *Daily*

News readers and their habits. He even took her with him into the foreign territory of Brooklyn and Coney Island.

But the America to which she returned was also a country she found diminished by the sudden death of Medill McCormick. He had been a joy to her while they were growing up, a handsome older cousin on whom she had had a crush for years. When she needed someone to bolster her during the ordeal of retrieving Felicia from Josef, Medill had been there. He was someone who knew her whole life, everything about her, and nevertheless loved her completely; like her brother, he had always been a man upon whom she could rely. But if it's true that when one door closes, another opens, it happened for Cissy after Medill departed and Elmer Schlesinger came back into her life. The New York lawyer, a Chicago native, was perhaps Medill's closest friend, and the two were similar to the point of physical resemblance. Moreover, both her life and Elmer's had changed since their platonic friendship during the 1912 political campaign. He was now divorced from Halle Schaffner of the Hart, Schaffner & Marx family, and the years of expatriation and successful writing had added a patina to Cissy's appeal. It seemed natural that she and Elmer would now see each other on a regular basis. They both enjoyed the theater, prizefights, racing and interesting, intelligent company. He had been in love with her for a long time, understood her and accommodated her.

Elmer was definitely a creature of the city; when Cissy invited him to Jackson Hole, he brought along an English valet, and his lack of aptitude in dealing with the Wyoming environment nearly ended their relationship. He was just another citified dude in the West, but fortunately in his own milieu he was a charismatic charmer who could hold his own with Cissy in any social situation. A distinguished lawyer and a partner in the New York firm Chadbourne, Stanchfield & Levy, he advised a number of the nation's largest corporations and such successful businessmen as automobile manufacturer W. C. Durant. Other clients included some of the greatest living figures in the art world internationally, among them the illustrious dealer Lord Duveen of Millbank, and Italian Renaissance expert Bernard Berenson. Elmer had inherited money, married money and made money—millions—and he spent it well. He belonged to the right clubs, kept a wine cellar at the Ritz, maintained a splendid Fifth Avenue apartment and owned a sixty-five-foot yacht.

Cissy's post-European world was much larger than her relationship with Elmer—or even her writing. She had returned to be immediately propelled into the milieu of *New York World* executive editor Herbert Bayard Swope, grandly known to himself and all others as Swope. The self-styled Swope was a natural force of superhuman velocity, vivifying any life into which he swept. Throughout the twenties, he and his formidable but delightful wife, Maggie, gave all-night parties in their twenty-eight-room duplex at 135 West 58th Street, with regulars who included neighbors Heyward Broun, Edna Ferber and Noël Coward. The couple and their two children enveloped Cissy, making her a part of their family, and Swope introduced her to *New Yorker* editor Harold Ross, George Kaufman, Joseph Pulitzer, Dorothy Parker and other members of the Algonquin Round Table group, as well as the Marx Brothers and Bernard Baruch. Swope knew everyone and so did Elmer; in fact, the two were very good friends, and the Swope friendship strengthened her bond with Schlesinger. For a time Swope and Maggie kept a Victorian mansion in Great Neck, Long Island, where neighbor Ring Lardner complained, "Mr. Swope lives across the way, and he conducts an almost continuous house party. . . . It is almost impossible to work at times and still more difficult to sleep." Occasionally, Lardner simply gave up, drove to New York and checked into a hotel to write.

Groups of Swope guests periodically wandered out of the house and through the neighboring woods, sometimes returning to the wrong house and expecting to have their drinks refreshed. But they could always follow the music back to the Swope estate, where invariably someone was at the piano: George Gershwin, or perhaps Irving Berlin, or, most often, Oscar Levant, who was a Swope household fixture for some twenty years. Arriving at these parties after the theater at night were Helen Hayes, Leslie Howard, Laurette Taylor and various

Barrymores, who, if they hadn't had enough make-believe on stage, joined in the games that were always under way. Later Swope and Maggie bought a Sands Point estate, Keewaydin, to be decorated by Elsie de Wolfe, the era's most fashionable interior designer. Given an almost unlimited budget, Elsie managed to exceed it with the antiques she and Maggie ordered from England and costly bedsheets from Paris. Although the Swopes lived far beyond his thousand-dollar-a-week salary from the *World*, they never thought about money; the subject bored them, and they allowed bills to age for at least a year before looking at them. Somehow their life continued blissfully.

ANOTHER DOOR OPENED, very slowly and only partially, when Cissy's daughter reappeared. After almost a year and a half of independence, lonely and unwilling to contact her mother, Felicia began corresponding with Drew Pearson, although she still regarded him as a stuffy old bore. "I had to write to *somebody*," she said. When she sent him pieces she had written in longhand and mentioned that she was saving to buy a typewriter, he had a typewriter delivered to her. Drew's career prospects were improving; he was writing, mainly interviews, for United Publishers Corporation for $125 a week. After several months' correspondence and a visit to San Diego, Drew—with Cissy's blessing—convinced Felicia to marry him for three years, enough time for her to become independent of her mother. In March 1925, she became Mrs. Drew Pearson in a simple ceremony conducted by a San Diego justice of the peace, without family or friends present, and the newlyweds settled into a small furnished apartment near Columbia University in New York's Morningside Heights.

Felicia was not the only Gizycka woman to marry during the spring of 1925; on April 11, Cissy accepted one of Elmer's proposals and they were wed in an impromptu civil ceremony at the New York City Municipal Building. Among their wedding gifts were his-and-hers Durant Locomobile limousines, with open seating for a chauffeur and footman in front, courtesy of Mr. Durant. After a honeymoon in Italy, Elmer and Cissy divided their time between his apartment at

1010 Fifth Avenue, her Dupont Circle house and Harbor Acres, a Long Island estate they acquired together.

Harbor Acres, formerly a property of Vincent Astor, sat on fifty-seven acres of one of the most enviable parcels of land anywhere, Sands Point, Long Island. With spectacular views of the New York skyline, Sands Point—as its name indicates—is a point of land surrounded by water on three sides: Long Island Sound on the north, Hempstead Harbor to the east and Manhasset Bay on the west. Home of America's very rich of the early twentieth century, the area was established in 1695 by the Sands brothers, who bought five hundred acres from the Cornwells, who preceded them by two decades. Along the way the Vanderbilts bought in and by the turn of the twentieth century Sands Point was the domain of fifty exceptionally rich families who built sumptuous estates there. The community's old money ambiance so impressed F. Scott Fitzgerald that he rechristened it East Egg and made it the home of Daisy Buchanan, heroine of his novel *The Great Gatsby*.

Harbor Acres was the quintessential summer place, a green-shuttered white clapboard house, surrounded by a great porch and situated high on a velvety green hill sloping down to Long Island Sound. Outbuildings and other amenities included a greenhouse, a writer's cottage for Cissy and a saltwater swimming pool. Set on land that had belonged to King Charles II of England, Harbor Acres was within walking distance of the constant revelry taking place at the Swope ménage and, throughout the summer, Elmer commuted from Sands Point to Wall Street on his yacht; by the time he had been shaved, finished breakfast and read the morning papers it was time to disembark and be driven to his office.

On Felicia and Drew's return from an extended working honeymoon through Europe and Asia, they lived at 15 Dupont Circle, vacated for them by Cissy. Drew began working as foreign editor of the Washington magazine that later became *U.S. News & World Report*. Felicia wrote film reviews for the *Washington Post*, still owned by Ned McLean. They declined the liberal allowance Cissy offered but were soon able to buy a house of their own in not-yet-gentrified George-town. The appearance of a happy union was completed by the birth of a baby girl, with Cissy's red hair, whom they named Ellen for an ances-tor of Drew's. Felicia, who was never in love with Drew and felt he was unable to become her social equal, stayed married for exactly the three years of their agreement. During the summer of 1928, while he was on one of his foreign trips, she traveled to Reno and, without warning or notification, divorced him. Drew discovered he was no longer her hus-band when he returned to Washington in August and chanced to see a newspaper story another passenger was reading in an elevator. Felicia further declared her independence by refusing to accept Cissy's money for herself but allowed her mother to pay Ellen's expenses, and she em-ulated Cissy by moving to Paris to write a novel. With odd timing, she, Ellen and a nurse sailed for France a day before the child was to be turned over to Drew for a six-month custody period. In a scenario echoing that of Felicia's parents, Drew followed them on the next ship, but it was months before he regained his child. After blithely settling into a flat near Nôtre Dame on the Quai d'Orléans, Felicia took a job with a magazine and began writing her novel.

She would have quite a challenge in matching the impact of her mother's first novel, from which Washington was still reeling. Cis-sy's relationship with Alice Longworth had been shattered by years of abuse, but none of the mischief with Alice's husband and her lover Borah offended Alice as much as Cissy's portrayal of her in *Glass Houses*. The book was widely reviewed and became a bestseller in 1926 with its American publication; however, its injured party should have been not Alice but rather Senator Borah, whose character was literally murdered on a hunting trip by the Cal Carrington figure, with Cissy's alter ego cast as the darling of both. The excitement the novel's publi-cation produced is understandable, particularly in Washington, where it created bitter enemies while supplying first-class material for weeks of dinner party gossip about the conduct of its thinly disguised central characters. Cissy would maintain her relationship with Cal, who made annual visits to stay with her in Washington for the remainder of her life, but Jackson Hole ceased to be on her summer agenda after the early 1930s.

Cissy continued to write for magazines and to work on a second novel, retreating whenever possible to her 61st Street studio or the Sands Point writer's cottage. Her second book, *Fall Flight*, was an intensely autobiographical account of her childhood relationship with her mother and her romance and marriage to Josef. When it was published in 1928, reviews were excellent and the book was serialized in newspapers nationally, with talk of a film version. A limited edition— only five hundred copies to be given to friends—carried a preface written by Cissy's analyst, Dr. Alvan Barach. In it Dr. Barach emphasized that Cissy's inability to love a man completely had grown from her relationship with a mother who withheld love and made her "continually conscious of her physical unattractiveness."

Cissy's interest in her second marriage did not last long. In February 1929, when she had begun to wonder why she had married Elmer and was contemplating divorce, he collapsed and died of a heart attack on a golf course in Aiken, South Carolina. He was fifty-three. Felicia and Drew Pearson had divorced a few months earlier, but Cissy called upon her former son-in-law to escort her for the sad trip to South Carolina to bring the body back for a funeral at 15 Dupont Circle. Always the actress and clotheshorse, Cissy ordered a black wardrobe hastily produced by New York designer Charles James, which she wore for two months after Elmer's death. Her formal mourning also extended to temporarily replacing her customary apricot silk sheets and pillowcases with black bed linens. Inexplicably bereaved, she mindlessly traversed the country in *Ranger* for two months but eventually pulled herself together, and legally changed her name, which had originally been Elinor Josephine Patterson, to Mrs. Eleanor Medill Patterson. The abrupt turnaround may have come from the revelation that Mr. Schlesinger, the great lawyer, had died without making a will; therefore property, for which she had paid, would go to his children. This discovery also led her to cancel plans for an elaborate mausoleum she had commissioned Raymond Hood to design. Hood, then living at 15 Dupont Circle while awaiting her green light, was dismissed without explanation; however, presumably the architect was becoming accustomed to the eccentric ways of the Medill family.

Both Cissy's husbands were now dead. Shortly after her second marriage, she had been napping in her Dupont Circle bedroom when she saw Josef Gizycki standing at the foot of her bed. "This was no drab, gray dream, it was bright Technicolor," she later reported, "and I was awake. He was wearing his cavalry uniform with dozens of bright campaign ribbons on his chest. As suddenly as he appeared, he vanished." She received a cable the following day: Josef had died in Vienna after a short illness at the time she had seen him at the foot of her bed.

Another demise came suddenly and unexpectedly in October 1929, when the prosperity and the gaiety of the 1920s skidded to a horrifying halt, but Cissy was one of the lucky few, who, with her capital virtually intact, would keep living as she always had.

THE COLONEL OF
CHICAGOLAND

WHILE Cissy searched for direction in her life and Joe pursued his calling with the *Daily News,* Bert was finalizing his transformation into the awesome Colonel Robert R. McCormick, who would personify the *Chicago Tribune* until midcentury. He was on the threshold of emerging as one of the nation's most visible figures, one who would replace Al Capone as the symbol of Chicago while exemplifying the extremes of archconservatism to observers everywhere. "His celebrity would be equal to a modern Rush Limbaugh, Larry King, and Dan Rather combined," wrote former *Tribune* managing editor F. Richard Ciccone in 1999. "No political figure in America today, save the president, is as renowned in these times as McCormick was in his."

Powerful, controversial and eminently effective, the notoriously backward-looking, almost cartoonish Colonel employed the same style of personal journalism his grandfather had practiced, and in many ways walked in the patriarch's footprints. To McCormick's distress, the nation he had known as a boy was changing, but, as much as he would attempt to maintain the America of his grandfather's time, he was unable to halt his country's progress or to move in the direction it was heading. Often said to have "the finest mind of the thirteenth century," in reality McCormick was stuck in the early twentieth century. It had been a serene era shaped in the courts of royal cousins on precarious European thrones and reflected in elitist clubs and drawing rooms across America. Many of the Colonel's generation spent the rest of their lives reminiscing about the golden years leading up to World War I, although most were able to accommodate at least some forward movement—but not McCormick. His *Tribune* was widely regarded by readers as antediluvian, but in Dick Ciccone's words "they took it. They took it because for most of the twentieth century the *Tribune* was the most complete newspaper in America. The *Tribune* had the best comic section, the widest sports coverage, the best color reproduction, the best magazine, the most interesting features, and, because it made the most money, could afford the widest distribution, the largest number of pages, the most reporters, and the most advertisements, which pleased its readers and its accountants." And at its helm was the Colonel.

Even in appearance, McCormick's style was close to Edwardian. Until the end of his days, he would wear the bristly military mustache he had grown to disguise his boyishness early in the century and he would maintain strict British tailoring, usually acquired from his father's bespoke London sources: suits tailored at Henry Poole, hats from James Lock and footwear made by John Lobb. His flawless shirts were customized for him in Paris, where he ordered Hermès monogrammed suitcases and trunks. The Colonel's eccentricity extended to his manner of speech, which was muffled, deep in voice and mid-Atlantic in diction; the fact that he was not easy to understand often worked to his advantage. The effect of his reminiscences could be impressionistic; the listener would hear the overall drama of his story, but not catch—and therefore be unable to verify—the details.

With an Anglo personal style but a distain for the British Empire and all it represented, he puzzled the public. He insisted he was not anti-British but pro-American; however, his chauvinism went deeper, into extreme regionalism; he expressed devotion to a portion of the nation populated by those who in no way looked, spoke or behaved as he did—the American Midwest. If there is any clue to why McCormick considered this part of the world superior to any other, it might be that it still consisted of the rural stretches and small towns of his grandfather's youth. Or perhaps it was that he considered it his personal realm; certainly it coincided with the *Tribune* circulation area, and the Colonel regularly addressed its residents—many of them farmers and small-town merchants—through his newspaper editorials and radio broadcasts. It was a wholesome, intact world, later celebrated by Norman Rockwell, where the local doctor made regular house calls, and the postman—having completed his second mail delivery of the day—sat at a drugstore soda fountain on Main Street, savoring a glass of milk and a slice of apple pie. This McCormick dominion stretched across a large area, spreading into significant portions of Illinois, Indiana, Wisconsin, Michigan and Iowa. He even had a name for his domain: he christened it Chicagoland.

Within a decade of Joe's departure for New York in 1925—and the paper's resulting shift to a consistently conservative point of view— the *Tribune*-style book began adopting elements of twenty-first-century computerese. In a surprising turn, the Colonel required staff to "simplify" language, substituting, for example, *tho* for *though* and *thru* in place of *through*. The word *freight* became *frate*, and the simplification of a word much used by McCormick himself was *burocracy*, for the hated modern system that seemed to engulf everything and everyone around him. The reform began in 1934, but the list grew over the years. And though there was loud denunciation from the teachers of Chicagoland, the *Tribune* continued simplified spelling until after the Colonel's death. McCormick continued to think outside the boundaries within which most mortal brains operate; for example, he wondered aloud why commuter trains turn around in an urban station when they could easily have an engine at each end of the string of cars. Railroad officials laughed, but then scratched their heads and did just that. Another innovation that industry leaders initially scoffed at but then adopted was the replacement of glass milk bottles with paper cartons. Repeatedly his sanity was questioned by more mundane minds—until the "crazy" suggestion was mulled over, seriously considered and ultimately implemented.

One of the oddities he shared with many other very rich men was that he seldom carried cash. Fortunately, there was usually a minion nearby who appeared in time to intercept security as the Colonel would start to leave a store with unpaid merchandise in hand. Some of the strangeness people felt when they were in his company may have been because he remained quite shy. One *Tribune* editor, Fanny Butcher, thought it was because he was so tall that he looked right over people. Other theories ranged from his poor eyesight to his increasing deafness. If his eyeglasses were hanging from one ear, as they often were, or if he wasn't looking at someone's face, he might not see or hear the speaker. On the other hand, no one ever gained from too great familiarity with the Colonel. He informed one underling who made a little joke at his expense, "that's the way you earn severance pay."

Eccentricity may have been a family characteristic, but within McCormick there was an extreme wee-hours craziness that seemed to emerge most fully during trips to Washington. Since he refused to stay in what he considered the provincial hotels of the nation's capital, he was a frequent guest at Cissy's Dupont Circle house. Always an attentive hostess to her cousin, she soon learned to Bert-proof the room in which he stayed. Invariably, each night during the predawn hour-of-the-wolf, the demons Kate had nurtured throughout her son's hellish childhood would burst forth from the dark room in shouts, screams of terror and crashes of battle. The following day, nothing was said by hostess, houseguest or servants, whose jobs it was to dismantle and remake the battleground. Cissy attributed his behavior to "Bertie's affliction," something beyond his control, which should therefore be overlooked.

THE COLONEL HAD almost single-handedly designed the structure of the modern Tribune Company. Among his contributions was the corporation's Canadian empire, which allowed it to produce an independent paper supply, freeing its newspapers from the unpredictability of the newsprint marketplace. Linked to this was the fleet of ships the company operated for transporting paper to Chicago and New York.

And he nurtured an international presence. Breaking news from cities and trouble spots around the world was cabled back by more than two dozen foreign correspondents, whose movements were monitored through colored pins stuck in a world map on the wall in his office; the men themselves gathered biannually to meet with their leader at the family's favorite Paris hotel, the Ritz, in Place Vendôme. *Tribune* readers crossing the Atlantic to Europe could read the news in the paper's Oceanic Edition, and when they arrived onshore there was the European Edition, until 1934, when McCormick sold the Paris *Tribune* to the *New York Herald* for fifty thousand dollars.

But never was the Colonel's prescience more remarkable than when he sensed the colossal potential of radio, and then television. He was the first newspaper tycoon to regard electronic media as an extension of print journalism, rather than its competitor. In 1921, within a year of the infant radio industry's first broadcast, he began picking up licenses; after acquiring the city's most powerful frequency, he purchased the call letters WGN and began to develop one of America's great radio superstations. It was James Keeley who had coined the phrase World's Greatest Newspaper, but McCormick was not embarrassed by its extravagance—especially since he could now extend and reinforce the *Tribune* brand through an exciting new medium. WGN's slogan, "broadcasting from atop the Drake Hotel," was accurate, but its first studios consisted of transmitting equipment placed on the bureaus and end tables of a few leased hotel guest rooms. Although music from a hotel dance band evoked fantasy and glamour to the listener, it was merely an illusion created by a skillful announcer stationed several floors away. During WGN's first year it broadcast the Memorial Day automobile races from Indianapolis and in 1925 listeners could hear the Kentucky Derby, the World Series and the Scopes "monkey trial." The dance bands of Wayne King, Ted Weems and others became household names with WGN broadcasts of their performances from Chicago's Trianon and Aragon ballrooms. Live reporting of an unfolding tragedy occurred in 1927 when a Lake Michigan excursion boat took on water and sank off

Oak Street Beach, mere steps from the Drake. WGN was perfectly situated to broadcast a minute-by-minute account of the accident in which families with their young children were drowned within view of announcer Quin Ryan, who leaned from a window of the make-shift studio to report the disaster.

In the same year, WGN's fight to protect its frequency from the infringement of rival broadcasters led to the Radio Act of 1927 and the Federal Radio Commission, which in turn produced the Federal Communications Commission. In the mid to late 1920s, McCormick spent almost a million and a half dollars broadcasting free programming to a growing audience, during which listeners developed the radio habit. He followed in the 1930s with paid sponsorship of pro football broadcasts and soon advertisers were paying for dramatizations of Joe's comic strips, including Ovaltine's *Little Orphan Annie,* which led to the birth of the soap opera. By 1934 radio was exploding throughout America and the newly organized networks were threatening to force out even the most powerful local stations; McCormick responded by constructing his own network in cooperation with stations in Cincinnati, Newark and Detroit, and within six years the Mutual Broadcasting System consisted of 109 stations in twenty-nine states. He was also shrewd in anticipating the possibility of television; in 1926 WGN engineers developed an early form of TV on a three-inch screen, preparing two decades in advance for the birth of WGN-TV, one of the nation's great television superstations.

Not the least of McCormick's accomplishments was to build on the law firm he had founded in 1909. Within six years, he and his law partner, Stuart G. Shepard, hired the brilliant young litigator Weymouth Kirkland and soon after engaged an associate, Howard Ellis. In 1938 Hammond E. Chaffetz would be lured from the U.S. Department of Justice, completing the trio that was to lead Kirkland & Ellis during much of the twentieth century. Meanwhile, the legal skills of Weymouth Kirkland had become indispensable for McCormick, especially in his fight to protect First Amendment rights for newspapers throughout the country. After *Tribune* encounters with Henry Ford and Big

Bill Thompson, this was an issue the two men had been studying for several years. When in 1925 a case surfaced involving the *Saturday Press*, an obscure—and somewhat unsavory—Minneapolis publication, they adopted it as their cause. The *Press* had published a piece leading the Minnesota legislature to pass a statute allowing any newspaper to be shut down by a judge under certain conditions. By involving the American Newspaper Publishers Association, McCormick and Kirkland were ready when the case came before the U.S. Supreme Court in 1931. The ruling was overthrown in a decision written by Chief Justice Charles Evans Hughes, a judgment that would serve McCormick well in the future, although there were times when he felt rival papers were behaving uncomfortably freely with his own name and reputation. Nevertheless, the Colonel would label the victory Freedom of the Press.

McCormick also led the Tribune Company in providing exceptional benefits for its employees, whose compensation ranked among the industry's highest. *Tribune* workers enjoyed medical aid, free dental cleanings, life insurance, silver flatware as wedding gifts, home financing and, in the volatile industry of journalism, job security. Full pay for an ill employee could last six months with half pay for another six, and in a business in which alcohol has always played a prominent role, the *Tribune* maintained a "drunk bank" for workers who found themselves without money the day after a bender. Throughout the Depression, employees received annual bonuses, except in 1931, when McCormick said he thought skipping them would remind his staff not to take these perks as a matter of course. And every employee who served in wartime had a job waiting on his return. The Colonel continued to pay pensions and annual bonuses in addition to Social Security after its founding, whereas New Deal enthusiast Joe discontinued the *Daily News* pension plan when the government measure came into effect. But there was a pragmatic facet to McCormick's paternalism. When a chapter of the Newspaper Guild was fleetingly installed at the *Tribune* in the late 1930s, with a $60 weekly salary requirement for experienced employees, McCormick saw that *every* employee's salary was at least $60 a week. The Colonel was a tough opponent, usually several steps ahead of the guild, which made the *Tribune* an impregnable fortress against organizers.

If the Colonel was a larger-than-life figure who, along with Mrs. O'Leary, Shoeless Joe Jackson and Al Capone, personified Chicago to the world, he was an awesome, godlike presence to his employees and perceived as thoroughly exotic by journalists who lived normal workaday lives. Some rarely saw him at all; when they did, he might be glimpsed marching through the city room in polo gear on his way to the roof to practice shots while riding his mechanical horse. And there were rumors about the great hall from which the Colonel ruled his dominion, a thirty-five-foot-long, walnut-paneled and Gothic-windowed office on the twenty-fourth floor of the Tribune Tower. This fortress to which few had access was the subject of many myths, among them rumors of hidden doors without exit knobs, vicious guard dogs lurking in the corners, a secret escape route known only to the Colonel and machine guns hidden behind a trap door in the ceiling. There was also said to be a telephone and an axe in McCormick's executive washroom for emergency exit in the event of a panic attack. As with so much about the Colonel, most of these myths, although perhaps not entirely accurate, were based on fact. On the same floor, further protecting the fortress, were three female secretaries, habitually at war with each other, and a small force of armed guards.

When McCormick was driven to the office each morning, it was by a bodyguard, usually former policeman Bill Bockelman, in a heavy bulletproof automobile, with a chassis so weighty it had to be replaced every other year. During the trip in, he tore pieces from the morning's *Tribune,* to which he added notes scratched in the margins. These he crammed in his pockets, while filling his head with random story ideas, among them that there are too many garden hoses being stolen in Chicago, or that stray dogs should be removed from city streets, or even, what is the relationship between unemployment and venereal disease? These would be conveyed to the appropriate employees to be further explored for publication. The whopper story idea of them all was assigned to the automobile editor after McCormick's car was stopped near his country house by a deranged panhandler named Indian Joe. The Colonel, who as usual carried no money, offered the crank a check instead. But Indian Joe's cheeky refusal to accept anything but cash prompted McCormick to launch a full-blown newspaper investigation focused on western suburban traffic bandits.

His editorial meetings were held at lunch in the Overset Club, a private enclave for executives in the Tribune Tower, where regulars sitting with McCormick were cartoonist John T. McCutcheon and editorial writers Tiffany Blake and Clifford Raymond. The Colonel's monologues at these lunches were carefully noted and sketches or drafts returned to him during the afternoon for approval before final development into cartoons and editorials. No one could eat in advance of the Colonel's arrival or leave before he did; fortunately he ate quickly and left the room promptly—unless of course a dignitary of the stature of Winston Churchill or Herbert Hoover was his guest. One Friday noon, McCormick entertained the Roman Catholic leader George Cardinal Mundelein, along with a distinguished local rabbi. The men both professed a loss of appetite when served ham but after a hearty chortle over his practical joke, McCormick gave the signal for salmon to be brought, restoring appetites.

WHEN MCCORMICK, THEN newly promoted to Colonel, and Amy had returned from Europe following the war, they were delighted to arrive at her house in Lake Forest, with its spacious stables and proximity to the equestrian activities of Onwentsia. But it took little time to realize they had been frozen out of proper North Shore society by the lingering effects of scandal. Whispering began every time they entered the Onwentsia clubhouse for a drink or the grandstands to watch a horse show. To minimize notoriety, Bert and Amy opted to spend the polo-playing, foxhunting and trail-riding months at Red Oaks Farm, Grandfather Medill's country house near Wheaton, which now belonged to the Colonel.

The couple directed the rebuilding of the estate's infrastructure, including electrical wiring, plumbing, insulation and heating facilities, and renamed the property Cantigny to commemorate the Colonel's World War I liberation of the French town. They hired farmers to work the estate and redesigned the property's basic landscaping, clearing views through dense woods and planting stands of leafy trees along roads within the grounds. A polo field was installed and the cellar stocked with enough of the best Scotch whiskey to last through the long Prohibition years. Amy hired staff, a cook and assistant, upstairs and downstairs maids and a butler, valet and chauffeur. For a time they joined the nearby Chicago Golf Club; the Colonel's father had once been president of the historic and notably selective club, and furthermore its membership was more broad-minded than that of Onwentsia.

Haven or not, Cantigny was still a part-time residence and the McCormicks spent the winter months at a house they acquired in town at 1519 Astor Street. The stately four-story limestone and brick residence was ivy-covered, with a formal garden encased in high walls, providing an elegant setting for occasional charitable benefits hosted by Amy, and such events as one she held for Queen Marie of Romania. As exquisite as the Astor Street house was, the McCormicks were without facilities for enjoying their beloved equestrian sports during the winter months, and a search was on.

IN THE 1920S, polo aficionados gravitated to a lovely town called Aiken set in the pine woods of South Carolina. Tall oak trees lined fifteen miles of broad nineteenth-century parkways, and in early spring the haunting fragrance of dogwood and wisteria drifted along riding trails and across the grounds of Aiken estates. Aiken's history began when Thomas Hitchcock, Long Island's ten-goal player, visited the spot in the 1880s and noted the sandy quality of the soil, ideal for cushioning horses' hooves. With William C. Whitney, he bought eight thousand acres of woods and in 1882 established the town's first polo club, a racetrack and miles of horse trails. Hitchcock and his wife, Lulie, treated the community as their own living room, closely monitoring real estate sales so that only those known to them and their social circle were allowed to buy. Soon the town was a center for Harrimans, Astors, Vanderbilts, Bostwicks and Leiters, with such guests as Winston Churchill, Prince Bernadotte, Edward, Prince of Wales and Will Rogers. Later Franklin Roosevelt would arrive quietly to visit his mistress Lucy Mercer there, and during high season a cluster of private railroad cars sat along the siding. Lulie Hitchcock established a preparatory school in town so that her sons and their friends could stay through the winter and perfect polo shots along with their studies. After learning the game on bicycles, some of the boys grew into formidable players, including Tommy Hitchcock, whose skill at polo and record of past performance earned him the same ten-goal handicap held by his father.

In 1924 the Robert R. McCormicks became Aiken winter regulars and three years later bought twenty-six acres of land from Marshall Field III on the town's prestigious Whiskey Trail. Their house, Whitehall, a high-ceilinged Georgian revival mansion designed by architect Willis Irvin of Augusta, Georgia, was completed in 1928 and furnished with antiques selected by Amy. The Colonel supervised rehabilitation of the Field stable and installation of practice jumps through the woods. But there was trouble ahead. Aiken was Long Island territory and as midwesterners the McCormicks had begun on unsteady ground, yet they managed to increase their vulnerability by building a house inappropriately grand for the horsey community. However, when Amy made the mistake of engaging in a legal battle with Hitchcock over an allegedly faulty horse she bought from him, sentiments in the community divided, and the McCormicks felt a frost similar to that in Lake Forest. It was time to seek another winter refuge.

Bert learned that a Yale classmate, Joseph Thomas, was forming Grasslands, a hunt club nestled in the countryside outside Nashville, and upon investigation he found that the new club promised to provide well for its guests. There would be spacious suites in the clubhouse, well-kept stables for the horses they would bring, and a fine pack of hounds imported from England. Both the Colonel and his cousin Chauncey McCormick went in as founding members and sent horses down for a season that began at Thanksgiving. But again, trouble was looming. Bert and Joe Thomas's wife, Clara, soon became lovers. Clara's father, James Fargo, had made money from the American Express traveler's check innovation and raised his daughter with wealth. She was beautiful, sexy, young—nineteen years younger than Amy—and a very sophisticated woman who had traveled in the highest social circles. Clara was also a talented artist whose work was collected by Vincent Astor and Percy Rockefeller. Although hunt season was in full swing, Amy soon departed; Grasslands had become as chilly for her as Lake Forest and Aiken. But the Colonel remained, making the three-hour flight back and forth from Chicago on his plane every weekend. As was his custom, he paid the bills at Grasslands while settling into a cozy relationship with Clara. The situation seemed destined to continue indefinitely, until the lovers were in an automobile accident, which scarred the lovely forehead of Clara Fargo Thomas. Although she was amenable to uprooting the lives of all concerned, McCormick would not agree to more scandal, and the affair drifted on until the Colonel ended it abruptly in the summer of 1934. It seems certain that Amy never recovered from the breach Grasslands created in their marriage, and while she received the gift of a Goya from her erring husband before the first year was out, their relationship was never the same again.

Following the Grasslands affair the Colonel and Amy led increasingly separate lives. Although they each had a private bedroom suite, they dined together every night at either end of an eight-foot-long table. Amy was a superb hostess and visitors were frequent; her parties, large or small, were impeccable and despite the fact that the Colonel invariably left the table mid-meal without explanation or excuses, not to be seen again that night, she made an effort to provide companions who would entertain him. Her friend and protégée Maryland Hooper was among the attractive women she invited repeatedly, not merely for dinner but as an overnight and weekend guest. Dinner was served at precisely seven o'clock—but *at Eastern Standard Time,* a detail the Colonel often neglected to share when issuing an invitation;

the customary tagline was "Don't mind being late. We won't wait for you," and they never did. Dinner was not delayed for Charles Lindbergh, Gloria Swanson or Lillian Gish, nor did the Colonel stay until the end of the meal for these distinguished guests. The lures upstairs were a bottle of fine Scotch whiskey and the first edition of the following morning's *Tribune*. The latter was delivered personally each night by a commuter train conductor who handed it to a local boy paid fifty cents a trip to bring the paper out from the station to Cantigny.

Amy's personal style was tailored and elegantly simple. She was attended by her French maid, Marie, an accomplished seamstress who custom-made satin sheets, lace negligees and occasional copies of dresses for her. Every day, no matter how she was dressed or what her activities, Amy wore the wedding pearls the Colonel had given her in defiance of his mother's fifty-thousand-dollar bribe. Apart from an interest in horses and foxhunting, her favorite daily occupations were working in the Cantigny gardens, walking the grounds with her Alsatians and overseeing a private art collection of works by Cézanne, Matisse, Renoir, Picasso, Modigliani and Degas. She was also an accomplished artist and painted regularly in her studio, Bois de Madame, a cottage nearly a mile from the house.

Horses were the very foundation of life at Cantigny. The autumn hunt season began toward the end of September, when the days were beginning to cool, and continued until the ground grew hard in December. Throughout the season, there were always several hunt members who were weekend houseguests at Cantigny, usually arriving late Friday afternoon. The Colonel would return from a day at the *Tribune* in time to change into a pink—actually red—hunting coat before the prehunt dinner. After rising at seven the following morning, the house party began a traditional ritual. Dressed in classic hunt attire, guests served themselves from an early breakfast set out on Amy's eighteenth-century English sideboard in the dining room and walked to the stables, where grooms had saddled the mount assigned to each. Riding as a group, they joined other hunt members who were gathering, silently signaling a greeting with a raise of whip or tap on the cap. Around nine o'clock, after the arrival of the hounds from Amy's kennel and a blast of the huntsman's horn, they were off. Through woods and over jumps the hounds followed a scent laid by a drag—a gunnysack with scrapings from a fox farm—for almost two hours, pausing now and again where the drag had been lifted to simulate the fox jumping into a tree or creek, or running along a fence. When the huntsman blew his horn to signal the hunt's end, the hounds departed for their kennels and riders led the horses back to the stables. It was time for the culmination of the morning chase, and its reward: a return to Cantigny for drinks and fellowship, followed by a hearty hunt breakfast.

In 1934, the Colonel revived a plan he had tabled in the 1920s for the renovation and enlargement of his grandfather's 1896 house. With funds from his private fortune newly enriched following his mother's death, he engaged Georgia architect Willis Irvin, who had designed Whitehall for him in Aiken. Irvin's overhaul of Joseph Medill's rural dream was extensive; by greatly expanding the floor plan and designing a new exterior, he converted the house of a gentleman farmer into an imposing country estate. Wings shot out in two directions, one to the east, chiefly to house the Colonel's vast library, and another to the west with bedrooms and servants quarters, all sheathed in red brick, painted white and then stripped. The effect was a subtle rosy shade. Because the house was one of the first to be air-conditioned—achieved by circulating cold water from Cantigny's well through an arrangement of pipes—its interior was always cool, summer and winter. What had been the Colonel's library became a sitting room, and his new library, forty-four feet long and twenty-two feet high, was paneled in Brazilian butternut with two large fireplaces. One hearth borrowed an innovation from Monticello; just as Thomas Jefferson had installed an elevator to bring wine from his basement, the Colonel devised a similar lift to raise logs from below. A further inventive device was a secret button in the library's paneled wall; when pushed the button opened a pair of hidden doors to a sleek Art Deco bar. According to Cantigny legend, houseguest Winston Churchill and the Colonel were once accidentally shut in the bar, without a means of opening the doors from within, and neither man called for help. Beneath the library, Irvin designed a movie theater, also Deco in style, with a gold-leaf-over-silver-leaf ceiling. Friday night was movie night, when neighbors in black tie joined formally dressed houseguests for a showing that began at precisely eight o'clock and was followed by drinks and conviviality.

Cantigny had long been a self-sufficient community with its own population of farmers and their families living on the estate; therefore its development into a complete working farm was a natural progression. The estate produced fresh vegetables, fruit and berries, and eggs, milk and honey, as well as fresh meat from chickens, geese, ducks, and beef animals. There were even occasional frog's legs from the estate pond. Amy's choice project was a herd of perfectly nurtured, petlike Guernsey cows, with the name of each on a bronze plaque above its stall. The quality of her cows' product was so high and their yield so great that the milk they gave three times a day was purchased, unpasteurized, by area hospitals. There was also an abundance of flowers from the Cantigny gardens, roses for the house, and peonies and lilacs, which Amy's driver took to nearby hospitals. In addition, Cantigny was registered as a wildlife preserve filled with protected deer, mink, possum, wild turkeys, pheasant, beaver and weasel, as well as rabbits, squirrels, groundhogs and raccoons. Inspired by Morton Salt founder Joy Morton, who also lived in the west suburban area, the Colonel collected rare trees he had planted at Cantigny and identified with brass plaques. Morton was a botanical enthusiast through his father, Arbor Day originator Sterling Morton, and Joy took his father's interest a step further by turning his estate into the internationally regarded Morton Arboretum.

Cantigny's greatest social ritual was conducted on Christmas Eve, when festivities began with an afternoon party for the families of all those farming the estate. The McCormick chauffeur, costumed as Santa, distributed toys to the children, and to each of the older girls he gave a dress, personally chosen for her by Amy. The children's parents received cash and all were treated to cakes, Christmas cookies and homemade ice cream. After sundown, twenty or so couples from

the McCormicks' social set began arriving to be greeted by a bonfire in front of the house and their host standing inside the door in a
hunting coat with a wassail-filled loving cup. Following drinks and a
buffet dinner, everyone filed into the library to observe two costumed
Cantigny staff members raise a Christmas-wrapped Yule log on the
Monticello-inspired device. In a perfect conclusion to the holiday evening, guests gathered in front of the burning log in the Colonel's richly
paneled library, where they sang a series of Christmas carols from a
booklet in which the McCormicks had collected their favorites. It was
one of the rare nights when the Colonel did not leave his guests mid-
evening for early retirement.

AMY PERFORMED WITH her customary grace and dignity throughout the early and mid-1930s, but there had been a fundamental
change. She continued to be a superb hostess, a loyal friend and
always a delightful companion. She managed the Colonel's household beautifully and was thoughtful in caring for his comfort and
needs. Although she appeared to be painting serenely in her studio
and energetically serving as master of the foxhounds for the DuPage
Hunt Club or calmly presiding over the impeccable McCormick parties, Amy was in fact deeply depressed. Following the Clara Thomas
affair, she had fallen into a prolonged despondency that eventually
segued into physical illness.

In October 1937, she entered Chicago's Passavant Hospital with
"chronic appendicitis," a euphemism for *cancer* when the word was not
used in polite society and certainly not in a discussion with a patient.
Accompanied home by a nurse who stayed during the nearly two years
following her surgery, Amy continued life as fully as her weakened
body would allow, including riding when she could. Her last hunt—
also Cantigny's last—was in the fall of 1938. On August 12, 1939, Amy
again entered Passavant Hospital for surgery, this time to address what
was described as "bowel stoppage." In the operating room the following day, surgeons discovered a body peppered with cancer. She did not
regain consciousness and died within hours.

The Colonel arranged a full-scale military funeral, with Amy's casket followed to graveside by a riderless horse, eyes hooded, and her boots reversed in its stirrups. Friends gathered with *Tribune* executives and employees while a live string quartet played her favorite hymns, and from above, a low-flying plane showered rose petals. A Fort Sheridan honor guard fired three volleys of shots at her grave and, finally, with the sounding of taps, the United States flag that had covered her coffin was folded and handed to the Colonel. Among Amy's personal mourners were Maryland and Henry Hooper, who had returned from fishing in Michigan to be there. Whether it was a courtly gesture or through embarrassment in having a wife eight years his senior, McCormick gallantly tweaked the birth date on the gravestone so that it bore the year of his birth, 1880, rather than hers, 1872. After mourners departed, the Colonel walked back to Amy's grave, sat down beside it and remained there until morning.

AMY HAD WILLED her Lake Forest house and personal property to her sister rather than to the Colonel, who "did not need it," but she did leave her superb art collection to him. The Colonel gave most of the paintings to the Art Institute of Chicago and divided the wedding gift pearls into three strands to present to her most intimate friends, one of whom was Maryland Hooper. As estranged as they were, Amy had been the core of McCormick's personal life and it was her spirit that vivified Cantigny. His Wheaton estate became a lonely and empty place for a man with few intimates and it would be especially gloomy with the nearing of the hunt season. Although he continued to dislike easterners, especially Manhattanites, the new widower spent much of the rest of 1939 in a large suite at the Ritz hotel in New York, a city in which he had no friends. *Tribune* reporters were invited to join him in his suite, particularly as the holiday season with its nostalgic memories of Christmas at Cantigny approached.

It was not long before the rich widower was being circled by aggressive unattached women, beginning with singing star Grace Moore. The operatic soprano, imported to present a WGN radio recital on Christmas night 1939, took one look at the Colonel and launched a campaign to become the next Mrs. McCormick, although it was a scant four months after Amy's death. Unhappily for Grace, she was missing the essential lure for snaring this particular quarry. As succinctly expressed by Weymouth Kirkland, "The Colonel likes women, but only if they are married to other men." Glamorous gossip columnist Hedda Hopper, to whom Cissy introduced him, and the beauteous redhead Arlene Dahl were among the unattached Hollywood women whose names would become linked with the Colonel's. For many years he kept a divorced woman, Mrs. Grace Parker Pickering, at New York's Biltmore Hotel and the Drake in Chicago, and there was a North Shore lady for whom he had to establish a trust in order to end an affair. But in none of these situations was there an existing husband to make the conquest interesting.

A few months after Amy's death, an interesting situation did arise. A married soprano, blond, vivacious, but almost talentless, appeared— or rather pushed herself—on the scene. Marion Claire had none of the talent, fame or star quality of Grace Moore but she did have the required accessory. She was married to Henry Weber, former conductor of the Chicago Civic Opera, who had become conductor of the WGN Orchestra. Marion's approach was to contact McCormick with a plea for him to take control of WGN's program content as only he could do. Flattered, and with the eager assistance of Marion, McCormick began shaping a series of musical programs known as "The Chicago Theater of the Air," which would be broadcast on Saturday nights over the Mutual network without commercials. The clincher was that during intermission each program would present "an outstanding speaker," the foundation of Colonel McCormick's fifteen-year reign as the Saturday-night speaker on whatever subject he chose, with the following day's Sunday *Tribune* carrying the full text of his talk. The program was an instant success; a light opera by Sigmund Romberg or one of the Strausses accompanied by a pompous address from the Colonel himself was just pretentious enough for members of Mutual's audience to feel they were receiving a week's quota of culture. Three hundred stations throughout America carried what would become the longest-running one-hour music program ever broadcast on radio.

The scene was now set. Marion and her husband lived in Lake Bluff, a few miles north of the house in which young Bert had visited Amy and Edward Adams. The combination of the Colonel's weekend visits, Marion's notable lack of talent and her blatantly imperious conduct toward *Tribune* and WGN employees convinced seasoned observers that another expensive uncoupling/recoupling was in the offing. In the heat of all this, Orson Welles released his film *Citizen Kane*. Although totally unrelated to the drama being carried out in the Midwest, the story of a newspaper baron and Susan Alexander, the talentless blond singer who became his paramour and then second wife, did nothing to dispel suspicions regarding hanky-panky being carried on at the house in Lake Bluff. Perhaps Marion began her aggressions toward the widower too quickly or possibly the Colonel had not spent enough time as a single man. In any case, he eluded the net of Marion Claire and was available prey for the next wife who would present herself for a possible trade-up—one who would have far better luck in landing the Colonel.

· 17 ·

THE EDITOR WORE EMERALDS:
MRS. ELEANOR MEDILL PATTERSON'S
WASHINGTON HERALD

THE 1920s had seen a winding down of the she-devil Medill sisters. Yet even in cranky old age they had lost none of their negative energy. When foreign correspondent George Seldes stopped in Paris early in the decade, he paid a courtesy visit to the Colonel's mother at the Ritz. After he told her he had been reporting for the *Tribune* from Berlin, she calmly replied, "Well, God damn the Germans." This led to similar wishes for the Japanese, Roman Catholics and Jews. As an afterthought she threw in the French, because "I fell out of bed in this damned country." Seldes left thinking that Kate's sentiments summed up the foreign policy of the *Tribune*. She lived on in similar temper until 1932, when she departed in appropriate fashion. On her deathbed in Versailles, a well-meaning but corpulent friend knelt beside her in prayer and, as the end neared, Kate's eyes flickered open for a moment. Catching sight of the woman's derrière, her hoarse voice shattered the morbid silence. "*My God*," she rasped, "what a bottom!" With that she expired, getting ahead of her sister for the last time. A senile Nellie caught up with her a year later.

AS THE LIVES of the Medill sisters drew to a close, Cissy's own began to move at an exhilarating new pace when a pair of influential journalists joined Walter Howey in believing she had the stuff of a newspaperwoman. One was longtime Hearst executive Arthur Brisbane, among the most talented American newsmen of the Park Row era. Brisbane had been the spectacularly successful editor of Joseph Pulitzer's *Sunday World* when Hearst recruited him in 1897. Like Joe Patterson he had a keen sense of popular taste and a signature writing style that began with a lead that captured the reader in the first line of his copy. When he joined Hearst, Brisbane requested a contract that would pay only a minimal salary but with bonuses for every thousand readers he added to the paper's circulation. His optimism was not unfounded; he was soon earning in excess of fifty thousand dollars a year, more than any other newspaper employee in the nation and second only to Mr. Hearst in the organization. Although most found Brisbane formidable, he was nothing but courtly and accommodating to Cissy, who had become increasingly itchy and was yearning to have her own newspaper. He discouraged her desire to buy a paper but was nonetheless a strong champion. With an intuition for raw talent, Brisbane sensed that beneath Cissy's unfocused energy was a rare gift, if only it could be harnessed. It would be an important judgment at the appropriate time.

Cissy's Hearst connections went beyond Brisbane. She was a favorite of both William Randolph Hearst and Marion Davies, the pretty blond chorus girl Mr. Hearst had built into a major film star and would have married in a heartbeat if his wife, Millicent, had consented to divorce. With Marion he presided over San Simeon, a California ranch nearly half the size of Rhode Island with breathtaking views of both the mountains and the Pacific Ocean. In addition to a majestic castle, San Simeon grounds held the largest private zoo in America, an airport, garages housing thirty-five automobiles, a dairy farm of ten thousand cattle, a multitude of horses and a cinema playing first-run films. Mr. Hearst, who entertained heads of state and other powerful figures worldwide, was routinely surrounded by film stars and other celebrated persons whom he considered quite ordinary. Cissy was another matter. She represented a dynasty that came close to his level in both wealth and journalistic power. He escorted her on private tours of the San Simeon grounds and early-morning horseback rides along its trails, and he placed her next to him in the castle's great dining hall. Furthermore, Marion adored her and appreciated her spunk and quick wit. They were co-conspirators who plotted jointly in everything from stashing liquor at San Simeon to pooling a couple of million dollars to save W.R.'s neck when he most needed it.

Cissy regularly visited the couple at the Hearst ranch, a pleasant cross-country jaunt in her private railway car. The Chief—as Mr. Hearst was known in the business—was familiar with her journalistic ambitions; he had been studying his frequent houseguest carefully and listening to recurrent hints that she would make a wonderful publisher. In June 1930 she decided to push the issue and asked Arthur Brisbane to plead her case with Mr. Hearst, which he did at once by cabling the Chief, who was traveling abroad. W.R. agreed to take a chance on channeling what both men sensed to be an uncommon instinct for journalism by making Cissy editor and publisher of his *Washington Herald*. The salary would be small compared to other Hearst executives—ten thousand dollars a year—plus a portion of any new advertising she brought in. With this seemingly erratic move, Brisbane and Hearst ignited a passion that had been lying dormant within Joseph Medill's granddaughter throughout her life, transforming Cissy's future as well as that of the *Washington Herald*.

Washington was one of the country's strongest home delivery cities, but with five daily papers it was oversupplied, and the circulation of the *Herald*, at less than sixty-three thousand, was not only paltry but also demographically low-end. Cissy's most formidable competition would be the city's prestige paper, the *Star*, which boasted the area's highest readership—almost double that of the *Herald*—as well as the envied department store advertising. Of the five, the *Star* was the only financially sound property; the remaining three were the *Post*, which still belonged to Ned McLean; the *News*, owned by the Scripps-Howard chain; and Hearst's evening paper, the *Times*. The Hearst and Scripps-Howard papers, produced at a loss, were kept operating by their owners in order to have the chains' opinions read by the men who ran the nation.

Cissy was determined to prove she could be as effective a journalist as her brother and cousin Bert. Earning their respect and carrying on in her grandfather's tradition gave new purpose to her life, along with presenting challenges. Achieving a level of journalistic excellence required a superb staff, and she made a priority of carefully assembling the best men she could find. She gave her new editors and reporters full autonomy, but she also wanted to monitor them as a major player on their team; therefore, when she moved into her *Herald* office she chose not the posh executive suite but a space adjacent to the city room formerly occupied by the sports department. The sole barrier separating the new editor/publisher from the chaos of her staff was a wall that stopped a few feet short of the ceiling, keeping her in the midst of the editorial action—which proved to be a successful strategy. Although her behavior toward them could be erratic, her editors, writers and reporters for the most part genuinely enjoyed working with her. Soon they were as reluctant to go home at the end of the day as Front Page newspapermen had been in Walter Howey's Chicago newsroom. In addition to their magnetic leader, there were always the late poker games and an abundance of drink. And for those who merited conferences in Cissy's office, chilled champagne quickly emerged from her personal refrigerator.

She replaced existing furniture in her office with antiques, ordered installation of a hardwood floor and had the room repainted a subdued shade of pink. Prominent among the pictures decorating the dusty pink walls was a portrait of Joseph Medill. To visitors it was a reminder of her heritage but to Cissy it was a reinforcement of his rule that a successful newspaper must be the voice of one person. At a Hearst newspaper the voice was that of the Chief, but W.R. did not reside in Washington and he had not been a flaming local personality off and on for three decades. The *Herald* continued to be a Hearst paper but Cissy would see that Washingtonians perceived it as Mrs. Eleanor Medill Patterson's paper. She would make her *Herald* read and talked about at the highest circles, the same elite group that had talked about her for most of the century.

IT WOULD HAVE been impossible for anyone passing a Washington newsstand to have been unaware of the *Herald* on August 1, 1930, Cissy's official first day at the helm. A box on page one, outlined in black lines, carried an enigmatic open letter headed "Arthur Brisbane Warns the Editor." The curious piece began, "Arthur Brisbane told me yesterday in New York that I've got to say something," and followed with a strange tale about a man who bought a multilingual parrot and presented it to his wife. The following night, the wife served him boiled parrot for dinner. " 'My God,' said the man . . . 'Didn't you know the parrot spoke five languages?' 'Well,' answered his wife, 'why didn't he say something?' " The letter, signed Eleanor Patterson, ended, "Now, Mr. Brisbane, I've said something." With this oblique message Cissy introduced herself as the paper's new editor, one from whom the reader could expect the unexpected—and the unexpected had only just begun.

Four days later she stood Washington on its ear and made her point about local focus when she took off on her old chum and rival Alice Longworth. The item was prompted by Ruth McCormick's quest for her husband's former Senate seat, and Alice's reported involvement in her campaign. This time Cissy's page-one box was headlined "Interesting But Not True." The copy read, "The news is that Mrs. Alice Longworth will not only be a confidential advisor to Mrs. Ruth Hanna McCormick, but that she will campaign publicly for her lifelong friend. Interesting but not true. Mrs. McCormick takes no advice, political or otherwise, from Mrs. Longworth. Mrs. Longworth gives no interviews to the press. Mrs. Longworth cannot utter in public. Her assistance will, therefore, resolve itself as usual into posing for photographs." When tout de Washington finished digesting this tasty morsel, the buzz crackled along telephone wires throughout the city, and then the country. Both Arthur Brisbane and Cissy's brother thought the item unprofessional, but Hearst was ecstatic. As fame of the piece spread, Brisbane changed his attitude and was pleased when Swope circulated the rumor that it was a Brisbane-ghosted editorial.

Cissy had not finished with this juicy subject. A follow-up editorial continued: "I was in error. I spoke hastily. Senator Borah, another *close* friend of Alice Longworth, has said that if Ruth McCormick is elected, he will vote to unseat her because of her excessive campaign expenditures. Mrs. Longworth may now present her real gifts. She may use her political influence, of which the country has for so long heard so much. She may soften this decision of the frugal gentleman from Idaho." Those who did not know about the Longworth-Borah-Patterson triangle from dinner party talk at the time learned of it by reading *Glass Houses*. The sexual rivalry of the women was infamous. And then there was the child Paulina. The circulation of the *Herald* exploded. Arthur Krock picked up the story in his *New York Times* column. And William Randolph Hearst cabled Brisbane from Germany, referring to Cissy as a brilliant business manager as well as a stellar editor. With these page-one boxes Cissy established once and for all that she fully grasped the most compelling ingredient any publication can have: to be known to offer exclusive, unexpected material to which only its readers are privy, material they will discuss with each other throughout the day and into the evening's social events, leaving anyone who is not a reader out of the loop. Cissy had given the signal: read my paper or be an outsider! Periodically over the next years, the front-page box would reappear with information it would be impossible to receive elsewhere.

Another Cissy ingredient was the look of quality she insisted the paper carry; it should be printed in good ink on the best paper, with an abundance of white space and an aesthetic balance to the page. There were times when Cissy's goals of excellence went beyond what the nation's newspaper editors could even imagine. In an early meeting with her staff, she announced that the *Herald* was "too black." When they comprehended that she was referring to the appearance of some of the ads, Irving Belt, who supervised printing, was called in. The Ryerson type he suggested gave Cissy the look she wanted, not just in ads but throughout the paper. It was so effective that production men from papers around the country later came to the *Herald* to learn the secret of its very dark gray—but less than black—headlines and print.

THE ELECTION OF November 1930 produced a Democratic landslide, causing the Republicans to lose their majority in the House, and on March 4, 1931, Nick Longworth made his last appearance as Speaker. Shortly afterward he left by himself to visit friends in Aiken, despite a mild late winter cold. The cold rapidly escalated into full-blown pneumonia, then a death sentence—particularly for a man of a certain age whose system had been as alcohol-abused as Nick's. Alice left for South Carolina immediately, but by the time she arrived Nick was in a coma. He died on April 10, and without sad songs from Cissy. Before the Longworth body had cooled, she managed to exceed even her own style of shock journalism by printing a photograph of the distinguished late Speaker surrounded by pictures of many of the women with whom he had been involved. Although her response to Nick Longworth's death was not admirable, it was quirky and unexpected, demonstrating that the instincts of William Randolph Hearst and Arthur Brisbane had been accurate in putting Cissy in the job. She was exactly what the paper needed to create excitement and boost circulation as well as, possibly, advertising sales.

Cissy and the two men who hired her were well aware she was a neophyte—a canny neophyte, but one who wisely counted on Brisbane to guide her. However, Brisbane had other concerns and was not on the scene with her as the need for decisions arose. What Cissy really needed was a seasoned newspaperman who could stand by her every day, someone who not only would steer her but could also vet her innovative ideas and instinctual decisions. Therefore, Hearst and Brisbane's second brilliant stroke was to send Walter Howey—now Hearst's troubleshooter-at-large—to guide the talented but inexperienced woman in overseeing the paper's content. What the two publishing geniuses did not know was that an electricity charging between Cissy and the charismatic newspaperman back in their Chicago years was now at risk of resurging. The editor who had created such journalistic legends as Charles MacArthur and Ring Lardner attracted intelligent, creative and original minds—journalists who were inspired by his brilliance and the unexpected twists of his personality and who in turn excited him. Cissy was no exception; they played off each other. Personally the two picked up where they had left off in 1920, except that Cissy had matured since then, and the added decade had honed her wit and originality. Howey, the alleged loner, who everyone believed only toyed with beautiful women while refusing to give his heart, was captivated by Cissy. And in a newsroom repetition of the Joe Patterson and Mary King romance, the intense attraction was mutual. He moved into 15 Dupont Circle and taught her how to run a newspaper.

Writer Adela Rogers St. Johns, also staying at the Dupont Circle house during part of this period, believed "Cissy and Howey were really in love. I asked Howey if he was in love with her, and he said, 'Yes, I am . . . I'm just plain nuts about her.' " After traveling out to San Simeon and back with Cissy in *Ranger* for Marion Davies's birthday, he told Adela that he had asked Cissy to marry him. Then, one day in a flash of anger, Howey fired the entire *Herald* staff—a fateful error for a man who hoped to marry Cissy. She was furious and rehired them all, but could not forget that Howey had overstepped his position at *her* paper. The chemistry was still there, and always would be, but marriage was now out of the question. The heat of the romance dwindled further when Hearst reassigned Howey to doctor a paper in another city. It was probably just as well. In his ardor Howey's promise to marry Cissy had been premature; he was still married to Liberty and would be until a 1935 divorce. Two years later Howey married another woman with a memorable name, Gloria Ritz, and the wedding was followed in a few months by the birth of their only child, William Randolph Howey.

That the *Herald* was part of a chain was limiting for Cissy because much of the material she had to print was canned and of no interest to Washington. But on October 12, 1931, less than fifteen months after she took over editorship of the sickly *Herald*, the paper ran a front-page streamer, which she described to Mr. Hearst as refined but sensational. LARGEST MORNING CIRCULATION IN THE NATION'S CAPITAL, it read, "easily 10,000 ahead of our competitor and going up." It wasn't merely circulation numbers Cissy had upgraded; she had raised *Herald* demographics from "a backstairs paper." Although it could not claim the prestige of the *Star* and never would, it was a publication the city's elite dared not miss. Emphasis on news was essential in a paper published by Joseph Medill's granddaughter, but Cissy knew it was also important to attract readers with sports, humor and fiction, elements considered crucial to newspapers of the era. To these Cissy added features of interest to women readers. When she discovered that 70 percent of the paper's readers were female, she perfected the modern woman's page in much the way Mary King had in the *Tribune*. She emulated upscale women's magazines in story ideas, layouts and photography, and incorporated fashion, health, beauty tips, local gossip and society coverage. In Washington, where policy is often formed at social occasions, society news is frequently inseparable from political news, even from breaking news. As someone who lived in the midst of the highest social circles, she was privy to what was happening behind the scenes in the city that was shaping the nation's policies, and she knew where to direct the staff of reporters she had assembled. And Cissy not only supervised the reporting of news, she created it.

MRS. PATTERSON'S DAILY schedule gave new meaning to the phrase "full-time job." Because the engine driving the *Herald*'s popularity was its editor's involvement in Washington's inner workings, she was entertaining or being entertained every night. When she awakened at around ten in the morning, the cycle began again. Breakfast was in bed, along with six poodles, her mail and the morning newspapers. While eating, she juggled the papers, mail and ringing telephones, while also giving the day's orders to her housekeeper and secretary. When at last Cissy was in the office, she looked like no other newspaper editor in the world. Her friend and colleague Adela St. Johns described Cissy sitting behind her desk in a Chanel suit, her red hair shining, and "the emerald clip on the lapel was real and matched her eyes." Back home her butler, housekeeper, houseman and several footmen were readying the household for the evening's activities while her lady's maid, seamstress and a pair of laundresses were keeping her wardrobe and boudoir in best-dressed order. An additional three men staffing her private railcar were on perpetual standby, ready to leave whenever she wished. Marguerite Cassini, no stranger to extravagance, wrote that Cissy was "probably the most luxurious person I ever knew, keeping her several homes always opened with her maids waiting, her bath ready and nightgown and slippers laid out in case she might drop in any hour of the day or night." But it was the Dupont Circle evenings that were legendary. Everything was top quality: the champagne, the brandy, the flowers, music, cuts of meat, cuisine and the people. Her guests mixed the men who governed the country, diplomats and the best of Washington society with a more raffish element of artists, writers and those with current celebrity. No one knew what to expect and news was often made at Cissy's table or after dinner in the ballroom.

When not in town, she was at her country estate, Dower House in Prince Georges County, Maryland, an hour's drive from Dupont Circle. When she found the property, it was a ruin of what had originally been the hunting lodge of Charles Calvert, the third Lord Baltimore, purportedly designed by the young Christopher Wren. It was also the site of the wedding of a member of George Washington's family and later a restaurant, but when Cissy first saw it, Dower House was a fire-charred shell attached to an enormous fireplace, in which six adults could stand with ease. She acquired the original plans and had the house restored to its initial design, with much of it decorated in the English country taste of floral chintz and yellow-and-white-striped satin. The drawing room was done in slate blue, and the dining room walls were hung with deep blue silk, covered with paintings of white flowers and large birds; the furniture throughout was largely English antiques. She directed greenhouses to be built for her orchids and the fresh flowers that abounded throughout her houses and in *Ranger*. The stable was renovated to her specifications, and she ordered an immense heated swimming pool installed for the pool parties she anticipated. Adela St. Johns, a frequent guest, said of it, "Of all the houses I have ever seen I would rather have lived in Dower House as Mrs. Patterson had restored the period, mood, hallowed warmth and stateliness of the past to it and still added every modern convenience. It lay among the sweet and friendly hills of Maryland, surrounded by meadows and streams, a fair land, at peace. It seemed impossible it had ever been anything else." It was the consummate weekend house; closer to Washington and the *Herald* than her Sands Point estate and the perfect site for house parties with her Washington friends.

LIKE CISSY, ADELA Rogers St. Johns was a particular pet of William Randolph Hearst. She was the Hearst organization's star female reporter, and the Chief appreciated the loose, wise-guy, syntax-be-damned-style of journalism St. Johns adopted whenever she sat at a newsroom typewriter. With the arrival of the Franklin Roosevelt administration, he moved her to Washington and assigned her to develop feature stories from the capital. "Mrs. Patterson is a great publisher for my paper there," he told her, but added, "I doubt if she knows its personalities on all levels." Adela's assignment was to add a Sweeney element to augment Cissy's coverage of the city's upper strata. Other women reporters began appearing at the *Herald*—young, pretty, well-connected women, who were not necessarily writers. They were there to contribute society columns and to cover parties, and if they couldn't write—well, who cared? In a way the idiosyncratic style of these women was an asset; they repeated in-group buzz phrases used by the social set and delivered information they gathered in a breezy format that conveyed intimacy with the subjects they were covering. They had known some of their quarry as children or at boarding school and had seen them on a regular basis for years; others were politicians and diplomats with whom they flirted at parties while collecting gossipy political "titbits," as Cissy liked to call them. There was another reason for the presence of these women: they were substitutes for Felicia, who in addition to the personal issues between the two was now well on her way to becoming a full-blown alcoholic. Cissy adored these young women, spoiled and coddled them; a current pet might be sent flowers from the Dower House greenhouse, invited to intimate lunches at Dupont Circle or even treated to travel on *Ranger*.

The quantity of attractive young women whose work was appearing in her paper was quickly noted by *Time* magazine, which dubbed the *Herald* "Cissy's henhouse." A significant perk of being a henhouse member was that Cissy periodically purged her fabulous wardrobe. Two full rooms on the top floor at Dupont Circle were filled with racks from which hung hundreds of dresses, suits, gowns, ensembles, Oriental pajamas and other costumes that made up Cissy's wardrobe. There were also coats, furs, riding habits, bathing costumes, hats, shoes, bags and miscellaneous accessories. They had all been photographed, numbered and recorded in a wardrobe book, which documented at least three hundred sets of lounging pajamas alone. When Cissy was ready to dress, she simply referred to the book and gave appropriate numbers to her maid. Whenever she felt burdened by her excessively large wardrobe, she would invite the hens in to plunder a segment of it. That Cissy was ranked as one of the twenty "Best Dressed" women in the world, she thought ridiculous. "How perfectly silly," she insisted. "I never spend more than twenty thousand a year on clothes." But with their "Best Dressed" benefactress, the *Herald* ladies were indeed well turned out.

An exemplary hire was Martha Blair, former wife of William Mitchell Blair, scion of several distinguished Chicago families. The attractive divorcée was writing a popular society column in that city when Cissy discovered her in 1932; she liked Martha's style and invited her for drinks at Chicago's Tavern Club. After engaging her new find to write a similar column for the *Herald*, Cissy forgot about the offer but Martha did not; with two children to support and an ex-husband who had just faced bankruptcy, she was motivated. When she showed up in Washington, Cissy, with no memory of employing her, was again enchanted; she suggested they call the new column "These Charming People" after Michael Arlen's book of the same name. Because it is almost impossible for a columnist to write about the society of a city in which she doesn't know the players, Cissy instructed Martha to throw parties at 15 Dupont Circle, using the Patterson guest list. Although the column was developing nicely, Martha received an unexpected boost when she slipped into a serious relationship with *New York Times* chief Washington correspondent Arthur Krock. Soon pillow talk involving exclusive material—gripping though not suitable for the *Times*—was finding its way into Martha's column, and her political titbits were drawing the city's top politicians to the *Herald*. Eventually the couple married and Martha retired to life as Mrs. Arthur Krock.

Even without Martha and her privileged status, confidential tales regarding the activities of celestial Washington persisted at the *Herald*, and elsewhere—particularly from the typewriter of Drew Pearson. Drew had continued to be a pet of Cissy's for several years after his divorce from her daughter, but in 1931 their relationship changed, together with a significant acceleration in his career. All of Washington—and much of America—was stunned that year by the publication of a sensational new book, *Washington Merry-Go-Round*, written anonymously by Drew and *Christian Science Monitor* Washington bureau chief Robert S. Allen. The book was filled with gossip verging upon scandal about the men who ran the nation and was followed a year later by a sequel, *More Washington Merry-Go-Round*. When the identity of the authors was exposed, both men lost their jobs, but Pearson was hired almost immediately by the *Baltimore Sun* as head of its Washington bureau. He and Allen also began writing the extraordinarily popular "Washington Merry-Go-Round" column, an institution eventually carried by more than six hundred papers with a readership of sixty million. Cissy emerged virtually unscathed in the first book when Pearson wisely defused the chandelier anecdote by changing the word "panties" to "shoes." But she didn't come off as lightly in the follow-up; this time her former son-in-law spun out a long, spicy yarn involving her apricot crêpe de Chine bedsheets. A livid Cissy, on the brink of printing one of her notorious page-one boxes, was saved by Arthur Brisbane. He convinced her that not only would she be giving Pearson a million dollars' worth of publicity, but she would also come away from the dispute looking small and lacking in dignity. She succeeded in persuading Drew's publisher, Liveright, Inc., to remove the story from future editions, and the winds of her displeasure with him soon blew over; within two years his column was appearing regularly in the *Herald*.

IN 1933 THE *Washington Post* was in receivership. Ned McLean, whose alcoholism led him to such excesses as confusing a White House fireplace with a pissoir, had suffered severe financial losses, followed by an emotional breakdown in 1929. By late spring 1933, the once proud McLean paper was a mere ghost of a property with $600,000 of debt and a pathetic fifty-thousand circulation. On the mild morning of June 1, a crowd gathered in front of the newspaper's building, then on Pennsylvania Avenue two blocks south of the White House, to witness a public auction of what was left of the *Post*—its antiquated building, an Associated Press franchise, a venerable name and debt. Those mingling on the building's steps and sidewalk that morning were primarily men in Panama hats and straw boaters, but among the three notable women present was Alice Longworth, an observer rumored to be a potential buyer. Cissy, inconspicuously dressed and almost obscured by the masculine crowd, stood on a top step beside an ornate gray column. And gazing out from an upstairs window was Evalyn McLean. The chronically drug-addled Mrs. McLean, her hair dyed pink, wore the Hope diamond against a conservative black dress; she hoped to keep the paper for her sons, but rumors were circulating that she would have to pawn the famous gem to back her bid.

Cissy would have loved to scoop up the bankrupt property but she couldn't cross Hearst; she was there on his behalf with a lawyer who was making the actual bids. Another bidder, a nameless Texan, dropped out at the quarter-million-dollar point. Evalyn McLean could only go to $600,000, and Cissy's Hearst representative fell away at $800,000. The prize went quickly, and cheaply, to a George E. Hamilton for $825,000. But who was he? A few days later it was revealed that the mysterious Mr. Hamilton was bidding for Eugene Meyer, who with his wife, Agnes, had—until then—been one of Cissy's closest friends.

Although she did not let their estrangement affect her fondness for Agnes, from that day to her death Cissy was at war with Meyer and she did everything she could to sabotage him. She already had the *Post* comic strips. Earlier, when the paper went into receivership, she had acquired exclusive Washington rights to distribute *Dick Tracy*, *Andy Gump*, *Winnie Winkle* and other crucial circulation boosters. But of course Eugene also wanted them. The two former friends went to court over the strips in litigation that lasted for almost two years. Meyer won and Cissy retaliated with a stunt that horrified their many mutual friends. She ordered precisely one pound of raw hamburger meat and placed it in an elaborately wrapped florist's corsage box surrounded with ribbons and flowers. The ornate package was delivered to Meyer by Cissy's driver with a note that read, "So as not to disappoint you—take your pound of flesh." Eugene's Christian wife, who watched him open it, noted the Shylock allusion, an outrageous dig at the Jewish Mr. Meyer. Because both Cissy and Meyer had been advised that only one morning paper could be profitable in Washington, the war was a real one, and Eugene Meyer an authentic enemy.

IN 1935 DREW Pearson remarried. The bride was Luvie Moore Abell, former wife of his best friend, George Abell, and once again a child was abducted. The angry George absconded to the British Isles with the former couple's five-year-old son, triggering litigation that resulted in the Pearsons receiving the boy's custody. The previous year, Felicia—who had been living in Europe and working on another novel—also remarried; the groom was English insurance broker Dudley de Lavigne, a socially aspiring member of the chic Prince of Wales set. Felicia was receiving a tax-free allowance of forty thousand dollars a year from Cissy, and Dudley was said to have tastes exceeding his income, a situation that did not bode well for the marriage. Within a year Felicia was single again, prompting Cissy to prevail upon Hearst general manager Tom White to facilitate a job for her daughter at

Harper's Bazaar in Paris. White did so, without Felicia ever knowing of Cissy's request, but the presence of Mr. White in her mother's life was becoming quite apparent to others.

Thomas Justin White was a married Roman Catholic, the father of five, and anything but eligible. Like Brisbane, he was a Hearst stalwart and well within the Chief's inner circle both professionally and personally. But he didn't have the high public visibility of his sister Carmel Snow, legendary *Harper's Bazaar* editor from 1933 to 1957, nor of his daughter, Nancy White, who ruled the same magazine until 1971. Tom White was charming, quick and witty, and with him Cissy truly enjoyed herself. They had known each other professionally at Hearst during the early thirties and gradually Cissy became besotted with the genial Irishman; by 1934 he was her devoted lover. A glimpse into their relationship—begun in earnest during a cross-country trip from Chicago to San Simeon and back on *Ranger*—is revealed in the note he wrote to her shortly after the lovers reeled off the train in Chicago. "Again and again, thanks, thanks, thanks, and a long restful sleep to you." Cissy promptly took an apartment in New York's Ritz Tower, a property owned by Mr. Hearst, and quite a clubby establishment. White kept a pied-à-terre on one floor; his sister, Mrs. Snow, on another; and Hearst and Marion Davies maintained quarters at its pinnacle. Cissy spent romantic days and nights with Tom there, at Dupont Circle, Sands Point and Dower House, and later in a house she rented for the purpose on Gramercy Park. In 1936 they traveled to Paris, where they spent time with Cissy's old flame Bill Bullitt, who had become United States ambassador to France. The ten-year difference in their ages no longer seemed as great as it had, nor as important—certainly not to Bullitt, who began courting Cissy with renewed fervor. She delighted in her role as the desired woman bracketed by the worldly ambassador and the convivial publishing executive; one polished and urbane, the other warm and lovable. It became a game with her, and Tom left.

Cissy would have given anything to marry Tom White, but when Bill Bullitt proposed to her after White's departure, she declined. She was accustomed to being the focal point of her universe and did not relish trailing after an ambassador, especially at the expense of giving up her role at the *Herald*. Following her return to Washington, she and Tom reconciled and the affair continued for another couple of years, with Cissy increasing in her desire to settle into a permanent, public relationship with him. She even contacted Tom's wife and asked for a meeting at New York's Carlton House. Cissy memorized a script of speeches and pleas, but when Virginia White arrived, all she could say was, "But you see, I *love* him." Mrs. White replied, "So do I," and that ended the matter. Although later Cissy reportedly offered Virginia a million dollars to divorce Tom, she stood firm.

CISSY ENJOYED HER feuds and had found her equal in Alice Longworth, who relished attention as much as she did and cared as little for middle-class decorum. Between them, Cissy, through sporadic gibes in the *Herald*, and Alice, in widely circulated dinner party pronouncements, made the feud a spectator sport—particularly after Alice's cousin Franklin became a national figure, making her again newsworthy. No less than George Kaufman collaborated in writing a 1935 Broadway play, *First Lady*, that spoofed the extraordinary pair and their ongoing quarrel. One day, when they met on the street in their mutual neighborhood, Cissy stopped, looked at Alice and said, "I think it's time we made up." Alice countered with "Oh, I don't think so. It's too soon."

A few months later, when Adela St. Johns was a guest at Dower House, she made a date to meet Alice. Over lunch at the Mayflower, Alice dished amusingly but indiscreetly about her first cousin Eleanor Roosevelt, now First Lady. She spoke of the president's wife, whom she had always disliked, in her customary booming volume, characterized by St. Johns as "a Barrymore voice that carries even when she whispers and she never whispers." When a Longworth monologue concerning an alleged flirtation between the president and a Norwegian princess became too vivid, Adela recalled that "I slid down in my chair" and changed the subject by saying, "You know Cissy's been ill?" And then she added, "I'm staying there and she knows I'm having lunch with you. . . . Why don't you come back with me?" Amazingly, Alice did just that, and when the two old friends met, she spoke first: "I should have believed you about the champagne. That was your weakness, not men." Cissy laughed, the former Graces fell into each other and then went for a long walk alone. What had begun as a defensive whim on Adela's part turned out to be a great success.

Alice remained cool with Marguerite Cassini, who returned to Washington in the 1930s after living in Europe for a number of years with her husband and two sons. Cassini was the surname of all four, based on a 1900 czar's decree awarding a hereditary title to the daughter of his loyal United States ambassador. Soon after her return, Alice passed Marguerite on a Washington street without stopping to speak, but later asked her to tea. In the countess's memoir, *Never a Dull Moment,* she recalled sitting across from her girlhood intimate in front of an open fire in the Longworth living room, saying to her, "It's strange, Alice, when you consider how inseparable we were that now we never see each other." Alice answered, "Well, we knew each other for such a short time." And that was the end of it, dismissed. Another who treated Marguerite cavalierly when she called on him at his *Daily News* office was Joe Patterson. "He remembered me. But to my surprise his manner when he received me was cold. No, not cold, hostile. His animosity was almost suffocating. I was bewildered and then it came to me unbelievably that it still rankled with this great newspaper titan that I had laughed at his youthful and impulsive proposal of marriage. It seemed incredible but Cissy later confirmed it was so."

Cissy, on the other hand, greeted the countess warmly—too warmly—and agreed to give her son Igor a job writing a column, but there was a catch. "I want your story," she said. "I've always wanted it. You will be paid, and I will assign one of my best writers to help you. You will write and say only what you choose. We'll call it 'Washington by Candlelight' or something of the sort." Before the story could be written, Marguerite was injured in an automobile accident, and while she was enduring a long, painful recovery, Cissy sent a reporter to interview her. Marguerite's story then morphed into a series of articles, titled not "Washington by Candlelight" but "I Lived for Love," based on the reporter's interviews and further fleshed out with clippings from *Town Topics,* a salacious turn-of-the-century society publication. Marguerite was mortified with the results, but she was paid a much-needed eight hundred dollars.

The job Cissy gave to Marguerite's son was decisive to his future as a journalist. By assigning him to take over Martha Krock's "These Charming People," she positioned Igor Cassini in line to become one of America's major twentieth-century society columnists. He pursued the job with such vigor that an item about a member of a prominent Virginia family resulted in his abduction from a country club party by five of the girl's angry relatives. The quintet took the columnist out to a remote road, where they stripped him and then covered his body with tar and feathers, with the warning that he would be "emasculated" were there ever a similar offense again. Igor turned the incident to his advantage by reporting on it in his column and basking in the national coverage it received. When he left to serve in World War II, Cissy replaced him with his beautiful first wife, Bootsie McDonnell, who successfully wrote "These Charming People" in spite of being confronted with a half-million-dollar libel suit from *New York Post* editor Dorothy Schiff.

Igor soon emerged as the *New York Journal American*'s Cholly Knickerbocker, covering mid-century international society—which he dubbed the Jet Set—with observations that garnered his column twenty million syndicated readers. Igor's finest moment came in 1958, when he hired Liz Smith as his assistant, giving the high-spirited Texas girl her introduction to the world of newspaper columns, and his nadir occurred in February 1963, with his failure to register as an agent of the former Trujillo dictatorship in the Dominican Republic. The latter episode led to a grand jury indictment, followed by the loss of his *Journal American* column and social ostracism. He was further humiliated when his then in-laws, Jayne and Charles Wrightsman, close Kennedy friends, insisted he and his wife, Charlene, remain away from Palm

Beach whenever the president was visiting. The banishment so destroyed Charlene—Charles's daughter—that she committed suicide in April 1963, intensifying the scandal.

Marguerite's other son, the late Oleg Cassini—once married to actress Gene Tierney and a lover of Grace Kelly during her wanton Hollywood phase—had better luck in his relationship with the Kennedys. His public image soared and design business surged after he became the fashion designer responsible for Jacqueline Kennedy's "look" during her White House years.

UNDER CISSY'S LEADERSHIP *Herald* circulation was continuing to increase, on its way to doubling by 1936, and it was read by Washington's finest. Yet she continued to be a Hearst employee and was required to use Hearst material even while yearning for the paper to be completely her own. She implored W.R. to sell either or both of his Washington newspapers to her but he would not, even though his losses in the capital were reaching $1.5 million annually. In addition, he had financial problems in non-newspaper areas of his life. In 1937 the Depression finally delivered Hearst a fundamental setback when he was informed on a Friday that payroll checks could not be issued for the following Tuesday. Concurrently, Marion—without consulting him—called Cissy and together they conspired to deposit $1 million each in the overdrawn bank account on Monday morning. Cissy loved the old man but she also learned that Eugene Meyer had made an offer to buy the *Herald*. Fearing he would acquire her beloved paper, strip it of all its best features, add them to the *Post* and then kill the *Herald*, she contacted the Chief.

"I called Mr. Hearst at three in the morning and commenced to cry on the phone," she remembered. "And he said, 'Well, Cissy, you tell me what you want to do and I will tell my folks to do it.' And in the morning, because they had to have the money, I went to the bank and borrowed a million dollars, and I made that loan to the Hearst Company." It took this crisis for W.R. to at last consider leasing Cissy the *Herald*. After several formal discussions among Cissy's representatives and Hearst's at her Long Island estate, the outcome was that she would enter into an option-to-buy lease of the *Herald* for five years, and absorb losses during that period. In addition, the agreement was bound by the million-dollar "loan" from Cissy to Hearst at 5 percent interest—a million dollars Cissy borrowed from the Morgan Guaranty Bank at a rate a shade less. In a deal engineered chiefly by Tom White, the loan would be a portion of the purchase price if Cissy were to buy the paper. The *Times* was included in the deal five months later. Even though the absorbed losses would cost her a million dollars, it was, all in all, a sweet transaction for Cissy.

But the two papers were bleeding cash and Cissy was losing big money during 1938, an assault to both her self-esteem and her bank account. Late in the year, she exercised her option, spending a half-million dollars of her capital to buy both papers, and at the end of January 1939 she took an innovative step, one that had never been taken by a metropolitan publisher. She combined the morning *Herald* with the evening *Times*, creating a twenty-four-hour newspaper. On any given date, features, cartoons and editorials remained the same, but as the day moved on with new stories breaking, fresh information was added. At a time before cable news television and in a company town where the company is the government of the nation, it was an inspired move. The unspoken agenda was not only to save money but also to present a package to department store advertisers that would give them the readers of two newspapers at the price of advertising in one. Her experiment was a success.

From the beginning, Cissy had received advertising support from the various retailers, suppliers and providers of services whom she had graced with her business through the years. She had also courted potential advertisers by including them in the heady milieu of Dupont Circle dinner parties. But in 1938 she staged an unexpected coup, one that not only brought in massive real estate advertising to the *Herald* but also stroked Cissy's desire to be an arbiter. There was no doubt that Washington was in need of a flamboyant new social hostess to succeed Evalyn McLean, but when Cissy elected Gwendolyn Detre de Surany

Cafritz to the position it was quite a stretch. Gwen was the flighty Hungarian wife of Morris Cafritz, a rich, indulgent husband who was Washington's most important real estate developer, and the Cafritzes had just moved into a new Foxhall Road mansion, furnished with Moderne décor, cutting-edge art and its own nightclub. The combination of the house and its nouveau riche occupants was just outré enough in staid Washington to make Cissy's anointment a success. With the name of the colorful, ambitious Gwen Cafritz repeatedly appearing in the *Herald* in the most glowing context, invitations to her parties were soon accepted by the city's most powerful guests. And a grateful Morris Cafritz became a major *Herald* advertiser.

CISSY'S POWER AND her sense of herself had grown to a point that she did not consider, nor did she care, what others might think. Her expensive wardrobe was that of the "Best Dressed" woman she was, but her elegant style could also be loose and, at times, entirely over-the-top; she often came into the office in riding clothes, accompanied by a pack of high-strung French poodles that were allowed to run wildly about the newsroom, skidding and yipping as they careered around the desks of working journalists. When the Ogden Armours gave a white-tie engagement party for their daughter Lolita at Chicago's Blackstone Hotel, Cissy showed up in western riding garb. It mattered little to her that other women guests were in ball gowns, tiaras and full-length white kid gloves or that hotel employees barred her entry until Mr. Armour came to her rescue. She casually explained that her train from Wyoming was late, she didn't have time to change—and that was that.

 Although known for her lovely voice, Cissy could use it to spew language rivaling that of a hardened newspaperman. And she was as fearless as any, having once secured an interview with Al Capone simply by walking up to him outside his Miami Beach house. With bodyguards standing nearby under the palm trees, Capone—fully aware of who Cissy was—took her on a tour of his garden, then into the house for a shot of his private stock bootleg whiskey and an informal chat. She described him for her readers as having the "the neck and shoulders of a wrestler, one of those prodigious Italians, thick-chested, close to six feet tall." And she continued with a colorful description of the gangster, one of the most vivid ever written. "Once I looked at his eyes. Ice-gray, ice-cold eyes. You can't any more look into the eyes of Capone than you can look into the eyes of a tiger. . . . Capone's eyes are dime-novel gangster's eyes. . . . I could feel their menace. The stirring of a tiger." She embarked on a similar impromptu interview with Albert Einstein outside Palm Springs, California, where both were staying. After quizzing the butler at the house where Einstein was a guest, Cissy followed a mountain trail where he was thought to be walking. When she found the legendary physicist, he was sunbathing in the nude. Well, not quite—his signature wild mop of hair was covered by a "white handkerchief," which, she wrote, was "knotted at each of the four corners." This was an intrusion that was more than even the intrepid Cissy could justify—she backed off but almost immediately reprimanded herself for bowing to conventionality.

Though she was a superb reporter, there was a limit to how much riveting copy Cissy could contribute herself; it was one reason why she would keep adding columnists through the years. A tribute to her instincts in selecting an unskilled journalist to write a column was the subsequent career of an actress she met at San Simeon. Hedda Hopper had a gift for gossip about Hollywood, and Cissy, listening to her stories about the stars, asked, "Why don't you write a gossip column? When you go home, dictate a letter to me. If I like it, I'll pay you for it." Cissy liked the letter, paid for it and launched a Hollywood gossip career rivaled only by that of Hearst columnist Louella Parsons. Cissy's theory was that almost any verbally adroit individual with access to the right people could produce a successful column, but it didn't always happen. She attempted to make a star columnist of Alice Longworth but then discovered—as anyone who has read Mrs. Longworth's memoirs can verify—that she was not an effective communicator on paper. Alice's monologues, without her impressionistic delivery style, singular body language and thunderous projection, did not translate effectively to the printed page. Another try was Evalyn McLean, whom Cissy assigned to write "My Say," a takeoff on Eleanor Roosevelt's successful column "My Day." That didn't work, either.

A trio of women, who had at least moderate success at the *Times-Herald*, would become historic figures because of their ties to John F. Kennedy. The future president's sister, Kathleen, or "Kick," joined the *Times-Herald* as assistant to executive editor Frank Waldrop for twenty dollars a week, and later reviewed plays and movies under her own byline. While at the paper she struck up a friendship with Inga Arvad, a glamorous Danish journalist who was writing a column profiling U.S. government officials. When Kick introduced her sophisticated friend to her brother, they began a sizzling romance approved by Joseph Kennedy, who believed the older, twice-married Inga would be an excellent love coach for Jack. But Inga brought a history with her; the former Miss Denmark had once interviewed Hitler, who was so charmed with her Nordic beauty that she was his much-photographed companion during the 1936 Summer Olympics in Berlin. Soon under FBI surveillance as a possible spy, she would be of even greater interest to J. Edgar Hoover after John F. Kennedy became president, and has remained an enduring footnote in the Kennedy legend.

Kick, more than a footnote, left the paper to move to England during World War II. In May 1944 she became the bride of the Marquess of Hartington, and within three months was a war widow, but she remained in England. Four years later she died tragically in the crash of a chartered plane while on a French holiday with her married lover, the eighth Earl Fitzwilliam. The senior Kennedys were horrified, but the scandal was moderated thanks to a *New York Daily News* article, which the Kennedys credited to Jack's friend Joe Patterson. The story, headlined CHANCE INVITE SENDS KENNEDY GIRL TO DEATH, suggested that Kick was flying to meet her father in the south of France and—unable to secure a seat on a commercial airline—accepted a ride from a casual friend. Reprinted internationally, the article softened the notoriety of her catastrophic escapade. The third in the Kennedy trio was Jacqueline Bouvier, who was hired as "Inquiring Camera Girl" by the *Times-Herald*—in 1951, after Cissy's death—for $42.50 a week, more than double Kick's starting wages.

Cissy's favorite columnist was tall, slender Evie Robert, considered the most glamorous Washington woman of the early Franklin Roosevelt administration. The gorgeous blue-eyed blonde was known for her wit, with its forthright, often risqué style. A sample of Evie's contribution to party chatter was her comment to a guest at a Dupont Circle dinner, "Don't talk of your sexual adventures with Cissy . . . because Cissy is like all the McCormick-Patterson clan—if there's any fucking to be done, they want to do it." Evie and her wealthy husband, Lawrence "Chip" Robert, lived in an apartment in the Mayflower hotel, where they entertained with notable flair. Evie's journalistic career began in July 1938 when she was in Ireland as houseguest of United States ambassador John Cudahy. While she was visiting, a plane piloted by Douglas Corrigan landed in an airfield outside Dublin. When the pilot claimed he had left New York the day before expecting to fly to Los Angeles, the legend of Wrong-Way Corrigan was born. Evie picked up a telephone and called Cissy in Washington with the story, and soon the glamour girl of the New Deal was writing a column. Cissy was particularly fond of the new columnist, whom she thought of as her younger self; she loved telling people that Evie had "the morals of a mink" and would sleep with anybody—which was probably true. A lawyer, in an effort to discredit Evie as a courtroom character witness, claimed to have a list of 165 of her lovers. And at a political dinner, Evie herself pointed toward one man after another announcing that she had slept with each; it was an anecdote Cissy loved to repeat. However, a man had his face slapped by Mrs. Patterson when he bragged that he had gone to bed with Evie the night before and "didn't even have to tell her I loved her." Cissy enjoyed Evie so much that she promised to bequeath her the black Cartier pearls, and kept her in line by periodically pointing to her own throat, with the words, "Now, now, Evie."

Though she adored Evie and identified with her, Cissy's closest woman friend at the *Herald* was her picture editor, photographer

Jackie Martin. They often dined together and Jackie was one of the few *Herald* employees invited to Cissy's small social evenings. They spent weekends together at Dower House, Sands Point and a place Cissy regularly rented at Lyford Cay in the Bahamas; Jackie often joined her on trips aboard *Ranger* and Cissy's gifts to her included fur coats and a Cadillac, all of which created rumors of a lesbian relationship between the two. But Jackie was not immune to the verbal abuse Cissy frequently heaped on employees; when she left in 1941 to become a war correspondent, she said, "I just couldn't take it any longer. . . . I carry away no grievances." One *Herald* employee quipped about Cissy's loss of her great friend, "Why should she care about Jackie when she's got Evie."

Evie stayed around; she was getting the Cartier pearls.

· 18 ·

ALICIA PATTERSON, SURROGATE SON

URING the years Cissy's daughter was growing up in Lake Forest, her closest summertime companions were Joe and Alice Patterson's three girls at nearby Westwood Farm. Elinor, a ladylike budding beauty, was two years older than Felicia, Alicia followed Elinor by three years and little Josephine trailed by another seven. So it was always the tomboy Alicia who instigated the girls' rough-and-tumble antics and led in daring adventures. By August the days were long and hot, with an unrelenting sun blazing down on the brick Georgian house and barren outbuildings. In the months of high summer Westwood was more midwestern farm than country estate— stark and desolate—with Alice's stately home standing off and alone within an island of cultivation. The surrounding roads were dusty and the terrain dismal. Crabgrass sprouted here and there among scattered rocks in the dark Illinois soil, fruit rotted into the earth where it fell and permeating everything was the heavy aroma of farm animals. Joe's farm was superb tomboy territory and the girls loved the freedom it gave them. They were usually able to elude Alice with her strict rules and, when possible, they dodged the ubiquitous governess; however, they could not avoid a bodyguard who arrived with the little countess and shadowed her wherever she went—even hiding with her in unsuccessful rounds of hide-and-seek. For the Patterson girls, a favorite activity of the Westwood Farm months was riding, and as far back as they could remember, ponies, horses and competing in Lake Forest horse shows were an important part of their lives.

But there was more to the Illinois summers than playing hide-and-seek and riding their ponies. Joe also taught his daughters to fish and shoot. His fixation about not having sons was so strong that when Alicia was born he stormed out of the house and stayed away for days. It remained with him during the long years before Jimmy's birth, prompting him to raise his girls as if they were sons, giving them harsh, character-building exercises to see what they were made of, and he encouraged them in hoydenish pranks. When they threw rotten apples at passing cars, he applauded, and leaving a dead cat on a neighbor's doorstep made him laugh. On rainy indoor days, the pace was more relaxed, and Joe would invent long stories, casting the girls as central characters in his plots and giving them intriguing roles to play. He sang to them and read aloud the dialogue from *Tribune* comic strips; when Alicia complained about the unwieldy size of the pages, he brought home comics he had specially printed on half pages.

ELINOR WAS TOO sedate and Josephine too young to be bona fide substitutes for the son Joe had so desired; therefore Alicia was the focus of his efforts to shape a pint-sized companion. When she was tiny, she fell off her pony while he was teaching her to ride. Although she was hurt, he lifted her back in the saddle and insisted she keep riding for another hour or more. He once ordered her to climb the twelve-foot diving board at Westwood's swimming pool, and she stood shivering at its top for hours until she summoned courage to dive into the water. After she finally made the plunge, he made her dive again repeatedly, which she did. In fact Alicia did everything her father asked—much of which was painful, even perilous—simply to be in his company. "Long after I had grown up, father continued to exert an almost hypnotic influence on me," she remembered. "I would have died rather than fail him. . . . Psychiatrists may suggest that pa felt an ambivalence toward me, a mixture of love and hate, a desire to test my nervous system to the snapping point. All I know is that he helped to make me unafraid. I felt at times like the Spartan boy who kept silent though the fox was gnawing at his vitals." A few years later she recalled, "Father seemed to get a kick out of having me do dangerous things. I kept getting so scared that finally I wasn't scared of anything anymore." Alicia believed that the slavish obedience to her father began one day when he found her sitting dejectedly on the floor and "asked me if I wouldn't go for a walk with him. It was the most wonderful invitation I had ever had. From that day on, I would have walked around the earth if he had asked me to."

Because both he and Alice felt it important for the girls to be multilingual, they engaged a series of signorinas, mademoiselles and frauleins as governesses, and in 1912 Joe took the two older girls to live in Berlin, hoping they would learn to speak pure German without an accent. After depositing them in a German-speaking pension with their current governess, Fraulein Klinger, he checked in for a stay at the fashionable Hotel Adlon on Unter den Linden. The project began well enough, but when Alicia's ear became infected, the Christian Scientist fraulein did not seek medical aid. It wasn't until the child's agony caused her to scream aloud in pain that she was taken to a specialist who removed an abscess. The Berlin experiment was a success for Elinor, who inherited her mother's facility with languages and became fluent in German, but it was a disaster for Alicia, not a linguist—then or ever.

At the beginning of each school year, the family moved into town. After first living for a few seasons at the Virginia Hotel, Joe leased a furnished house at Three East Banks Street, which today would stand almost back-to-back with the celebrated Pump Room. They spent winters there for five and a half years in the late 1910s before renting a rambling apartment in 232 East Walton Place. School was confining for the irrepressible Alicia, who was repeatedly sent to the principal's office at the progressive Francis Parker School. After a few semesters she transferred to the University School for Girls on Lake Shore Drive, where she was memorable as being "the ringleader." But Alicia wasn't the only Patterson who was memorable at the University School.

According to an often-repeated anecdote, the headmistress was looking out a window one morning when she noticed the casually attired Joe delivering Alicia to school. Within minutes, she was on the telephone with Alice. "I thought I ought to tell you," she said with some alarm, "that I saw your houseman kiss your little girl this morning."

But Alicia never stayed in any school long and a European education was beckoning. This time it was Alice who packed up the girls and accompanied them to the Continent; Elinor and Alicia attended Les Fougères, a boarding school in Lausanne, while their mother and Josephine lived in hotels in Nice and then Versailles, where Josephine was enrolled in local day schools. Again the unspoken mission was to learn a foreign language, but not for Alicia. Les Fougères was one in a series of institutions from which she was dismissed for infractions ranging from speaking English to sneaking out a window after hours, which she did both there and at Miss Risser's School for Girls in Rome. When she was expelled from St. Timothy's near Baltimore it was simply for "general obstreperousness," but none of her outlaw behavior displeased her father, who seems to have appreciated his daughter's stylish show of high spirits. Finally, Foxcroft in the horse country of Virginia—with its heavy emphasis on the equestrian activities at which Alicia excelled—did graduate her; she finished second in the class of 1924 and came away with a permanent Middleburg drawl.

Her schooling completed, Alicia joined her mother in wandering around Europe with Josephine and a tutor, visiting museums and other cultural destinations. During a stay in Rome, she sneaked out for a night on the town with a handsome Italian suitor of noble birth. The escapade ended when Alice chanced to recognize one of her own dresses on a girl, who looked like Alicia, walking along the street with an exotic-looking man. For once Alice was stymied; not knowing what to do and considering the possibility of a convent for her errant daughter, she cabled Joe for advice. His return cable reply: KEEP ALICIA MOVING. She did just that, traveling on to Biarritz with the girls and more amorous adventures for Alicia, who remembered, "Around eighteen, I had a passion for broken-down Russian princes and things like that. I guess I was hard to handle." But, while at Les Fougères, she had also begun to think about her future and possibly pursuing a newspaper career. When Joe suggested Columbia University Graduate School of Journalism as a far distant goal, she wrote back that she was interested and "would like to go there awfully."

Throughout all of Alicia's transgressions, Elinor continued to conduct herself with restraint as she matured into a great beauty, graduating with an unblemished record from Spence and making her debut at Chicago's Blackstone Hotel during Christmas week in 1923. After her blazing start as the nun in *The Miracle,* Elinor continued to act for a time, appearing onstage in *Behold the Dreamer* opposite Glenn Hunter. In 1926 she married socially prominent Bostonian Russell Sturgis Codman Jr., whom she divorced two and a half years later to wed Chicago steel scion Griffith Mark; after that she effectively dropped out of sight. But the younger Patterson girls did not. They were destined for continuing attention from the national press as they became prototypes for the madcap tomboy heiresses played by Carole Lombard and Katharine Hepburn in the Hollywood screwball comedies of the following decade.

WHEN ALICIA WAS nineteen, Alice and Joe presented her at an elaborate coming-out party in Chicago's Blackstone Hotel, the largest debutante ball of the 1925 season. The Pattersons were a handsome trio standing at the doorway of the double-tiered Crystal Ballroom to receive guests that night—Alicia, wearing wisteria tulle, her mother in a gown of pale green velvet and Joe uncharacteristically impeccable in white tie and tails. She may not have possessed her sister Elinor's fragile beauty, but Alicia had grown into a handsome young woman with the lean, supple body of a natural athlete, although at five foot three, she was disarmingly tiny. She inherited her father's stubborn chin, and both her smile and brown-eyed gaze were straightforward and direct. Her official arrival in the adult social world coincided with the publication of F. Scott Fitzgerald's *The Great Gatsby,* a synchronicity not lost on the fun-loving post-deb who plunged directly into the frenetic Jazz Age milieu of flaming youth and remembered, "I read all the books, and took them to heart." She attended a typing class a few hours a week but spent the rest of her time collecting Chicago swains at the same rate she had been accumulating Roman aristocrats and Russian princes on the Continent. Her escorts were the most popular men-about-town, among them lawyer Adlai E. Stevenson II, six years her senior, and restaurant chain heir Daggett Harvey, with whom she attended the Yale prom in February 1927. She managed to wedge the New Haven weekend between houseguesting in Memphis and a holiday in the Bahamas. Added to this hectic pace was a pull to New York, with her father now established there, and to Boston, where her favorite suitor, James Simpson Jr., was a student at Harvard.

Alicia's New York visits and her Boston weekends at the Copley Plaza were growing in frequency during early 1927 as the romance—encouraged by her father—became more serious. Jim Simpson was son of the president of Marshall Field & Company, familiar territory for Joe and, furthermore, he was Patterson's kind of guy, a horseman, an aviator and a developer of Arlington Park Race Track. Less enthusiastic about a prospective union was Jim's father, a Scotsman by birth and protégé of the conservative Marshall Field from age eighteen. He gave his reluctant consent, although he had hoped that, after Harvard, Jim would go England to study at Cambridge and "become a man of polish and a man of the world." At the end of March, Joe wrote Alice about a long talk he had had with Alicia, reporting that Simpson had urged their daughter to "quit traveling around with the bunch of neurotics with which she has been associating. . . . Alicia wants to go to work in New York and Jim is strongly for it, since it would keep her away from the neurotics and, I suppose, give him a chance to come down for week-ends. I told Alicia if she wanted to go to work I would give her a start until she learned a little something about newspaper technique, and after that she could go on another paper where she would get more experience."

A thirty-dollar-a-week job at the *Daily News* was exactly what Alicia needed; she plunged into her new career with enthusiasm, not daring to return from an assignment empty-handed. She worked conscientiously but also benefited from watching her father in action. "He was geared with invisible antennae that alerted him to the shifting moods of the times," she noted. And she told *Editor & Publisher* that working for the *News* was "the most fun in the world. Far better than going to school, and you learn so much more, too." Some years later she added, "father told me I would become a member of a triumvirate that would operate and control the *Daily News* after his death, the others being executives of the newspaper. It was a wonderful plan, but it never came true." Joe made a point of showing her no favoritism. After a stint of "sitting in a corner clipping out filler items from other newspapers for use in the *Sunday News*," Alicia was elevated to minor human interest assignments in the outposts of Brooklyn or Hoboken, though undeterred, she kept at her work.

Her turning point at the *News* came with the next assignment, a big one with the promise of a byline; she was to interview the mother of the prospective divorcée in a case heavily covered in the press. Successfully snagging the interview by posing as a Junior League member, she unfortunately mistook the battling pair for another similarly named—although contented—couple, resulting in a libel suit against the *News*. It was then that Joe gave his daughter a devastating lesson, one that outdid any of the distressing experiences he designed for her as a child. He fired her. The fatal session appeared to begin harmlessly when her father and Uncle Bertie invited her to lunch at a fashionable New York restaurant, but once in the formal, dignified atmosphere, the two men gave her the news. Joe later revealed that he would have discharged her anyway; he had planned to do so from the outset so that she would have to beat the sidewalks to find another job. "That's a regular part of newspaper life," he said.

Alicia outsmarted him. Rather than job hunt, she went back to Chicago and a life of partying, shooting, hunting and playing tennis, but most often partying. Without a job to channel her energies, the flaming youth tempo of her life accelerated. Joe, always a resourceful adversary, countered with a solution to her unbridled restlessness:

Marriage to Jim Simpson, and soon. Her engagement was announced immediately, August, 18, 1927, but on the day of the announcement, a rival suitor, J. Ledyard Smith, applied for a marriage license in Wisconsin, exasperating both the Simpsons and the Pattersons, who canceled the planned church wedding. A contrite Smith issued a statement: "She did not know my intention. . . . When it became obvious that I was not to be successful in my suit I returned the license to the Waukegan courthouse." Nevertheless, it provided wonderful juice for rival Chicago newspapers and a vigilant national press. In a renegotiation, Alicia promised her father she would marry Simpson and stay with him for at least a year. Joe accepted the deal and a few weeks later, on September 28, the couple was married at Westwood Farm with Robert S. Pirie, son of an owner of rival department store Carson Pirie Scott & Company, as best man. Although only thirty family members and close friends were present, Alicia was formally attired in the white satin and heirloom alençon lace gown she would have worn to a large church wedding, and Josephine, her only attendant, was gowned in a fashionably short dress of flesh pink chiffon with a pink velvet hat.

The couple set off for a long European honeymoon but the omens were not promising. Aboard the outbound RMS *Laconia*, Alicia wrote her father asking him to join them later in England, an invitation he wisely declined. By the time they reached Paris, the Simpsons' arguments had reached such a pitch that Alicia cabled a Lake Forest friend, Janet Chase, to meet them in England and stay for the rest of the trip. After Janet arrived in early January, the remainder of the unconventional honeymoon went smoothly. Jim successfully competed in English steeplechases, while Alicia and Janet engaged in foxhunting in the Melton Mowbray district, giving Alicia material for a successful *Liberty* magazine piece. She lived up to her agreement to stay with Jim for one year—seven months of which was the honeymoon trip. The short-lived marriage ended when she divorced Simpson in 1930, legally resumed use of her maiden name and plunged into a new avocation.

*   *   *

A WORLD-CHANGING PHENOMENON—ONE that would have a powerful impact on the Patterson-McCormick clan—exploded in early-twentieth-century America, capturing public imagination and creating heroes and heroines on a colossal scale. It was the marvel of aviation, and the first of the dynasty to feel its force had been the Colonel on a breezy afternoon in 1908. The twenty-eight-year-old Sanitary District president was checking a site south of Chicago when he saw a man with wings attached to his arms running along the sand dunes like a lunatic. Periodically the latter-day Icarus was picked up by the wind, only to soar a few feet before dropping back down to the sand, but he stopped long enough to inform Bert of a pair of brothers, bicycle mechanics from Ohio, who had constructed a flying machine they would be demonstrating for the army at Fort Myer in Arlington, Virginia. Fascinated by the eccentric story, Bert almost immediately left for Washington by train, and over lunch with Alice Longworth he convinced her, with her father's influence, to reserve a spot for the two of them to view a demonstration.

The prospect was just offbeat enough for Alice, who drove with him over to Fort Myer in her electric automobile and waited patiently while Wilbur and Orville Wright delayed their flight until a fierce wind died down. When conditions were favorable, the brothers steered their fragile machine across the grass until it was caught by an air current; Bert and Alice watched while the men propelled the plane up and around the field once before landing. The experience was a vivid one for the Colonel, who classified it as "the greatest thrill of my life." He would circle the globe by plane many times during the remainder of his days, and although he survived three crashes, he never feared flying. The blasé Alice was also taken with the afternoon's expedition and soon made excursions to Fort Myer part of her daily routine, creating a new Washington craze for the fashionable set, to whom she supplied drinks and sandwiches. "I would go over at about five in the electric, taking a picnic basket and a half a dozen vacuum bottles filled with iced tea and 'Tom Collins,' " she wrote in her 1933 memoirs. "Indeed I ran a most popular 'lunch wagon.' "

Joe never acquired his cousin's extraordinary passion for flying, but it became an absorbing pursuit as he neared fifty. From 1928 to 1931 he was a flight student at Curtiss Field near Mineola, Long Island, later Roosevelt Field, but despite his enthusiasm, flying was not a natural activity for him. *Time* magazine, always quick to take a poke at Joe, reported that "Capt. Patterson's heart is in the air; notwithstanding that he never learned to fly. He tried hard. He spent weeks, months under the patient tutelage of Lieut. Frederick H. Becker at the Curtiss Field School. He got along all right when Becker was with him. But on his first solo flight he sat frozen at the controls, and missed collision in a crowded sky by sheer act of God." Lieutenant Becker reported a more restrained version of the incident in the plane's pilot's log: "Mr. Patterson swiped his ship while I was at a football game, soloed all over the place, landing on the third attempt."

Nevertheless, Joe was smitten with flying, and though he would never excel in the cockpit, he became an adequate pilot. In 1928 he acquired a $75,000, three-ton Sikorsky amphibian, with two 520-horsepower Hornet engines and a speed of 140 miles per hour. Although awkward appearing on the exterior, this precursor of today's private jet was a lavish air yacht, featuring a luxurious red leather and lacquer cabin with commodious chaise lounges. Joe christened his new toy *Liberty* after his magazine. That December, he, Becker and twenty-two-year-old Alicia launched a cruise of the Caribbean in *Liberty*, taking with them Joe's old friend and colleague, the dashing one-eyed foreign correspondent Floyd Gibbons. Never one to overlook an opportunity, Gibbons contracted with the *New York Times* to send back dispatches on the voyage. Also aboard were an engineer and a radioman who joined the foursome in grazing the Caribbean area for almost a month, first flying to Cuba, where they spent four days in Havana, then cruising the neighboring sea and setting down in the harbor of one island port after another. It was a leisurely sampling of cockfights, jai alai matches and other island attractions, under the surveillance of the American press, led by Floyd Gibbons's lively reports to the *Times*.

The Pattersons were on the vanguard of a rapidly advancing

development, one that had already begun to fundamentally transform history. Charles Lindbergh's nonstop solo flight to Paris in 1927 had made him an international hero to a degree that no other United States civilian has since matched, and although most Americans did not themselves fly, they were enthusiastic spectators. Among the few who became committed participants were Joe and Alicia, soon joined by sixteen-year-old Josephine. Both girls joined their father as pupils of Lieutenant Becker, and under his guidance all three passed tests for pilot licenses, earning Becker the bonus of a gold watch. Having met the challenge of acquiring a license, Joe's interest in flying soon wore off and by 1932 he stopped entirely. But Alicia and Josephine continued to be enthusiastic pilots; Joe gave each her own Laird biplane and watched with pride as his daughters became expert aviatrixes following in the footsteps of Amelia Earhart. Five years after Lindbergh's phenomenal crossing, Earhart became the first woman to conquer the Atlantic alone. The boyish Amelia exuded a certain sex appeal, as did almost any pretty young woman dressed to fly. An aviator's helmet, with goggles propped high on the forehead, was flattering to the features, the lamb collar of a leather flight jacket framed the face prettily and a pilot's jumpsuit about a shapely form was subtly seductive. It was also a utilitarian look and one the Patterson women adopted concurrently with Earhart while setting flight records and embarking on aeronautic exploits of their own.

Alicia was the eighteenth woman in the United States to earn the demanding transport pilot's license, and she was soon setting a series of women's one-way speed records, including routes between Cleveland and New York, Philadelphia and New York and the round-trip record between Albany and New York. But her flight history was not without blemish; in early 1930 she landed her plane on top of a mowing machine at the Miami municipal airport, injuring two city employees. By that year Josephine was flying professionally; at age seventeen she had managed to wangle a job as a commercial pilot, transporting mail between St. Louis and Chicago, the youngest pilot to do so.

The aeronautic adventures of Joe's daughters soon gained a global dimension. In January 1931, Alicia and Libby Chase—sister of Janet Chase, who had joined Alicia on her honeymoon—flew from Sydney, Australia, across the continent's interior nineteen hundred miles to Darwin, almost all of which was unpopulated desert. They relieved the journey by stopping along the way to hunt kangaroo at an oasis in intense heat of more than 110 degrees in the shade. From Australia they journeyed to Java by ship before flying 775 miles to Singapore. Two years later, following Josephine's January 1933 coming-out party, Josephine, Alicia and Libby traveled to India to stalk wild boar and hunt tigers in an expedition that would grip the imagination of Depression-era America. By day they flew—Alicia and Josephine sharing the controls—or indulged in sightseeing; at night they partied and slept in an assortment of exotic metropolises. After arriving in Marseilles, the trio hopscotched their way by air from Marseilles to Rome, and on to Athens, where, Alicia reported, they were able to hire a car and driver for fifteen cents an hour, buy a bottle of fine wine for ten cents and stay cheaply in an acceptable hotel.

From Athens it was a five-and-a-half-hour hop to Cairo and such adventures as riding camels to visit the Sphinx and the pyramids. Next was Baghdad, and then Djask in Persia to catch their breaths before flying the final thousand miles to Jodhpur. Once in India, the women proceeded to pursue the dangerous sport of pig-sticking. Libby succeeded in killing a wild boar, becoming the first woman ever to do so. When it came time for the big hunt in which Alicia was to kill a tiger, Josephine instead shot the tiger. Infuriated, Alicia insisted that her sister stay out of the next hunt; Josephine obliged by bringing along only a book, which she read sitting in a tree. When a leopard leapt up behind her, she hurled her makeshift weapon, hitting the elegant creature in the nose. However, in the words of the *New York Times*, "Alicia finished it off."

The glamour and currency of aviation prompted Alicia to write trendy articles on the subject for such national publications as *Vogue* and her father's *Liberty*. But she was more often the subject of news stories than their writer, and frequently they involved her romantic life. Six months after the divorce from Simpson, she was reportedly engaged to Shanghai businessman Peter Grimm, whom she had met aboard a ship bound for Tokyo from French Indochina, where she had bagged a rare and ferocious water buffalo, the sladang. Alicia called the engagement item absurd, insisting she had never been alone with the man for more than a half hour. The sladang was another matter. Alicia was the first white woman to kill such a beast, and members of the Moi aboriginal tribe—her guides in the hunt—celebrated the feat with a tom-tom ceremony. At its end they marked a cross in blood on Alicia's forehead, dubbing her "hunt lady," before settling down to feast on the animal's carcass.

Competing with aviation and big-game hunting for Alicia's time was bona fide employment. She continued to write for her father's *Liberty*, and in one well-received series, she assumed the identity "Agnes Homberg," writing a succession of how-to pieces on finding a job without experience. In researching the articles she sold magazine subscriptions, cashiered at a movie theater and trained to be a house detective. Josephine, also aspiring to a journalism career, hoped to be a newspaper reporter but her father would not hire her. She nevertheless triumphed by landing not merely a reporting job but an authentic *Front Page*-style beat with the *Chicago Daily News*, covering murder trials in the criminal courts and interviewing such notorious killers as Baby Face Nelson.

Alicia continued to be Joe's sidekick and protégée, perhaps more than ever before. He took her with him to visit Lord Beaverbrook in England and along on his New York subway expeditions. She also accompanied him on a trip to inspect drought areas of the Southwest, as always a willing companion and eager student. Of the years she worked for Joe and was his cohort, Alicia said, "To live up to father was my ambition, and to be his companion a priceless education. I traveled with him wherever in the world news was breaking. It was a fine experience, and always fun, but it shut me off from the day-to-day grind of big and little news assignments that transform a cub reporter into a pro." She later added, "the best thing about him was his wonderful curiosity and interest. He taught me to see things and to be curious."

JOE ALSO ENJOYED the time they spent together, but once again he decided Alicia should marry, and this time his candidate was Joseph W. Brooks, another robust American man in the style Patterson appreciated. A onetime all-American football tackle, sportsman, aviator and, like Joe, a captain in World War I's illustrious Rainbow Division, Brooks had continued a close friendship with Patterson after the war. Physically he was everything Joe was or wanted to be—and even taller than the six-foot Patterson. A successful insurance broker, Brooks was solvent if not fabulously rich, the son of a top executive of Western Union Telegraph Company, single and fifteen years older than Alicia. Patterson set up the match. He was aware of Brooks's interest in aeronautics, an enthusiasm so intense he piloted his own racing plane and installed an airfield at his trout-fishing camp in the Adirondacks. When Brooks invited Joe to spend a weekend at the six-hundred-acre camp, it was a perfect opportunity for him to show off his daughter, and he asked if Alicia could join them. It was not the love-at-first-sight Patterson had anticipated, but their mutual passion for flying brought the two together regularly, and before long a spark ignited. By fall 1931 they were engaged.

Alicia became Mrs. Joseph Brooks on December 23 in New York's Broadway Tabernacle, in the presence of the couple's families, including Cissy and Felicia. This time the bride was more chic than traditional in a maroon crepe afternoon gown by Paris couturier Madeleine Vionnet, which she accessorized with a maroon velvet turban and a high-fashion bouquet of brown and yellow orchids. After the ceremony, guests traveled up to Joe's building at Fifth Avenue and 84th Street for a wedding breakfast in the apartment he had built for Alicia. The honeymoon, spent flying through the American South, was again chaperoned; however, this time Alicia and her bridegroom were accompanied not by a childhood friend but a mechanic who kept their plane in shape throughout the tour. Among their stops were Greensboro, North Carolina, for quail hunting; the Miami area, where they went deep-sea fishing; and Tampico, Mexico.

Joe was determined that this marriage succeed. He had always provided for Alicia, but he wanted to ensure that finances would never be a problem in a union he had so carefully engineered. He settled an income of twenty-five thousand dollars a year on his daughter, and while the newlyweds were on their honeymoon, he bought three choice acres of Sands Point for a house to be designed by Raymond Hood. The finished product was a gracious machine for entertaining, with a handsome living room, dining room and library, as well as a game room/taproom and spacious porches and terracing. There were also his-and-her bedrooms for Alicia and Brooks, three guest bedrooms and a trio of servants' rooms. For all of this, Joe charged the couple one dollar a year in rent.

It was a generous gift, but once again Patterson had imposed his will on his daughter. Raymond Hood, whose style had recently progressed from Art Deco to cutting-edge modern, created a design that, according to a contemporary issue of *Arts & Decoration* magazine, "could only have been built today" and "is really of no previous style." Unfortunately, neither her father nor the architect had considered Alicia's personal taste, which tended toward the English country–style. Therefore the interiors created by her decorator, Chez Nous, featuring the traditional elements of chintz and Chippendale, were at war with the basic lines of Hood's design. To complete the idiosyncratic mélange, bathroom walls throughout were decorated with primitive jungle murals of tigers, palm trees and flying monkeys in bright secondary colors. The artist was the ubiquitous Janet Chase.

Throughout Alicia's party-prone life, there was always a parent or a spouse endeavoring to keep her "busy" or "moving." Most often it was her father, who now offered her a job in the advertising department of the *News*. She countered by saying she would rather be in editorial, but then commented, "The main thing is I want to learn the newspaper game backwards and forwards. Who knows? I might be a great publisher myself someday." Although she worked sporadically for the *News*, mainly as a book reviewer, what she really did with her time was play. Alicia truly enjoyed her charming husband; together they hunted, fished, flew, toured nightclubs and attended social events in Manhattan and Long Island. With Alicia's income, she and Brooks were able to buy eighteen hundred acres on the St. Marys River near the Okefenokee Swamp in Georgia, where at river's bend they built a six-room quail-shooting lodge. The simple building, constructed of clear cypress, blended into its environment with shutters painted a muted pink, the same shade as the fungus growing on the trees around it. Their informal name for the property was Kingsland, for a nearby town. The natural simplicity of Kingsland, where alligators swam in the black waters of the river and Spanish moss hung from live oak trees surrounding the property, was in contrast to the sophistication of the rest of Alicia's life and it would be her much-loved haven as long as she lived.

Alicia's marriage to Brooks was idyllic, perhaps too much so as years passed without children to mark their passage. Her one pregnancy was ectopic, after which she was unable to bear a child, and Brooks had added to his sporting activities by gambling and rolling up debts, which she paid. By the time the couple passed the seven-year point Alicia was feeling that a life built on sports and attending parties was frivolous. She was feeling a strong desire to make a change.

NOT FAR FROM Joe and Alicia Brooks's house in Sands Point was the estate of copper smelting heir Harry Frank Guggenheim, whose passion for aeronautics was, if anything, stronger than that of those in the extended Patterson clan; in fact, Harry Guggenheim was possibly American aviation's earliest and greatest aficionado. Concerned about lack of governmental support for flight in the mid-1920s, Harry had convinced his father to back the new industry philanthropically, and in January 1926 they announced establishment of the Daniel Guggenheim Fund for the Promotion of Aeronautics. When Charles

Lindbergh took off for Paris from Curtiss Field in May 1927, aviation's new patron saint Harry Guggenheim had been there to wish him God-speed. Although dubious about the young barnstormer's chances of making a successful crossing, he said, "When you get back from your flight look me up."

A major goal of the multimillion-dollar Guggenheim Fund was to convince the American public of the safety of flight, and with the unprecedented success of the Lindbergh expedition Harry had the perfect tool for this purpose. Guggenheim believed that the public, although fascinated by Lindbergh, was continuing to keep commercial aviation at arm's length because of a general concern about its hazards. He wanted to demonstrate the ease and safety with which air transportation could be incorporated into everyday life, and the triumph of the Lindbergh flight provided a perfect opportunity to communicate his position to the American public. To this end the Guggenheim Fund sponsored Lindy and his plane, the *Spirit of St. Louis,* in an eighty-two-city transcontinental tour, resulting in a large increase in pilot's license applications and airplane sales, as well as a sizable swelling in the use of airmail. The tour also began a close lifelong connection between Guggenheim and Lindbergh.

At any number of Sands Point parties, Alicia, increasingly dissatisfied with the purposelessness of her life, was thrown together with the rich, and exceedingly purposeful, Harry Guggenheim, whose devotion to the cause of aviation gave them a substantial interest in common. He too had reached a crisis in his second marriage.

·19·

THE BITTERSWEET REVENGE
OF ALICIA'S *NEWSDAY*

H ARRY Guggenheim was not merely a rich man; he was among the richest men in America. His Swiss grandfather Meyer Guggenheim arrived in the United States in 1847 and began making money almost immediately. The Midas-fingered Meyer first peddled goods door-to-door in the Pennsylvania coal-mining region, but when the most popular product in his pack proved to be stove polish, he became a manufacturer of stove polish. He followed by successfully importing spices and herbs, before building a substantial business in laces and embroidery, and then he made a profit in railroad stocks. Next was mining, where he hit the jackpot. After initially investing in Colorado lead and silver mines, Meyer graduated to other metals and their refinement. Eventually the family occupied a presence in mines internationally: Mexico, Alaska, Bolivia, Chile and even in the diamond mines of South Africa, but its great wealth came from smelting, a process for extracting a metal from its ore. As Stephen Birmingham states in his 1967 bestselling book, *Our Crowd,* Meyer's heirs "amassed what may have been the greatest single fortune in America. The only fortune that may outweigh the Guggenheims' is that of John D. Rockefeller."

But rarely was gentlemanly conduct involved. Wherever Guggenheims ventured they were aggressive—and tough. They thrashed the railroads on transport fees and were uncompromising strikebreakers.

They pitted armed ruffians against the miners who worked for them and forcefully evicted those who did not. Of Meyer Guggenheim's seven sons, Daniel, born in 1856, was the leader and most determined, and Daniel's son Harry was his father's equal. When the dynasty emerged from World War I with a total worth of as much as $300 million, Guggenheim ranked second only to Rothschild as the world's wealthiest Jewish family. Further riches poured into Guggenheim coffers with the sale of its Chilean copper company to the Anaconda Copper Mining Company for a dizzying $70 million in the early 1920s; it was the largest private mining transaction that had ever occurred internationally.

Daniel Guggenheim's personal dominion from 1910 was an Irish-style castle on 216 acres of that abundantly moneyed territory Sands Point, Long Island, not far from the future estates of Cissy and the Swopes, or the property Joe would buy for Alicia and Joe Brooks. Daniel named his castle Hempstead House and in 1923—when Sands Point was entering its Gatsby heyday—he gave a large portion of the land overlooking Long Island Sound to Harry and his second wife, Carol. There the younger Guggenheims built Falaise, a thirty-room Norman-style manor house and furnished it with museum-quality furniture, paintings, tapestries and objets d'art. It was in the splendor of Falaise that the unhappily married Harry Guggenheim was living during the late 1930s when he and his neighbor Alicia Brooks repeatedly found each other together at the community's many social events. Harry was also a regular at Saratoga Springs, to which Alicia, her husband and much of the Sands Point crowd would gravitate during the August race meet. While the affable Joseph Brooks was gambling and neglecting his wife, Harry spent time charming her with his courtly attentions.

If in the arena of sex and romance opposites attract, Harry and Alicia were fateful magnets for each other and proved the theory, initially. She was a liberal; he was a die-hard conservative. She was a frivolous thirty-two-year-old woman who, despite her big-game hunting and aviation glamour, had never really held a job or accomplished anything of note. At almost forty-nine, Harry was an intensely serious former executive of the Chile Copper Company, who had spent four years as United States ambassador to Cuba during the Herbert Hoover administration, and he had the foresight to back the rocket experiments upon which the American space program would be built. In addition to being a consummate philanthropist who presided over two of the family's multimillion-dollar foundations, Harry was a former World War I naval officer and owner of a fine Thoroughbred racing stable, later to produce 1953 Kentucky Derby winner Dark Star. And his personal visibility in New York would increase with his role as board president of the Frank Lloyd Wright–designed Solomon R. Guggenheim Museum, established by an uncle. Possibly the most important, and ominous, difference between the two was money. Alicia had never thought about it; everything she needed had always been provided by her father. But money was power to the Guggenheims, who had used it carefully, and none of his predecessors had been more wary in guarding the family wealth than Harry, as Alicia would discover.

Their score was even in the marriage department. In 1910 Harry wed Helen Rosenberg, with whom he had two daughters in a marriage that lasted a dozen years. After divorcing Helen, he married Caroline "Carol" Morton Potter of the Morton Salt family. A gentile and a divorcée with two daughters, Carol was emotionally unstable and a heavy drinker; their one child together, Diane, was born in 1924. It was a difficult marriage that grew more so during Harry's years as Cuban ambassador from 1929 to 1933, when their incessant quarreling became more intense. Harry's assignment ended with the election of Franklin Roosevelt and the marriage hobbled along for another four years until they separated in 1937. Central to the couple's difficulties were underlying sexual problems, but it is unclear who was to blame. The outwardly courtly Harry would always say that both his first and second wives were "wonderful women" and that he was the cause of the breakdown of both marriages. But it would not be the last time sexual inactivity would be a factor in a marriage of his.

*   *   *

AFTER TWICE FOLLOWING her father's matrimonial wishes, Alicia had decided when she would marry and to whom. In the summer of 1939, she and Harry traveled to Florida, where they rented separate houses and divorced their spouses. On July 1 they were married by a judge in the Jacksonville home of an old Chicago friend of Alicia's. Again it was a peculiar honeymoon. The never frivolous Harry made Roswell, New Mexico, the destination of their wedding trip, combining it with a visit to physicist Robert Hutchings Goddard. The space scientist's theories about the future of space travel, including a possible flight to the moon, had been ridiculed by the news media and many fellow scientists. But Harry bankrolled Dr. Goddard's rocket experiments and would continue to do so, even though he never saw one of the rockets rise above the ground. Almost alone he believed in the success of the man who would become known as the father of modern rocket propulsion, and as in many matters involving money, Harry's judgment would prove to be correct.

If Joseph Brooks was everything Joe Patterson wanted in his daughter's husband, Harry Guggenheim was all he was against. Not only was Joe furious that Alicia had thrown over his good friend Brooks, but he also held a fundamental aversion to Guggenheim, whom he called a "Goddamn old stuffed shirt." Harry's personal style, that of a gentleman of the Old World, was counter to all Joe stood for, but he had two other major strikes against him as a son-in-law: he was only eleven years Patterson's junior and he was Jewish. "Patterson didn't warm up to Guggenheim," wrote Charles Wertenbaker in 1951. "Perhaps he saw that here was a man—middle-aged, quiet, urbane, determined—with whom he could not compete for Alicia's affections. After her marriage, he sometimes saw Alicia alone, but she wouldn't go to his house without her husband. Finally Patterson called up Guggenheim and asked him to come to dinner. 'No, Joe,' said Guggenheim, 'I think it would be better if you came to my house.' Patterson went. Thereafter the men maintained a cautious friendship."

The house to which Patterson was summoned was, to put it mildly, impressive. Charles Lindbergh, who wrote his bestselling book, *We*, in one of its guest rooms, called Falaise "the most desirable home I have ever been in." Set on a cliff high above Long Island Sound, the house was Guggenheim's 1923 vision of a medieval manor in Normandy; its name was both that of the Norman town where William the Conqueror was born and the French word for cliff. The estate managed to be opulent without being pretentious, exuding a quiet elegance that signaled old money. A drive into Harry's ninety-acre property evoked the image of entering the grounds of Daphne du Maurier's Manderley. After passing through a high black iron gate, surmounted by the letter *G*, visitors continued along a driveway that wound toward another iron gate. Beyond the second gate—silhouetted against the sky— stood a large house of dark red brick, topped by a sharply inclined tiled roof. An enclosed cobblestone-paved courtyard fronted the manor, and along its rear stretched a terrace with a heart-stopping view of Long Island Sound two hundred feet below. Arches and a round tower embellished the manor's exterior and within the house, further arches, heavy dark wood beams, stone fireplaces and thickly plastered walls continued the impression of medieval France. Also on the estate were stables for Harry's Thoroughbred horses, garages housing a fleet of automobiles, miscellaneous outbuildings and an enclosed swimming pool. Throughout the grounds Harry's gardeners tended lush lawns edged with flowering bushes and expanses of seasonal blossoms. The effect was not merely imposing, it was romantic; the impact was not lost on Francis Ford Coppola, who used Harry's stables and a room at Falaise, with a portrait of Alicia on the wall, as location sets for a palatial estate in *The Godfather*.

Regardless of Joe's aversion to him, Harry was an attractive man. At forty-eight, the blue-eyed Guggenheim was still fit, impeccably turned out and, with his patrician bearing and superb manners, he was agreeable company. But perhaps his greatest appeal for Alicia was that he appreciated her for her intelligence. On the other hand Harry was from rigid Swiss-German stock, annoyingly measured and controlling in all he did—though dominating Alicia Patterson would not be an easy task. In the beginning the two were immensely attracted to each other, but after about a year, Harry lost interest in her physically— providing Alicia with a second father figure when what she needed was a sexual partner.

BUT HARRY GAVE Alicia something that was better than sex. He gave her a newspaper. He saw the unfocused intelligence and drive, as well as her need for an interest beyond hunting, shooting, tennis and attending parties. "Everybody ought to have a job," he said, in announcing that he would buy his bride a paper to occupy her energies. "People who make a business of pleasure seldom are happy." At the time, Alicia thought she would inherit a powerful position at the *Daily News;* certainly Harry believed she would and he wanted her to prepare by publishing a small newspaper. Almost immediately, a facility became available within a short drive of Falaise. It was the *Nassau County Daily Journal*—the only paper ever founded by the senior S. I. Newhouse—but it had folded within nine days to avoid a labor dispute from spreading to a sister paper, the *Long Island Press*. Before putting down cash, the cautious Harry first commissioned a four-month feasibility study to determine whether he was making a viable investment. He was. Although in 1940 no one could have imagined the astonishing post–World War II expansion of Nassau County, the study's projection of sufficient growth, coupled with weak competition, was adequate. So Harry spent fifty thousand dollars to buy the paper and its presses, all housed in a former automobile showroom in Hempstead. The weak competition referred to in the study was the *Nassau Daily Review-Star*, a stiff, staunchly Republican paper, whose publisher was a party committeeman, James E. Stiles, with close ties to the county Republican leader.

Alicia had a formidable task ahead: a staff to be assembled, secondhand equipment restored to working order and the design and concept of a newspaper created. But she did it all, beginning with the paper's fundamental style. "I favored a tabloid," recalled the daughter of the genre's king, "despite discouragement from my father, who thought a standard size paper would be more acceptable in a suburban community where the population is considered more conservative."Again she called on Janet Chase. Her girlhood friend had married Fred Hauck, a commercial artist, who rolled up his sleeves and designed a tabloid like no other. A horizontal format replaced the expected vertical tabloid design, and Hauck banished column rules, giving a cleaner look to the page. The day's top news stories were assigned to front and back pages. And each column contained either editorial copy or ads, never both. The effect was an upscale, magazine-style appearance— fresh and new. Hauck's design was a compatible showcase for Alicia's concept for the paper's content. She wanted to publish a sparkling, energetic paper that covered local news but in a sophisticated style. National and international news would be covered, but with the emphasis on its significance to Long Island readers. In her words, "My job is to make *Newsday* readable, entertaining, comprehensive, informative, interpretive, lively, but still sufficiently serious-minded so that no Long Islander will feel compelled to read any New York City paper." After hiring staff and holding a contest to select a name for the new paper, Alicia published the first issue of *Newsday* on September 3, 1940. In spite of Hauck's brilliant design, the maiden issue was filled with errors and glitches, prompting Alicia to exclaim, "I'm afraid it looks like hell." It didn't help her mood to learn that a member of her staff had immediately taken a copy into the city to show her father, who made no comment on her achievement, then or ever.

Harry had been correct. The carefree, partying, rich man's bride did benefit from having a job; however, editing *Newsday* was far more than "a job" for Alicia. As Stanton Peckham, an early *Newsday* columnist, confidant and sometime playmate of Alicia's, put it, "The burning ambition she had, all she gave a damn about, was to prove to her goddamn family—and she would call them her goddamn family—that she was just as good a newspaperman as any of them." Edith Wyckoff, another Long Island newspaperwoman, added, "People who knew her said, 'Wait, she's not Joe Patterson's daughter for nothing. She's not

Cissy Patterson's niece for nothing.' "Nor was she Joseph and Kitty Medill's great-granddaughter for nothing. After years during which her father honed her competitive nature while impeding her creative instincts, Alicia Patterson now had a newspaper to craft day by day. But Harry owned the paper; he had bankrolled *Newsday* and would continue to do so until it broke even in 1946. Alicia was in effect his unpaid employee, although he gave her an initial equity of a four-thousand-dollar "participation" and a document that read, "In lieu of salary, you are to receive one-half of the net profits to me from *Newsday* that may accrue in any calendar year"—profits that would be far in the future.

Fundamental differences between the two, which may have been charming during courtship, were beginning to impact not only their relationship but also the publication of *Newsday*. Alicia was and always would be a liberal. And Harry was a dyed-in-the-wool conservative, creating a fundamental schism in their marriage that would ultimately destroy the long-range dreams she held for her beloved paper. It was also creating an editorial predicament in the short term. The 1940 presidential election was looming; Alicia was pro-FDR and Harry was backing Wendell Willkie. It might have been a hopeless dilemma were there not a family precedent for precisely this type of editorial schizo-phrenia. Just as the liberal Joe and conservative Bert had performed a balancing act at the *Chicago Tribune* decades earlier, Alicia, *Newsday*'s editor and publisher, wrote a column supporting the incumbent Roo-sevelt while Harry, the paper's owner and president, penned an oppos-ing column favoring Willkie, the Republican candidate.

"THOSE WERE RUGGED days," Alicia remembered of the first years of *Newsday*. "The presses broke down regularly. Our editorial staff of less than twenty-five had to queue up for the available desks and typewriters. The cartoonist and editorial writer worked in the com-posing room, alongside the typesetting machines. My first office had no windows, and reminded me of the black hole of Calcutta. The floor was so cold in winter that I kept my feet in a desk drawer or in the wastebasket." And that was before the war. With Pearl Harbor came government curtailment of every sort, and newsprint rationing was soon based on mid-1941 circulation. As *Newsday* happily grew from its twenty-six-thousand circulation of that period, Alicia scrimped on paper by rationing ad space for the duration. At first she thought of joining the war effort herself; aviatrix Jacqueline Cochran had established a group of women flyers, who were transporting planes to air bases from factories, and Alicia considered going to England with her. But Harry stopped that. They couldn't both go and he was committed. The World War I veteran, now over fifty, returned to the navy as commandant of Mercer Field, a naval air station outside Trenton, New Jersey. He later served in combat in the Pacific, and emerged as the sole navy pilot to have served in action in both world wars. She wanted to take in some English children for the war's duration, as many American families were, but Harry thought it wrong to expose ordinary children to the luxe Guggenheim lifestyle. When Alicia found a brother and sister from a wealthy, highborn family, he agreed, hence Patrick and Janka Koenigswarter, whose baroness mother was a Rothschild, spent the war years at Falaise with their nanny.

World War II created domestic upheaval for families internationally, and Alicia and Harry—with their barren intimate life—were not exceptions. According to Guggenheim family chroniclers Irwin and Debi Unger, Harry "had girl friends" while married to Alicia; the most visible was a WAVE, referred to only as Miss Sullivan, with whom he had a liaison while at Mercer Field. During the same period, Alicia was spending personal time with *Newsday* columnist and editorial writer Stan Peckham in a relationship he described as "quite romantic." Peckham, then an army lieutenant, visited her regularly at Falaise, as well as at the Savoy Plaza in New York, and they corresponded through a post office box she leased under an assumed name. Alicia also continued to see Joe Brooks after her marriage to Harry. They fished together at his camp in the Adirondacks and made quail-shooting trips to her Georgia hunting lodge. She never lost her fondness for him, and Brooks—still hurt by the end of their marriage—implied to her nephew Joe Albright, another fishing companion, that he hoped she would leave Harry. The relationship would come to an irrevocable end in November 1953 when the rugged Brooks, sixty-two and in poor health, died of a self-inflicted gunshot wound in his Park Avenue apartment.

In her home front capacity, Alicia proved to be a hands-on executive who managed to be "everywhere" at the paper's small plant. In the early days she had dealt with a series of alcoholic editors, but as they were drafted to serve in World War II her staff became increasingly female. She did not cosset her new, sometimes inexperienced, women employees; she championed them, pushing them to excel. She was also pushing herself—and the paper. Fearlessly, she took on the *Nassau Daily Review-Star*, which was growing rich from the hugely profitable county legal ads awarded it. She argued against a monopoly the paper held on taxpayer-supported advertising, brought in by its Republican committeeman publisher, and further noted that the ads were being printed in inappropriately large type. Hammering away editorially on both points, she insisted *Newsday* could run the same ads more economically and save taxpayer money. Eventually she won. After that, the *Review-Star*'s days were numbered.

Following the war, *Newsday* fought in favor of low-cost housing for veterans and supported Levitt & Sons, the real estate developer planning massive tracts of affordable houses on slabs. The paper fought aggressively for a change in the local ordinance requiring basements, and won. Thus Levittown, the famous postwar expanse of look-alike houses, sprang up in *Newsday*'s backyard, swelling its circulation base and producing advertisers wishing to reach new residents occupying the houses. It was the beginning of a newspaper phenomenon, and Alicia was its dynamic leader. She may not have anticipated the unprecedented population explosion in her circulation territory, but she maximized the miracle that brought in thousands of new families needing furniture, appliances, automobiles, food, clothing and other goods, along with the merchants eager to reach them through advertising. Echoing her ancestor Judge Patrick, who had sent his sons out on horseback across neighboring Ohio fields to deliver the *Tuscarawas Chronicle*, *Newsday* employed the children of the new residents to distribute the paper to subscribers. As many as eighteen hundred newsboys at a time were not only employed by *Newsday* but also treated as valuable star athletes.

IN MARCH 1949, three and a half years after the war's end, *Newsday* moved to a shining new Garden City plant, fifteen miles from Falaise. With the progression of the 1950s, Alicia's status as a distinguished personage in her industry became assured; those in New York City media circles routinely referred to her paper as "Alicia Patterson's *Newsday*." The fact that it carried more advertising than any evening newspaper in Manhattan was in itself an impressive achievement. Her editorial excellence was recognized when *Newsday*'s coverage of graft and corruption at New York racetracks won the top Pulitzer Prize for the most "disinterested and meritorious public service rendered by a U.S. newspaper" in 1953. It was an amazing accomplishment, and furthermore the paper was now hers, at least 49 percent hers. When she received a sizable bequest in 1946, she had written Harry asking to become an owner. This message was in keeping with the couple's custom of carrying on communication about *Newsday* in writing, as was his reply. "As you know, I desire to retain a controlling interest in the enterprise, and accordingly I am prepared to sell you a 49 percent interest in NEWSDAY, which on the overall value of $165,000, comes to $80,850." Their mutual friend *New York Post* publisher Dorothy Schiff confirmed what Alicia suspected: "Harry told me he kept control because he knew she would leave him if she had that additional two percent." Although there were challenges and setbacks at the office, it had become a happier place for Alicia than her home. She was now an owner rather than Harry's employee, but the 2 percent difference was an inequality that triggered almost nightly arguments between them.

Alicia's daily schedule had continued unchanged, her attention completely absorbed in running the paper, with management of the household turned over to a secretary and six servants. After rising at eight in the morning and breakfasting in bed with the New York papers, she drove her Oldsmobile coupe to the Garden City plant, where she worked in a small office off the city room from ten-thirty in the morning until cocktail time. Most evenings the Guggenheims entertained friends and neighbors, who included assorted celebrities of the day, among them actress Katharine Cornell, theatrical producer George Abbott, financier Bernard Baruch, war hero Jimmy Doolittle and publisher Bennett Cerf, with his wife, Phyllis, who later married New York's mayor Robert Wagner. Alicia made time for a few diversions: tennis, chess and riding her horses—Newsboy, Copyboy and Alicia P. Periodically she would retreat alone to Kingsland to shoot quail and swim or boat in the river's black water. Summers she visited Josephine in Wyoming, enjoying the time she spent at her sister's ranch with Josephine and her children, but it was always back to the paper.

Newsday was increasingly the only glue holding Alicia in her marriage. It was simple: without marriage to Harry, she had no hope of controlling her beloved paper, but as passionate as she was about *Newsday*, she also felt an overwhelming desire to leave the deteriorating relationship. In addition, there was a powerful exterior pull. She had been in a youthful romance with future Democratic presidential candidate Adlai E. Stevenson II during the 1920s and in 1947 she began seeing him again. Both were married to others, but his marriage to Ellen Borden was crumbling toward their 1949 divorce. Despite rumors to the contrary, fueled by Ellen, Stevenson was immensely attracted to the opposite sex, and vice versa. He particularly enjoyed beautiful, well-dressed women of means and sophistication. After his marriage dissolved, he had warm relationships with a number of cultivated, glamorous—and usually strong-willed—women, who had in common an illustrious male relative. Among them were Susie Morton Zurcher, granddaughter of Morton Salt founder Joy Morton; Marietta Peabody Tree, whose grandfather, the Reverend Endicott Peabody, founded Groton School; Dorothy Fosdick, daughter of the Reverend Harry Emerson Fosdick, for whom John D. Rockefeller Jr. built New

York's Riverside Church; and the widows of Marshall Field III, advertising tycoon Albert Lasker and Walter Paepcke, founder of Aspen, Colorado.

The woman Adlai had chosen to marry was Ellen Borden, a beautiful, artistic but tragically disturbed heiress who was surrounded by achieving relatives. Her grandfather, mining engineer William Borden, and his father had joined Marshall Field and Levi Leiter in a Leadville, Colorado, silver mining venture, from which each of the four netted a million dollars. William parlayed his stake into a real estate fortune, which enabled his children to lead colorful, and usually artistic, lives that brought them international prominence. Among the four celebrated Borden siblings was Ellen's father, John, a fabled professional explorer, whose harrowing expeditions made national front-page news, and her mother, the former Ellen Waller, rivaled Mrs. Potter Palmer as "queen of Chicago Society." Adlai had married a lovely, talented woman who was thwarted by a family of competitive superstars.

Adlai Stevenson and Harry Guggenheim were quite different men, and Adlai found Alicia very desirable physically. Between 1947 and 1951 they were locked in a passionate affair, and as torrid as it was, their relationship was also lighthearted and fun. After *Newsday*'s circulation went over one hundred thousand in 1949, he wrote her, "So you've made it—you indomitable little tiger. I could just bite your ears with savage joy." And he added, "I *know* you're a hard little empire builder—but I *love* a woman—a gentle, wise, compassionate woman—not a mighty, ruthless, determined conqueror! Or do I?" At the time they were considering marriage, although neither was free. Stevenson biographer and United Nations colleague Porter McKeever believed that it was Alicia "to whom more than anyone else he communicated his innermost thoughts." Addressing her as "Darling Elisha," or just "E," his letters were charmingly lyrical, "Somewhere the sun is shining—and you're in it—in a pool of bright light, your hair is glistening and reddish & tumbling all about your shoulders, your delicate little face serene—and your eyes half shut in reverie. And in a moment I'm going to kiss you and you're going to be all alive again—and so am I." He often referred to the fantasy-like quality of their affair—"I brood about this mysterious dream that's enveloped me for a year and a half"—and wrote of his "reveries of a drowsy, contented man high in the clouds. There is something fitting about coming to you on the wings of wind and floating away from you in the clouds. . . . I'll resist the awful temptation to sweep you up into a soft white ball, that magically, unfolds a sharp, savage little tigress. . . . Then the cocoon will unfold in the moonlight—very soft, very tender, and my heart will stop."

Both were absorbed in their careers but managed to meet, sometimes at his Libertyville estate—not far from the Westwood Farm of her childhood—or in Springfield at the Governor's Mansion, where he once contrived to have columnist Marquis Childs present as a beard, or even at Kingsland. Adlai referred to the river running by her lodge as the Black River, and in one letter he described her retreat as "the fairy land of the Black River . . . with the forest and solitude and you." And in another, "As always it was a charmed moment by the blessed black river with you. I feel reborn, well, strong and peaceful." With the development of Stevenson's career, Alicia was finding her political loyalties going beyond complications with her father and her husband. She had begun championing the former general Dwight D. Eisenhower for president shortly after World War II. When it developed that Stevenson would run against Eisenhower in the 1952 election, she solved the problem by printing editorials that straddled the party fence. "We feel that the country needs a change of administration," began one, "in short, needs Eisenhower. Nevertheless, an honest appraisal of Adlai E. Stevenson makes clear that if the nation prefers another Democrat, Stevenson will make a magnificent president." When she gave a dinner at New York's posh River Club to introduce Adlai to a group of New Yorkers including Dorothy Schiff, Gardner Cowles and Harry and Clare Boothe Luce, Guggenheim wired his regrets: TELL ADLAI HOW SORRY I AM. . . . I WOULD LIKE TO DINE WITH HIM ANYWHERE—EVEN IN THE WHITE HOUSE—IF WE ARE BOTH GUESTS OF IKE.

*   *   *

ALICIA INSISTED ON complete control of the paper's news and editorial content, leaving the business side to Harry, but he was determined to have more presence editorially, thus greater visibility. Although he had been the subject of a 1929 *Time* magazine cover story as Cuban ambassador, he was annoyed when a massive 1954 *Time* piece on *Newsday* scarcely mentioned him and showcased Alicia on the cover. And when the *Saturday Evening Post* published two major pieces on *Newsday* during the 1950s, both focused completely on her. The issue of editorial control rose to a crescendo during the 1956 campaign. Believing Alicia would again endorse Eisenhower, Guggenheim told Republican National Committee chairman Leonard Hall that *Newsday* was behind his candidate. Instead Alicia backed Stevenson. The ensuing storm prompted her to write a letter of resignation, which said in part, "I have chosen to resign because I cannot be a part of transforming a living newspaper put out by journalists into a balance sheet controlled by businessmen." Although she did not follow through by leaving *Newsday*, the Guggenheim marriage reached a new level of domestic hell. At one point she left him and moved in with Phyllis and Bennett Cerf for a few weeks. And she toyed with the idea of selling her *Newsday* stock to S. I. Newhouse—which would infuriate Harry—and use the proceeds to buy the faltering *New York Daily Mirror*, a *Daily News* competitor—revenge against both husband and father. But she did neither, and as unhappy as she was, she remained with both the paper and her marriage.

Alicia may have stayed with Harry because there was no longer urgent motivation to leave. In July 1951 she was confronted by an overwhelming shock when she wrote Stevenson that she was contemplating a divorce, and he pulled back. "Elisha dearest," he wrote, "I am sorely distressed by this turn of events. . . . Certainly to seek a divorce impetuously would be, I should think, a great mistake." His contemporaries believed that Stevenson had been deeply hurt by the breakdown of his marriage to Ellen Borden and thus consistently avoided embarking upon another union that might ultimately dissolve. Two of Adlai's closest lifetime friends were A. B. Dick Company heir Edison Dick and his wife, Jane, who had grown up with Alicia. Jane Dick was moved to write Stevenson that she knew Alicia well and liked her, "but to say that she is temperamentally unstable, self-centered and demanding puts it very mildly. Qualities that may be interesting, amusing, even appealing in a friend are often not those that work out very satisfactorily in a more intimate sort of relationship. . . . BEWARE AND BE FIRM."

Although Alicia would never again mention the possibility of divorce, with its implication of their subsequent marriage, she and Adlai continued to be magnetically bonded, maintaining a loving exchange of letters and repeatedly turning up in the same place at the same time in various parts of the world. In the fall of 1952 she became so gravely ill that she didn't expect to survive, and Adlai—by mail—was tender and caring. In late September she underwent exploratory surgery at New York's Doctors' Hospital to discover the cause of abdominal pains and a high fever she was experiencing. A preliminary diagnosis indicated uterine cancer; however, further surgery uncovered a large tumor in her colon, resulting in removal of the tumor as well as a hysterectomy and a temporary colostomy. On October 12 he wrote, "A letter from Josephine brings me the shocking news about your operations, that you can't talk by phone etc." And on October 28, after receiving a feeble written answer from her, Adlai replied that her letter "sounds so tired." Seven years later Alicia wrote of the experience. "I completely lost the will to live. It was Josephine who restored it to me. She sat by my bedside for hours at a time and cussed me out as a yellowbelly until I got so mad I decided to 'show her.' "

THE MOST STABLE relationship of Alicia's adult life was with Josephine, then divorced from Jay Frederick Reeve, whom she had married in 1936 when she was twenty-three. Fred Reeve was a high-powered litigator twenty years Josephine's senior who, according to their son, "virtually fell apart when he lost an important case." The marriage disintegrated soon after and they divorced in 1944. Josephine took their children, Joseph, seven, and Alice, four, with her to Dubois, Wyoming, where she raised horses.

In 1946 she married the celebrated painter Ivan Le Lorraine Albright, identical twin of artist Malvin Marr Albright. Ivan was a meticulous realist who specialized in uncomfortably detailed, decaying subjects typified by the ghoulish portrait of actor Hurd Hatfield he painted for the MGM film *The Picture of Dorian Gray*. His wedding present to Josephine was a painstaking rendering of a wax funeral wreath on a door, evaluated—by the artist—at $125,000. After their marriage, Ivan adopted Joseph and Alice, who assumed the Albright surname, and were followed by Adam, born in 1947, and Blandina, or Dina, in 1949. With her newspaper background and four children, Josephine was a perfect fit to write the column "Life with Junior" for *Newsday*. During the school year the family lived in a house at 55 East Division Street in Chicago and in the summer months Josephine took the children to her Wyoming ranch. When eighteen-year-old Alice was a student at Radcliffe in 1959, she was the first woman writer named to the editorial board of the Harvard *Crimson*. The occasion prompted her to announce that her ambition was to run a newspaper that would be "*The New York Times* with guts."

While a Williams College student, Joe Albright spent the summer of 1957 working as an intern for the *Denver Post*, where he met and fell in love with Madeleine Korbel, a fellow intern who also hoped for a career in journalism. When they married in June 1959, three days after Madeleine's Wellesley graduation, she became Madeleine Albright, the identity she would bear as U.S. ambassador to the United Nations and U.S. secretary of state. The newlyweds first settled in Chicago, where Joe worked for the *Chicago Sun-Times* and Madeleine, as she recalled in her autobiography, *Madam Secretary*, attempted to "figure out how to socialize with local debutante types, some of them former girlfriends of Joe." She also evoked the bizarre domestic atmosphere that Ivan's artistic style lent to her in-laws' house on the city's conventional Near

North Side. "I never got used to his depiction of the Temptations of St. Anthony," she remembered, "with drowning corpses being devoured by half-eaten fish while slavering wolves looked on. This spectacle hung above the dining room table."

"It was a very hard family to be a part of," a tangential family member told Ann Blackman, one of Madeleine's several biographers. "Josephine was a rather mean alcoholic and acted very nasty to Madeleine. . . . She had a lot of anger in her that would focus on whoever happened to be around." Josephine's onetime son-in-law James Hoge Jr. added that she "could be very impatient, very upfront with her emotions. You could tell when she didn't like you. She sizzled a lot. . . . There were days when you just couldn't do anything right." Madeleine more kindly characterized her new mother-in-law as "a mixture of rebel and socialite . . . alternately charming and blunt." And she was even more restrained in describing the behavior of her new sister-in-law Alice, whom she asked to be a bridesmaid at her wedding. Alice "hated" the pale green dress Madeleine selected for her to wear, and "after the wedding and the picture taking she ripped it in two and left it in the trash basket in the bathroom."

It was Madeleine's "larger than life" Aunt Alicia whom she found especially fascinating. "She looked like Katharine Hepburn in *The Lion in Winter* and dressed like the Duchess of Windsor. She was also just plain gutsy. She smoked, drank, hunted big game and quail, played tennis and bridge, all with elegant style." And Madeleine was charmed by the septuagenarian Alice Patterson, whom she remembered as "less than five feet tall, frail and beautiful." Fortunately she accepted Madeleine warmly as her grandson's fiancée and took her to lunch at the Casino in Chicago, where the future diplomat noticed all the lunching ladies surrounding them at the elite club wearing hats. When she defensively mentioned to Joe's grandmother that she wasn't able to find a hat she liked at Wellesley and thought she would buy one in Chicago, Alice said, "Wonderful idea," and took her directly over to Bes-Ben, a fabled local milliner, where she had Madeleine fitted for a two-hundred-dollar custom-made hat, "an Easter present." Continuing to

be extravagant as her age advanced, Alice would present her grandchildren Alice and Joe Albright each with a red Mercedes-Benz automobile in 1961, because she thought the cars they were driving were
"beneath them."

AS ALICIA'S SUCCESS with *Newsday* had continued to build, so had
the disappointments in her personal life. She was deeply saddened
when Adlai Stevenson made it clear there would be no wedding in
their future, and her domestic life had become a living hell, but these
setbacks could not compare with the deterioration of her relationship
with her father. Colonel McCormick had called her "the ablest woman
publisher this country has ever had." She had won the Pulitzer Prize
for reporting; she was editor and publisher of America's most profitable new daily newspaper of the postwar period; and she drove and
oversaw every detail of it, yet the father who had nurtured her with
such dedication could not forget that she had thrown over his friend
Joe Brooks for Harry Guggenheim. Of all Joe Patterson's peculiar behavior perhaps the oddest was his inability to respect his daughter's
towering achievement. Her unparalleled success in creating *Newsday*
ranked with his own tour de force in giving birth to the *Daily News;*
she had designed and propelled the great journalistic phenomenon of
mid-century America and, although Long Island's astonishing post–
World War II growth was the wave that swept *Newsday* to its stunning
triumph, Alicia did more than merely ride that surge to its crest. Only
she had recognized the opportunity that was there; amazingly, it never
occurred to any of the New York metropolitan papers—including to
her father's *Daily News*—to even attempt to compete for the enviable
circulation and advertising that *Newsday* enjoyed alone.

Joe's retribution had begun soon after her divorce from Brooks and
the new marriage he so despised. Initially he countered by diminish-
ing her through remarks about *Newsday*. When a mutual colleague inquired about Alicia, Joe answered, "Oh, she's all right. She's got a little
paper out in Hempstead, but it isn't going anywhere." He refused to
allow her to publish his comic strips, crucial builders of reader loyalty

for any newspaper of the time, and she never forgot his words of rejection: "I wouldn't give them to anyone else in my circulation area, so why should I give them to you?" He didn't so much as visit *Newsday* until it had been publishing for several years. "He walked in," Alicia recalled, with tears in her eyes, "and he looked around, and he walked out. He didn't say anything." Devastated, she wrote him: "When I started *Newsday* I thought you would be proud and happy that I was trying to follow your lead. But it took the greatest persuasion to get you even to look at the plant. And you never take any interest anymore in anything I do." To the world, Alicia Patterson had scored a great triumph, but because of her father's indifference, it would always have a hollow core.

HUBRIS: FDR AND THE
McCORMICK-PATTERSON AXIS

WHILE Alicia was creating her Long Island newspaper during the middle years of the Franklin Roosevelt administration, the grandchildren of Joseph Medill were at the height of their collective power. Between them they controlled the largest-circulation newspapers in three of the nation's most influential markets: Joe held New York; Bert, Chicago; and Cissy, Washington. By 1941 they were reaching more than three million American readers six days a week and, on the seventh, almost five million, with a combined impact rivaled only by William Randolph Hearst. And long after much of the industry had moved toward an attitude of objectivity, all three were publishing in their grandfather's style of personal journalism—though persuading their readers in individual directions.

Throughout the 1930s the archconservative Colonel opposed Franklin Roosevelt; he deplored the New Deal agencies and was certain his old Groton schoolmate was a communist. Joe and Cissy were, however, both personally close to the president, and their newspapers, particularly the *News*, supported him on most issues. As one of the New Deal's most enthusiastic advocates, Joe not only backed Roosevelt editorially, he advised him, and during the president's first five years in office, Patterson was personally influential in molding New Deal policies. But it was Joe's enthusiastic editorial endorsement to his massive New York readership for which FDR was most grateful.

Cissy became an ardent Roosevelt admirer while covering the 1932 Democratic convention and three weeks after his election traveled in her railroad car to Warm Springs, Georgia, where she interviewed the president-elect and followed with a party in *Ranger* for members of his new "brain trust." Her cordial relationship with FDR stretched back through the years to memories of Roosevelt as the active young man he had been before polio crippled his legs. During an intimate lunch alone at Hyde Park before the 1932 election, the two old friends reminisced about their youth together, and how he had cracked a suitor of hers "on the shinbone at the Chevy Chase Club with one of those marvelous long balls" he was then able to drive. (The discreet candidate didn't mention that he had hit the young man because he had not seen him lying on the grass with Cissy behind a line of bushes.) She also had a long friendship with the First Lady and greatly admired her; FDR's wife was the daughter of Elliott Roosevelt, Theodore's tragically alcoholic brother, but very unlike her cousin Alice Longworth. Cissy thought Eleanor "the noblest woman I have ever known. I adore her above all women." The new First Lady was serenely purposeful and without the vanity of so many of her other friends, qualities Cissy admired and envied. But most of all she was thrilled with the rumor of a romance between Mrs. Roosevelt and a handsome state trooper while she was first lady of New York state. And she was furious when Alice Longworth, dining in a chic Washington restaurant, announced loudly enough to be heard throughout the room, "I don't care what they say, I simply *cannot* believe that Eleanor Roosevelt is a lesbian."

At the Roosevelt inauguration on March 4, 1933, Cissy sat shivering in her sable coat within an inner circle of observers while the new president declared, "the only thing we have to fear is fear itself." She appreciated the historic moment but felt relieved to move into the warmth and geniality of the White House for a reception that followed. Her *Herald* was the only Washington paper to support the new president, but Cissy went beyond all expectations by giving her picture retoucher standing orders to improve the appearance of the unfortunately homely First Lady. The Roosevelts reciprocated. FDR made

Cissy chairman of the Inauguration Ball Patroness Committee and his wife asked her to join the Committee on Human Needs; she was also invited to serve as associate chairman of the Democratic Central Committee. Cissy supported Roosevelt throughout his first term, although the other Hearst papers had turned on the president by 1936; but even she was beginning to cool, personally feeling that Roosevelt's policies were not sufficiently effective in ending the Depression. As always, Cissy was tremendously influenced by her brother and continued to be torn between the two most significant men in her professional life, Joseph Medill Patterson and William Randolph Hearst. In thanking the president for a message he sent to be read at her annual newsboys dinner, Cissy added a postscript inviting him to "drive out some day" to Dower House. When he replied he would do so "when the nice weather starts," she took a further step in suggesting a personal dialogue between the president and Hearst.

Cissy's idea for a meeting between the two men evolved into a White House weekend for Hearst that did not include Marion Davies. To compensate, Marion became Cissy's houseguest for a merry weekend that began on the eve of W.R.'s overnight stay at the executive mansion, with a dinner party for fifty guests, followed by dancing and midnight supper for another two hundred. In Marion's eyes the party truly began at one o'clock and she didn't retire until eight the next morning, making her Dupont Circle visit far more successful than the White House weekend. FDR, while charming, had disagreed with his houseguest on various matters, and Hearst reported he had scarcely slept in the drafty old mansion, swearing to Marion that he would never again "spend a weekend at someone else's house, whether it was the White House or Buckingham Palace." Cissy remained on the presidential fence, but not for long. Her dropping away from Roosevelt began innocently enough during a friendly interview at the White House in which she suddenly accused the president of doing nothing constructive to remove fear in businessmen. He struck back with "All right. You go ahead. Write out exactly what you think I should do to banish fear!" She did, and she did so very publicly.

*   *   *

CISSY'S PAGE-ONE OPEN letter in the *Herald* began: "You once said, with eternal truth, that the only thing to fear is fear itself. . . . This fear is fear of you." In conclusion she wrote, "You have been a great leader and a great man. You can be again." Her brazen knuckle-rapping of the president was itself a national news story; the *New York Times* and other papers published articles about it and Hearst's newspapers reprinted the letter in full. But Cissy was just warming up. Her next hostile move was to launch a campaign against the then-proposed Jefferson Memorial, which she turned into a harangue against the tearing out of cherry trees lining the Tidal Basin in front of the proposed monument. This escalated to a 1960s-style women's march on the White House, followed by a delegation of women who chained themselves to the trees. The cherry trees were torn down and the memorial built, with irreparable damage to the relationship between Cissy and the president.

In Chicago the Colonel was steadfast in his opposition to the incumbent, prompting Roosevelt to claim the McCormick venom had sprung from their Groton days, when Franklin stole a girlfriend of Bert's. The Colonel countered by saying this was just "another one of Frank's shallow lies" and kept up the anti-Roosevelt pressure. Only Joe remained a loyal Roosevelt supporter. To provide a degree of balance in the *News*, he introduced a "battle" page during the 1936 campaign; the regular feature included both parties, but support was clearly for the Democratic candidate. After backing Roosevelt in his second election bid, Patterson received a letter from the president addressed "Dear Joe," which assured him that "the NEWS was worth more to us in the city in the way of votes than all the political meetings and speeches put together." The following September, Patterson lunched with Roosevelt on the yacht *Potomac* and later he and Mary King joined FDR and Eleanor for an afternoon at Hyde Park in a pattern of relative intimacy that would continue through the next several years. Joe's support of the president went beyond editorial endorsement; the *News* was instrumental in raising twenty-seven thousand dollars to install the White House swimming pool so essential for the paralyzed president's daily exercise. And the relationship between the two men became so close that Joe was reportedly in line to be ambassador to the Court of St. James's.

While Roosevelt could not wish for a more loyal supporter than Patterson, his archenemy continued to be McCormick of Chicago, who was rabidly against every aspect of the FDR regime. Bert's growing conservatism had pushed the two cousins further apart ideologically than ever before, finally to the point that his anti-Roosevelt rants became more than Joe could tolerate. However, Bert was stunned when he asked to break up the Tribune Company to provide an equitable financial division between the Chicago and New York newspapers. McCormick, with his business mind, attempted to rationally explain tax ramifications of such a separation, as well as increased difficulty in dealing with Canadian properties and other interests under mutual ownership. Fortunately for the economic welfare of the company, Patterson's attention was being diverted in another direction, and the issue passed.

JOE'S PERSONAL LIFE had continued to evolve during the 1930s. Despite Alice's resistance to a divorce, he optimistically began preparing a home for Mary and Jimmy. After buying 108 acres overlooking the Hudson River at Ossining, New York, in 1930, he commissioned Raymond Hood to design an appropriate country house he would name Eagle Bay. Genuinely wishing to avoid an appearance of affluence, he nevertheless asked for the unusual flourish of a domed rooftop observatory to accommodate a powerful telescope for viewing the heavens at night. The provocative modernist in Hood leapt at the challenge and designed a sprawling boxy but asymmetric house, very open and severely contemporary in style. To tone down a mansion that was now anything but ordinary, Joe had the house painted in World War I naval camouflage, consisting of jagged lightning bolt thrusts of yellows, grays and blues, to make it "inconspicuous." The result—both indoors and out—was a bewildering shock to the Depression-era eye. When

Arts & Decoration magazine published an article and photo layout on the estate in November 1935, writer Fay Hines, stunned by the stark, yet open, design of the house, wrote, "Inside the owner wanted a nice unobstructed view of the countryside. And he got it. There are windows, windows everywhere . . . one feels like a cross between a Nudist Colony and that poem of Edna St. Vincent Millay's about lying on a hilltop and being alone with God, Nature, the sky and a pine tree. For it is bare—but in a way that would be very restful to a febrile New Yorker."

One quirky request was for steel doors in the master bedroom and other upstairs rooms. "I have often been troubled by doors jamming in bad weather," he wrote the architect in April 1930, "and I don't think it is safe to have a door into the hall so that it might jam. Likewise, if possible and advisable would like to have steel frames for the windows." Air-conditioning was added to the house, with Joe paying twenty-three thousand dollars to have central air installed in the living room, master bedroom, his dressing room and the upstairs hallway, an extraordinary amenity—and expense—at the time. Butler and housekeeper accommodations were located in the main house, but scattered nearby were quarters for other servants, a large garage/chauffeur's dwelling and several other smaller houses, including one for the property superintendent. Among the automobiles in the garage were a Packard limousine, a Ford town sedan and a Ford truck; further installations on the grounds included a barn/cowshed, an all-weather ice- and roller-skating rink, a greenhouse, hog house, toboggan slide, beehives, grape arbor and marine housing for five boats.

In the early years it was only Jimmy—now elementary school age—who lived with him, while Mary remained in Riverdale with her sisters but joined Joe and her son most nights for dinner. In a note regretting a 1935 Manhattan dinner invitation, Joe politely detailed a rigid early-morning schedule of study and exercise. "Dining in town throws it out of whack," he explained. There was no way for the gently rebuffed hostess, or anyone else in the outside world, to know that, although still legally married to Alice, Joe spent quiet evenings with his new family and retired early; work began at six in the morning with three uninterrupted hours spent reading papers sent out to him from town, including the *Daily Worker, Wall Street Journal* and *Journal of Commerce*.

In June 1938, after years of steadfast refusal, Alice finally agreed to a divorce. The *Daily News* printed the story in detail on page two—the equivalent to page one in the picture-obsessed *News*. Alice's terms included lifetime annual allowances of a least twenty thousand dollars to each of their daughters, as well as the transfer to them of Tribune Company stock at his death. Joe made his break from Chicago complete that year by resigning from his North Shore country clubs, Onwentsia in Lake Forest in June, and Lake Bluff's Shoreacres in October. He had transferred his membership in the Saddle & Cycle, a family club at the northeast edge of the city, to Alice in late 1935. With a satisfactory home life, his always marginal interest in social organizations had further declined; he did, however, join New York's Lotus Club in March 1938. When Joe and Mary were wed in a New York ceremony a month after the divorce, it was a small family occasion with Bert and Cissy among the witnesses. It had been a long wait for the couple, whose son was sixteen and publicly thought to be Joe's adopted child. This time the *News* played the story of the fifty-nine-year-old publisher marrying fifty-three-year-old Mary on page four, along with a photo of the newlyweds—now quite mature in appearance—preparing to sail on the *Queen Mary* for a honeymoon in Scotland, Ireland and Wales.

Eagle Bay was a stable, tranquil retreat for Joe, Mary and Jimmy, who attended Mary Immaculate School in Ossining. The Patterson partnership was an orderly twenty-four-hour routine. Mary joined Joe in reading the papers at six in the morning, followed by breakfast at seven with more newspapers. After Joe's morning exercise of skating on their personal rink, they boarded a commuter train to Manhattan, a bodyguard riding in the seat behind, and arrived at the Daily News Building between ten and eleven. The quiet routine resumed at night; Joe finished his day with an after-dinner walk before settling down for an evening of reading the history, biography or military books preferred by his grandfather, believing they produced some of his best ideas. He continued to see afternoon movies during the week, and on Sundays Mary joined him in driving to a movie house in nearby Peekskill. The big losers in the happy rearrangement of his domestic life were Joe's daughters, especially Alicia, with what was left of their close father-daughter relationship now eroded. Both she and Josephine regarded their Catholic stepmother as a usurper and referred to her as "Bloody Mary." Although Mary had been Joe's beloved and trusted partner for many years, her presence by his side every day around the clock increased her influence. Furthermore, with an authentic son, Joe no longer needed a substitute in Alicia.

From early childhood Jimmy had been fascinated by the military and was determined to attend West Point. An appointment was no problem, but his school marks were not up to academy requirements, which Joe attributed to his being "taught by women," Mary Immaculate's sisters of the Dominican order. After testing that began in October 1938, and seeking advice from authorities at Princeton and Fordham, Joe enrolled his son at Scarborough School in nearby Scarborough-on-the-Hudson to begin preparing for the academy's entrance examination; after Scarborough the boy attended a six-month West Point preparatory course at the Millard School in Washington, D.C. Meanwhile, a preliminary West Point physical examination disclosed that, though Jimmy was without disqualifying physical disabilities, he did have flat feet, which added corrective exercises to the regime. Joe also signed him up for a schedule of fifty private French lessons at Berlitz during the summer of 1939. Finally, after this long program of preparation, Jimmy was accepted at West Point.

Balancing the boy's fascination with the military was an interest in newspapers, prompting him to spend summers at the *Daily News*, beginning at the lowest rung on the ladder, copy boy. He cheerfully ran errands, brought in lunch and coffee for reporters and politely thanked them for tips. Immediately following his 1944 West Point graduation, Jimmy married Dorothy Clarke, his sweetheart since their elementary school days in Ossining, and spent five years of active army duty, serving in Europe with General George Patton's Third Army and in Japan as liaison pilot.

JOE HAD BACKED Franklin Roosevelt in 1940 but was losing enthusiasm. Despite publishing a Pulitzer Prize–winning series supporting FDR's decision to run for a third term, he had become openly critical in print of the president's increasingly interventionist foreign policy. In Washington, Cissy's attitude toward Roosevelt—even when critical—had been tempered by her feelings for her brother. And there had been an element of capriciousness in her criticisms of the president— in the "fear is you" open letter, for example, or her stand against removal of the Tidal Basin cherry trees, and even in her impatience with the ineffectiveness of his anti-Depression measures. But now her disapproval of FDR toughened along with Joe's and she joined him in a stand against the president's interventionism. Both he and Cissy were raised on isolationism. Their grandfather and father had been isolationists, and Cissy's feelings were further reinforced by her lover Senator Borah and dear friends Senators Burton Wheeler and Hiram Johnson, all firm isolationists. But the turning point for both publishers came on December 17, 1940, when FDR put forth his lend-lease plan and submitted it to Congress. The measure, which would allow the United States to transfer war supplies, including food, ammunition, tanks, planes and other equipment, to opponents of the Axis, pushed Joe to the wall ideologically, and Cissy went with him. His *Daily News* editorialized that the bill "gives the President virtual power to take us into war on the side of any country or countries he thinks we should be allied with, and to run our entire war effort without consulting Congress." The lend-lease bill, Joe further stated, would "make the President Dictator of the United States, and hence its right name is the 'dictatorship bill.' "

Joe had defended the president to a greater extent than any other publisher; now he felt deceived. They had been fellow aristocrats who shared a concern for the common man; they had been friends and together had sold the New Deal to the American people. Joe continued to back the president as he edged toward an interventionist stand, but FDR's latest move was more than he could support. In offering supplies to one side in the foreign war, Joe felt Roosevelt had crossed the line. Lend-lease passed and was signed by the President on March 11. In talking with Senator Henrik Shipstead about the man he felt had betrayed him, an emotional Patterson blurted, "He lied to me." Breaking into tears, he repeated, "He lied to me."

Bert was already so publicly vehement in his criticism of the president that when a crowd organized by the Fight for Freedom Committee gathered in support of the Roosevelt foreign policy during the summer of 1941, its constituents bought every copy of the *Tribune* available and burned them all. The three grandchildren of Joseph Medill, with their powerful collective following, now lined up against White House policy. FDR was devastated by Joe's about-face, and his editorials saddened him in a way that McCormick's could not, prompting the president to spit back at the three cousins, characterizing the trio as the McCormick-Patterson Axis.

NEW YORK AND Washington supported newspapers capable of counteracting the anti-FDR influence of the Medill grandchildren, but not Chicago; thus Roosevelt had shrewdly begun measures to correct the situation. Without Joe's liberal influence moderating *Tribune* policy, the Colonel's rigid conservatism had become so uncontrolled that toward the end of the thirties the president had implored "richest boy in the world" Marshall Field III to back a more moderate Chicago newspaper. In doing so FDR tapped the best-equipped man in the country to produce a formidable weapon for his war against the *Chicago Tribune*.

The immense fortune amassed by the first Marshall Field had been preserved through a modified form of primogeniture in the remarkable will drafted by Isham, Lincoln & Beale. The substance of his considerable capital was left in trust for Field's two grandsons in the male line, Marshall III, born in 1893, and Henry, two years later, and each was to inherit the principal of his share on his fiftieth birthday. Three-fifths was earmarked for Marshall III and two-fifths for Henry; if either were to die without an heir, his portion would go to his brother. In 1917 the charming, magical young Henry died, shockingly, of bizarre complications following an elective tonsillectomy, leaving his brother sole heir to the fabulous estate. The Eton- and Cambridge-educated Marshall III was a larger-than-life personality, a horseman and big-game hunter who raced speedboats and piloted his own airplane. He and his glamorous wives occupied New York, Chicago and Long Island's most lavish houses, apartments and country estates, while they partied, traveled, launched African game-hunting expeditions and survived several plane crashes. But there was change on the horizon.

The breakup of Marshall III's second marriage in the mid-1930s coincided with the arrival in his life of the Russian-born Dr. Gregory Zilboorg and psychoanalysis. The intensive probing he underwent in the Russian doctor's care transformed Field from a fun- and adventure-loving rich boy into one of the nation's most visible liberal opinion makers. In 1940, he spent almost $2 million in creating the left-leaning New York tabloid *PM* and hired as his publisher Ralph Ingersoll, already established as one of twentieth-century America's great journalistic talents, as well as being a Zilboorg patient. If Field wanted to launch a major liberal money drain, he did so in a colossal manner; *PM* editorial policy was so far to the left that it prompted newspaper veteran Ben Hecht to characterize its slant with the quip "man bites underdog." The publication, which accepted no advertising, lost significant money, providing Field with a substantial tax write-off. The following year Marshall III radically reworked a version of *PM* to create the soft, popular appeal Sunday supplement *Parade*, which he later sold. So he was ripe for the president's urgent plea for wartime patriotism, and in 1941 he founded the *Chicago Sun*. Field's liberal *Sun* proved to be precisely the instrument needed by the Roosevelt administration to combat McCormick's rabidly anti–New Deal daily rant to Chicago readers. Six years later, he expanded the paper by buying the existing afternoon *Times* and merging the two papers into the *Chicago Sun-Times*, a twenty-four-hour tabloid. After dropping the evening editions in 1950, the *Sun-Times* became a morning paper and would continue so into the twenty-first century.

ON SUNDAY MORNING, December 7, 1941, at seven minutes before eight o'clock, a dark mass of Japanese planes suddenly swept out of the Hawaiian sky, striking the United States Pacific Fleet's base in Pearl Harbor in a brutal assault, sinking or severely damaging the eight battleships anchored there. More than 2,400 human lives and 188 airplanes were destroyed in the surprise attack.

It was early afternoon in Chicago's fashionable north suburbs, where ominous overcast skies and gusting south winds had plunged the midthirties temperature to a gray, foreboding chill. Inside the Lake Bluff house where the Colonel was ensconced in his current domestic situation, it was warm and safe by the fire. After finishing a pleasant lunch, he, Marion Clare and Henry Weber had settled down to listen to a WGN broadcast of the champion Chicago Bears's final game of the season. At 1:29 Chicago time, just after kickoff, announcer Ward Quaal interrupted the broadcast with a heart-stopping announcement of the attack. The Colonel's first act was to telephone the station to order continuous reporting of the enemy strike and the nation's entry into World War II, coverage that would air without interruption for the next ten days. He followed by directing Quaal to instruct WGN staff on Pacific geography and pronunciation of unfamiliar placenames for the extensive reporting he had requested.

In Washington, Cissy's executive editor, Frank Waldrop, was in the office alone—acting on a premonition—when the bulletin came through the news wire. Cissy called her staff together, many of whom heard the request announced on the public address system at a football game they were attending. They rushed back to the *Times-Herald* offices to plan the comprehensive coverage the momentous event warranted, and did so with speed. Thanks to Waldrop's presentiment, a *Times-Herald* extra, full of detailed information, was on the streets four hours ahead of the competition, perhaps the first in any city. During their planning of the Pearl Harbor coverage, a bitter Cissy sat on the floor of her office listening to the radio. She turned to Chalmers Roberts, her Sunday editor, who was sitting with her, and interjected suspicion of a Roosevelt conspiracy by asking, "Do you think *he* arranged this?"

Joe didn't learn the news until the following day. He was hunting at Cain Hoy, the Guggenheim plantation in the Carolinas, removed from all outside news because Harry insisted on no radios or telephones on the premises. It wasn't until Monday morning, while Joe was stalking wild turkey in the field, that a Guggenheim chauffeur back at the estate switched on a car radio and heard the news. Patterson was with Alicia and his outdoors editor, Hal Burton, when they heard a jeep coming toward them; Harry was at the wheel, with Mary Patterson calling out, "My God, you don't know what's happening? Pearl Harbor was bombed yesterday." Joe immediately drove to Charleston, phoned instructions to his office and followed a plan to drive up to Washington to confer with the *Daily News* bureau there. His first task was to write an editorial for the *News*, which Cissy reprinted: "Well, we're in it, God knows Americans didn't want it. But let's get behind our President and fight for America first." Both editors meant every word. Also on Monday, the president appeared in the Capitol to address the nation. Proclaiming December 7, 1941, "a date which will live in infamy," Roosevelt asked Congress to declare that "a state of war has existed between the United States and the Japanese empire" retroactive to the time of the attack. Meanwhile, Fred Pasley, in his capacity at the *News* Washington bureau, suggested to White House aide Steve Early that it might be an appropriate time for the newspaper baron and the nation's chief executive to meet. When Joe was told of the arranged meeting, he had little hope for a happy outcome, but he had no idea how devastating the encounter would be. On Wednesday, the day before he was to meet with the president, he wrote a letter to the War Department applying for readmission into the army "in any capacity in which I may be useful." A year and a half earlier he had been approached indirectly to serve as secretary of the navy, but that was before the lend-lease issue had arisen. What he really hoped to fill was a new cabinet post, secretary for air, not for the prestige it would bring him but rather to lend his own status to the post.

THE WHITE HOUSE meeting was scheduled for noon on Thursday, December 11, in the president's study. When Joe was admitted to the room, he found Roosevelt seated at his desk, head down, signing papers—which he continued to do for a full ten minutes while Joe stood, hat in hand, on the other side of the desk. When the president did look up, Joe offered his hand, which FDR took. "I am here, Mr. President," Joe said, continuing to stand, "to tell you that I wish to support your war effort." According to a memorandum Joe recorded of the meeting, "I remained standing for fifteen minutes while he gave me a pretty severe criticism for the way the *News* had conducted itself during the year 1941." The job that FDR assigned him "was to read over the *News* editorials for 1941. This I have since done." The president further told Patterson "that as a result of our conduct we had delayed 'the effort' by from sixty to ninety days . . . at the end he seemed a bit mollified and told me to pass on the word to Cissy to behave herself also."

Joe's meeting with Roosevelt at the White House would irrevocably transform his life, and Cissy's. In the words of Joe's Washington bureau chief, Walter Trohan, "It took balls for Joe to go to the White House to see Roosevelt—after he called Roosevelt a dictator. But Joe had been a wounded hero in World War I, and now his country had been attacked." Trohan was with Joe that night at Cissy's, where Joe expounded bitterly about the White House session, saying, "That man did things to me that no man should ever do to any man." And then he made his often quoted statement, "All I want to do now is outlive that bastard." To Bert he said, "Until today the *News* has been for Roosevelt. Starting tomorrow we are against him." Cissy was as furious as he, not only because of Roosevelt's conduct toward her beloved brother—which she never forgave—but also for the message to "behave herself." Both Pattersons joined their McCormick cousin in removing all support of Roosevelt permanently. However, this was a country at war, and others who had previously been isolationists pulled together in support of their nation. Inevitably, the patriotic American public at large, as well as powerful individuals who had been Patterson-McCormick friends, stood by the president and scorned the three, which did not perturb the Colonel but devastated both Joe and Cissy.

Cissy heard first from the fiercely right-wing Clare Boothe Luce, wife of *Time* magazine publisher Harry Luce, one of journalism's greatest interventionists. Within days of Pearl Harbor, an immense tribute of roses arrived on Cissy's doorstep with the note, "Hiyi: How do you like everything now? Affectionately, Clare Luce." Then Democratic representative Elmer Holland of Pennsylvania spoke from the floor of the House against the Pattersons, referring to them as "America's No. 1 and No. 2 exponents of the Nazi propaganda line." He accused them of "doing their best to bring about a fascist victory, hoping that in the victory they were to be rewarded." Joe responded with the only editorial he ever signed; the headline read, YOU'RE A LIAR, CONGRESSMAN HOLLAND. Hate mail was pouring into the *Times-Herald;* someone even tossed a bomb into the building, and then one day in the real estate section of the classified section, Cissy found the words "SHIT ON ELEANOR JEW PATTERSON." She was horrified at the invasiveness of the action; but it was also perplexing in the midst of wholesale accusations of anti-Semitism, some of them on the part of the city's Jewish advertisers.

Regardless of how Americans felt before Pearl Harbor about entering a conflict fought on foreign soils, they were patriotic as soon as the nation was officially at war. Young men flocked to enlist in the army, navy, marines and air force to serve their country. Soon their female contemporaries were enlisting in the WAACs, WAVEs and SPARs, and those too young or too old to serve were giving up their automobiles, donating pots and pans and even wads of tinfoil to the "war effort," as well as cheerfully tendering rationing stamps at the grocery and gasoline station. Blue service stars in residential windows were replaced by gold stars as sons, husbands and fathers were killed in action. Virtually every man, woman and child in America was involved in the war in some way and supportive of those putting their lives on the line to protect the nation. It was within this American atmosphere of intense patriotism that the *New York Herald-Tribune* and other newspapers throughout New York and elsewhere began insinuating that the *Tribune* was pro-Axis. In March 1942, at a Washington meeting of the Overseas Writers Association, speakers talked of ending the criticism of FDR's administration. One was former *Tribune* correspondent George Seldes, who accused McCormick and Joe Patterson of publishing "news, editorials and cartoons which must please Hitler." Soon after the meeting, three of the speakers, including William L. Shirer, called on Attorney General Francis Biddle to ask that he find grounds to indict McCormick, Patterson and William Randolph Hearst.

In the midst of this outcry, McCormick received a letter from former employee Jacob Sawyer asking how, with a war on, the Colonel could continue to criticize the government. It was much milder than McCormick's usual mail, prompting him to reply in part: "You do not know it, but the fact is that I introduced the R.O.T.C. into the schools; that I introduced machine guns into the army; that I introduced mechanization; that I introduced automatic rifles; that I was the first ground officer to go up in the air and observe artillery fire." After continuing in this vein for four paragraphs, he concluded with "The opposition resorts to such tactics as charging me with hatred and so forth, but in view of the accomplishment, I can bear up under it." The amazed Sawyer innocently took the letter over to the rival *Chicago Daily News*, which printed it in full. When Carl Sandburg's heading "And On the Seventh Day He Rested" was considered blasphemous, the *News* captioned the letter with "Whatta Man!" Even FDR joined in the ridicule by joking to General Hap Arnold, "I think we should give Colonel Robert R. McCormick the next title higher than Field Marshal." The Colonel's fight had always been with Franklin Roosevelt the man, and yet when his staff in Washington pushed for authorization to reveal the president's apparently adulterous relationships with Lucy Rutherfurd and Marguerite "Missy" LeHand, he refused. "The *Tribune* doesn't fight that way" was his response.

In New York, Joe's devastation over the humiliation Roosevelt dealt him did not abate. *Daily News* columnist John O'Donnell hammered away relentlessly at the president on Joe's behalf; FDR was fully aware of the barrage, so aware that during the 1942 Christmas season a gift for O'Donnell arrived from the White House, a Nazi Iron Cross from the president of the United States. And even Joe's daughter—who had sat at his knee, absorbing his views most of her life—had become a supporter of the man who had so humbled him. Bitterness and melancholy were aging Joe; he was losing his characteristic vigor and edge—and he was drinking heavily. It wasn't merely the rejection by Roosevelt and other powerful figures; the love and esteem of his *Daily News* readers had been essential to him and now it was gone. Joseph Medill Patterson, along with his sister and cousin, had committed an act of extreme hubris and together they were reaping the wrath of Nemesis.

THE COUSINS IN WINTER

T HE 1940s were crushing years for Cissy. Surrounded by disapproval for her stand against Roosevelt, she became depressive, and her already excessive alcohol consumption increased. In 1942 she and Drew Pearson, her not-quite-son but not-entirely-lover, had broken completely. She also split that year with the controversial Walter Winchell in a conflict over the war. Ben Hecht may have insisted the hyperkinetic columnist wrote "like a man honking in a traffic jam," but she enjoyed Winchell's energetic sense of adventure and participated in his nocturnal excursions around New York. His car radio was furnished with a police receiver and when code 1030 broke through his self-absorbed rat-tat-tat monologue, he and Cissy knew an armed crime was in progress and sped to its site. But those days were over.

Cissy's insomnia had become so severe her bedroom was a blaze of lights throughout the night; the Dupont Circle parties continued, but they were smaller and more subdued, and often the hostess retired to her private quarters before guests left. In desperation she began consulting Eugene de Savitsch, a local Dr. Feelgood. The urbane Russian émigré—witty, single and an accomplished conversationalist—appeared first as an extra man at Cissy's dinner table. Although there were rumors of his incompetence, de Savitsch's charm made him a favorite society doctor, who blithely provided illicit drugs along with Vitamin B12 shots for such patients as Evalyn McLean and Alice Longworth. Cissy was smoking three packs of cigarettes a day and her alcohol use began with a magnum of breakfast champagne every morning, but he nevertheless treated her with cocaine to relieve depression. The copious alcohol intake interacted with Dr. de Savitsch's drugs, making Cissy's eccentric behavior increasingly erratic and argumentative. Old friends fell away, sometimes supplanted by new acquaintances, soon also to leave, causing further dejection. Her health appeared to be deteriorating and at times she felt faint, experiencing chest pains doctors casually diagnosed as heart problems. She was advised to slow down but did not. When she appeared to have suffered a heart attack in the humid Washington heat of July 1943, medical help was not summoned until she became incapacitated; at this point Dr. de Savitsch was called.

De Savitsch solemnly pronounced Cissy near death, sedated her and left an order for no visitors; after that the matter drifted. When Evie Robert appeared, breaking the visitor ban, she insisted de Savitsch be fired, but the patient was too feeble to act. After Cissy had been in a semiconscious state for weeks, her secretary called Waldrop at the *Times-Herald* for guidance. While he was there, Cissy roused long enough to say, "Get me a doctor. . . . This man is trying to kill me." De Savitsch was not only dismissed but when Cissy recovered she published an exposé, the FBI stepped in, and Dr. Feelgood left the country. Next the celebrated Dr. Paul Dudley White was engaged. The eminent cardiologist—later world famous for treating President Eisenhower following a 1955 heart attack—thoroughly examined Cissy and announced that she had "a nice little heart."

Dr. White's cheery diagnosis did nothing to decrease the patient's continued abuse of alcohol and drugs, making her even more capricious and confrontational. As her contentiousness grew, she sometimes became physically violent and several times went so far as to strike an employee or even a mere acquaintance during a quarrel. One day she and the long-suffering Waldrop were discussing a photograph when she slapped him and fled the room. Her extreme behavior had reached the point that it even tested the bond with her adored brother. When she told Joe she might hand the *Times-Herald* reins to Alicia, he broke her heart by telling her to stay away from his daughter: "You'll only hurt her the way you've hurt everyone else." Cissy was no longer in control; she was gaining weight and had lost interest in her appearance. Bizarre stories were flowing as her conduct became progressively more outlandish. Wasn't something going on between Cissy and her good-looking chauffeur? And hadn't she been seen checking out local homosexual houses of ill repute with columnist and right-wing extremist Westbrook Pegler? What about those orgies that were occurring at Dower House, with Cissy a voyeur? Her servants reported the last was true, and that drugs were involved.

CIRCUMSTANCES WERE HAPPIER for the Colonel, who didn't last long as a single man. Within five years of Amy's death, he was caught up in another triadic arrangement involving an insistent lady married to a compliant husband in need of McCormick cash. The bride-to-be was Amy's protégée Maryland Mathison Hooper, a bright, witty, good-looking woman, who, like Amy, was a skilled horsewoman and an enviable hostess. The former Baltimore belle was regarded by some as an adventuress but had received the certification of her respected predecessor. Maryland was twenty-six years her junior, but Amy viewed her as the woman she herself had been during her marriage to Ed Adams, and considered Maryland one of her best friends. The Hoopers lived in a McCormick-owned house on the Cantigny estate and they had socialized as a couple with Amy and Bert for fifteen years in both Chicago and Wheaton. McCormick felt comfortable with the alcoholic Henry Hooper and his decorative wife, and he enjoyed the time he spent with them. As it had in his affair with Amy, the relationship with Maryland ripened; eventually she separated from Henry after a twenty-one-year marriage and he gladly moved to the Lake Shore Club. In November 1944, Maryland traveled to Mexico City and sued for divorce on grounds that her husband was chronically drunk. She returned divorced, but the Colonel wanted no complications this time and insisted she also file locally. The bride-to-be was forty-seven and the prospective groom sixty-four.

The couple was married in a late-afternoon ceremony at the Lake View Avenue apartment of the Chauncey McCormicks on December 21, 1944, with Joe Patterson as best man. The event was widely covered not only by newspapers locally but also by *Life* magazine, at the time a must-read in households throughout the country. The *Life* reporter commented, "The ceremony was unpretentious and the Colonel, usually gloomy and aristocratically aloof, was as excited and misty-eyed as any young swain."

When the newlyweds arrived at Cantigny following the ceremony they were greeted with a bonfire in front of the house and a large heart stomped in the snow by household staff. Because everyone involved sensed the estate would be immediately invigorated by the presence of Maryland and her daughters, there was genuine cause for rejoicing. The Colonel no longer hosted a hunt, and the polo field now produced crops, but with Maryland as hostess the social pace of Cantigny quickly returned to the heyday of Amy's years. The new energy extended beyond the Wheaton estate when the couple, with portions of their staff, traveled to houses in Chicago and Palm Beach, a suite in New York's Waldorf Towers and quarters they would maintain in Washington. Rounding out the portable household were the Colonel's English bulldog, Buster Boo, and a series of dachshunds and Pekinese for Maryland.

On April 12, 1945, Franklin Roosevelt suffered a cerebral hemorrhage at Warm Springs, Georgia, and died instantly. Tribune Tower flags flew at half-mast and McCormick's circumspect editorial read, "The whole nation is plunged into mourning; those who opposed him in politics no less than those who followed him." When Maryland called the *Tribune* to ask whether she should cancel a dinner party they were giving that night, the Colonel replied no, then added, "Don't serve champagne. I don't want anyone to say we are celebrating." But on his way out of the Tower, he distributed ten-dollar bills to various employees he passed, and on arrival at Cantigny his reply to Maryland about lowering the estate's American flag was "I don't know of anyone for whom I'd rather do this."

Jubilation was less subdued for Joe, who had finally achieved his supreme ambition by outliving "that bastard." His *Daily News,* perhaps the nation's only major newspaper not to print an obituary editorial immediately after the president's death, instead carried a column of Roosevelt's major quotations in its first postmortem issue. In Washington, Cissy temporarily snapped out of her malaise and when Waldrop began the obituary on page one with a photograph of the late president, she changed it. In her version page one carried a very large picture of FDR with only his birth and death dates and no copy. "You don't need his name," she said. "Everybody knows who he is." The following day, she ordered the paper filled with material about his successor, Harry S. Truman. "He's the story now."

There was a more personal milestone for Cissy that year when she found herself "divorced" by Felicia, at great sacrifice. Severance meant that her daughter, now sober and a member of Alcoholics Anonymous, would give up a tax-free forty-thousand-dollar annual income and two houses. Instead she proposed to live on money earned from her writing and thirty-five hundred dollars a year from her grandmother's estate, though she still planned to keep her horses stabled at Dower House. Before the final split, Felicia took her mother to an AA meeting; it was not successful and there was never a repeat of the gesture. In 1946 Felicia's daughter, Ellen, married George Arnold, son of Thurman Arnold, a distinguished lawyer and close friend of her father. Predictably Cissy's relationship with her granddaughter was as troubled as with her daughter and son-in-law, and when the Arnolds produced a red-haired son, they named him Drew Pearson Arnold, which did not please Cissy.

CRUSHING DEVELOPMENTS CONTINUED to accumulate for Cissy, but with 1946 came a sadness that surpassed all others and was the greatest sorrow she would ever know. Joe, who had spent his adult years drinking in the newsman style of his era, never completely recovered from a 1945 bout with pneumonia, and during the months when he should have been rebuilding his physical condition, his alcohol consumption escalated at an alarming rate. Despite fragile health, he accepted an invitation from General MacArthur to visit occupied Japan and hoped to attend his fiftieth reunion at Groton in the spring; instead he entered New York's Doctors' Hospital in early May. The women in his life gathered around, turning his hospital room into a battleground where his daughter Josephine and his drunken sister tore mercilessly into Mary. In the midst of this chaotic bedside carnival the Colonel appeared, with a mission to enlist Joe in a plan to keep *Little Orphan Annie* creator Harold Gray from carrying out a threat to leave the syndicate. But Joe, the center of silence in the room, was near the end and had no idea who McCormick was.

On May 26, 1946, sixty-seven-year-old Joseph Medill Patterson was dead of cirrhosis of the liver. Reactions were mixed. A. J. Liebling praised Joe's journalistic achievements in his five-column *New Yorker* obituary but referred to him as a "strange and fearsome man." Cissy was inconsolable. He had been her rock. She had adored him as a child when both were without a mother's love and nurturing. And she had been devoted to him throughout adulthood, though never more than in the later years when they were bound by their stand against Roosevelt and together faced the hatred of patriotic America. The *Daily News* published appropriate eulogies, along with a remark attributed to Douglas MacArthur that Joe was "one of the greatest natural-born soldiers who ever came under my command." The *Times-Herald* and *Tribune* reprinted much of the *Daily News* material, but Liebling noted the *Tribune* omitted MacArthur's quote, because, he pointed out, "Everyone on the *Tribune* knows that Colonel McCormick is the most brilliant, natural-born soldier that ever served under anyone."

Joe's body was taken first to his house in Ossining, where it lay in state, then moved to 15 Dupont Circle until burial with full military honors at Arlington National Cemetery. Cissy managed to thrust herself into the role of widow that day, displacing Mary and upstaging her. She prepared by advising her sister-in-law to dress in simple, unadorned black, which Mary did, wearing, like Joe's daughters, a somber black suit, hat and accessories with dark hose. When the limousines drew up at Dupont Circle for the procession to Arlington, the family was gathered outside the house, except for Cissy. While other mourners stood and watched, she swept out of the door heavily veiled in classic full mourning with yards of black crepe flowing over her face and about her body in the spring breeze. She brushed by the others and entered the lead car, usurping Mary's position. Walter Trohan, who was with Cissy in her house after the service, said, "It was the only time I've seen her cry. She should have married her brother. He was the only one she ever really loved." Influenced by his second wife, Joe had become a Catholic, which inspired Cissy. She began consulting Father Edmund Walsh, whom she had met through Evalyn McLean, and faithfully listened to the radio sermons of Monsignor Fulton J. Sheen. There was no conversion; although Father Walsh helped to reduce her need for drinking, for a while.

Scarcely was Joe's body in the ground when fighting resumed among the women he left behind. His final word was delivered from the grave: control of the *Daily News* would go to his widow, the despised usurper, and to two of the paper's top executives, not even family. Mary and Joe's now-grown son, Jimmy, were considered "new" members of the clan and Joe's daughters were furious. Alicia was particularly devastated. Her beloved father left her a mere 3 percent interest in the Tribune Company, which owned both the *Daily News* and the *Chicago Tribune*, a shocking blow and the greatest rejection of her life, from the most important man in it. Cissy, in a throwback to the she-devil days, hopped into the fray, again aligning with her nieces against Bloody Mary and their son, to the displeasure of the Colonel, who was exhausted by a lifetime of dealing with Medill women.

McCormick's relationship with Cissy deteriorated after Joe's death.

The two were made trustees of the *New York Daily News* three months after Joe's death, and the Colonel injected himself into the paper's management, usually without involving her. Maintaining the Patterson power balance was paramount to Cissy; she suggested that Alicia fill Joe's vacant chair on the *Tribune* board, but McCormick refused. She also nominated Alicia to replace her as McCormick-Patterson Trust trustee, but the Colonel steadfastly declined to allow Alicia to occupy any position in company operations. At one point Cissy even returned to the idea of leaving the *Times-Herald* to Alicia—with a proviso that she thought would have pleased Joe: Alicia would have to divorce Harry and return to Joe Brooks.

CISSY HAD BECOME a severely damaged woman, desperately clutching at the rim of reality. Her paranoia was extreme; *Time* magazine had declared her "the most hated woman in America" and she reacted by keeping guns everywhere: next to her bed, in her handbag, a stash of twenty-five revolvers at Dower House and several more in her automobile, even though an armed guard followed in a second car. Still reeling from the loss of Joe, she received another traumatic jolt in 1947 with the death of sixty-year-old Evalyn McLean. Cissy—accompanied by Evalyn's lawyer, Thurman Arnold, and Frank Waldrop with their wives—was at her friend's deathbed while Father Walsh administered last rites. She had fallen to her knees in prayer, but the moment Evalyn breathed her last, Cissy disappeared to the *Times-Herald* office to oversee the obituary, leaving a curious security detail to the Waldrops and Arnolds. The two couples dutifully scooped up the celebrated McLean jewels, which were spread about the room, and dumped them in a shoe box. Because no banks were open, they took the package to FBI head J. Edgar Hoover, who gave them a receipt: "Received, one shoebox, said to contain . . ." Evalyn's death was one more devastating upset for Cissy, whose drinking returned to pre–Father Walsh severity, and she was again greeting each day with a magnum of breakfast champagne. She had entered a tragic and irreversible decline, aggravated in 1948 by the July 9 death of Tom White. She attended his funeral at St.

Patrick's Cathedral—at the invitation of his amazingly magnanimous wife, Virginia—and after that she lost her desire to live; it would be only a matter of days before she joined her adored Irishman.

Cissy had planned to travel out west at the end of July and arranged for a private railroad car; she would visit Jackson Hole and then San Simeon with the Waldrops, her personal maid and a cook. On Friday night, July 23, her dinner guests left Dower House early and by 11 P.M. Cissy was in bed with the *Times-Herald,* her poodle Butch and a few books. Her bedroom at Dower House was on the first floor behind the immense drawing room; it was a small space dominated by a classic four-poster canopied bed, but even in domestic isolation and the quiet of night she was guarded. A watchman, assigned to spend the long, sultry night sitting in a hallway outside her door, was close enough to hear if she should ring for service, which she did. At approximately one o'clock, Cissy asked the man to take Butch for a walk. Both spent the remainder of the oppressive July night in the cooler air outside, and when the watchman left at seven he let Butch back into the house.

Cissy did not stir that morning. There was no eight o'clock ringing of her bell in the kitchen to order breakfast and an outing for Butch; staff waited, fearing to disturb her, even when a forlorn-looking poodle wandered alone into the kitchen. At eleven o'clock Waldrop telephoned to discuss his editorial and was told by her butler, Robert Lye, that Mrs. Patterson had not yet awakened. Finally, around noon Lye and Cissy's personal maid opened the bedroom door to peer in. The room was a still, lifeless vacuum with a human form lying across the bed, lights on, a book in hand and face on the book. Waldrop called again and once more Lye told him that she had not yet risen, then he suddenly announced, "I think she's dead." Lye followed his abrupt declaration by telephoning Cissy's personal physician, Dr. Bernard J. Walsh, and the Prince Georges County coroner. When the deputy county medical examiner announced that death had occurred at 1:08 A.M., servants remembered hearing the banshee cry of a dog just outside the house around that time. Although the medical examiner signed a certificate stating death was from natural causes, police were in and out of Cissy's bedroom, combing the scene for evidence of suicide or foul play. Waldrop and Dr. Walsh arrived, and soon friends and acquaintances were all over the house, but Cissy's undraped body, pajamas askew, was still on the bed.

On the following Tuesday a short Episcopal service was held in the Dupont Circle ballroom with flowers everywhere—an estimated $35,000 worth of tributes—and a blanket of yellow roses on the casket. Washington's elite turned out, socialites, diplomats and high governmental officials. Later that day, flowers filling two railroad boxcars traveled to Chicago, leaving an equal amount in Washington. Felicia, accompanied by close family and friends, rode in a private railcar to attend additional services at Chicago's Graceland Cemetery on Wednesday morning. Cissy's body was cremated there and buried next to her mother's grave in the resting grounds of the city's privileged. Drew Pearson wrote, "A great lady died the other day—a lady who had caused me much happiness—and much pain." The Colonel was at the Paris Ritz with Maryland when he learned of Cissy's death by telephone. After a few moments he began whistling and retreated to a bathroom of the suite where he sang, "I'm the last leaf on the tree. . . ." However he publicly lauded her and honored her memory in a *Tribune* editorial praising her effectiveness as a publisher.

WHATEVER GLEE MCCORMICK may have felt as the tree's "last leaf" would soon disappear. In fact, Cissy dead was more disruptive than Cissy alive. "They'll have a damned good fight when I've gone," she promised before she died. "I've fixed that!" It was more than a good fight. Her will was the eighth such document she was known to have written and there may have been others, including an alleged new will that was never found. Furthermore, there was blood spilling all around, beginning with the violent death of one former employee and the suicide—or possible murder—of another. Then there were accusations that Cissy herself had been murdered—including a prediction of her own—further police investigations, inexplicable disinheritances, frantic searches for the missing will, the ransacking of her daughter's apartment, telephone tapping and dispositions regarding Cissy's mental deterioration. And all this was before her cousin Bert was delivered his own comeuppance.

Cissy's estate, including her beloved newspaper, was worth more than $16.5 million, but her most recent will delivered an unexpected shock—with Felicia the big loser. It announced that Cissy had left only a lifetime annual income of twenty-five thousand dollars to her daughter, with the *Times-Herald* going to seven of its employees— soon to be mischievously known as the Seven Dwarves. Felicia was outraged, even though the income would be tax-free and thrown in with it were her mother's Long Island estate, some North Dakota real estate and personal effects, including furniture, jewelry and Cissy's immense wardrobe. But it was a mere pittance against more than $16 million. The Dupont Circle house went to the American Red Cross, Cissy's niece Josephine Albright received the Jackson Hole ranch, and Evie Robert was soon possessor of the imperial Russian black pearls, a sable wrap and Washington real estate said to be worth half a million dollars. Another Cissy pet, Ann Bowie Smith, received Dower House, its livestock and furnishings, and the six hundred acres surrounding it. Mrs. Smith, a descendant of original Dower House owner Lord Calvert, was also to be paid five thousand dollars a year for five years. Although Cissy had left numerable bequests to such organizations as one "aiding Polish refugee children of Catholic origin," she left nothing to her only grandchild, who was one-quarter Polish of Catholic origin.

Felicia sued to break the will, charging that her mother was not "of sound mind and memory" when she wrote the latest version. But it was the accumulation of the various legacies and random charitable contributions that gave Felicia sufficient motivation to sue, on counsel of her advisors, who questioned whether there would be capital left to provide her income. The breaking of a will can be messy, and this one was becoming so. When dispositions from acquaintances and servants regarding alcohol, drugs, perversions, orgies and even lesbianism began piling up, Felicia backed off. She did not want to destroy what was left of her mother's reputation and jeopardize her own. In the meantime, a settlement was arranged and she came away with four hundred thousand dollars. Felicia considered this an improvement, but it was a long way from the provisions made for her in the first of Cissy's previous wills. In 1924 she was her mother's sole heir, but slowly through the years, through mother-daughter conflicts and succeeding wills, her legacy had eroded. In the spring following Cissy's death Felicia sold the awesome collection of clothes she inherited from her mother, believing the items would be recycled anonymously in resale shops. Instead the wardrobe was put up for sale in the embarrassment of a well-publicized five-hour auction at 15 Dupont Circle.

The "missing will" was never found, but there was a trail of clues that began five months before Cissy's death when she contacted *New York Daily News* president Jack Flynn, asking him to meet with her in early March at a house she had bought in Sarasota, Florida. He was stunned when she told him she was rewriting her will and wanted to leave him either the *Times-Herald* or her *Tribune* stock, and possibly both. He declined, having all he wished for and not wanting to enter into what could be a family squabble, but he offered to help in any way he could. Flynn also advised her that estate taxes might overwhelm assets, necessitating the sale of *Tribune* stock or the *Times-Herald* to pay them. She was impressed with Flynn's honesty, but when he told her the seven *Times-Herald* employees of her current will would not be in agreement in their operation of the paper, he thought he saw a sly grin come across her face. Then she said, "But what do I care. I'll be dead." When Flynn suggested she leave the newspaper to Alicia, her answer was that she didn't like Alicia's husband but that she might do so anyway. Those with whom Cissy talked while she was developing the "missing will" believe the new document would have made Alicia the paper's heir. Joe's daughter certainly had the cushion to absorb operating costs when necessary, which few other candidates had— including *Tribune* Washington bureau chief Walter Trohan, who was another person Cissy conferred with about receiving the paper. She was talking with Trohan up until a week before she died and even discussed the new will with her dinner guests the night of her death, telling them that there would be "great changes." The fact that she was considering drastic revisions intensified rumors she had been murdered, gossip that continued for several decades after her death.

Nineteen forty-eight would not be an easy year for the Colonel, either. A humiliation not even he could overlook occurred with the presidential election in November and the legendary page-one headline that followed it. Although McCormick swore that when he retired at eleven o'clock on election night he was certain Truman had won, those who were following the tight returns throughout the predawn hours at the *Tribune* determined otherwise. The DEWEY DEFEATS TRUMAN headline in the morning edition ascended to the Valhalla of American errata when the beaming reelected president was photographed holding the immortal front page above his head. It was a twin victory for Truman, a longtime McCormick victim, as well as an occasion to snicker for newspaper editors throughout North America. But late-life irritations were only beginning for the sixty-eight-year-old publisher.

Flynn had been correct: the Seven Dwarves soon proved incapable of sustaining the *Times-Herald*. A capital fund was necessary to meet operating expenses during the lag a newspaper can experience while waiting for income from delayed advertising revenues. The inheritors found themselves repeatedly borrowing money to meet payroll, prompting one to wail, "She left us a gold mine and forgot to give us a shovel." There was also the predicted conflict among the seven, chiefly on the issue of keeping their inheritance, with four preferring to cash in. If they were to sell, there was pressure from the executors for them to do so within the tax year; otherwise the balance of the estate might be eroded. Prospective buyers, including William Randolph Hearst Jr. and Eugene Meyer, were circling the property, and not the least of the prospects was Robert R. McCormick. As much as the Colonel loathed Washington, he was even more unnerved by the specter of Meyer buying the *Times-Herald*. He knew the *Washington Post* owner would kill Cissy's paper, the city's sole conservative voice, after first incorporating its best features into his own liberal paper. Therefore, the reluctant Colonel bought the paper from the Dwarves, although the last place he wished to spend his twilight years was in Washington, D.C., running his late cousin's newspaper. It was a dim prospect for the aging tycoon now well into retirement age, but appeared to be the only solution.

ENTER BAZY MILLER. Ruth and Medill's only son and presumed *Tribune* heir, Medill Jr., had died in 1938. The twenty-one-year-old college dropout, known as Johnny, was attempting an ascent in the Sandia Mountains near his mother's home in Albuquerque when he and a climbing partner were struck by a bolt of lightning and thrown in different directions. The following day, a search party sent by Ruth found his companion's body but not Johnny's. Six days later searchers discovered the boy's remains at the bottom of a two-thousand-foot cliff on the other side of the ridge, overwhelming Ruth with grief. The Colonel, who had expected Johnny to one day take over the *Tribune,* was more shocked than bereaved by the boy's sudden death. He was in the *Tribune* newsroom when he learned of the loss, and his immediate reaction was "Now everything will go to Joe's boy." Even with a powerful female cousin publishing the *Washington Times-Herald,* it had not yet occurred to him that a woman could operate the *Tribune.*

When Ruth died of a ruptured pancreas at the end of 1944, she left two remaining offspring. Both were strong, fearless women, politically active clones of their mother—except that the elder, Katrina, or Triny, had swung far to the left, predating America's radical chic movement by three decades. In 1935 she had married stockbroker and New York blueblood Courtlandt Barnes Jr., with whom she lived in a Manhattan coach house, produced a son, Medill, and plunged into the activities of the city's fashionable liberal set. It followed that she would soon decide to divest herself of her embarrassingly conservative *Tribune* holdings. The Colonel, then tied up in Canadian dealings, borrowed $2.2 million to buy her out and graciously congratulated her on doing what was appropriate for her. Triny's next move was to become publisher of the left-leaning magazine *Common Sense* and to anonymously contribute most of her inheritance—which she called "blood money"—to liberal causes, telling reporters, "I've always hated Uncle Bertie." Eventually she went back to McCormick to redeem the six shares of *Tribune* stock she still held. Asking for a higher price—which he refused—she sold the stock elsewhere and gave the money away because she did not want to gain from a business she thought "evil."

That left the conservative twenty-eight-year-old Ruth, or Bazy, in whose DNA was embedded the family passion for newspapers. She was also the Colonel's favorite niece and the family member he now hoped would eventually hold the reins at the *Tribune*. Bazy had already demonstrated a strong interest in journalism through her purchase of the *News-Tribune* in LaSalle, Illinois, which she was publishing with her thirty-year-old husband, Peter Miller. In addition to solving McCormick's immediate need, the hands-on practice of running the *Times-Herald* would give her big-city newspaper experience and demonstrate her ability to handle a major paper. It was an ideal fit, and Bazy leapt at the opportunity to take over the *Times-Herald* as publisher, with Peter, who had recently begun suffering from epilepsy, joining her in a mechanical capacity.

Despite her lack of familiarity with Washington and its politics, Bazy quickly began carrying out her role with panache. The Colonel, though impressed with the newsgathering aggressiveness she often exhibited, sometimes questioned her editorial judgment, and was quoted as saying, "She's getting too big for her britches." Yet all in all things were going well until Eros once again raised his tempting presence in the newsroom in the guise of city editor Garvin "Tank" Tankersley. It wasn't long before Bazy was repeating a family tradition begun by Joe Patterson and Mary King and continued with Cissy and Walter Howey. McCormick soon learned of the affair and Bazy's subsequent separation from Peter Miller, father of her two young children. The Colonel, who had so cavalierly shattered two marriages and humiliated his elegant first wife with his amorous extramarital conduct, was incensed. He transferred Tank to Chicago and notified Bazy through Weymouth Kirkland that she could not continue her relationship with Tankersley and also run the *Times-Herald*. But Bazy desperately wanted both, and when McCormick would not give her the paper—or even sell it to her—she resigned. She also divorced Miller, giving him custody of their children and full ownership of the Illinois paper. After marrying Tank, she proceeded to do what she said she enjoyed most, raise Arabian horses. Although McCormick had been determined to maintain a conservative voice in Washington, the *Times-Herald* had been losing money through his ownership and he found the capital as tiresome as ever. The paper plodded on, now run by *Tribune* executives who knew nothing of Washington or how to edit a newspaper for its residents. The *Times-Herald* had definitely lost its Cissy zing.

In early 1954 an enterprising new figure entered the scenario. Kent Cooper had been general manager of the Associated Press and was close enough to McCormick to occupy a house on his Palm Beach property without charge. He was also sufficiently familiar with the situation to determine that the Colonel might part with the *Times-Herald* if he could recoup the $4.5 million cost of the paper, plus an additional $4 million he had paid for a new plant. He further believed McCormick would now sell to Eugene Meyer, whom he liked and respected as a newspaper publisher despite the discrepancy in their political views. The most important factor in Meyer's favor was that he had become increasingly convinced that in order to endure, the *Post* would have to be Washington's sole morning paper, which made him the only prospective buyer with both the capability of paying the price and the motivation to do so. A few weeks into the year, Cooper wrote a letter to the *Post* owner referring to a "business matter" he thought would be of interest to him. In her Pulitzer Prize–winning book, *Personal History,* Katharine Graham, Meyer's daughter and wife of the paper's publisher, Philip Graham, described the excitement surrounding what she considered "one of the most important newspaper purchases in history."

"Dad arrived at our door that morning, waving the letter in his hand, obviously excited asking, 'Where's Phil?' I explained he had gone to Jacksonville." According to the late Mrs. Graham, Meyer then called Cooper and asked, " 'Kent, this "business matter" to which you refer, is it in the field of journalism?' Cooper said that it was. 'Is it in Washington?' my father probed. Again Cooper said yes. This was the moment we had fought for, worked for, and prayed for since 1933. After the disappointment in 1949, when the Colonel had stepped in, our hopes that he would sell at all—much less sell to us—had all but vanished, so the excitement aroused by Kent Cooper's letter was immense." It was essential that the $8.5 million deal—plus another $1 million or more for severance pay to redundant *Times-Herald* employees—proceed in complete secrecy. McCormick wanted to bring the matter up before *Tribune* directors and stockholders, which could not happen until March; meanwhile, terrified that Bazy would learn of the impending transaction, he kept it a secret from even his wife and his lawyer. "Cooper told us there was nothing to worry about," remembered Mrs. Graham, "because we had McCormick's word, which was good, but six weeks of holding our collective breaths seemed a lifetime." In mid-March the imminent sale was announced during a *Tribune* stockholders meeting at the *Times-Herald* building. Bazy Tankersley, learning of the matter for the first time, appeared to have been "struck by a thunderbolt."

When Bazy asked to have time to raise $10 million to meet Meyer's offer, Mary Patterson stood up in front of her chair in support of Medill and Ruth's daughter. The Colonel agreed, giving his niece forty-five hours to find the backing; the sale to Meyer was then approved, pending the outcome of Bazy's quest to raise the money. The list of men she reportedly called—depending on the source of information— included Sears chairman General Robert Wood, Joseph P. Kennedy and Texas high rollers of the 1950s, including H. L. Hunt, Sid Richardson and Clint Murchison, but she was able to produce only $4 million by the deadline. McCormick declined to give her an extension and the paper was sold to Meyer. Katharine Graham wrote, "The time was 12:44 p.m., St. Patrick's Day, 1954—a supreme moment in the history of The Washington Post Company." Thus was laid the foundation for the powerful base from which Mrs. Graham would be able to rock the nation two decades later with her Watergate investigation.

WHEN THE ROBERT R. McCormicks reached the age when many affluent couples spend weeks at a time traveling the world, they did so frequently but not as commercial tourists. Eschewing ocean liners and cruise ships, Maryland and the Colonel toured in their own plane, a converted B-17 bomber McCormick had bought in 1948. The wartime aircraft was transformed into a luxurious passenger conveyance with comfortable bunks, luxurious carpeting, an extensive library and a well-stocked bar. Over the next several years, the McCormicks made a series of seven "around the world" trips in it. Wherever they went, they were greeted at the airport as VIPs, frequently by ambassadors. The State Department arranged sessions with cabinet ministers, heads of state and sometimes dictators. They met with Jawaharlal Nehru in India and, in Japan there was an audience with former emperor Hirohito as well as a reunion with the Colonel's longtime hero Douglas MacArthur. When they met with Juan Perón and his equally notorious wife Evita in Argentina, Maryland was charmed with the couple and declared the Peróns principals in a great love story. After it was mentioned that Perón was a dictator, McCormick blandly replied, "Argentina is not ready for democracy." In Spain they were with Generalissimo Francisco Franco, whose hunting lodge the Colonel described as "about the size of the late Potter Palmer's mansion." He then managed to anger liberals worldwide by naming the hated Spanish chief of state "the father of modern warfare." McCormick did draw the line at acceptance of Fulgencio Batista, whom he saw during a visit to Cuba. He inexplicably developed a strong dislike for the dictator, saying, "He's an awful man," and refused future meetings suggested by the State Department. The McCormicks' last tour was in 1953, to France, Germany, Italy and England, where the visit included an excursion out to the Colonel's alma mater Ludgrove. It was a sentimental afternoon, made more so by a stop on their way back to Claridge's hotel, to look over the Brook Street house where he and Medill had lived with their parents as boys.

The legend of the Colonel, for decades a near-mythical figure, was growing larger with time. In meeting him many people were astonished to discover the ferocious publisher was, in the flesh, quite docile. Atomic Energy Commission chairman David Lilienthal, a frequent *Tribune* target, found him "rather courtly, courteous in the extreme, and with no slight hint that I was one of the devils that for years and years he had been whamming vigorously." Arriving for lunch at the Tribune Tower, Lilienthal remembered being greeted by both the Colonel and "with no little exuberance by a waddling, gallumping English bull, the kind that is terrifying to see but actually very friendly." Another to discover McCormick to be quite benign in the flesh was British reporter Frank Walker, who wrote, "The fire-breathing colonel whose paper has spoken of the degenerate aristocracy of Britain drank whiskey and soda and chatted pleasantly for half an hour with Scotland's premier nobleman, the Duke of Hamilton, in his private apartments in the Palace of Holyroodhouse." When he visited Hollywood, with Hedda Hopper as his hostess and guide, the worldly and somewhat cynical Frank Sinatra pronounced him "a great man" and the wife of formidable producer and master of malapropism Samuel Goldwyn told him, "I don't know why I was afraid of you. Why, you're as comfortable as an old shoe."

Maryland, whose million-dollar prenuptial agreement was considerable for the time, was as pretentious as the Colonel and her personal style was so studied that—in the manner of the chatelaine of a great European castle—she carried a small handbag and lace handkerchief around her own houses. She proved to be a spectacular hostess, presiding over frequent and elaborate parties at Cantigny, including a lavish soiree that was among those to celebrate the 1947 centennial of the *Tribune*. More public was the party for two thousand at the former Stevens Hotel and another for thirty-five hundred at the Tribune Tower. The mammoth centennial blast of them all was an event in Burnham Park that three hundred thousand attended to watch a breathtakingly extravagant display featuring fireworks portraits of *Tribune*-related personalities ranging from Abraham Lincoln to Little Orphan Annie and Dick Tracy.

At home, Maryland maintained a reputation as a hostess, giving small dinner parties and large soirees. One of her great evenings at Cantigny was the seventieth birthday party she gave for her husband in July 1950. Three hundred and fifty guests arrived before sundown and gathered in a striped tent that stretched above satin-clothed tables on the lawn. Among his surviving friends and relatives celebrating this milestone on a perfect summer evening was his niece Bazy, then expected to succeed her doting uncle at the *Tribune*. After dinner, toasts were made and messages read to applause and laughter, but no one surpassed Weymouth Kirkland, who began his toast with "People ask me how in the world I have gotten along with McCormick all these years. It is really very simple. I find out what he wants and I give it to him." As night fell and a full moon rose, hundreds of Chinese lanterns were lit and guests danced under the moon, lanterns and stars. It was a party the Colonel did not leave. Maryland followed with a similar grand Cantigny evening two years later when, during the 1952 Republican convention, guests included Cecil B. DeMille, Irene Dunne, John Wayne, Clare Boothe Luce and Alice Longworth.

Maryland was a decorative spouse who fussed over her husband as his mother never had. He appreciated the attention and her skills as a hostess, but she often annoyed him with her fluttering femininity and fervent interest in his investments. Acquaintances began to notice that when he mentioned "my wife," it was Amy, not Maryland, to whom he referred. Apparently, however, his carnal interest in his current marriage had not waned; McCormick was seventy-two when Maryland asked a doctor at what age a man loses his libido. "Sometimes at ninety" was his immediate answer. "Good God!" was hers.

The following year, the Yale class of 1903 celebrated its fiftieth reunion. The Colonel rented a private railroad car for the trip from New York to New Haven and invited a group of classmates to join him. He also provided a little book of Yale songs for each of the men to refer to as they sang their Boola Boola all the way north. After a disagreement about placement of the railroad car in the New Haven yard, local police calmed the unhappy group with a siren-screaming escort to the Yale Bowl for the Yale-Harvard football game.

While the Colonel was winding down his visibility at the newspaper and WGN, Maryland was increasing her position as a journalist. She had written a weekly column for the *Times-Herald,* and now her byline was appearing in the Sunday *Tribune*, among other papers. When after buying and closing down the *Times-Herald*, Eugene Meyer took Maryland's column to the *Post*, the Colonel told him, "Be careful, she has had no experience and has never written anything beyond a check, and her signature on that is illegible."

A CHILDHOOD OF fragile health and adult bouts of scarlet fever and jaundice had inspired the Colonel to build his body through exercise. However, alcohol continued to be his closest companion; he read—and drank—himself to sleep at night, often polishing off a full bottle of Scotch before sleeping, and yet he never experienced a hangover. "The only man I know who can drink more liquor and hold it better than I can," he told his doctor, "is Winston Churchill." His body, however, was feeling the consequences, especially in the liver and bladder, but he would not give up alcohol, announcing to the same doctor, "Young man, everyone of us has his idiosyncrasy. Scotch is one of the few pleasures in my life. I will determine when I give it up." Yet in his seventies he was still appearing at the *Tribune* six days a week, arriving shortly before noon for lunch and editorial conferences at the Overset Club, and remaining in the office until almost five, when he crossed the river to the Tavern Club for drinks with Maryland before returning by air to Cantigny.

McCormick survived a serious bout with pneumonia in 1953 and during the late summer of 1954 he was feeling ill enough to have a *Tribune* nurse join the Cantigny household, although he continued to go into the office for a portion of most days. His appetite began to decrease and, most ominously, he lost his taste for Scotch. In mid-December he and Weymouth Kirkland polished his will and he signed it; most of his estate would go to charity. Two years before, he had established the Robert R. McCormick Foundation, which formalized his philanthropic donations. Maryland would be left a million dollars to be paid in ten annual installments; nevertheless, she had become increasingly aggressive in demanding to be made a trustee of the Tribune Company. The situation became so obvious to Kirkland that he contacted the Colonel's physician, Dr. Charles B. Wyngarden, saying that Mrs. McCormick was "pestering the life out of the Colonel," and candidly asked him whether the Colonel possessed sufficient mental alertness to protect himself from her unrelenting demands. The doctor replied, "As far as I'm concerned, he does not." As the year drew to a close, Maryland was becoming even more insistent; shortly before Christmas 1954, a dinner table argument suddenly rocketed into a dispute so extreme that Maryland presented a formal catalog of demands: two secretaries must be fired; she would be named executor of his estate, as well as chief *Tribune* trustee; hefty trust funds were to be established for her daughters, plus a million dollars for herself— and a divorce!

On Christmas night the Colonel gave his last WGN address, and the following Sunday, New Year's Day, an announcer read his talk for him. In early January 1955 he added a codicil to his most recent will, and, although only his lawyers knew what either new document held, Maryland continually agitated for possible changes in her interest. By January 18 he was in Passavant Hospital, where Amy had died, but when he was discovered walking down the hospital corridor in his hospital gown, trailing tubes, doctors agreed to allow him to return home. The McCormicks' town address was now an apartment in the very proper 209 East Lake Shore Drive, where Joe Patterson had owned an apartment but which the Colonel jokingly referred to as "the tenement."

The Colonel spent the winter at his Palm Beach house, always with a trusted *Tribune* executive nearby. A handful of men, known as Watchers of the Night, were there to guard against the uncertainties growing out of Cissy's death, not to mention the domestic chaos surrounding Joe's. He terrified all those around him by insisting upon shaving himself with a straight razor as he always had, although his hands quivered and wobbled as he held the lethal device to his face and throat. When, on March 10, doctors returned him to Chicago for bladder surgery at Passavant, even he must have known time was growing short. He contacted Bazy, now living at her horse farm outside Washington, asking her to visit him; he wanted to ask forgiveness for treating her "outrageously" during the *Times-Herald* sale. A nonflyer in a family of aviators, she was in her automobile within five minutes and drove all night to be with him. He was under sedation and groggy but knew she was there; they silently held hands until he completely lost consciousness. It was a definite reconciliation; still, his intention to leave the *Tribune* in her hands had died in Washington with her departure from the *Times-Herald*.

On St. Patrick's Day doctors determined that, between his heart and his liver, there was nothing more that could be done. He was taken to Cantigny, where doctors and nurses joined the *Tribune* watchmen, who were now especially important to help him through the night he was growing increasingly to fear. Although the presence of his dear bulldog Buster Boo in the room was an added comfort whenever he became lucid, the Watch was there to ensure that Maryland did not benefit from his deteriorating condition to reverse previous documents. As it was, her behavior was more than unpleasant. At one point she stood over him, saying, "You know you are going to die—why make it so hard on everyone else?" Providentially she was sleeping when her husband breathed his last a few minutes before three o'clock on the morning of April 1, 1955. Official cause of death was myocardial insufficiency due to arteriosclerotic heart condition and cirrhosis of the liver.

A few days later, lying in the specially built oversized casket he had ordered years before, his World War I uniform tucked carefully around his shrunken form, the Colonel was buried beside Amy in the hard April earth of the garden at Cantigny. It had been one hundred years since the chilly spring morning in 1855 when, thirty miles to the east, young Joseph Medill stood in the rotunda of the Tremont House shaking hands with Charles Ray, his new partner in the purchase of the *Chicago Daily Tribune*. The last leaf of the great tree had fallen and with it had come the end of the turbulent, but splendid, Medill century.

EPILOGUE:
AFTER THE MEDILL
CENTURY

I N February 1962, Alicia Patterson added a postscript to her family's history of White House visits that might have earned her father's respect. Twenty years after his life was irrevocably tarnished by the disastrous confrontation with Franklin Roosevelt—and a century following his grandfather's Civil War scolding from Abraham Lincoln—Joe's daughter made a call on President John F. Kennedy that was a triumph.

The Kennedy White House of 1962 was the epicenter of power and glamour in America, in the world. The tensions of the president's Cold War dealings with Russian premier Nikita Khrushchev and Cuban leader Fidel Castro—punctuated by the suspense of such white-knuckle dramas as the Cuban Missile Crisis—were balanced by the magic of Camelot. The unparalleled style and urbanity of the executive mansion during the early 1960s would never again be matched. Only a few nights before Alicia's visit, viewers in three out of four American households had watched Jacqueline Kennedy guide the CBS television network's Charles Collingwood on a tour of the newly redecorated executive mansion. A month earlier, composer Igor Stravinsky, conductor Leonard Bernstein and other distinguished guests from the arts had gathered for a highly acclaimed dinner in the State Dining Room next to the room in which she was meeting with the president. And later that spring, at a banquet hosted by the Kennedys for forty-nine

Nobelists, JFK would famously refer to the evening as the most "extraordinary collection of talent, of human knowledge that has ever been gathered together at the White House with the possible exception of when Thomas Jefferson dined alone."

On the drab February afternoon of Alicia's visit, not unlike the misty day of Joseph Medill's meeting with President Lincoln a few rooms away, she was seated next to John F. Kennedy for a private lunch in the cheerful formality of the White House Family Dining Room. She had a mission. She was with the president to ask his support in closing Mitchel Field, the former military air base located in a heavily populated portion of *Newsday*'s circulation area. It was a complex issue with hearings held the month before, and the key figure in the drama was Federal Aviation Administration head Najeeb Halaby. The former skydiver, test pilot and Yale-educated lawyer would later become president of Pan American World Airways and—upon the marriage of his daughter Lisa, now Queen Noor—he would be father-in-law of King Hussein of Jordan.

Alicia and the president talked pleasantly over a first course of clear soup, followed by the entrée of veal, green beans and salad. When a dessert of ice cream cake arrived, the question of Mitchel Field came to a head and Kennedy suddenly sprang into action, rolling his chair back to a telephone. "Get me Jeeb Halaby," he began with uncharacteristic urgency in his familiar halting Boston diction. Then, "Jeeb, we don't need Mitchel Field, do we? Let's shut the damn thing." After a few moments of pleasantries, he hung up the phone and turned to Alicia with the words, "It's closed."

"She persuaded him," Halaby remembered of the incident; "she was a very persuasive and powerful woman."

IN JUNE 1963, Alicia entered New York's Doctors' Hospital with a bleeding ulcer. Ignoring the protests of her doctors, she ran the paper from her bed, arguing with editors by phone, developing projects, commanding stories and driving *Newsday* as she always had. Although the ulcer would have healed through a bland diet and abstention from alcohol, the impatient Alicia insisted upon surgery. The first operation caused bleeding that required a second surgical procedure. The bleeding persisted. Doctors opened her abdomen again for a third operation, to no avail, and on the night of the third surgery, Alicia Patterson died. She was fifty-six years old.

Alicia's dream that her nephew Joe Albright, a young newsman in training at the paper, and his sister Alice would succeed her at *Newsday* was not to be. The staunchly conservative Harry Guggenheim still held controlling interest and was concerned—as Colonel McCormick had been with the *Washington Times-Herald*—that the newspaper could become a thoroughly liberal vehicle. He felt this was a very real possibility if Alicia's heirs gained editorial control. When the Albrights, who inherited Alicia's 49 percent interest, tried to buy Harry's share, he told Josephine, "Your children are all New Left, and I don't approve of that." In 1970, *Newsday* was sold to California's Chandler family, owners of the Times Mirror Company, which published the *Los Angeles Times*. Harry's 51 percent interest brought a reported $31.6 million, somewhat less than the $37.5 million paid to the Albrights for their smaller share. Guggenheim died several months later at age eighty.

A few years before the plan for Alice and Joe Albright to run *Newsday* was destroyed by Harry's sale of the paper, Alice had fallen in love with fellow journalist James Fulton Hoge Jr.; they were married in 1962. Jim Hoge, a golden-haired Robert Redford look-alike and brother of the former *New York Times* reporter and editor Warren Hoge, joined the *Chicago Sun-Times* as a financial writer in 1958. He rose quickly from city editor to managing editor and then executive editor. His title was editor in 1971 when the Hoges divorced. Alice left for New York and married Michael J. Arlen, whose father, Michael Arlen, was author of the groundbreaking 1924 novel *The Green Hat*, one of the most popular books of that decade. *Exiles*, the junior Arlen's book about his glamorous parents, was a runaway bestseller of 1970.

In 1982, after twenty-three years of marriage, Madeleine Albright received an overwhelming surprise, a shock, from her husband. One day he announced, "This marriage is dead and I am in love with someone else." She soon discovered that, during the political conventions of 1980, he had met Marcia Kunstel, an *Atlanta Journal* reporter who was more than a decade younger than she. The revelation broke Madeleine's heart, but it also released her to launch one of the most spectacular diplomatic careers of any woman in history, ultimately becoming United States secretary of state. She also emerged from the marriage with a handsome Georgetown house, a 370-acre Virginia farm and a fortune of as much as $10 million. Joe and Marcia, whom he married, now own and operate Cissy's much-loved Flat Creek Ranch in Jackson Hole.

After his divorce from Joe's sister Alice, Jim Hoge remained in Chicago and continued his rise at the *Sun-Times*. He was the paper's publisher when it was sold to Rupert Murdoch in 1984—ending his career as a Chicago newspaperman, as well as the last vestige of the Medill-McCormick-Patterson presence in the city's journalistic arena. Coincidentally, in a stroke of irony—and symmetry—he was almost immediately recruited to serve as president and publisher of Joe Patterson's *New York Daily News,* where he spent the next seven years at the helm of the phenomenally successful newspaper created by his former wife's grandfather.

THE MEDILLS, THE McCormicks and the Pattersons were a family of vibrant, dynamic individuals who, for four generations, sustained their passionate involvement in a tradition that may soon drift as far into history as the dynasty itself. The talents of Joseph Medill and his descendants were honed while producing newspapers during the decades the medium grew and developed, and they in turn were vital to molding the contemporary media industry. Creating new formats and stretching concepts of journalism, they pressed for quality and repeatedly advanced their profession. Although the Medills often espoused controversial viewpoints and created turmoil and upheaval, they could not be ignored. Their newspapers—bright, entertaining and informative—contributed to the shaping of modern America and were a piece of the fabric of an era that is now changing so rapidly and fundamentally that it will likely soon disappear—along with the newspapers themselves. The Medill achievement was, however, monumental and should be remembered not only with nostalgia but also with respect.

ACKNOWLEDGMENTS

I am grateful to Arthur H. Miller, archivist and librarian for special collections at Lake Forest College, for providing access to the J. M. Patterson Papers and Patterson Family Papers in the Lake Forest College Library Special Collections, and for directing me through an invaluable collection of correspondence, photographs, invoices, newspaper clippings, memorabilia and further material relating not only to Mr. Patterson but also to other family members, often revealing significant interaction between these individuals. I am similarly obliged to Eric Gillespie, director of the McCormick Research Center in Wheaton, Illinois, for his guidance through the abundance of comparable material in the McCormick Papers in the Colonel Robert R. McCormick Research Center, as well as an illuminating personal tour of Colonel McCormick's estate, Cantigny, and its grounds. The rich store of family letters in these two repositories has been vital to me in uncovering nuances in personal relationships unavailable elsewhere.

I wish also to acknowledge the Newberry Library in Chicago and the Research Center of the Chicago History Museum for supplying material to which I have referred throughout the book, particularly in the early chapters. Miscellaneous papers in the Chicago History Museum's Medill Collection were extremely helpful in assembling portraits of Joseph and Katherine Medill and offering insight into their daily lives. For factual material pertaining to people and events occurring during the many decades covered by this book, I am also beholden to the newspaper archives of the *Chicago Tribune* and the *New York Times*. Additionally, I found *Time* magazine, in its obsessive fascination with the McCormicks and the Pattersons, a valuable resource. The publication's sometimes weekly attention to family members offered a continuing reference for their activities during the years from 1924 onward.

As with any book of this nature—about people who have been dead for many years, along with those who could offer memories of them—much research was accomplished through existing publications. The following sources, along with many others, are acknowledged more specifically in the chapter endnotes that follow; however I particularly wish to express my gratitude to the authors and publishers of the following books: *Chicago Tribune: The Rise of a Great American Newspaper* (Chicago: Rand McNally, 1979) by Lloyd Wendt, an outstanding chronicle of the paper and the individuals behind it throughout many decades; Philip Kinsley's three-volume history, *The Chicago Tribune: Its First Hundred Years* (New York: Knopf, 1943–46); . . . *Pictured Encyclopedia of the World's Greatest Newspaper* (Chicago: Tribune Company, 1928); and *Chicago Days: 150 Defining Moments in the Life of a Great City* (Wheaton, IL: Cantigny–First Division Foundation, 1997). Together these references provided an excellent fund of information about the *Chicago Tribune* and the various family members associated with it.

Previous biographies of principals in the family saga offered a magnificent store of specifics and quotes. Especially notable is Richard Norton Smith's fine book *The Colonel: The Life and Legend of Robert R. McCormick 1880–1955* (Boston: Houghton Mifflin, 1997), an amazingly comprehensive account of the life of the complex publisher. I am also grateful for Frank C. Waldrop's *McCormick of Chicago: An Unconventional Portrait of a Controversial Figure* (Englewood Cliffs, NJ: Prentice-Hall, 1966); Joseph Gies's *The Colonel of Chicago* (New York: Dutton, 1979); Gwen Morgan and Arthur Veysey's *Poor Little Rich*

Boy (Carpentersville, IL: Crossroads Communications, 1985); and John Tebbel's *An American Dynasty* (1947; reprinted Westport, CT: Greenwood Press, 1968).

Three riveting biographies of Cissy Patterson provided factual information about other members of the family in addition to their primary subject and were thus important in verifying details throughout the book. They are *Cissy: The Extraordinary Life of Eleanor Medill Patterson* by Ralph G. Martin (New York: Simon & Schuster, 1979); Paul Healy's *Cissy: A Biography of Eleanor M. "Cissy" Patterson* (Garden City, NY: Doubleday, 1966); and *Cissy Patterson: The Life of Eleanor Medill Patterson, Publisher & Editor of the Washington Times-Herald* (New York: Random House, 1966) by Alice Albright Hoge, now Alice Arlen.

Mrs. Arlen is a granddaughter of Joseph and Alice Patterson and niece of Alicia Patterson; her book, to which she brought enviable access and unquestionable accuracy, is a superb and reliable account of the life of Cissy Patterson. Similarly, I am obliged to Kristie Miller for the candid biography of her grandmother, *Ruth Hanna McCormick: A Life in Politics 1880–1944* (Albuquerque: University of New Mexico Press, 1992), which illuminated facets in the often difficult life of Ms. Miller's grandfather, Medill McCormick, as well as that of his remarkable wife. I am also deeply indebted to Robert F. Keeler for his excellent *Newsday: A Candid History of the Respectable Tabloid* (New York: William Morrow, 1997). Keeler, a longtime member of the *Newsday* staff, produced a comprehensive history of the newspaper yet also managed to focus tightly on its founder, Alicia Patterson. His book is an outstanding store of information not only about this fascinating woman, but also about her father, Joseph Medill Patterson, and other family members.

John Chapman's *Tell It to Sweeney: The Informal History of the New York Daily News* (Garden City, NY: Doubleday, 1961) and *The News: The First Fifty Years of New York's Picture Newspaper* by Leo E. Mc-Givena and Others (New York: News Syndicate, 1969), two books devoted to the *New York Daily News*, together provided an invaluable supply of details about the founding and growth of that astonishing publication.

I am especially indebted to Eric Gillespie and Arthur Miller for permission to use the photographs and portraits reproduced in this book. Gillespie graciously supplied images from the Colonel Robert R. McCormick Research Center, along with consent for their use, as did Miller for photographs and portraits from the J. M. Patterson Papers, Lake Forest College Library Special Collections; Patterson Family Papers, Lake Forest College Library Special Collections; and Mrs. Michael Arlen Collection, Lake Forest College Library Special Collections.

Finally, I am beholden to the late managing editor Merrill Panitt for hiring an inexperienced college graduate to write for his phenomenally successful new weekly, *TV Guide*, and to publisher Frank Sullivan, who much later selected me to be editor of Chicago's *Avenue M* magazine, as well as to so many others since. Most of all, I wish to thank those who supported *The Magnificent Medills* from the outset. I am particularly grateful to my agent, Agnes Birnbaum of Bleecker Street Associates, who has been steadfast in her loyalty for countless years. After patiently vetting my many concepts for a book about Chicago dynasties, she suggested that I focus on the McCormick-Patterson clan. How right she was!

At HarperCollins, I was greeted with immense warmth and courtesy by executive editor Gail Winston and senior vice president and publisher Jonathan Burnham, who welcomed my proposal with enthusiasm. I feel unbelievably fortunate to have had the amazingly talented Ms. Winston as my editor; she subtracted here and added there, while tactfully and gently shaping my manuscript to its final form. With the capable assistance of Maya Ziv, Gail then skillfully organized and massaged the many ingredients that create a successful book. In conclusion, I appreciate the sage but witty legal counsel of Kyran Cassidy, whose parting advice was to "enjoy the ride!" And, because of the talents of the professionals at HarperCollins, I know that I can.

NOTES

1: FERTILE SOIL

1   Wolf Point at a fork: A. T. Andreas, *History of Chicago*, vol. 1, *To 1857* (Chicago: A. T. Andreas, 1975), 106.

1   "I plays de fiddle": Donald L. Miller, *City of the Century: The Epic of Chicago and the Making of America* (New York: Simon & Schuster, 1996), 57.

1   all races, ranks and classes: James R. Grossman, Ann Durkin Keating, and Janice L. Reiff, *The Encyclopedia of Chicago* (Chicago: University of Chicago Press, 2004), 467.

1   And they were there every night: Ibid., 228.

2: THE PATRIARCH

4   on the site: Edwin Oscar Gale, *Reminiscences of Early Chicago and Vicinity* (Chicago: Fleming H. Revell, 1902), 139.

4   Thurlow Weed, shepherding: Gordon Leidner, *Washington Times*, August 10, 1996.

4   Boss Weed also brought: Lloyd Wendt, *The Chicago Tribune: The Rise of a Great American Newspaper* (Chicago: Rand McNally, 1979), 117–18.

5   where they handed out: Emmett Dedmon, *Fabulous Chicago: A Great City's History and People* (New York: Random House, 1953), 55.

5   By then most spectators: Wendt, *The Chicago Tribune*, 120.

5   Illinois Republican chairman Norman Judd: Philip Kinsley, *The Chicago Tribune: Its First Hundred Years*, vol. 1, *1847–1865* (New York: Knopf, 1943), 76.

5   Lincoln's convention manager, Judge David Davis: Ibid., 94.

5 backroom deals: Ibid., 116–17.

5 "I AUTHORIZE NO BARGAINS": Wendt, *The Chicago Tribune*, 121.

5 secured Indiana's twenty-six votes: Kinsley, *The Chicago Tribune*, vol. 1, 116.

6 Caleb B. Smith, would be named: Ibid., 153.

6 Medill and Judd: H. I. Cleveland, *Saturday Evening Post*, August 5, 1899.

6 arrive at the Wigwam: Wendt, *The Chicago Tribune*, 121.

6 delegates could barely hear them: Chicago Tribune, *Chicago Days: 150 Defin-ing Moments in the Life of a Great City* (Wheaton, IL: Cantigny–First Division Foundation, 1997), 23.

6 "the meanest trick": Cleveland, *Post*, August 5, 1899.

6 Others in the running: Kinsley, *The Chicago Tribune*, vol. 1, 117.

6 On the second ballot: Ibid., 117–18.

6 "one who when bought": Wendt, *The Chicago Tribune*, 121.

6 "If you can throw": Cleveland, *Post*, August 5, 1899.

6 "H-how d-d'ye know?": Ibid.

6 "I know, and you know": Ibid.

7 "Mr. Chairman! I-I-I a-arise": Wendt, *The Chicago Tribune*, 122.

7 An astonished moment: Mabel McIlvaine, ed., *Reminiscences of Chicago During the Civil War* (New York: Citadel Press, 1967), 48.

7 all sensed history in the making: Wendt, *The Chicago Tribune*, 122–23.

7 Prairie yells resounded: Ernest Poole, *Giants Gone: Men Who Made Chicago* (New York: Whittlesey House, 1943), 50.

7 "It is absolutely impossible to describe": Kinsley, *The Chicago Tribune*, vol. 1, 118.

7 "There was more management": Cleveland, *Post*, August 5, 1899.

7 where he was replacing a teacher: Elias Colbert, notes for a paper read before the Chicago Historical Society, 1903.

7 "In the name of common sense": Richard Norton Smith, *The Colonel: The Life & Legend of Robert McCormick 1880–1955* (Boston: Houghton Mifflin, 1997), 5.

7 When Medill's fury exploded: Colbert, notes for CHS paper.

8 She was Katherine "Kitty" Patrick: Ibid.

8 eight years his junior: Obituary, Mrs. Joseph Medill, *Chicago Daily Tribune*, October 2, 1894.

8 by appointment of John Quincy Adams: Ibid.

8 where "sons of gentlemen went": Ralph G. Martin, *Cissy: The Extraordinary Life of Eleanor Medill Patterson* (New York: Simon & Schuster, 1979), 13.

8 a professor of mathematics: Obituary, *Tribune*, October 2, 1894.

8 Books in the library he amassed: Smith, *The Colonel*, 5.

8 Judge Patrick fancied pretty women: Martin, *Cissy*, 13.

8 She was quick to enlighten Ohioans: Obituary, *Tribune*, October 2, 1894.

9   distinguished himself: Wayne Andrews, *Battle for Chicago* (New York: Harcourt, Brace, 1946), 50.

9   the stash of gold dollars: Smith, *The Colonel*, 6.

9   kinship with Sir Walter Scott: Kinsley, *The Chicago Tribune*, vol. 1, 34.

9   objected to the union: Gwen Morgan and Arthur Veysey, *Poor Little Rich Boy: The Life and Times of Col. Robert R. McCormick* (Carpentersville, IL: Crossroads Communications, 1985), 13.

9   eldest of the nine children: Cissy Patterson's scrapbook, J. M. Patterson Papers.

9   Because of the border change: Smith, *The Colonel*, 3.

9   outside the town of Massillon: Wendt, *The Chicago Tribune*, 39.

9   farm in Pike Township nearby: Smith, *The Colonel*, 4.

9   From Mr. Wales: Wendt, *The Chicago Tribune*, 39–40.

9   On Saturdays he walked: Ibid., 40.

10 legal association with: Kinsley, *The Chicago Tribune*, vol. 1, 35.

10 "It was hard work": Smith, *The Colonel*, 4.

10 Nineteenth-century journalism: Frank Waldrop, *McCormick of Chicago: An Unconventional Portrait of a Controversial Figure* (Englewood Cliffs, NJ: Prentice-Hall, 1966), 15.

10 The great barons of journalism: Allen Churchill, *Park Row: A Vivid Re-Creation of Turn of the Century Newspaper Days* (New York: Rinehart, 1958), 4.

10 They believed that a newspaper: Ibid., 33.

10 He also peppered area newspapers: Wendt, *The Chicago Tribune*, 40.

10 newspaper offices were lures: John Tebbel, *An American Dynasty* (1947; reprinted Westport, CT: Greenwood Press, 1968), 8.

10 Joseph began spending: Wendt, *The Chicago Tribune*, 40.

11 And she encouraged him: Ibid., 39.

11 Bolstered by Kitty: Ibid., 41.

11 As soon as he had the press repaired: Ibid.

11 "I have determined to make": Joseph Medill to Katherine Patrick, McCormick Papers, Colonel Robert R. McCormick Research Center.

12 he founded the *Daily Forest City:* Kinsley, *The Chicago Tribune*, vol. 1, 36.

12 "My prospects are bright": Joseph Medill to Katherine Patrick, McCormick Papers.

12 *New York Tribune*'s Cleveland correspondent: Smith, *The Colonel*, 7.

12 "Father says he never intended": Joseph Medill to Katherine Patrick, McCormick Papers.

12 "My God!": Ibid.

13 "My madly loved Kate!": Ibid.

13 On September 2, 1852: Wendt, *The Chicago Tribune*, 43.

13 She was in the *Leader* office: Waldrop, *McCormick of Chicago*, 15.

13 With the progression: Leo E. McGivena and Others, *The News: The First Fifty Years of New York's Picture Newspaper* (New York: News Syndicate, 1969), 8.

13 During his short practice: Kinsley, *The Chicago Tribune*, vol. 1, 35.

14 Another political group in play: John J. McPhaul, *Deadlines & Monkeyshines: The Fabled World of Chicago Journalism* (Englewood Cliffs, NJ: Prentice-Hall, 1962), 28.

14 destroyed the Whig Party forever: Wendt, *The Chicago Tribune*, 43.

15 Opposed to the historic: Kinsley, *The Chicago Tribune*, vol. 1, 37.

15 "Go ahead": Obituary, Joseph Medill, *Chicago Tribune*, March 17, 1899.

15 Medill kept pressing onward: Kinsley, *The Chicago Tribune*, vol. 1, 36.

15 the group had adopted: Cleveland, *Post*, August 5, 1899.

15 In autumn 1854: Wendt, *The Chicago Tribune*, 46.

16 He and Kitty: Ibid., 45–46.

16 "Go West": Smith, *The Colonel*, 7.

16 True or not: Wendt, *The Chicago Tribune*, 46.

16 A similar letter: Ibid.

16 Medill had made: Cissy Patterson's scrapbook, J. M. Patterson Papers.

17 also had eighty-five thousand: Smith, *The Colonel*, 7.

17 the Sands: Lloyd Lewis and Henry Justin Smith, *Chicago: The History of Its Reputation* (New York: Harcourt, Brace, 1929), 76.

17 "Compared with Cleveland": Wendt, *The Chicago Tribune*, 47.

17 In 1855, the city council: Lloyd and Smith, *Chicago*, 67.

3: JOSEPH MEDILL AND THE MAKING
OF THE PRESIDENT (1860)

19 Medill bought one-third: John J. McPhaul, *Deadlines & Monkeyshines: The Fabled World of Chicago Journalism* (Englewood Cliffs, NJ: Prentice-Hall, 1962), 27.

19 with each receiving: Lloyd Wendt, *The Chicago Tribune: The Rise of a Great American Newspaper* (Chicago: Rand McNally, 1979), 57.

19 Joining them were: Philip Kinsley, *The Chicago Tribune: Its First Hundred Years*, vol. 1 (New York: Knopf, 1943), 43.

19 Medill colleagues: McPhaul, *Deadlines*, 27.

19 existing Adams printing equipment: Ernest Poole, *Giants Gone: Men Who Made Chicago* (New York: Whittlesey House, 1943), 47–48.

19 Richard March Hoe: James Brough, *Princess Alice: A Biography of Alice Roosevelt Longworth* (Boston: Little, Brown, 1975), 128.

20 a cleaner, smarter appearance: Kinsley, *The Chicago Tribune*, vol. 1, 43.

20   they began making the paper: Tim Jones, *Chicago Tribune*, June 10, 2007.

20   the stern, rheumatic: Poole, *Giants Gone*, 47.

20   "He was a very tall": H. I. Cleveland, *Saturday Evening Post*, August 5, 1899.

21   "Please tell me": Ibid.

21   Before long Old Abe: Ibid.

21   "Get your damn feet": Ralph G. Martin, *Cissy: The Extraordinary Life of Eleanor Medill Patterson* (New York: Simon & Schuster, 1979), 12.

21   sleighs and bustling bobsleds on the streets: Wendt, *The Chicago Tribune*, 139.

21   Soon the river: Elizabeth McNulty, *Chicago Then and Now* (San Diego: Thunder Bay Press, 2000), 78.

22   long drives together: Wendt, *The Chicago Tribune*, 145.

22   Washington and Morgan: Ibid., 71.

22   a reliable bridge: A. T. Andreas, *History of Chicago*, vol. 1, *To 1857* (Chicago: A. T. Andreas, 1975), 202.

22   an important artery: Daniel Bluestone, *Constructing Chicago* (New Haven, CT: Yale University Press, 1991), 65.

22   the old town bell: Joseph Kirkland and Caroline Kirkland, *The Story of Chicago*, vol. 2 (Chicago: Dibble, 1894), 23.

22   "Tomorrow I hope": Wendt, *The Chicago Tribune*, 71.

23   tall black hats: James R. Grossman, Ann Durkin Keating, and Janice L. Reiff, *The Encyclopedia of Chicago* (Chicago: University of Chicago Press, 2004), 786.

23   replace an overbearing father: Gwen Morgan and Arthur Veysey, *Poor Little Rich Boy: The Life and Times of Col. Robert R. McCormick* (Carpentersville, IL: Crossroads Communications, 1985), 17.

24   *Tribune*'s Washington correspondent: Wendt, *The Chicago Tribune*, 71.

24   pen name "Chicago": Ibid., 140.

24   His Washington home: Ibid., 73.

24   he missed Chicago: Ibid., 145–46.

24   "Lincoln sat": Cleveland, *Post*, August 5, 1899.

24   shrill, high-pitched voice: Wendt, *The Chicago Tribune*, 75–76.

25   "on the top of the table": Cleveland, *Post*, August 5, 1899.

25   "paralleled or exceeded": Kinsley, *The Chicago Tribune*, vol. 1, 56.

25   "My belief is": Kinsley, *The Chicago Tribune*, vol. 1, 57.

25   Joseph advised him: Stephen B. Oates, *With Malice Toward None: The Life of Abraham Lincoln* (New York: Harper & Row, 1977), 26–27.

25   but not the Senate seat: Chicago Tribune, *Chicago Days: 150 Defining Moments in the Life of a Great City* (Wheaton, IL: Cantigny–First Division Foundation, 1997).

25   Nevertheless, Lincoln had made: Chicago Tribune, *Chicago Days*, The Lincoln-Douglas Debates.

26   Horace White joined the staff: Wendt, *The Chicago Tribune*, 90.

26 And then, in July 1858: Richard Norton Smith, *The Colonel: The Life & Legend of Robert McCormick 1880–1955* (Boston: Houghton Mifflin, 1997), 13.

26 merged with the *Democratic Press:* Wendt, *The Chicago Tribune,* 84.

26 owned by William Bross: Kinsley, *The Chicago Tribune,* vol. 1, 66.

26 Bross was a Williams College graduate: Ibid.

26 Known as "Deacon": Ibid., 21.

26 able to repay: John Tebbel, *An American Dynasty* (1947; reprinted Westport, CT: Greenwood Press, 1968), 18.

26 while also absorbing: Wendt, *The Chicago Tribune,* 23.

26 The name would revert: Ibid., 128.

26 again face ruin: Tebbel, *An American Dynasty,* 18.

26 During 1859: Smith, *The Colonel,* 15.

26 scored a coup: *Chicago Tribune,* May 16, 2010.

26 most significant of their machinations: McPhaul, *Deadlines,* 5.

26 would give the Illinois candidate: Kinsley, *The Chicago Tribune,* vol. 1, 104–5.

27 *Tribune* wasted no time: Ibid., 120.

27 "The labor of six years": Ibid., 133.

27 THE GREAT VICTORY: Ibid.

27 The distribution: Wendt, *The Chicago Tribune,* 143–44.

28 directly from the nation's capital: Ibid., 138.

28 "We made Abe": Ibid., 140.

28 twenty-seven correspondents: Ibid., 165.

28 including two Medill brothers: Ibid., 167.

28 Joseph, prevented from serving: Ibid., 22.

29 nation's only major paper: Poole, *Giants Gone,* 54.

29 In February 1865: Wendt, *The Chicago Tribune,* 17.

29 Secretary of War Edwin Stanton: Ibid., 20.

29 This room was the heart: www.mrlincolnswhitehouse.org.

29 "I cannot do it": Wendt, *The Chicago Tribune,* 18.

30 "You called for war": Tebbel, *An American Dynasty,* 27.

30 "I couldn't say anything": Ibid., 27–28.

30 He went back: Poole, *Giants Gone,* 55.

30 Medill escorted the president's body: Kathryn Maddock, *Joseph Medill: An Editor of the Old School* (Unpublished thesis, University of Illinois, 1916), 24.

31 "I wish I could go to America": Robert G. Spinney, *City of Big Shoulders: A History of Chicago* (Dekalb: Northern Illinois University Press, 2000), 46.

31 The four years: Wendt, *The Chicago Tribune,* 176.

31 the newspaper had grown: Ibid., 171.

31 The war had made money: Tebbel, *An American Dynasty,* 48.

4: THE GREAT CHICAGO FIRE:
MAYOR MEDILL'S PERSONAL PHOENIX

32 the handsomest in Chicago: Frederick Francis Cook, *Bygone Days in Chicago* (Chicago: A. C. McClurg, 1910), 260.

32 Joseph's deafness was selective: Chicago Tribune, *Joseph Medill: A Brief Biography and an Appreciation* (Chicago: Chicago Tribune, 1947), 37.

32 a power shift: Lloyd Wendt, *The Chicago Tribune: The Rise of a Great American Newspaper* (Chicago: Rand McNally, 1979), 206.

33 latest headquarters, on "Newspaper Row": Lloyd Lewis and Henry Justin Smith, *Chicago: The History of Its Reputation* (New York: Harcourt, Brace, 1929), 118.

33 did not invest in fire insurance: Wendt, *The Chicago Tribune*, 222.

33 pseudonym that fooled no one: John J. McPhaul, *Deadlines & Monkeyshines: The Fabled World of Chicago Journalism* (Englewood Cliffs, NJ: Prentice-Hall, 1962), 56.

33 "Chicago is a city": John Tebbel, *An American Dynasty* (1947; reprinted Westport, CT: Greenwood Press, 1968), 49.

34 scarcely an inch and a half of rain: Emmett Dedmon, *Fabulous Chicago: A Great City's History and People* (New York: Random House, 1953), 96.

34 the worst drought in history: Donald L. Miller, *City of the Century: The Epic of Chicago and the Making of America* (New York: Simon & Schuster, 1996), 144.

34 High winds: Caroline Kirkland, *Chicago Yesterdays: A Sheaf of Reminiscences* (Chicago: Daughaday, 1919), 197.

34 prematurely parched leaves: Dedmon, *Fabulous Chicago*, 96.

34 flames jumped the river: Stephen Longstreet, *Chicago 1860–1919* (New York: David McKay, 1973), 124.

34 business district was ablaze: Miller, *City of the Century*, 147–48.

35 A distraught mayor: Dedmon, *Fabulous Chicago*, 100.

35 one hundred and fifty: Ibid.

35 The courthouse bell: Ibid.

35 bridges were choked with humanity: David Lowe, *The Great Chicago Fire in Eyewitness Accounts and 70 Contemporary Photographs and Illustrations* (New York: Dover, 1979), 13.

35 fire again vaulted the river: Dedmon, *Fabulous Chicago*, 103.

36 cowered in the newly opened graves: Longstreet, *Chicago 1860–1919*, 133.

36 the city's rich and powerful: Miller, *City of the Century*, 150.

36 It appeared to be business as usual: Wendt, *The Chicago Tribune*, 234.

36 scoop every other newspaper in town: Ernest Poole, *Giants Gone: Men Who Made Chicago* (New York: Whittlesey House, 1943), 101–3.

36 "Our faces were black": Ibid.

37 burst into flame and melted into nothing: Lowe, *The Great Chicago Fire*, 45.

37 Joseph quickly leased space: Wendt, *The Chicago Tribune*, 235.

37 "and the wind raging": Ibid.

37 "Go to Chicago now!": Miller, *City of the Century*, 169.

38 "Cheer Up": *Chicago Tribune*, October 11, 1871.

38 "Rebuild the City": *Chicago Tribune*, October 12, 1871.

38 "Let the watchword": Ibid.

39 Joseph put the five thousand dollars: A. T. Andreas, *History of Chicago*, vol. 2, *1857–1871* (Chicago: A. T. Andreas, 1975), 771.

39 at the behest of Carter Harrison: Frank Thomas Moriarty, *The Life and Public Service of Joseph Medill* (Unpublished thesis, Northwestern University, 1933), 81.

39 powers of the mayor's office: Smith, *The Colonel*, 30.

39 appropriate taste and conduct: Miller, *City of the Century*, 448.

40 The question of Sunday closings: Wendt, *The Chicago Tribune*, 60.

40 During the first portion: A. T. Andreas, *History of Chicago*, vol. 3, *From the Fire to 1885* (New York: Arno Press), 845.

40 Lester Legrand Bond: Kinsley, *The Chicago Tribune*, vol. 2, 176.

40 He subsequently declined offers: Chicago Tribune, *Joseph Medill: A Brief Biography and an Appreciation*, 3.

40 "Politics and office seeking": Wayne Andrews, *Battle for Chicago* (New York: Harcourt, Brace, 1946), 65.

40 for a year of travel: Kinsley, *The Chicago Tribune*, vol. 2, 176.

40 Together the five Medills: Smith, *The Colonel*, 32.

40 Joseph had added: Wendt, *The Chicago Tribune*, 230.

40 he borrowed: Ibid., 246–47.

41 "Now we meet again": McPhaul, *Deadlines*, 66.

41 Joseph held undisputed control: Kinsley, *The Chicago Tribune*, vol. 2, 200.

41 "This was probably": Ibid.

41 More than ever before, Medill: Tebbel, *An American Dynasty*, 4–5.

5: THE WORST TWO SHE-DEVILS IN ALL OF CHICAGO

42 "Is it my fault": Ralph G. Martin, *Cissy: The Extraordinary Life of Eleanor Medill Patterson* (New York: Simon & Schuster, 1979), 15.

42 It's also probable: Gwen Morgan and Arthur Veysey, *Poor Little Rich Boy: The Life and Times of Col. Robert R. McCormick* (Carpentersville, IL: Crossroads Communications, 1985), 17.

43 "a truly awesome woman": Alice Hoge, *Cissy Patterson: The Life of Eleanor*

Medill Patterson, Publisher & Editor of the Washington Times-Herald (New York: Random House, 1966), 4.

43 "shrewder, brighter": Ibid., 7.

43 her father's favorite: Lloyd Wendt, *The Chicago Tribune: The Rise of a Great American Newspaper* (Chicago: Rand McNally, 1979), 278.

43 a clue to his true priorities: Richard Norton Smith, *The Colonel: The Life & Legend of Robert McCormick 1880–1955* (Boston: Houghton Mifflin, 1997), 32.

44 Obsessed with images: Morgan and Veysey, *Poor Little Rich Boy*, 3.

44 His scholarly: Frank Waldrop, *McCormick of Chicago: An Unconventional Portrait of a Controversial Figure* (Englewood Cliffs, NJ: Prentice-Hall, 1966), 20.

44 The mighty Cyrus: John Tebbel, *An American Dynasty* (1947; reprinted Westport, CT: Greenwood Press, 1968), 41.

44 It was a catastrophic: Ibid., 43.

45 He and Leander: Ibid.

45 It was a distinction: Ibid.

45 "He would like": Wayne Andrews, *Battle for Chicago* (New York: Harcourt, Brace, 1946), 43–44.

45 When the young: Ibid., 44.

45 The gentle, tragic William: Smith, *The Colonel*, 25.

45 Just when his emotional balance: John Tebbel, *The Inheritors: A Study of America's Great Fortunes and What Happened to Them* (New York: G. P. Putnam's Sons, 1962), 217.

45 He was fifty years old: Andrews, *Battle for Chicago*, 45–46.

45 there was a personal grudge: Martin, *Cissy*, 20.

45 Cyrus had encroached: Smith, *The Colonel*, 16.

46 after William's death: Andrews, *Battle for Chicago*, 46, 116.

46 McCormick, Adams & Company: A. T. Andreas, *History of Chicago*, vol. 3, *From the Fire to 1885* (New York: Arno Press), 363.

46 Cyrus Adams: Albert Nelson Marquis, *The Book of Chicagoans* (Chicago: A. N. Marquis, 1911), 13.

46 loans he was never able to repay: Andrews, *Battle for Chicago*, 200.

46 recently completed Miss Porter's: Elinor Medill Patterson obituary, *New York Times*, September 6, 1933, 21.

46 Second Presbyterian Church: Franz Schulze, Rosemary Cowler, and Arthur H. Miller, *30 Miles North: A History of Lake Forest College, Its Town, and Its City of Chicago* (Chicago: University of Chicago Press, 2000), 14.

46 America's Presbyterian Rome: Waldrop, *McCormick of Chicago*, 20.

47 In 1855, when public disorder: Schulze, Cowler, and Miller, *30 Miles North*, 10–11.

47 "the stubborn, aggressive": Tebbel, *An American Dynasty*, 4.

47 "The Robert Sanderson McCormicks": Arthur Meeker, *Chicago, with Love* (New York: Knopf, 1955), 248.

47 "religiously dogmatic Pattersons": Tebbel, *An American Dynasty*, 4.

48 A Williams College graduate: John Leonard, *The Book of Chicagoans* (Chicago: A. N. Marquis, 1905), 449.

48 considered him weak: Martin, *Cissy*, 16–17.

48 Patterson resigned: Ibid., 17.

48 Patterson was a man: Paul Healy, *Cissy: A Biography of Eleanor M. "Cissy" Patterson* (Garden City, NY: Doubleday, 1966), 20.

48 With the progression: Ibid., 19.

48 three servants: United States Census, 1870.

48 Kitty, slightly less polished: Tebbel, *An American Dynasty*, 59.

48 charter members of Fortnightly: Muriel Beadle, *The Fortnightly of Chicago: The City and Its Women: 1873–1973* (Chicago: Henry Regnery, 1973), 13.

48 series of fashionable South Side addresses: McCormick Papers, Colonel Robert R. McCormick Research Center, also Chicago City Directories, Chicago Social Directories.

49 Sunlight streamed: Tebbel, *An American Dynasty*, 60.

49 two rooms: *Chicago Tribune*, February 25, 1935.

49 The library: *Graphic*, December 2, 1891.

49 one of Chicago's finest: Wyatt Rushton, "Joseph Medill & the Chicago Tribune," manuscript, Chicago Historical Society, 16.

49 history and science, no fiction: Chicago Tribune, *Joseph Medill: A Brief Biography and an Appreciation* (Chicago: Chicago Tribune, 1947), 38.

49 He wrote editorials: *Graphic*, December 19, 1891.

49 met with Robert Patterson: Tribune, *Joseph Medill*, 38.

49 attracting skilled engineers: Carl W. Condit, *The Chicago School of Architecture* (Chicago: University of Chicago Press, 1964), 34.

50 "that might stand side by side": Bessie Louise Pierce, *As Others See Chicago: Impressions of Visitors 1673–1933* (Chicago: University of Chicago Press, 1933), 228.

50 "Getting ahead": Hoge, *Cissy Patterson*, 7.

51 she vowed she would name Katrina II: Beadle, *Fortnightly of Chicago*, 77.

51 a boy—the future Colonel: Smith, *The Colonel*, 39.

51 addressed the boy as Roberta: Beadle, *Fortnightly of Chicago*, 77.

51 sometimes even Katrina: Robert Keeler, *Newsday: A Candid History of the Respectable Tabloid* (New York: William Morrow, 1997), 10.

51 dressed little Roberta: Beadle, *Fortnightly of Chicago*, 77.

51 because Joe: Healy, *Cissy*, 20.

51 addressed each other: Hoge, *Cissy Patterson*, 6.

51 Robert retreated to his stable: Ibid.

52 serious sexual disappointment: Joseph Gies, *The Colonel of Chicago* (New York: Dutton, 1979), 26.

52 an autocratic Scottish nanny: Smith, *The Colonel*, 40.

53 "My mother hated me": Morgan and Veysey, *Poor Little Rich Boy*, 24.

53 "My mother and aunt": Ibid.

53 Lost in the drama of inheritance rights: Ibid., 4.

53 "She tried to adopt me": Ibid., 5.

53 But Bert was not the only: Alan Brinkley, *The Publisher: Henry Luce and His American Century* (New York: Knopf, 2010), 17.

53 After praying over: Isaiah Wilner, *The Man Time Forgot: A Tale of Genius, Betrayal, and the Creation of* Time *Magazine* (New York: HarperCollins, 2006), 19.

54 "He is self-contained": Elinor Medill Patterson to Alice Higinbotham Patterson, February 9, 1914, J. M. Patterson Papers.

54 with a book on her head: Healy, *Cissy*, 23.

54 "I am a snob": Eleanor Gizycka, *Fall Flight* (New York: Minton, Balch, 1928), 90.

54 "To understand Cissy": Martin, *Cissy*, 11.

54 climbing the steeple: Tebbel, *An American Dynasty*, 307.

54 operating a lemonade stand: Healy, *Cissy*, 22.

54 "It was like ringing doorbells": Gizycka, *Fall Flight*, 201.

55 "I *don't* come": Joseph Medill Patterson to Alice Higinbotham Patterson, J. M. Patterson Papers.

55 When she climbed: Martin, *Cissy*, 22.

55 Joseph Medill saw extraordinary: Ibid., 24.

55 he wrote to her regularly: Ibid., 24–25.

55 had not inherited: Hoge, *Cissy Patterson*, 9.

55 "Your teeth": Gizycka, *Fall Flight*, 88.

55 "your mouth": Ibid.

56 "I was so handsome": Ibid., 38.

56 "You're very underdeveloped": Ibid., 45.

56 "Your shoulders": Ibid., 86.

56 "I had been brought up": Louise de Koven Bowen, *Open Windows* (Chicago: Ralph Fletcher Seymour, 1946), 51–52.

56 joined their mother: A. T. Andreas, *History of Chicago*, vol. 2, *1857–1871* (Chicago: A. T. Andreas, 1975), 766.

56 Their cooperation: Andreas, *History of Chicago*, vol. 2, 771.

56 Organizations promoting: Bessie Louise Pierce, *A History of Chicago*, vol. 2, *1848–1871* (Chicago: University of Chicago Press, 1913), 456.

57 Socialites gathered : Frances M. Glessner, "Journals 1870–1921," manuscript, Chicago Historical Society.

57 raise funds in support: Pierce, *As Others See Chicago*, 403–4.

57 charter members: Susan Dart, *The Friday Club: The First Hundred Years 1887–1987* (Published privately, 1987), 206.

57 "to encourage every literary": Ibid., 5.

58 gaslit parlors: Arthur Meeker, *Prairie Avenue* (New York: Knopf, 1949), 15.

58 one of several such deliveries: Ibid., 27.

58 While separately making: Hoge, *Cissy Patterson*, 11.

6: THE MEDILL SISTERS' UPWARD SCRAMBLE

59 At Kate's behest: Richard Norton Smith, *The Colonel: The Life & Legend of Robert McCormick 1880–1955* (Boston: Houghton Mifflin, 1997), 43.

59 "Her father": Frank Waldrop, *McCormick of Chicago: An Unconventional Portrait of a Controversial Figure* (Englewood Cliffs, NJ: Prentice-Hall, 1966), 30.

59 Bert didn't mention: Katherine Medill McCormick obituary, *New York Times*, July 5, 1932, 15.

60 Kate was moved to tinker: Waldrop, *McCormick of Chicago*, 32.

60 Dispatched to Harrow: Ibid., 8.

60 Of Ludgrove: Ibid., 33.

60 "One cup of tea": Gwen Morgan and Arthur Veysey, *Poor Little Rich Boy: The Life and Times of Col. Robert R. McCormick* (Carpentersville, IL: Crossroads Communications, 1985), 9.

61 "Ah, a nice little English boy": Ibid., 10.

61 "I am an American": Ibid.

61 Bert recalled only: Ibid., 11.

61 becoming fluent: Waldrop, *McCormick of Chicago*, 35.

61 arsenic as: Morgan and Veysey, *Poor Little Rich Boy*, 11.

61 A highlight of the visit: Cissy Patterson's scrapbook, J. M. Patterson Papers.

61 in early January Josie caught a cold: McCormick Papers, Colonel Robert R. McCormick Research Center.

61 She lived only: Cissy Patterson's scrapbook, J. M. Patterson Papers.

62 DEAREST MOTHER: Katherine Medill McCormick cable draft, McCormick Papers.

62 "Mrs. McCormick": Cissy Patterson's scrapbook, J. M. Patterson Papers.

62 "the coffin was": Ibid.

62 the vast space never: *Chicago Tribune*, February 25, 1935.

62 Her casket was transported: Cissy Patterson's scrapbook, J. M. Patterson Papers.

63 she had been his companion: Lloyd Wendt, *The Chicago Tribune: The Rise of a Great American Newspaper* (Chicago: Rand McNally, 1979), 280.

63 He most missed: Ibid.

63 so similar to trips: Ibid., 145.

63 unit of beds in a Paris hospital: Cissy Patterson's scrapbook, J. M. Patterson Papers.

63 The opportunity: John Franch, *Robber Baron: The Life of Charles Tyson Yerkes* (Urbana: University of Illinois Press, 2006), 154.

63 "Chicagoans must not expect": Ibid.

63 "Such a golden apple": Ibid.

63 "It takes too many": Ibid., 155.

64 George Pullman could not resist: Ibid.

64 only Chicago: Mrs. Carter H. Harrison, *Strange to Say—Recollections of Persons and Events in New Orleans and Chicago* (Chicago: A. Kroch & Son, 1949), 65.

64 At nearly ten times: Russell Lewis, "From Shock City to City Beautiful," *Chicago History*, Fall 2010, 18.

64 Florenz Ziegfeld Jr.: Emmet Dedmon, *Fabulous Chicago: A Great City's History and People* (New York: Random House, 1953), 234–36.

64 Joseph had stepped up: Morgan and Veysey, *Poor Little Rich Boy*, 12.

64 Nellie became a member: Smith, *The Colonel*, 39.

64 Robert McCormick served: Wendt, *The Chicago Tribune*, 300.

65 Writers were especially interested: *Chicago Tribune*, November 15, 1898.

65 "is as good": *Chicago Tribune*, February 3, 1893.

65 Residents and tourists: *Chicago Tribune*, January 20, 1906.

65 "Their stylishness": Bessie Louise Pierce, *As Others See Chicago: Impressions of Visitors 1673–1933* (Chicago: University of Chicago Press, 1933), 311–12.

66 equipped with electric bulbs: Arthur Meeker, *Prairie Avenue* (New York: Knopf, 1949), 154.

66 Gas had moved: Ibid.

66 Designed to produce: Larissa MacFarquhar, "East Side Story," *New Yorker*, February 25, 2008, 59.

66 A primary aim: Ibid.

67 Nellie sent him off: John Tebbel, *An American Dynasty* (1947; reprinted Westport, CT: Greenwood Press, 1968), 279.

67 Joe went out of his way: Joseph Gies, *The Colonel of Chicago* (New York: Dutton, 1979), 14.

67 he was very lonely there: Wayne Andrews, *Battle for Chicago* (New York: Harcourt, Brace, 1946), 223.

67 "I will die": Joseph Medill Patterson to Elinor Medill Patterson and Robert W. Patterson, J. M. Patterson Papers.

67 his grades: Robert Keeler, *Newsday: A Candid History of the Respectable Tabloid* (New York: William Morrow, 1997), 11.

67   "You tell them": Morgan and Veysey, *Poor Little Rich Boy*, 35.

68   "sectional arguments": Ibid.

68   Mrs. Roosevelt traveled: Smith, *The Colonel*, 56.

68   ranches in Montana: Morgan and Veysey, *Poor Little Rich Boy*, 38.

68   Idaho: Gies, *Colonel of Chicago*, 18.

68   Hudson Bay: Ibid.

68   Arizona cattle drive: Smith, *The Colonel*, 79.

68   camping out: Morgan and Veysey, *Poor Little Rich Boy*, 38.

68   During one school: Ibid.

68   entire student body prepared: Smith, *The Colonel*, 53.

69   They could eat: Morgan and Veysey, *Poor Little Rich Boy*, 56.

69   participate in: Gies, *Colonel of Chicago*, 16.

69   herding cattle: Keeler, *Newsday*, 11.

69   "love for Yale": *New York Times*, May 12, 1913, 9.

69   "Groton was very strict": Keeler, *Newsday*, 24.

69   But he did glean: Joseph Medill Patterson, *A Little Brother of the Rich* (Chicago: Reilly & Britton, 1908), 360.

69   He was accepted: Gies, *Colonel of Chicago*, 17.

70   He also embraced polo: Morgan and Veysey, *Poor Little Rich Boy*, 57.

70   "Don't dally": Ibid., 59.

70   Joseph's mother: Cissy Patterson's scrapbook, J. M. Patterson Papers.

70   Kitty's father: Ibid.

70   "must take steps": Joseph Medill to William Medill, Medill File, Chicago History Museum.

70   "Mrs. M. worked": Annie Hitchcock letter, Medill File, Chicago History Museum.

70   During their later years: Cissy Patterson's scrapbook, J. M. Patterson Papers.

70   Kitty suffered: Ibid.

71   "I desire": Katherine Patrick Medill will, McCormick Papers.

71   "My beloved": Joseph Medill to Katherine Patrick Medill, McCormick Papers.

71   Nursing her husband: Morgan and Veysey, *Poor Little Rich Boy*, 34.

71   She was sixty-three: Katherine Patrick Medill obituary, *Chicago Tribune*, October 2, 1894.

71   On its grounds: Chicago Tribune, *Joseph Medill: A Brief Biography and an Appreciation* (Chicago: Chicago Tribune, 1947), 42.

71   The young Pattersons: Waldrop, *McCormick of Chicago*, 39.

71   his idol Benjamin Franklin: Smith, *The Colonel*, 4.

72   Even more against: John Chapman, *Tell It to Sweeney: The Informal History of the New York Daily News* (Garden City, NY: Doubleday, 1961), 29.

72   Although not officially ill: Morgan and Veysey, *Poor Little Rich Boy*, 46.

72 His grandfather's suggestion: Waldrop, *McCormick of Chicago*, 39.

72 pointed him in the direction: Morgan and Veysey, *Poor Little Rich Boy*, 46.

72 Serious problems: Smith, *The Colonel*, 65.

72 developed a kidney infection: Wendt, *The Chicago Tribune*, 349.

73 Flags were flown: Hoge, *Cissy Patterson*, 15.

73 His body was buried: Ibid.

73 "That's where": Ibid.

73 Joseph left: Andrews, *Battle for Chicago*, 201.

73 "The *Tribune*": Morgan and Veysey, *Poor Little Rich Boy*, 53.

73 Performing as usual: Ibid.

74 The handsome: Ralph G. Martin, *Cissy: The Extraordinary Life of Eleanor Medill Patterson* (New York: Simon & Schuster, 1979), 29.

7: CISSY COMES OF AGE

75 The city's most remarkable: Nigel Nicolson, *Mary Curzon* (New York: Harper & Row, 1977), and Kenneth Rose, *Superior Person: A Portrait of Curzon and His Circle in Late Victorian England* (New York: Weybright & Talley, 1969).

76 While the patriarch's death: Wayne Andrews, *Battle for Chicago* (New York: Harcourt, Brace, 1946), 201.

76 the widowed Mrs. Marshall Field: Arthur Meeker, *Chicago, with Love* (New York: Knopf, 1955), 59.

76 Nellie's own capital climb began: Alice Hoge, *Cissy Patterson: The Life of Eleanor Medill Patterson, Publisher & Editor of the Washington Times-Herald* (New York: Random House, 1966), 17.

76 His design for Nellie: Ibid.

76 Turn-of-the-century Washington: Nicolson, *Mary Curzon*, 26.

76 The paved streets: Ibid.

77 Washington's continuous: Ibid., 27.

77 member of the public library board: Richard Norton Smith, *The Colonel: The Life & Legend of Robert McCormick 1880–1955* (Boston: Houghton Mifflin, 1997), 77.

77 Dramatic coloring: Hoge, *Cissy Patterson*, 9, 19.

77 "Watch the way": Ibid., 24.

77 At fifteen: Ibid., 12–13.

77 her first beau: Ralph G. Martin, *Cissy: The Extraordinary Life of Eleanor Medill Patterson* (New York: Simon & Schuster, 1979), 32.

78 accompanied by: Hoge, *Cissy Patterson*, 18.

78 She lavished Worth: Ibid., 19.

78 monitored the girl's: Ibid., 20.

78 Her imitations: Ibid.

78 Among her admirers: Ibid.

78 Freddy: Albert Nelson Marquis, *Who's Who in Chicago 1931* (Chicago: A. N. Marquis, 1931), 659.

79 This enraged: Martin, *Cissy*, 42.

79 March 7, 1901: Frank Waldrop, *McCormick of Chicago: An Unconventional Portrait of a Controversial Figure* (Englewood Cliffs, NJ: Prentice-Hall, 1966), 54.

79 elevated to ambassador: Ibid.

79 Nellie recognized: Hoge, *Cissy Patterson*, 21.

79 In addition to formal balls: Ibid.

80 Among the Austrians: Martin, *Cissy*, 45.

80 After entering a large marble foyer: Ibid.

81 There was the Archduke Otto: Ibid., 44.

81 Three sharp raps: Ibid., 45.

82 "felt her fingertips turn icy cold": Hoge, *Cissy Patterson*, 22.

82 "heavy, sickening thuds": Ibid.

82 lady-in-waiting to Franz Josef's mother: Paul Healy, *Cissy: A Biography of Eleanor M. "Cissy" Patterson* (Garden City, NY: Doubleday, 1966), 28.

82 His Polish father: Martin, *Cissy*, 49.

82 unhappily married Austrian mother: Ibid.

82 lavished affection: Ibid., 83.

83 "I don't believe": Ibid.

83 droit du seigneur: Ibid., 89.

83 "I think it was": *The Times* (London), May 1, 2003.

83 Nellie was rather pleased: Hoge, *Cissy Patterson*, 23.

83 Robert McCormick was transferred: Gwen Morgan and Arthur Veysey, *Poor Little Rich Boy: The Life and Times of Col. Robert R. McCormick* (Carpentersville, IL: Crossroads Communications, 1985), 65.

83 dazzling in the world: Miranda Carter, *George, Nicholas and Wilhelm: Three Royal Cousins and the Road to World War I* (New York: Knopf, 2010), 185.

84 the McCormick carriage: Martin, *Cissy*, 53.

84 Their Majesties' entrance: Eleanor Gizycka, *Fall Flight* (New York: Minton, Balch, 1928), 104.

84 Once inside the palace: Ibid., 106.

84 "Their Imperial Majesties": Ibid.

84 As the doors swung open: Robert K. Massie, *Nicholas and Alexandra* (New York: Atheneum, 1967), 9.

85 Nicholas to the men: Esther Singleton, *Romantic Castles and Palaces as Seen and Described by Famous Writers* (New York: Dodd, Mead, 1901), 124–32.

85 "a vision in flashing jewels": Gizycka, *Fall Flight*, 106–7.

85 "a face from which every vestige": Ibid.

85 "And do you like St. Petersburg?": Ibid.

85 "like a crystal statue": Ibid.

85 "And is this your first visit here?": Ibid.

85 "her immense silver": Ibid.

85 Once the polonaise: Singleton, *Romantic Castles and Palaces*, 124–32.

85 thirty degrees below zero: Martin, *Cissy*, 55.

86 suddenly rose to their feet: Gizycka, *Fall Flight*, 116.

86 The czar: Ibid.

86 the carousel: Healy, *Cissy*, 27.

86 Cissy's equestrian skills: Ibid.

86 he was there: Martin, *Cissy*, 56.

86 a subject of the czar: Hoge, *Cissy Patterson*, 23.

87 Robert Patterson demanded: Healy, *Cissy*, 29.

87 "to show these foreigners": Hoge, *Cissy Patterson*, 23.

87 "in honor . . . made her debut": Cissy Patterson's scrapbook, J. M. Patterson Papers.

8: THE MALE COUSINS: HEIRS, PAWNS,
VICTIMS, SURVIVORS

88 the grandchild: Lloyd Wendt, *The Chicago Tribune: The Rise of a Great American Newspaper* (Chicago: Rand McNally, 1979), 360.

88 his parents sent him: Gwen Morgan and Arthur Veysey, *Poor Little Rich Boy: The Life and Times of Col. Robert R. McCormick* (Carpentersville, IL: Crossroads Communications, 1985), 37.

89 bringing unexpected: Joseph Gies, *The Colonel of Chicago* (New York: Dutton, 1979), 15.

89 he was seated: Frank Waldrop, *McCormick of Chicago: An Unconventional Portrait of a Controversial Figure* (Englewood Cliffs, NJ: Prentice-Hall, 1966), 39.

89 Medill fell in love: Kristie Miller, *Ruth Hanna McCormick: A Life in Politics 1880–1944* (Albuquerque: University of New Mexico Press, 1992), 15.

90 headquarters at: Richard Norton Smith, *The Colonel: The Life & Legend of Robert McCormick 1880–1955* (Boston: Houghton Mifflin, 1997), 73.

90 Washington correspondent: Miller, *Ruth Hanna McCormick*, 26.

90 a career in politics: Ibid.

90 association with Theodore Roosevelt: Ibid., 29.

91 "Mother must": Ibid., 27.

91 "but she must bridle": Ibid.

91 The scale of the wedding fully: *New York Times*, June 11, 1903.

91 "feebleminded": Miller, *Ruth Hanna McCormick*, 14.

91 there would be no children: Ibid., 27.

91 "spent hours sitting": Ibid., 14.

91 unaware that: Ibid., 158.

92 all twelve hundred: *New York Times* June 11, 1903, and Miller, *Ruth Hanna McCormick*, 30–31.

92 they had fun together: Miller, *Ruth Hanna McCormick*, 31, 35.

92 Senator Hanna: Ibid., 33–34.

92 Ruth was forced to admit: Ibid., 35.

92 Kate's chronic interference: Ibid.

92 one of the three: Ibid., 150.

92 income far greater: Ibid., 35.

92 Kate considered avant-garde: Ibid., 36.

93 "Don't forget": Ibid.

93 a quarter of a million dollars: Smith, *The Colonel*, 84.

93 its afternoon companion: Wendt, *The Chicago Tribune*, 360.

93 moved to Cleveland: Morgan and Veysey, *Poor Little Rich Boy*, 66.

93 made treasurer: Wendt, *The Chicago Tribune*, 360.

93 an emotional breakdown: Smith, *The Colonel*, 113.

93 twenty-thousand-dollar: Ibid.

93 Medill sold the Cleveland papers: Morgan and Veysey, *Poor Little Rich Boy*, 100.

94 joining the wives: Smith, *The Colonel*, 110.

94 largest carrier: Morgan and Veysey, *Poor Little Rich Boy*, 104.

94 titles of vice president: Wendt, *The Chicago Tribune*, 360.

94 twenty thousand dollars: Morgan and Veysey, *Poor Little Rich Boy*, 100.

94 city editor: Ibid., 42.

95 While peddling papers: Ibid., 41–42.

95 "News is a commodity": Jay Robert Nash, *People to See: An Anecdotal History of Chicago's Makers and Breakers* (Piscataway, NJ: New Century, 1981), 40.

95 recognition for community service: Edwin Emery, *The Press and America: An Interpretive History of Journalism* (Englewood Cliffs, NJ: Prentice Hall, 1962), 726.

95 reliable news tips: Nash, *People to See*, 40–41.

95 a pompous: Burton Rascoe, *Before I Forget* (Garden City, NY: Doubleday, Doran, 1937), 240.

95 he commanded respect: Nash, *People to See*, 41.

95 J. God Keeley: Ben Hecht, *Charlie: The Improbable Life and Times of Charles MacArthur* (New York: Harper & Brothers, 1957), 39.

96 as Saturday drew: Ibid.

96 "A good newspaperman": Wendt, *The Chicago Tribune*, 345.

96 "There are 10,000 men": John J. McPhaul, *Deadlines & Monkeyshines: The Fabled World of Chicago Journalism* (Englewood Cliffs, NJ: Prentice-Hall, 1962), 106.

96 hired first: John T. McCutcheon, *Drawn from Memory* (Indianapolis: Bobbs-Merrill, 1950), 61.

96 employment with the *Tribune:* Ibid., 190–91.

97 The cartoonist's unique personal qualities: Ibid., and author interviews with Paula McCutcheon and the late Cleveland Amory.

97 "my dear child": Miller, *Ruth Hanna McCormick*, 45.

97 "unless you and Medill": Ibid.

97 leave of absence: Wendt, *The Chicago Tribune*, 361.

97 "infantile relations": Miller, *Ruth Hanna McCormick*, 47.

97 "World's Greatest Newspaper": Tribune Company, *Pictured Encyclopedia of the World's Greatest Newspaper* (Chicago: Chicago Tribune, 1928), 336.

98 long holiday in Japan: Wendt, *The Chicago Tribune*, 367.

98 follow Medill McCormick's: Ibid.

98 "Keeley's somewhat amused": Ibid.

98 "respectable villains": Author's quotes.

98 some of Chicago's: Ibid.

98 directors voted: Smith, *The Colonel*, 127.

98 reappearance of Keeley: Ibid.

98 "Lock it up": Morgan and Veysey, *Poor Little Rich Boy*, 102.

98 put his arm around: Wendt, *The Chicago Tribune*, 367–68.

98 This third nervous breakdown: Smith, *The Colonel*, 126.

99 still a virgin: Morgan and Veysey, *Poor Little Rich Boy*, 68.

99 Central America: Leo E. McGivena and Others, *The News: The First Fifty Years of New York's Picture Newspaper* (New York: News Syndicate, 1969), 27.

99 becoming a judge: John Chapman, *Tell It to Sweeney: The Informal History of the New York Daily News* (Garden City, NY: Doubleday, 1961), 28.

99 possibly governor: Wendt, *The Chicago Tribune*, 374.

99 for a Chicago practice: Gies, *Colonel of Chicago*, 19.

99 will that kept: John Tebbel, *The Marshall Fields: A Study in Wealth* (New York: E. P. Dutton, 1948), 112.

100 squalid: Gies, *Colonel of Chicago*, 20.

100 resembled: Wendt, *The Chicago Tribune*, 377.

100 addressing him as "Mac": Gies, *Colonel of Chicago*, 21.

100 one of the boys: Ibid.

100 notoriously corrupt: Waldrop, *McCormick of Chicago*, 76.

100 Sanitary District of Chicago: District has since been renamed the Metropolitan Water Reclamation District of Greater Chicago.

101 river soon to: Gies, *Colonel of Chicago*, 22.

101 "If you were to say": Ibid.

101 seven patents in his name: Morgan and Veysey, *Poor Little Rich Boy*, 158.

101 disregarded younger brother: Waldrop, *McCormick of Chicago*, 81.

101 Bert became an expert: Morgan and Veysey, *Poor Little Rich Boy*, 89.

102 widespread favorable regard: Gies, *Colonel of Chicago*, 23.

102 electricity from Lockport: Chapman, *Tell It to Sweeney*, 28.

102 Stuart Gore Shepard: Morgan and Veysey, *Poor Little Rich Boy*, 108.

102 Tribune Building's: Gies, *Colonel of Chicago*, 25.

102 finally graduated: Ibid., 26.

102 almost died: Jack Alexander, "Vox Populi II," *New Yorker*, August 13, 1938, 20.

102 assistant Sunday editor: Wendt, *The Chicago Tribune*, 375.

103 work shirt open: Rascoe, *Before I Forget*, 241.

103 "wearing two pairs": *American Mercury*, December 9, 1944, 676.

104 "does not go slumming": George Seldes, *Lords of the Press* (New York: Julian Messner, 1938), 38.

104 another cosseted: Jack Alexander, "Vox Populi I," *New Yorker*, August 6, 1938, 16.

104 she was twenty-one: Cissy Patterson's scrapbook, J. M. Patterson Papers.

104 reception that followed: *Chicago American*, November 19, 1902.

104 The bride: Ibid.

104 Medill's then-fiancée: *New York Times*, November 20, 1902, 7.

105 platform of "municipal ownership": Wendt, *The Chicago Tribune*, 375–67.

105 "Capitalism has seen the end": Ibid., 376.

105 presented Joe's resignation: Ibid.

105 "always wanted": Joseph Medill Patterson to Elinor Medill Patterson, March 6, 1905, J. M. Patterson Papers.

105 "It seems to me": Wendt, *The Chicago Tribune*, 376.

105 including his father-in-law's: Smith, *The Colonel*, 106.

106 pushing family: McGivena, *The News*, 18.

106 "Money is power": *New York Times*, March 4, 1906, 5.

106 "It isn't fair": Ibid.

106 "I am really undecided": Ibid.

106 designed by architect: Virginia A. Greene, *The Architecture of Howard Van Doren Shaw* (Chicago: Chicago Review Press, 1998), 123.

107 his lavish-spending: Smith, *The Colonel*, 125.

107 they would stay at the Virginia: Elinor Medill Patterson to Alice Higinbotham Patterson, March 9, 1909, J. M. Patterson Papers.

107 "He hated parties": Robert Keeler, *Newsday: A Candid History of the Respectable Tabloid* (New York: William Morrow, 1997), 16.

107 second woman: Michael Dobbs, *Madeleine Albright: A Twentieth-Century Odyssey* (New York: Henry Holt, 1999), 175.

107 "She would have preferred": *Saturday Evening Post*, February 21, 1959, 45.

107 "In fact, she took": Ibid.

108 national campaign manager: Waldrop, *McCormick of Chicago*, 68.

108 Joe was bagging: Alexander, *New Yorker*, August 13, 1938, 21.

108 "The work of": George Seldes, *Lords of the Press*, 22.

108 feeling a "money pinch": Rascoe, *Before I Forget*, 249.

108 "People who do not know me very well": *Saturday Evening Post*, February 21, 1959, 44.

109 "Wish Joe would go": Elinor Medill Patterson to Alice Higinbotham Patterson, June 8, 1908, J. M. Patterson Papers.

109 "Dear Aluss": Joseph Medill Patterson to Alice Higinbotham Patterson, May 14, 1908, en route to Plymouth, then Cherbourg, J. M. Patterson Papers.

110 collaborated with James Keeley: Chapman, *Tell It to Sweeney*, 35.

110 Joe's message: Alexander, *New Yorker*, August 13, 1938, 21.

110 earliest serious: Kim Coventry, Daniel Meyer, and Arthur H. Miller, *Classic Country Estates of Lake Forest* (New York: Norton, 2003), 113.

110 Another *Post* piece: Ibid.

111 "deliberately trying": *New York Times*, May 12, 1913, 9.

111 "right in line with": Ibid.

9: CISSY: DEBUATANTE COUNTESS

112 After settling into: Cissy Patterson's scrapbook, J. M. Patterson Papers.

112 "Cabinet Circle": Alice Hoge, *Cissy Patterson: The Life of Eleanor Medill Patterson, Publisher & Editor of the Washington Times-Herald* (New York: Random House, 1966), 25.

112 an even more exclusive: Ibid. 25.

112 Count Arthur Cassini: Marguerite Cassini, *Never a Dull Moment* (New York: Harper & Brothers, 1956), 99, 101.

112 "the Three Graces": Hoge, *Cissy Patterson*, 25.

113 "Alice Blue": Carol Felsenthal, *Alice Roosevelt Longworth* (New York: G. P. Putnam's Sons, 1988), 59.

113 First Daughter's shocking: James Brough, *Princess Alice: A Biography of Alice Roosevelt Longworth* (Boston: Little, Brown, 1975), 144.

113 betting on racehorses: Felsenthal, *Alice Roosevelt Longworth*, 64.

113 Alice climbed onto: Brough, *Princess Alice*, 118.

113 "I can be President": Ibid., 151.

113   she buried a voodoo idol: Ibid., 15.

113   an ultrasophisticated: Cassini, *Never a Dull Moment*, 94.

113   She spoke six languages: Ibid., 95.

113   "too much physical charm": Ibid., 176.

113   swansdown puff: Brough, *Princess Alice*, 143–44.

114   child of the count's: Cassini, *Never a Dull Moment*, 11.

114   "Could there be a better": Ibid., 112.

114   Nicholas Longworth: Ralph G. Martin, *Cissy: The Extraordinary Life of Eleanor Medill Patterson* (New York: Simon & Schuster, 1979), 62–63.

114   "Be careful": Brough, *Princess Alice*, 157.

114   "And you be careful": Ibid.

114   Nick's former loves: Felsenthal, *Alice Roosevelt Longworth*, 97.

115   seat her next to Joe: Cassini, *Never a Dull Moment*, 201–2.

115   "Never did I work": Ibid., 202.

115   "All right, you win": Ibid.

115   "I won't be": Ibid.

115   the amazing revelation: Ibid., 335.

115   Fearing elopement: Hoge, *Cissy Patterson*, 25.

115   April 14, 1904 at noon: *New York Times*, April 15, 1904.

116   presented with a silver cigarette case: Paul Healy, *Cissy: A Biography of Eleanor M. "Cissy" Patterson* (Garden City, NY: Doubleday, 1966), 30.

116   "Suppose he is marrying": Hoge, *Cissy Patterson*, 26.

116   "Darling, remember": Ibid.

116   A veil of white tulle: Martin, *Cissy*, 80.

116   bouquet of white roses: Healy, *Cissy*, 32.

116   Count Ivan Rubido-Zichy: Cassini, *Never a Dull Moment*, 202.

116   lavish floral displays: Healy, *Cissy*, 32.

116   ribbons tied there: Martin, *Cissy*, 81.

117   reneged on the dowry: Hoge, *Cissy Patterson*, 26–27.

117   would meet Cissy: Ibid.

117   accounting error was corrected: Cassini, *Never a Dull Moment*, 202.

117   large picture hat: Healy, *Cissy*, 32.

117   "Darling, remember": Martin, *Cissy*, 81.

117   "I always felt": Cassini, *Never a Dull Moment*, 202.

117   "Now go to bed": Martin, *Cissy*, 81.

117   "Ugh!": Ibid., 82.

117   "But he was a *man*": Ibid.

118   "little girls, little snowfields": Ibid., 83.

118   Sacher Hotel: Hoge, *Cissy Patterson*, 31.

118   "for a few days": Martin, *Cissy*, 85.

118   Narvosielica: As spelled by the *New York Times*, April 15, 1904.

118   Halfway between: Martin, *Cissy*, 86.

119   "Our village": Eleanor Gizycka, *Fall Flight* (New York: Minton, Balch, 1928), 164.

119   a huddle of mud huts: Ibid.

119   children's faces bore: Martin, *Cissy*, 89.

119   "This is the beginning": Gizycka, *Fall Flight*, 165.

119   flowers and ribbons: Ibid.

119   "This is our private park": Ibid.

119   "My father never finished": Ibid., 166.

119   "He had several": Ibid.

120   brought a personal maid: Healy, *Cissy*, 36–37.

120   with a child: Martin, *Cissy*, 90.

120   mistress for five years: Healy, *Cissy*, 46.

120   "quite a lot of other rooms": Gizycka, *Fall Flight*, 172.

120   The count's rages: Hoge, *Cissy Patterson*, 31.

120   as much as a million dollars: It was "close to $500,000," according to Martin, *Cissy*, 79, but other sources speculated that the figure was a million dollars.

120   between twenty: Martin, *Cissy*, 78.

120   thirty thousand dollars: Healy, *Cissy*, 37.

120   "A man marries to get": Gizycka, *Fall Flight*, 218.

120   "Otherwise, why would he": Ibid.

121   exercise her horses: Hoge, *Cissy Patterson*, 38.

121   Josef, expecting a male: Ibid.

121   Vienna hospital twenty-four: Healy, *Cissy*, 38, 46.

121   feminine frailties displeasing: Hoge, *Cissy Patterson*, 3.

121   catalog of his many: Martin, *Cissy*, 107.

121   Nellie arrived: Ibid., 106.

121   a peasant midwife: Healy, *Cissy*, 37-38.

122   In December 1907: Martin, *Cissy*, 113.

122   a train to Paris: Healy, *Cissy*, 38.

122   bound for London: Ibid., 38–39.

122   Robert Patterson, in London: *New York Times* January 29, 1911.

122   Hampden, Middlesex: Martin, *Cissy*, 116.

122   take the child for a drive: *New York Times*, January 29, 1911.

122   demand in damages from his brother-in-law: Hoge, *Cissy Patterson*, 41.

123   czar's mother: Martin, *Cissy*, 122.

123   "Child, I have had": Healy, *Cissy*, 40.

123   their position with the *Tribune*: Lloyd Wendt, *The Chicago Tribune: The Rise of a Great American Newspaper* (Chicago: Rand McNally, 1979), 360.

123   health failed rapidly: Joseph Gies, *The Colonel of Chicago* (New York: Dutton, 1979), 28.

123   3000 Massachusetts Avenue: Frank Waldrop, *McCormick of Chicago: An Unconventional Portrait of a Controversial Figure* (Englewood Cliffs, NJ: Prentice-Hall, 1966), 91.

124   He was arrested on arrival: Martin, *Cissy*, 126–27.

124   Medill and Ruth McCormick: Healy, *Cissy*, 42.

124   August 18, 1909: Ibid., 35.

124   a decree of separation: Healy, *Cissy*, 43.

10: DYNASTY IN JEOPARDY

125   Boston sanitarium: Lloyd Wendt, *The Chicago Tribune: The Rise of a Great American Newspaper* (Chicago: Rand McNally, 1979), 378.

125   she assumed his seat: Wayne Andrews, *Battle for Chicago* (New York: Harcourt, Brace, 1946), 231–32.

125   a coup against his father: Richard Norton Smith, *The Colonel: The Life & Legend of Robert McCormick 1880–1955* (Boston: Houghton Mifflin, 1997), 126.

125   "he should not": Joseph Gies, *The Colonel of Chicago* (New York: Dutton, 1979), 29.

126   "never before identified": *Chicago Evening Post*, February 16, 1910, 1.

126   " 'We will correct that' ": Gies, *Colonel of Chicago*, 29.

126   unless Medill McCormick: Frank Waldrop, *McCormick of Chicago: An Unconventional Portrait of a Controversial Figure* (Englewood Cliffs, NJ: Prentice-Hall, 1966), 92.

126   "absolute authority": Leo E. McGivena and Others, *The News: The First Fifty Years of New York's Picture Newspaper* (New York: News Syndicate, 1969), 10.

126   rare visit to his wife: Gies, *Colonel of Chicago*, 29.

126   dying mother: Smith, *The Colonel*, 128.

126   succeed him at the *Tribune:* Gwen Morgan and Arthur Veysey, *Poor Little Rich Boy: The Life and Times of Col. Robert R. McCormick* (Carpentersville, IL: Crossroads Communications, 1985), 116.

127   strengthen its morning: Ibid.

127   extension of a series: Wendt, *The Chicago Tribune*, 361.

127   "Had Patterson lived": Gies, *Colonel of Chicago*, 30.

127   price war against: Morgan and Veysey, *Poor Little Rich Boy*, 117.

127   "an overdose of Veronal": Smith, *The Colonel*, 128.

127   city completely out: Waldrop, *McCormick of Chicago*, 92.

127   a double funeral: John Tebbel, *An American Dynasty* (1947; reprinted Westport, CT: Greenwood Press, 1968), 76.

127   one of the most notable funerals: Waldrop, *McCormick of Chicago*, 92.

127   "Nellie sure got ahead": Alice Hoge, *Cissy Patterson: The Life of Eleanor Medill Patterson, Publisher & Editor of the Washington Times-Herald* (New York: Random House, 1966), 7.

128   a necessary move: Smith, *The Colonel*, 128 fn.

128   leave without salary: Ibid., 129.

128   "someone vitally interested": Ibid.

128   this was the opinion: Gies, *Colonel of Chicago*, 29–30.

128   White's stake: John J. McPhaul, *Deadlines & Monkeyshines: The Fabled World of Chicago Journalism* (Englewood Cliffs, NJ: Prentice-Hall, 1962), 215–16.

128   "Would it make any difference": Wendt, *The Chicago Tribune*, 382.

128   "It certainly would": Ibid.

128   convincing them to hold out: McPhaul, *Deadlines*, 216.

128   price of the *Record-Herald:* Wendt, *The Chicago Tribune*, 382.

129   Tobias Annenberg: Christopher Ogden, *Legacy: A Biography of Moses and Walter Annenberg* (Boston: Little, Brown, 1999), 9.

129   "Those who were accustomed": Burton Rascoe, *Before I Forget* (Garden City, NY: Doubleday, Doran, 1937), 269.

130   "the Annenbergs": Ibid.

130   contract were illegal: Jay Robert Nash, *People to See: An Anecdotal History of Chicago's Makers and Breakers* (Piscataway, NJ: New Century, 1981), 29.

130   "to give them to understand": Andrews, *Battle for Chicago*, 234.

130   "wild man": Jay Robert Nash, *People to See*, 31.

131   Moe remained: Wendt, *The Chicago Tribune*, 383–84.

131   became reciprocal: Gies, *Colonel of Chicago*, 36.

131   *Tribune* won the war: Wendt, *The Chicago Tribune*, 383.

131   Some of the thugs: W. A. Swanberg, *Citizen Hearst* (New York: Charles Scribner's Sons, 1961), 322.

131   Mossy murdered Dutch: Andrews, *Battle for Chicago*, 239.

131   "I had to get him": Richard Lindberg, *Chicago by Gaslight: A History of Chicago's Netherworld 1880–1920* (Chicago: Academy Chicago 1996), 180.

131   Bert's law firm: Smith, *The Colonel*, 150.

131   His déclassé background: Rascoe, *Before I Forget*, 270.

132   Max crossed over: Ibid., 272–73.

132   Al Capone era: Nash, *People to See*, 27–32.

132   "Max Annenberg": Robert R. McCormick radio broadcast, 1952.

132   it was for cash: Lindberg, *Chicago by Gaslight*, 181.

132   penitentiary at Lewisburg: Ogden, *Legacy*, 232.

132   feared that he would: Ibid.

132   died at the age of sixty-five: Ibid., 243–44.

132 largest such case: Ibid., 218.

133 ambassador to the Court of St. James's: Ogden, *Legacy*, 3.

133 future in Congress: Gies, *Colonel of Chicago*, 31.

133 "I shall go to work": John Chapman, *Tell It to Sweeney: The Informal History of the New York Daily News* (Garden City, NY: Doubleday, 1961), 34.

133 "as a minor irritation": Rascoe, *Before I Forget*, 242.

134 Joe became chairman: Ibid, 385.

134 Keeley agreed to continue: Ibid.

134 "The family knew": Ibid., 400.

134 halt to the puff pieces: Gies, *Colonel of Chicago*, 39.

134 autonomy to business: Ibid., 40.

134 "invented the science": Wendt, *The Chicago Tribune*, 94.

135 By the July board meeting: Gies, *Colonel of Chicago*, 41.

135 *Tribune*'s newsprint needs: Chapman, *Tell It to Sweeney*, 31.

135 clause within the 1861 *Tribune*: Wendt, *The Chicago Tribune*, 100.

135 They voted an expenditure: Gies, *Colonel of Chicago*, 41.

135 spruce forests of Canada: Wendt, *The Chicago Tribune*, 3.

135 one of the country's major industries: Ibid., 4.

135 Sunday editor left abruptly: Smith, *The Colonel*, 140.

135 Sunday edition is the flagship: Frank Luther Mott, *American Journalism: A History of Newspapers in the United States Through 250 Years 1690 to 1940* (New York: Macmillan, 1941), 585.

136 *Tribune*'s flagship was losing: Wendt, *The Chicago Tribune*, 392.

136 Mary had been secretary: Rascoe, *Before I Forget*, 248.

136 "gave me a new attitude": Kristie Miller, *Ruth Hanna McCormick: A Life in Politics 1880–1944* (Albuquerque: University of New Mexico Press, 1992), 37.

136 counterproductive: Rascoe, *Before I Forget*, 249.

137 coverage of film stars: Wendt, *The Chicago Tribune*, 392–93.

137 grew to seventy-two pages: Mott, *American Journalism*, 584.

137 "mildly insane on the subject": Rascoe, *Before I Forget*, 250.

137 make magazines obsolete: Ibid.

137 By 1914: Mott, *American Journalism*, 584–85.

137 added such audience builders: Ibid.

137 empty life of the idle rich: Morgan and Veysey, *Poor Little Rich Boy*, 67.

138 "Thank you very much": Joseph Medill Patterson to Elinor Medill Patterson, J. M. Patterson Papers.

138 "show yourself": Miller, *Ruth Hanna McCormick*, 49.

138 career in politics: Ibid., 48.

139 Senator Robert La Follette: Morgan and Veysey, *Poor Little Rich Boy*, 116.

139 joined TR's team: Ibid., 124.

139 condemned Medill as a traitor: Waldrop, *McCormick of Chicago*, 67.

139 She threw her energies: Ralph G. Martin, *Cissy: The Extraordinary Life of Eleanor Medill Patterson* (New York: Simon & Schuster, 1979), 146.

139 the tall, rangy: Ibid., 145.

139 interesting human being: Ibid., 146.

139 Woodrow Wilson: Wendt, *The Chicago Tribune*, 331.

139 climbing off a train: Smith, *The Colonel*, 142–43.

140 her brother Daniel in Ohio: Miller, *Ruth Hanna McCormick*, 101.

140 battling alcoholism: Ibid., 14.

140 should be institutionalized: Ibid., 101.

140 "Finally, Medill appeared": Ibid.

140 "he may have stopped drinking": Ibid.

140 Borden Company: Miller, *Ruth Hanna McCormick*, 104.

141 Victor Lawson was still involved: Tebbel, *An American Dynasty*, 93.

142 "The ironbound agreement": Wendt, *The Chicago Tribune*, 397.

142 until both had died: Ibid.

142 little comment: Gies, *Colonel of Chicago*, 44.

142 *Tribune* circulation increased: McPhaul, *Deadlines*, 224–25.

142 Pullman Building: Smith, *The Colonel*, 144.

143 production of the suburban edition: Ibid.

11: THE COUNTESS AND HER ADMIRERS

144 "the most glamorous": Scott Donaldson, *Hemingway vs. Fitzgerald: The Rise and Fall of a Literary Friendship* (Woodstock, NY: Overlook Press, 1999), 31.

145 Cissy sued Count Gizycki: *New York Times*, January 29, 1911.

145 "the count struck": Ibid.

145 half-million-dollar ransom: Ibid.

145 custody of her daughter: Paul Healy, *Cissy: A Biography of Eleanor M. "Cissy" Patterson* (Garden City, NY: Doubleday, 1966), 48.

145 "like opium": Ralph G. Martin, *Jennie: The Life of Lady Randolph Churchill*, vol. 2 (Englewood Cliffs, NJ: Prentice-Hall, 1971), 2.

145 "as the most graceful human": *Vogue*, April 1, 1965, 200.

145 Freddy McLaughlin: Ralph G. Martin, *Cissy: The Extraordinary Life of Eleanor Medill Patterson* (New York: Simon & Schuster, 1979), 131.

145 The coffee company heir: Healy, *Cissy*, 49–50.

146 A rival suitor: Martin, *Cissy*, 136.

146 raced off without his lady: Healy, *Cissy*, 50–51.

146   reflect poorly on Cissy: Alice Hoge, *Cissy Patterson: The Life of Eleanor Medill Patterson, Publisher & Editor of the Washington Times-Herald* (New York: Random House, 1966), 46.

146   Designed by Howard Van Doren Shaw: Kim Coventry, Daniel Meyer, and Arthur H. Miller, *Classic Country Estates of Lake Forest* (New York: Norton, 2003), 94.

146   Newport: Hoge, *Cissy Patterson*, 52.

146   "before the lamps went out": Geoffrey Marcus, *Before the Lamps Went Out: Britain's Golden Age, Christmas 1913–August 1914* (Boston: Atlantic/Little, Brown, 1965).

147   his troubled marriage: Martin, *Cissy*, 138–39.

147   grow in print: Ibid., 144.

147   Cissy's acting phase: Hoge, *Cissy Patterson*, 53.

147   Hull House: Healy, *Cissy*, 49.

147   best amateur he had seen: Ibid.

147   Although critics: Martin, *Cissy*, 140–41.

147   "nervous" and "high strung": Elinor Medill Patterson to Alice Higinbotham Patterson, February 14, 1912, J. M. Patterson Papers.

147   "a delicate woman": Martin, *Cissy*, 130.

147   Felicia remembered watching: *Vogue*, April 1, 1965, 200.

148   "She looked like a big wildcat": Ibid., 200, 203.

148   a brutal shock: Healy, *Cissy*, 55.

148   immediately sent home: Hoge, *Cissy Patterson*, 57.

148   free of a nanny: Ibid., 56.

148   Initially Cissy stayed: Ibid., 57.

148   "my mother enchanted Cal": *Vogue*, April 1, 1965, 203.

148   stalking her bull elk: Hoge, *Cissy Patterson*, 58.

148   It was a new kind: Ibid.

148   Carrington, then in his: Martin, *Cissy*, 156.

148   He named himself: Ibid., 156–57.

149   she saw Cal's spread: Hoge, *Cissy Patterson*, 61.

149   His valley: Martin, *Cissy*, 157–58.

149   Moose, elk, bear: Ibid., 166.

149   "I could see the sheriff": *Vogue*, April 1, 1965, 203.

149   "put up two": Martin, *Cissy*, 158.

149   Cissy insisted: Ibid., 165, 206.

149   Her cook: Ibid., 166.

149   Soon furniture: Ibid., 206–7; Hoge, *Cissy Patterson*, 61.

149   "born with nineteen legs": Martin, *Cissy*, 173.

149   She felt comfortable: Ibid., 171.

150   All urban pretension: Healy, *Cissy*, 69.

150   "Cal was a quiet drunk": Martin, *Cissy*, 209.

150   first woman to navigate: Hoge, *Cissy Patterson*, 63; Healy, *Cissy*, 69.

150   Forbidden River: Martin, *Cissy*, 192.

150   buried the year before: Ibid., 193.

150   The relationship: Ibid., 173.

150   He respected: Hoge, *Cissy Patterson*, 60.

150   *Field & Stream*: Ibid., 63.

151   *Chicago Herald-Examiner* to commission: Healy, *Cissy*, 53–54.

151   *Omaha World Journal*: Martin, *Cissy*, 175.

151   first newspaper article: Healy, *Cissy*, 58.

151   "She'd like to sit": Martin, *Cissy*, 161.

151   She took Cal: Ibid., 198–99.

151   She sent him to Italy: Ibid., 199.

151   shanty-Irish bitches: Hoge, *Cissy Patterson*, 67.

151   "I've laughed with you": *Vogue*, April 1, 1965, 205.

151   "the greatest influence": Healy, *Cissy*, 60.

151   "she could do anything": Ibid.

151   "Her curiosity about people": *Vogue*, April 1, 1965, 205.

152   "fiercely when they were together": Martin, *Cissy*, 147.

152   buy a house on R Street: Ibid.

152   Ruth and Medill: Ibid., 165.

152   The two enjoyed: Ibid., 204.

152   In 1905: Evalyn Walsh McLean, *Father Struck It Rich* (Ouray, CO: Bear Creek, 1981), 148–51.

152   eloped on a whim: Ibid., 167.

152   In the years: Carol Felsenthal, *Alice Roosevelt Longworth* (New York: G. P. Putnam's Sons, 1988), 191–92 fn.

152   Marion Davies's sister Rose: Ibid., 191 fn.

152   suffered a nervous breakdown: Ibid.

153   potential presidential candidate: Martin, *Cissy*, 190.

153   Senator William Edgar Borah: Ibid., 164.

153   "Stallion of Idaho": Felsenthal, *Alice Roosevelt Longworth*, 147.

153   conveniently away from Washington: Ibid.

153   "Aurora Borah Alice": Ibid.

153   a barren marriage: James Brough, *Princess Alice: A Biography of Alice Roosevelt Longworth* (Boston: Little, Brown, 1975), 268.

153   the baby resembled: Felsenthal, *Alice Roosevelt Longworth*, 157.

153   naming the child Deborah: Ibid.

153   honor of the Apostle Paul: Brough, *Princess Alice*, *269*.

153   "I said a lot of things": Martin, *Cissy*, 10.

153   "If any man ever caused": Ibid., 190.

154   When someone opened: Ibid.

154   "I believe they are yours": Ibid., 189.

154   "And if you look": Ibid.

154   "Stop the presses": Healy, *Cissy*, 9.

154   led Ben Hecht to insist: Martin, *Cissy*, 178.

154   he was her masculine: Ibid.

154   Cissy respected: Ibid.

155   an error the *Tribune*: Hoge, *Cissy Patterson*, 70.

155   Mr. Hearst was backing: Ibid., 71.

155   Elmer Schlesinger: Martin, *Cissy*, 186.

155   soon-to-become-historic: Ibid., 111.

155   "We've got a lot": Ibid., 187.

155   "The day of giants": Ibid.

155   "on a couch": Ibid.

156   the plausible rumor: Ibid., 206.

156   "a lion": Ibid., 186.

156   BORAH IS COUNTESS: Hoge, *Cissy Patterson*, 71–72.

12: WORLD WAR I AND THE CREATION OF COLONEL ROBERT R. MCCORMICK

157   more than the greens: Gwen Morgan and Arthur Veysey, *Poor Little Rich Boy: The Life and Times of Col. Robert R. McCormick* (Carpentersville, IL: Crossroads Communications, 1985), 71, 266.

157   Bert's affair with the wife: Joseph Gies, *The Colonel of Chicago* (New York: Dutton, 1979), 51.

157   daughter of Bernard J. D. Irwin: Ibid.

158   she was a handsome: Frank Waldrop, *McCormick of Chicago: An Unconventional Portrait of a Controversial Figure* (Englewood Cliffs, NJ: Prentice-Hall, 1966), 108.

158   Originally known as Amie: Ibid.

158   begun innocently enough: Ibid., 107.

158   became inseparable: Morgan and Veysey, *Poor Little Rich Boy*, 126.

158   becoming lovers: Richard Norton Smith, *The Colonel: The Life & Legend of Robert McCormick 1880–1955* (Boston: Houghton Mifflin, 1997), 146.

158   "Poor poor Bertie": Ibid.

158 "It is his Mother's fault": Elinor Medill Patterson to Alice Higinbotham Patterson, February 9, 1914, J. M. Patterson Papers.

158 "Poor Bertie—Amy": Elinor Medill Patterson to Alice Higinbotham Patterson, September 6, 1914, J. M. Patterson Papers.

158 "That old tart": Smith, *The Colonel*, 147.

158 "Who could live": Ibid.

158 The divorce: Ibid.

159 New York and Milwaukee: Morgan and Veysey, *Poor Little Rich Boy*, 130.

159 the "old strumpet": Smith, *The Colonel*, 153.

160 fifty-thousand-dollar enticement: Morgan and Veysey, *Poor Little Rich Boy*, 131.

160 George Bakhmeteff: Lloyd Wendt, *The Chicago Tribune: The Rise of a Great American Newspaper* (Chicago: Rand McNally, 1979), 149.

160 "preserved the best": Gies, *Colonel of Chicago*, 51.

160 "a distinguished foreigner": Ibid.

160 aboard the S.S. *Adriatic*: Gies, *Colonel of Chicago*, 52.

160 Mary Garden: Arthur Meeker, *Chicago, with Love* (New York: Knopf, 1955), 99.

160 married in London: Gies, *Colonel of Chicago*, 52.

160 "Amie de Houle Adams": Smith, *The Colonel*, 159.

161 "of full age": Ibid.

161 two pearl necklaces: Morgan and Veysey, *Poor Little Rich Boy*, 134.

161 Lord Northcliffe: Smith, *The Colonel*, 155.

161 Tsarskoe Selo: Robert K. Massie, *Nicholas and Alexandra* (New York: Atheneum, 1967), 117–18.

161 gunfire incident: Sir Bernard Pares, *A History of Russia* (New York: Knopf, 1926), 448.

162 his surroundings: Morgan and Veysey, *Poor Little Rich Boy*, 142.

162 variety of books: Ibid.

162 simple olive uniform: Smith, *The Colonel*, 164.

162 "I am very pleased": Morgan and Veysey, *Poor Little Rich Boy*, 143.

162 "the largest eyes": Gies, *Colonel of Chicago*, 55.

162 "less of an accent": Morgan and Veysey, *Poor Little Rich Boy*, 143.

163 cheese sandwich: Waldrop, *McCormick of Chicago*, 123.

163 An awesome figure: Massie, *Nicholas and Alexandra*, 287.

163 a legend throughout: Ibid., 316.

163 presided from a private car: Ibid., 294.

163 a favorable impression: Smith, *The Colonel*, 169.

164 "There was one": Gies, *Colonel of Chicago*, 56.

164 She and her sister: Massie, *Nicholas and Alexandra*, 244.

164 "the black peril": Marguerite Cassini, *Never a Dull Moment* (New York: Harper & Brothers, 1956), 99, 151.

164 fulfilled the long-held: Ibid.

164 He was correct: Edvard Radzinsky, *The Last Tsar: The Life and Death of Nicholas II* (New York: Doubleday, 1992), 26.

164 She would survive: Robert K. Massie and Jeffrey Finestone, *The Last Courts of Europe* (New York: Greenwich House, 1981), 25.

165 Having achieved: Waldrop, *McCormick of Chicago*, 132.

165 This bit of gossip: Smith, *The Colonel*, 218.

165 rented a furnished house: Real Estate file, J. M. Patterson Papers.

165 the Greenbrier: Cleveland Amory, *The Last Resorts* (New York: Harper & Brothers, 1948), 4.

165 Joe's letters: Joseph Medill Patterson to Alice Higinbotham Patterson, J. M. Patterson Papers.

165 TO ALICE: Ibid.

166 I SHALL: Ibid.

166 FOR THE LOVE: Ibid.

166 Eventually she returned: Ibid.

166 "poor wrongheaded goat": Smith, *The Colonel*, 168.

166 "for a worthless antique": Ibid.

166 "Poor baby boy": Ibid., 178.

167 recorded a visual account: *Time*, May 7, 1928.

167 The footage: Wendt, *McCormick of Chicago*, 415.

167 The success: Gies, *Colonel of Chicago*, 61.

167 "He would come in": Burton Rascoe, *Before I Forget* (Garden City, NY: Doubleday, Doran, 1937), 265–66.

168 "an anarchistic enemy": Richard Lindberg, *Chicago by Gaslight: A History of Chicago's Netherworld 1880–1920* (Chicago: Academy Chicago, 1996), 189–90.

168 The furious Ford: Ibid., 192.

168 Eventually promoted: John Tebbel, *An American Dynasty* (1947; reprinted Westport, CT: Greenwood Press, 1968), 289.

169 "Lord, how I wish": Smith, *The Colonel*, 188.

169 On their arrival: Gies, *Colonel of Chicago*, 67.

169 "the funny side": Ibid.

170 Spring 1918: Smith, *The Colonel*, 191.

170 In late May: Waldrop, *McCormick of Chicago*, 172.

170 some seventy-five miles: McCormick Papers, Colonel Robert R. McCormick Research Center.

170 near the village: Waldrop, *McCormick of Chicago*, 170.

170 McCormick suffered: Gies, *Colonel of Chicago*, 72.

170 dearth of experienced: Ibid.

170 he had to remain: Ibid.

170 remained with his men: Smith, *The Colonel*, 204.

170 several other factors: Ibid., 205.

171 taking of Cantigny accomplished: Gies, *Colonel of Chicago*, 73.

171 Although his veracity: Waldrop, *McCormick of Chicago*, 170.

171 promoted to the rank: Gies, *Colonel of Chicago*, 73.

171 returned with Amy: Ibid., 74.

171 commission as brigadier general: Ibid.

171 Distinguished Service Medal: Waldrop, *McCormick of Chicago*, 172.

171 War Department citation: Ibid., 173.

13: THE JAZZ AGE COLLIDES WITH THE *CHICAGO TRIBUNE*

173 Hollywood discovered: TCM, *The Golden Age of the Gangster Film*, 2008.

174 Maurine Dallas Watkins: *Chicago Tribune*, April 24, 2009, 4.

174 model for Walter Burns: Jay Robert Nash, *People to See: An Anecdotal History of Chicago's Makers and Breakers* (Piscataway, NJ: New Century, 1981), 47.

174 disdain for marriage: Ibid.

174 "Give me Liberty": Author interviews with Judith Hargrave Coleman.

174 Howey to leave: Ibid.

175 "And what's more": Paul Healy, *Cissy: A Biography of Eleanor M. "Cissy" Patterson* (Garden City, NY: Doubleday, 1966), 110.

175 enticed Cissy: John J. McPhaul, *Deadlines & Monkeyshines: The Fabled World of Chicago Journalism* (Englewood Cliffs, NJ: Prentice-Hall, 1962), 129.

175 By switching hangouts: Jay Robert Nash, *People to See*, 48–49.

175 signed an employment: Ibid., 49.

175 knew every policeman: Joseph Gies, *The Colonel of Chicago* (New York: Dutton, 1979), 46.

175 "I address you": Ibid.

175 successful in severing: Gies, *Colonel of Chicago*, 46.

175 oafish, boisterous: Robert G. Spinney, *City of Big Shoulders: A History of Chicago* (Dekalb: Northern Illinois University Press, 2000), 182.

176 headquarters of the Roaring Twenties: Richard F. Ciccone, *Chicago and the American Century* (Lincolnwood, IL: Contemporary Books, 1999), 42.

176 police were virtually powerless: James R. Grossman, Ann Durkin Keating, and Janice L. Reiff, *The Encyclopedia of Chicago* (Chicago: University of Chicago Press, 2004), 511.

176 enemy of the McCormicks: Kristie Miller, *Ruth Hanna McCormick: A Life in Politics 1880–1944* (Albuquerque: University of New Mexico Press, 1992), 131.

176 "bankrupt, insolvent": Gwen Morgan and Arthur Veysey, *Poor Little Rich Boy: The Life and Times of Col. Robert R. McCormick* (Carpentersville, IL: Crossroads Communications, 1985), 271.

176 "expert consultants": Ibid., 272.

176 voters on Election Day: Ibid.

176 grateful Mr. Capone: Ciccone, *Chicago and the American Century*, 42.

176 "from a curtained automobile": Gies, *Colonel of Chicago*, 89.

177 "I liked the kid": Ibid.

177 "I paid him plenty": Ibid.

177 valued for his "connections": Lloyd Wendt, *The Chicago Tribune: The Rise of a Great American Newspaper* (Chicago: Rand McNally, 1979), 529–36.

177 Capone to special friends: Ibid.

177 Under their leadership: Ibid., 471.

177 By 1922: Richard Norton Smith, *The Colonel: The Life & Legend of Robert McCormick 1880–1955* (Boston: Houghton Mifflin, 1997), 245.

177 first rotogravure press: Gies, *Colonel of Chicago*, 47.

178 fifty thousand dollars each: Wendt, *The Chicago Tribune*, 471.

178 recession of 1921–22: Ibid., 490.

178 rich men from their bonuses: Ibid., 485.

178 "The greatness": Smith, *The Colonel*, 236.

178 today's Michigan Avenue: Elizabeth McNulty, *Chicago Then and Now* (San Diego: Thunder Bay Press, 2000), 58–59.

178 The first step: Morgan and Veysey, *Poor Little Rich Boy*, 227.

178 printing plant: John W. Stamper, *Chicago's North Michigan Avenue: Planning and Development, 1900–1930* (Chicago: University of Chicago Press, 1991), 65.

178 "the world's most": Wendt, *The Chicago Tribune*, 488.

179 because of his workload: Rem Koolhaas, *Delirious New York* (New York: Monacelli Press, 1994), 164.

179 keep the fee if they won: Leo E. McGivena and Others, *The News: The First Fifty Years of New York's Picture Newspaper* (New York: News Syndicate, 1969), 178–79.

179 333 North Michigan: Ira J. Bach, *Chicago's Famous Buildings* (Chicago: University of Chicago Press, 1965), 61–62.

179 When the award: Wendt, *The Chicago Tribune*, 488.

179 his wife took the check: Koolhaas, *Delirious New York*, 164.

180 He would rescind: *American Mercury*, December 9, 1944, 676–77.

180 lost in the primary: Miller, *Ruth Hanna McCormick*, 141.

180 British ambassador: Ibid., 149.

180 Dr. Joseph De Lee: Ibid., 150.

181 poisoned himself: Ibid., 150–51.

181   widow was a survivor: Ibid., 162, 200.

181   She lost: Wendt, *The Chicago Tribune*, 541.

182   unrelated caricatures: Ibid., 315.

182   an innovation exploded: W. A. Swanberg, *Pulitzer* (New York: Charles Scribner's Sons, 1967), 238.

182   Yellow Kid: Joyce Milton, *The Yellow Kids: Foreign Correspondents in the Heyday of Yellow Journalism* (New York: Harper & Row, 1989), xi.

182   Richard F. Outcault: Allen Churchill, *Park Row: A Vivid Re-Creation of Turn of the Century Newspaper Days* (New York: Rinehart, 1958), 67.

182   "yellow journalism": Swanberg, *Pulitzer*, 239.

183   Joe worked closely: Chicago Tribune, *Chicago Days: 150 Defining Moments in the Life of a Great City* (Wheaton, IL: Cantigny—First Division Foundation, 1997), 106.

183   *Gasoline Alley*: McPhaul, *Deadlines*, 235.

183   "Youngsters for kid": Wendt, *The Chicago Tribune*, 405.

184   consoling his wife: *Chicago Daily Journal*, April 18, 1919.

184   architect David Adler: Stephen M. Salny, *The Country Houses of David Adler* (New York: Norton, 2001), 196.

184   Communication between: Joseph Medill Patterson to Alice Higinbotham Patterson, January 19, 1921, J. M. Patterson Papers.

184   Alice would allow Elinor: Joseph Medill Patterson to Alice Higinbotham Patterson, January 24, 1921, J. M. Patterson Papers.

184   "I certainly think": Joseph Medill Patterson to Alice Higinbotham Patterson, March 24, 1921, J. M. Patterson Papers.

184   "I had lunch with Insull": Joseph Medill Patterson to Alice Higinbotham Patterson, August 8, 1921, J. M. Patterson Papers.

184   interest in experimental farming: Kim Coventry, Daniel Meyer, and Arthur H. Miller, *Classic Country Estates of Lake Forest* (New York: Norton, 2003), 203.

184   Insull's Hawthorne Farms: Ibid., 200.

185   "five cents a day": Joseph Medill Patterson to Alice Higinbotham Patterson, October 10, 1922, J. M. Patterson Papers.

185   "make a practice": Joseph Medill Patterson to Alice Higinbotham Patterson, October 12, 1922, J. M. Patterson Papers.

185   The venture had begun: John Chapman, *Tell It to Sweeney: The Informal History of the New York Daily News* (Garden City, NY: Doubleday, 1961), 14.

186   "In Paris": John T. McCutcheon, *Drawn from Memory* (Indianapolis: Bobbs-Merrill, 1950), 287–88.

186   Lord Northcliffe: Chapman, *Tell It to Sweeney*, 16.

186   "New York's": Wayne Andrews, *Battle for Chicago* (New York: Harcourt, Brace, 1946), 245–46.

186   "simple and bright": Jack Alexander, "Vox Populi II," *New Yorker* August 13, 1938, 19.

186   The language: Morgan and Veysey, *Poor Little Rich Boy*, 221.

186   James Gordon Bennett Jr.: Chapman, *Tell It to Sweeney*, 17.

187   cousins to operate separately: Morgan and Veysey, *Poor Little Rich Boy*, 222.

14: THE RISE OF THE *NEW YORK DAILY NEWS*:

LOVE, SEX, MONEY AND MURDER

188   rich enough to retire: Leo E. McGivena and Others, *The News: The First Fifty Years of New York's Picture Newspaper* (New York: News Syndicate, 1969), 32.

188   "This is Joe Patterson's": Ibid.

188   one of the most valuable: Ibid.

188   seed money: Gwen Morgan and Arthur Veysey, *Poor Little Rich Boy: The Life and Times of Col. Robert R. McCormick* (Carpentersville, IL: Crossroads Communications, 1985), 225.

188   directors authorized Field: Lloyd Wendt, *The Chicago Tribune: The Rise of a Great American Newspaper* (Chicago: Rand McNally, 1979), 461.

188   either with the purchase: Morgan and Veysey, *Poor Little Rich Boy*, 226.

189   Carson Pirie Scott chairman: *Chicago Tribune, Ultimate Address* supplement, June 18, 2010, 18.

189   his choice of Arthur L. Clarke: Wendt, *The Chicago Tribune*, 461.

189   a seasoned newspaperman: John Chapman, *Tell It to Sweeney: The Informal History of the New York Daily News* (Garden City, NY: Doubleday, 1961), 67.

189   "That the officers": Wendt, *The Chicago Tribune*, 461.

189   *Evening Mail* might lease: McGivena, *The News*, 34–35.

189   provide personnel: Chapman, *Tell It to Sweeney*, 19.

189   a floor of his building: Morgan and Veysey, *Poor Little Rich Boy*, 226.

189   created a dummy: Ibid., 233.

189   presence of Joe Patterson: Chapman, *Tell It to Sweeney*, 61.

189   the three subjects: Burton Rascoe, *Before I Forget* (Garden City, NY: Doubleday, Doran, 1937), 277.

190   A fourth: Ibid.

190   GERMANS BLOCK: Morgan and Veysey, *Poor Little Rich Boy*, 234.

190   "Newport to": Ibid.

190   small photo caption: Ibid.

190   On the third day: Morgan and Veysey, *Poor Little Rich Boy*, 234.

191   "Remember": Chapman, *Tell It to Sweeney*, 75.

191   Joe bounced back: Ibid.

191 "In its early days": Jack Alexander, "Vox Populi III," *New Yorker*, August 20, 1938, 19.

191 Max deposited: *Time*, June 3, 1946.

191 distribution to subway: Ibid.

191 *Editor & Publisher* interviewed: Chapman, *Tell It to Sweeney*, 77.

192 "For goodness sake": Ibid., 70.

192 "I hear people": Ibid., 71.

193 "A princess from": McGivena, *The News*, 51.

193 cattle census: 1929 Livestock Inventory, J. M. Patterson Papers.

193 As the twenties: *Time*, June 3, 1946.

194 Joe approached: Morgan and Veysey, *Poor Little Rich Boy*, 236.

194 Sunday edition: Jack Alexander, "Vox Populi II," *New Yorker*, August 13, 1938, 19.

195 "to make you": Richard Norton Smith, *The Colonel: The Life & Legend of Robert McCormick 1880–1955* (Boston: Houghton Mifflin, 1997), 221.

195 He also convinced: Chapman, *Tell It to Sweeney*, 134.

195 An important: Ibid., 87.

196 Pacific & Atlantic Photos: McGivena, *The News*, 235.

196 "like a regular fellow": Ibid., 237.

196 Stanley Baldwin: Ibid., 244.

196 "Remember one thing": Walter E. Schneider, "Fabulous Rise of N.Y. Daily News Due to Capt. Patterson's Genius," *Editor & Publisher*, June 24, 1939, 45.

196 "to have a picture": Ibid.

196 "to anticipate": Ibid.

196 "a chilly-looking blonde": John J. McPhaul, *Deadlines & Monkeyshines: The Fabled World of Chicago Journalism* (Englewood Cliffs, NJ: Prentice-Hall, 1962), 143.

196 Tom Howard: Ibid.

197 Four hundred thousand: Alexander, *New Yorker*, August 20, 1938, 20.

197 The *News* had: W. A. Swanberg, *Citizen Hearst* (New York: Charles Scribner's Sons, 1961), 419.

197 Trucks filled: Ibid.

197 Retailers: Chapman, *Tell It to Sweeney*, 120.

197 Slowly department stores: Ibid., 124.

198 Lower East Siders: Ibid., 139.

198 avid *News* readers: Ibid., 145.

198 "Tell it to Sweeney": Ibid., 133.

199 he would remain: Ibid., 39.

199 "until further notice": Joseph Medill Patterson to Alice Higinbotham Patterson, October 1, 1922, J. M. Patterson Papers.

199   "Gentlemen": Joseph Medill Patterson to Cartier New York, August 17, 1923, J. M. Patterson Papers.

199   She lived first: Mary King file, J. M. Patterson Papers.

199   later at the Gotham: Ibid.

199   by 1923: Lease, June 9, 1923, Real Estate file, J. M. Patterson Papers.

199   He would keep: Real Estate file, J. M. Patterson Papers.

199   Joe's prolific association: Robert Keeler, *Newsday: A Candid History of the Respectable Tabloid* (New York: William Morrow, 1997), 47.

200   Mary took a leave: Ibid.

200   The success: Swanberg, *Citizen Hearst*, 433.

200   "pornoGraphic": Chapman, *Tell It to Sweeney*, 128.

200   *Time* magazine: Joseph Gies, *The Colonel of Chicago* (New York: Dutton, 1979), 76.

201   "The *News's*": *Time*, June 3, 1946.

201   In October 1925: Real Estate file, J. M. Patterson Papers.

201   The units: Neil Harris, *Chicago Apartments: A Century of Lakefront Luxury* (New York: Acanthus Press, 2004), 156–59.

201   Patterson apartment: Real Estate file, J. M. Patterson Papers.

201   A bathroom: Morgan and Veysey, *Poor Little Rich Boy*, 238.

202   the stage version: *Time*, February 15, 1926.

202   "Folk who": Ibid.

202   also fallen in love: Rem Koolhaas, *Delirious New York* (New York: Monacelli Press, 1994), 164.

203   The commission: Christopher Gray, "Streetscapes: 3 East 84th Street: An Art Deco Precursor of the Daily News Building," *New York Times*, November 12, 1995.

203   "that damned":" Jack Alexander, "Vox Populi I," *New Yorker*, August 6, 1938, 20.

204   thirty-six-story skyscraper: Smith, *The Colonel*, 266.

204   "He made": Morgan and Veysey, *Poor Little Rich Boy*, 264.

204   Patterson's ninth-floor office: Schneider, *Editor & Publisher*, June 24, 1939, 45.

204   The room's chief: John Tebbel, *An American Dynasty* (1947; reprinted Westport, CT: Greenwood Press, 1968), 278.

205   "Sid said": Bruce Smith, *The History of Little Orphan Annie* (New York: Ballantine Books, 1982), 8.

205   "So the kid": Ibid.

205   "The kid": Smith, *Orphan Annie*, 9.

205   "Who ever heard": Chapman, *Tell It to Sweeney*, 156.

205   PLEASE DO: Ibid., 157.

205 *Little Lefty*: Tebbel, *An American Dynasty*, 137.

206 "Collectively the comics": *American Mercury*, December 9, 1944, 672.

206 He didn't return: Chapman, *Tell It to Sweeney*, 52.

206 His appearance: Ibid., 42.

207 "Let's try": Ibid., 43.

207 "Don't you think": Ibid.

207 "I kept on": Ibid., 43–44.

207 "Don't give": Alexander, *New Yorker*, August 6, 1938, 16.

207 "Joe, you always": Ibid.

207 After dinner: Ibid.

208 "Memo to Max": Chapman, *Tell It to Sweeney*, 42.

208 His idols: Alexander, *New Yorker*, August 6, 1938, 17.

208 Jack London: Rascoe, *Before I Forget*, 241.

208 Among those: Ibid.

208 It was a stand: Alexander, *New Yorker*, August 6, 1938, 18.

208 lost $5 million : Frank Waldrop, *McCormick of Chicago: An Unconventional Portrait of a Controversial Figure* (Englewood Cliffs, NJ: Prentice-Hall, 1966), 213.

208 "We're off": Tebbel, *An American Dynasty*, 258.

208 Although sex and crime: Ibid., 259.

209 This philosophy: E. J. Kahn Jr., *The World of Swope* (New York: Simon & Schuster, 1965), 342.

209 annual bonuses: Schneider, *Editor & Publisher*, June 24, 1939, 45.

209 made an exchange: Wendt, *The Chicago Tribune*, 461.

209 *Detroit Daily Mirror*: Chapman, *Tell It to Sweeney*, 28.

209 "the kindly tyrant": Schneider, *Editor & Publisher*, June 24, 1939, 46.

209 "Newspapers start": Wayne Andrews, *Battle for Chicago* (New York: Harcourt, Brace, 1946), 229.

15: THE CARTIER LIFE

211 "fuzzy-minded": Alice Hoge, *Cissy Patterson: The Life of Eleanor Medill Patterson, Publisher & Editor of the Washington Times-Herald* (New York: Random House, 1966), 75.

211 she became convinced: Elinor Medill Patterson to Alice Higinbotham Patterson, February 21, 1923, J. M. Patterson Papers.

211 Also to be lit: Ralph G. Martin, *Cissy: The Extraordinary Life of Eleanor Medill Patterson* (New York: Simon & Schuster, 1979), 238.

211 full-length portraits: Ibid., 201.

211 Heads of caribou: Ibid., 201–2.

212   the set: Rita Reif, *The New York Times*, April 6, 1984.

212   signed a blank check: Hoge, *Cissy Patterson*, 78.

212   She also acquired: Ibid.

213   "When I reached": Ibid., 79.

213   maturing into: Ibid.

213   "older than God": Martin, *Cissy*, 198.

213   planter's punch: Ibid.

213   "I was always": Ibid., 208.

214   "She and I": Ibid.

214   "You bore me": Ibid., 209.

214   Among those: Ibid., 215–16.

214   She sold: Ibid., 214.

214   In 1926: Paul Healy, *Cissy: A Biography of Eleanor M. "Cissy" Patterson* (Garden City, NY: Doubleday, 1966), 114.

215   she became a necessary: Martin, *Cissy*, 215.

215   Scott Fitzgerald: Ibid., 215–16.

215   first depression: F. Scott Fitzgerald, *Ledger: A Facsimile* (Washington, DC: NCR, 1972), 179.

215   marveled at: Martin, *Cissy*, 216.

215   Gertrude Stein's studio: James R. Mellow, *Charmed Circle: Gertrude Stein* (New York: Praeger 1974), 6.

215   Among them: Ibid.

215   Sherwood Anderson: Ernest Hemingway, *A Moveable Feast* (New York: Charles Scribner's Sons, 1964), 28.

216   "If you brought": Ibid.

216   She even stopped: Mellow, *Charmed Circle*, 249.

216   upwardly aspiring: Carol Felsenthal, *Alice Roosevelt Longworth* (New York: G. P. Putnam's Sons, 1988), 246.

216   ten years Cissy's junior: Ibid.

216   Aimee Ernesta Drinker: Virginia Gardner, *"Friend and Lover": The Life of Louise Bryant* (New York: Horizon Press, 1982), 236.

216   Louise Bryant: Ibid., 243.

216   Bullitt was: Ibid., 236–37.

216   chronic impotence: Ibid., 242.

216   a hideout: Martin, *Cissy*, 244.

217   He even took: Ibid., 226.

217   He was someone: Ibid., 220.

217   an English valet: Healy, *Cissy*, 82.

217   Other clients: Ibid., 96.

218   sixty-five-foot yacht: Healy, *Cissy*, 98.

218   Throughout the twenties: E. J. Kahn Jr., *The World of Swope* (New York: Simon & Schuster, 1965), 289–90.

218   "Mr. Swope lives": Ibid., 291.

218   Occasionally, Lardner: Ibid., 292.

218   follow the music: Ibid., 294.

218   after the theater: Ibid., 295.

219   Keewaydin: Ibid., 315.

219   Elsie de Wolfe: Ibid., 318.

219   thousand-dollar-a-week: Ibid., 289.

219   allowed bills to age: Ibid., 318.

219   "I had to write": Martin, *Cissy*, 227.

219   When she sent: Ibid.

219   Drew's career: Ibid.

219   newlyweds settled: Ibid., 229.

219   Felicia was not: Ibid., 230.

219   Durant Locomobile: Healy, *Cissy*, 97.

219   After a honeymoon: Hoge, *Cissy Patterson*, 82.

220   Harbor Acres: Healy, *Cissy*, 96.

220   area was established: www.sandspointpreserve.org.

220   Along the way: Ibid.

220   quintessential summer place: Martin, *Cissy*, 234.

220   Set on land: Ibid.

220   Elmer commuted: Healy, *Cissy*, 98.

220   Drew began working: Martin, *Cissy*, 239.

221   not-yet-gentrified Georgetown: Ibid.

221   Drew discovered: Ibid., 248.

221   a flat near Nôtre Dame: Ibid., 263.

221   portrayal of her in *Glass Houses:* Eleanor Gizycka, *Glass Houses* (New York: Minton, Balch, 1926).

221   Cissy would maintain: Martin, *Cissy*, 461–62.

222   Cissy continued: Ibid., 240.

222   "continually conscious": Ibid., 245.

222   In February 1929: Healy, *Cissy*, 107.

222   Felicia and Drew: Ibid.

222   ordered a black wardrobe: Ibid., 108.

222   mindlessly traversed: Hoge, *Cissy Patterson*, 84.

222   Elinor Josephine Patterson: Frank Waldrop, *McCormick of Chicago: An Unconventional Portrait of a Controversial Figure* (Englewood Cliffs, NJ: Prentice-Hall, 1966), 30.

222   died without: Hoge, *Cissy Patterson*, 84.

222   cancel plans: Ibid.

223   "This was no drab": Healy, *Cissy*, 105.

223   She received: Ibid.

16: THE COLONEL OF CHICAGOLAND

224   "His celebrity": F. Richard Ciccone, *Chicago and the American Century* (Lincoln-wood, IL: Contemporary Books, 1999), 16.

224   "No political figure": Ibid.

224   patriarch's footprints: John Tebbel, *An American Dynasty* (1947; reprinted Westport, CT: Greenwood Press, 1968), 4, 107.

225   "they took it": Ciccone, *Chicago and the American Century*, 193.

226   "simplify" language: Joseph Gies, *The Colonel of Chicago* (New York: Dutton, 1979), 5–6.

226   began in 1934: Lloyd Wendt, *The Chicago Tribune: The Rise of a Great American Newspaper* (Chicago: Rand McNally, 1979), 568.

226   continued simplified spelling: Ibid.

227   a minion nearby: Gwen Morgan and Arthur Veysey, *Poor Little Rich Boy: The Life and Times of Col. Robert R. McCormick* (Carpentersville, IL: Crossroads Communications, 1985), 447–48.

227   looked right: Fanny Butcher, *Many Lives—One Love* (New York: Harper & Row, 1972), 189.

227   "that's the way": Morgan and Veysey, *Poor Little Rich Boy*, 451.

227   "Bertie's affliction": Frank Waldrop, *McCormick of Chicago: An Unconventional Portrait of a Controversial Figure* (Englewood Cliffs, NJ: Prentice-Hall, 1966), 163–64.

228   first newspaper tycoon: Morgan and Veysey, *Poor Little Rich Boy*, 253.

228   first broadcast: David Halberstam, *The Powers That Be* (New York: Knopf, 1979), 27.

228   most powerful frequency: Tebbel, *An American Dynasty*, 119.

228   "broadcasting from atop": Ibid.

228   hotel guest rooms: Ibid.

228   merely an illusion: Ibid.

228   WGN's first year: Ibid.

228   dance bands: Ibid., 120.

229   Ovaltine's: *Chicago Tribune*, January 26, 2010.

229   networks were threatening: Tebbel, *An American Dynasty*, 121.

229   birth of WGN-TV: Morgan and Veysey, *Poor Little Rich Boy*, 388.

230   Chief Justice Charles Evans Hughes: Wendt, *Chicago Tribune*, 547.

230   *Tribune* workers: Tebbel, *An American Dynasty*, 215.

230   Throughout the Depression: Waldrop, *McCormick of Chicago*, 213.

231   at least $60: Richard Norton Smith, *The Colonel: The Life & Legend of Robert Mc-Cormick 1880–1955* (Boston: Houghton Mifflin, 1997), 360.

231   he might be glimpsed: Tebbel, *An American Dynasty*, 213.

231   random story ideas: Ibid., 147–49.

232   prompted McCormick: Ibid., 221.

232   editorial meetings: Wendt, *The Chicago Tribune*, 387.

232   The Colonel's monologues: Tebbel, *An American Dynasty*, 215.

232   No one could eat: Smith, *The Colonel*, 260.

232   restoring appetites: Ibid.

232   Whispering began: Morgan and Veysey, *Poor Little Rich Boy*, 225.

232   rebuilding of the estate's: Morgan and Veysey, *Poor Little Rich Boy*, 265.

233   Cantigny to commemorate: Gies, *Colonel of Chicago*, 74.

233   Chicago Golf Club: Morgan and Veysey, *Poor Little Rich Boy*, 266.

233   Aiken: Smith, *The Colonel*, 319.

233   Hitchcock and his wife: Morgan and Veysey, *Poor Little Rich Boy*, 278.

234   Franklin Roosevelt: Ibid., 279.

234   a preparatory school: Ibid., 280.

234   from Marshall Field III: Smith, *The Colonel*, 319.

234   supervised rehabilitation: Morgan and Veysey, *Poor Little Rich Boy*, 280.

234   house inappropriately grand: Ibid., 282.

234   felt a frost: Ibid.

234   founding members: Ibid., 319.

235   Joe Thomas's wife, Clara: Smith, *The Colonel*, 340.

235   talented artist: Ibid.

235   every weekend: Morgan and Veysey, *Poor Little Rich Boy*, 319.

235   automobile accident: Smith, *The Colonel*, 341.

235   gift of a Goya: Ibid.

235   protégée Maryland Hooper: Morgan and Veysey, *Poor Little Rich Boy*, 359.

236   "Don't mind": Smith, *The Colonel*, 383.

236   Dinner was not delayed: Ibid.

236   Bois de Madame: Smith, *The Colonel*, 339.

236   prehunt dinner: Morgan and Veysey, *Poor Little Rich Boy*, 293.

236   Dressed in classic: Ibid.

237   Through woods: Ibid., 293–94.

237   hearty hunt breakfast: Ibid., 294–95.

237   architect Willis Irvin: Ibid., 322.

237   Wings shot out: Smith, *The Colonel*, 337.

237   sheathed in red brick: Morgan and Veysey, *Poor Little Rich Boy*, 327.

237   first to be air-conditioned: Gies, *Colonel of Chicago*, 118.

237 innovation from Monticello: Morgan and Veysey, *Poor Little Rich Boy*, 323.

237 houseguest Winston Churchill: Ibid., 322.

238 movie theater: Ibid., 324.

238 The estate produced: Ibid., 346.

238 petlike Guernsey: Smith, *The Colonel*, 339.

238 The quality: Morgan and Veysey, *Poor Little Rich Boy*, 345–46.

238 Cantigny was registered: Ibid., 346.

238 Salt founder Joy Morton: Ibid., 340–41.

238 chosen for her by Amy: Ibid., 359.

238 twenty or so couples: Ibid., 360.

239 In October 1937: Ibid., 355.

239 did not regain consciousness: Smith, *The Colonel*, 385.

240 military funeral: Waldrop, *McCormick of Chicago*, 263.

240 three volleys of shots: Gies, *Colonel of Chicago*, 150.

240 Maryland and Henry Hooper: Morgan and Veysey, *Poor Little Rich Boy*, 363.

240 After mourners departed: Ibid.

240 Amy had willed: Ibid., 364.

240 most of the paintings: Ibid.

240 wedding gift pearls: Ibid.

240 *Tribune* reporters: Smith, *The Colonel*, 394.

240 operatic soprano: Ibid., 395.

241 "The Colonel likes women": Ibid.

241 Grace Parker Pickering: Ibid.

241 to end an affair: Morgan and Veysey, *Poor Little Rich Boy*, 389.

241 Henry Weber: Tebbel, *An American Dynasty*, 123.

241 "an outstanding speaker": Smith, *The Colonel*, 396.

241 Sunday *Tribune:* Tebbel, *An American Dynasty*, 123.

242 Three hundred stations: Morgan and Veysey, *Poor Little Rich Boy*, 383.

242 Although totally unrelated: Smith, *The Colonel*, 397.

17: THE EDITOR WORE EMERALDS: MRS. ELEANOR MEDILL
PATTERSON'S *WASHINGTON HERALD*

243 "Well, God damn": Frank Waldrop, *McCormick of Chicago: An Unconventional Portrait of a Controversial Figure* (Englewood Cliffs, NJ: Prentice-Hall, 1966), 226.

243 "I fell out": Ibid.

243 *"My God"*: Alice Hoge, *Cissy Patterson: The Life of Eleanor Medill Patterson, Publisher & Editor of the Washington Times-Herald* (New York: Random House, 1966), 77.

243   Nellie caught up: Waldrop, *McCormick of Chicago*, 226.

243   One was: Paul Healy, *Cissy: A Biography of Eleanor M. "Cissy" Patterson* (Garden City, NY: Doubleday, 1966), 6.

244   Brisbane requested a contract: W. A. Swanberg, *Citizen Hearst* (New York: Charles Scribner's Sons, 1961), 106.

244   San Simeon: Ralph G. Martin, *Cissy: The Extraordinary Life of Eleanor Medill Patterson* (New York: Simon & Schuster, 1979), 261.

245   recurrent hints: Healy, *Cissy*, 127.

245   W.R. agreed: Ibid.

245   The salary: Ibid.

245   Washington was: Ibid., 142.

245   the circulation: Ibid., 3.

245   the *Star* was: Ibid., 5.

246   chains' opinions read: *Redbook*, October 1937, 24.

246   The sole barrier: Healy, *Cissy*, 2.

246   there were: Ibid., 170.

246   those who merited: Ibid., 176.

246   She replaced: Hoge, *Cissy Patterson*, 92.

246   portrait of Joseph Medill: Martin, *Cissy*, 271.

247   box on page one: Ibid., 269–70.

247   "Arthur Brisbane Warns": Ibid.

247   "Arthur Brisbane told": Ibid.

247   "Now, Mr. Brisbane": Ibid.

247   "Interesting But": Carol Felsenthal, *Alice Roosevelt Longworth* (New York: G. P. Putnam's Sons, 1988), 162.

247   "The news is": Healy, *Cissy*, 7.

247   When tout de Washington: Felsenthal, *Alice Roosevelt Longworth*, 162.

248   Brisbane changed: Martin, *Cissy*, 275–76.

248   "I was in error": Healy, *Cissy*, 8.

248   Hearst cabled: Martin, *Cissy*, 276–77.

248   quality she insisted: Ibid., 333.

248   "too black": Martin, *Cissy*, 273.

249   papers around the country: Ibid.

249   Nick Longworth: Felsenthal, *Alice Roosevelt Longworth*, 163.

249   visit friends in Aiken: James Brough, *Princess Alice: A Biography of Alice Roosevelt Longworth* (Boston: Little, Brown, 1975), 126.

249   alcohol-abused: Felsenthal, *Alice Roosevelt Longworth*, 164.

249   He died on April 10: Brough, *Princess Alice*, 286.

249   Speaker surrounded by: Marguerite Cassini, *Never a Dull Moment* (New York: Harper & Brothers, 1956), 337.

250 Howey, the alleged loner: Martin, *Cissy*, 282–83.

250 "Cissy and Howey": Ibid., 283.

250 Cissy to marry him: Ibid., 285.

250 The heat: Ibid., 285–86.

250 Two years later: Colleen Moore's Scrapbooks, courtesy of Judith Hargrave Colman.

251 LARGEST MORNING: Martin, *Cissy*, 297.

251 Cissy knew it: Healy, *Cissy*, 141–42.

251 modern woman's page: Martin, *Cissy*, 278.

251 As someone who: Healy, *Cissy*, 142.

251 While eating: Hoge, *Cissy Patterson*, 95–96.

251 "the emerald clip": Adela Rogers St. Johns, *The Honeycomb* (Garden City, NY: Doubleday, 1969), 387.

252 private railcar: Hoge, *Cissy Patterson*, 97–98.

252 "probably the most": Cassini, *Never a Dull Moment*, 349.

252 Her guests mixed: Hoge, *Cissy Patterson*, 98.

252 young Christopher Wren: Hoge, *Cissy Patterson*, 100.

252 It was also: Martin, *Cissy*, 310.

252 English country taste: Ibid., 310–11.

252 The drawing room: Ibid.

252 The stable: Ibid., 311.

253 "Of all the houses": St. Johns, *Honeycomb*, 396.

253 "Mrs. Patterson": Ibid., 368.

253 "titbits": Hoge, *Cissy Patterson*, 137.

254 Cissy adored: Ibid., 145.

254 A significant perk: Healy, *Cissy*, 192.

254 When Cissy was ready: Ibid., 10.

254 "Best Dressed": *Time*, December 24, 1934.

254 "How perfectly silly": Martin, *Cissy*, 339.

254 The attractive divorcée: Hoge, *Cissy Patterson*, 143.

254 "These Charming People": Healy, *Cissy*, 200–1.

255 *New York Times:* Hoge, *Cissy Patterson*, 143.

255 "panties" to "shoes": Healy, *Cissy*, 231.

255 a long spicy yarn: Ibid., 232–34.

256 Liveright, Inc., to remove: Ibid., 235.

256 Ned McLean, whose alcoholism: Martin, *Cissy*, 265.

256 $600,000: Katharine Graham, *Personal History* (New York: Knopf, 1997), 59.

256 June 1: Martin, *Cissy*, 329.

256 two blocks south: Hoge, *Cissy Patterson*, 122.

256 Associated Press franchise: Graham, *Personal History*, 59.

256 Those mingling: Ibid., 58.

256 Mrs. McLean: Martin, *Cissy*, 329–30.

256 have to pawn: Marquis Childs, *Saturday Evening Post*, June 5, 1943, 14.

256 Evalyn McLean could only: Graham, *Personal History*, 59.

256 Hearst representative fell: Ibid.

256 But who was he?: Childs, *Post*, June 5, 1943, 14.

257 Mr. Hamilton was bidding: Healy, *Cissy*, 253.

257 "So as not to disappoint": Ibid., 255.

257 Eugene's Christian wife: Martin, *Cissy*, 331.

257 only one morning paper: Healy, *Cissy*, 253.

257 The angry George: Martin, *Cissy*, 362.

257 tastes exceeding his income: Ibid., 361–62.

258 without Felicia ever knowing: Ibid., 364.

258 Thomas Justin White: Hoge, *Cissy Patterson*, 116.

258 his sister Carmel Snow: *New York Times*, May 29, 2002.

258 Tom White was charming: Martin, *Cissy*, 368.

258 "Again and again": Penelope Rowlands, *A Dash of Daring: Carmel Snow and Her Life in Fashion, Art, and Letters* (New York: Atria Books, 2005), 226.

258 White kept a pied-à-terre: Ibid., 222–23.

258 Cissy spent romantic: Martin, *Cissy*, 369.

258 Bill Bullitt: Ibid., 371.

258 She delighted: Ibid.

259 "But you see": Ibid., 397.

259 "So do I": Ibid.

259 million dollars to divorce: Ibid.

259 *First Lady*: Healy, *Cissy*, 237.

259 "I think it's time": Ibid., 238.

259 "Oh, I don't": Ibid.

259 "a Barrymore voice": St. Johns, *Honeycomb*, 381.

259 "I slid down": Ibid., 382.

259 "You know Cissy's": Ibid.

260 "I'm staying there": Ibid.

260 "I should have believed": Martin, *Cissy*, 294.

260 What had begun: Healy, *Cissy*, 239.

260 a hereditary title: Cassini, *Never a Dull Moment*, 137–38.

260 "It's strange": Ibid., 347.

260 "Well, we knew": Ibid.

260 "He remembered": Ibid., 335.

260 "I want your story": Ibid., 337–38.

261   Marguerite's story: Ibid., 340.

261   paid a much-needed: Ibid.

261   tar and feathers: Igor Cassini obituary, *New York Times*, January 9, 2002, B8.

261   half-million-dollar libel suit: *Newsweek,* July 3, 1944, 62.

261   Igor soon emerged: *Times*, January 9, 2002, B8.

261   The latter episode: Charlene Cassini obituary, *New York Times*, April 10, 1963, 18.

262   The banishment: Ibid.

262   Yet she continued: Healy, *Cissy*, 144–45.

262   financial problems: Ibid., 145.

262   Marion—without consulting him: Waldrop, *McCormick of Chicago*, 250.

262   "I called Mr. Hearst": Hoge, *Cissy Patterson*, 162–63.

263   bound by the million-dollar: Swanberg, *Citizen Hearst*, 581.

263   absorbed losses would cost: Hoge, *Cissy Patterson*, 163.

263   a sweet transaction: Ibid., 162.

263   spending a half-million: Ibid., 163.

263   On any given date: Waldrop, *McCormick of Chicago*, 250.

263   The unspoken agenda: Healy, *Cissy*, 149.

263   Washington was in need: Ibid., 316.

264   just outré enough: Hoge, *Cissy Patterson*, 142.

264   a grateful Morris Cafritz: Healy, *Cissy*, 317.

264   She casually explained: Martin, *Cissy*, 177.

265   "the neck and shoulders": Healy, *Cissy*, 206.

265   "Once I looked": Ibid.

265   "white handkerchief": Ibid., 205.

265   "Why don't you": Martin, *Cissy*, 393.

266   Another try: Hoge, *Cissy Patterson*, 141.

266   The future president's sister: Lynne McTaggart, *Kathleen Kennedy: Her Life and Times* (Garden City, NY: Dial Press, 1983), 93.

266   Inga Arvad: Ibid., 94.

266   love coach for Jack: Ibid., 103.

266   Inga brought a history: Ibid.

266   Four years later: Ibid., 136.

266   Reprinted internationally: Ibid., 243.

267   $42.50: PBS special, *Jackie*.

267   Cissy's favorite columnist: Healy, *Cissy*, 344.

267   known for her wit: Ibid., 372.

267   "Don't talk": Martin, *Cissy*, 421.

267   Lawrence "Chip" Robert: Healy, *Cissy*, 268.

267   Mayflower hotel: Ibid., 228.

267 When the pilot: Ibid., 344.

267 Cissy was particularly: Martin, *Cissy*, 386.

267 "the morals of a mink": Ibid., 385.

267 A lawyer: Ibid.

267 Evie herself pointed: Ibid., 421.

267 "didn't even have": Ibid.

267 "Now, now, Evie": Ibid., 441.

268 They spent weekends: Ibid., 387.

268 Jackie often joined: Healy, *Cissy*, 350.

268 rumors of a lesbian: Martin, *Cissy*, 388.

268 Jackie was not immune: Healy, *Cissy*, 350.

268 "I just couldn't": Martin, *Cissy*, 388.

268 "Why should she care": Ibid.

18: ALICIA PATTERSON, SURROGATE SON

269 brick Georgian house: Alicia Patterson as told to Hall Burton, "This Is the Life I Love," *Saturday Evening Post*, February 21, 1959, 44.

269 an island of cultivation: Kim Coventry, Daniel Meyer, and Arthur H. Miller, *Classic Country Estates of Lake Forest* (New York: Norton, 2003), 112.

269 fruit rotted: Robert Keeler, *Newsday: A Candid History of the Respectable Tabloid* (New York: William Morrow, 1997), 15.

269 They were usually: Charles Wertenbaker, "The Case of the Hot-Tempered Publisher," *Saturday Evening Post*, May 12, 1951, 37.

269 bodyguard who arrived: Arthur Meeker, *Chicago, with Love* (New York: Knopf, 1955), 92.

270 Joe also taught: Alicia Patterson cover story, *Time*, September 13, 1954.

270 he stormed out: Alicia Patterson official *Newsday* biography.

270 raise his girls: Cover story, *Time*, September 13, 1954.

270 invent long stories: *Post*, May 12, 1951, 37.

270 He sang: Keeler, *Newsday*, 22.

270 Although she was hurt: *Post*, May 12, 1951, 37.

270 After she finally: Cover story, *Time*, September 13, 1954.

270 "Long after": *Post*, February 21, 1959, 44.

271 "Father seemed": Keeler, *Newsday*, 21.

271 "asked me": Ibid., 17.

271 in 1912 Joe took: Joseph Medill Patterson to Alice Higinbotham Patterson, May 7 and May 10, 1912, J. M. Patterson Papers; Joseph Medill Patterson to Elinor Medill Patterson, October 12, 1912, J. M. Patterson Papers.

271 It wasn't until: Keeler, *Newsday*, 16.

271   at the Virginia Hotel: Elinor Medill Patterson to Alice Higinbotham Patterson, March 9, 1909, J. M. Patterson Papers.

271   Joe leased a furnished house: Real Estate file, J. M. Patterson Papers.

271   232 East Walton Place: Ibid.

271   sent to the principal's office: *Post*, February 21, 1959, 44.

271   "the ringleader": *Post*, May 12, 1951, 37.

272   "I thought I ought": *Post*, February 21, 1959, 44.

272   expelled from St. Timothy's: Ibid.

272   Foxcroft in the horse country: *Post*, May 12, 1951, 113.

272   Her schooling completed: *Newsday* biography.

272   During a stay in Rome: Cover story, *Time*, September 13, 1954.

272   KEEP ALICIA MOVING: *Post*, May 12, 1951, 113.

272   "Around eighteen": Ibid.

273   "would like": *Newsday* biography.

273   opposite Glenn Hunter: *Chicago Tribune*, January 20, 1928.

273   In 1926 she married: *Time*, February 14, 1926; December 10, 1928; January 21, 1929; October 7, 1929.

273   The Pattersons were a: *Chicago Tribune*, December 30, 1925.

274   "I read all the books": *Post*, May 12, 1951, 113.

274   attended a typing class: *Newsday* biography.

274   Adlai E. Stevenson II: Keeler, *Newsday*, 29.

274   She managed to wedge: *Chicago Tribune*, February 1 and 4, 1927.

274   Jim Simpson was son: *Post*, May 12, 1951, 114.

274   "become a man": Joseph Medill Patterson to Alice Higinbotham Patterson, March 31, 1927, J. M. Patterson Papers.

274   "quit traveling": Ibid.

275   "He was geared": *Newsday* biography.

275   "the most fun": *Time*, July 18, 1927.

275   "father told me": *Post*, February 21, 1959, 21.

275   "sitting in a corner": *Post*, February 21, 1959, 45.

275   libel suit against the *News: Post*, May 12, 1951, 113.

275   The fatal session: *Post*, February 21, 1959, 45.

275   "That's a regular part": Keeler, *Newsday*, 28.

276   Marriage to Jim Simpson: *Post*, May 12, 1951, 113-14.

276   Her engagement: *Chicago Tribune*, August 18, 1927.

276   "She did not know": *Chicago Tribune*, August 19, 1927.

276   at least a year: *Post*, May 12, 1951, 114.

276   Although only thirty: *Chicago Tribune*, September 29, 1927.

276   Aboard the outbound: Keeler, *Newsday*, 30.

276   Alicia wrote: *Newsday* biography.

276 After Janet arrived: *Chicago Tribune*, January 9, 1928.

276 Jim successfully: *Chicago Tribune*, January 20, 1928, and March 8, 1928.

276 She lived up: *Chicago Tribune*, October 8, 1930.

276 The short-lived marriage: Ibid.

277 marvel of aviation: Gwen Morgan and Arthur Veysey, *Poor Little Rich Boy: The Life and Times of Col. Robert R. McCormick* (Carpentersville, IL: Crossroads Communications, 1985), 107.

277 the latter-day Icarus: Ibid.

277 "the greatest thrill": Ibid.

277 circle the globe: Morgan and Veysey, *Poor Little Rich Boy*, 428.

277 The blasé Alice: Carol Felsenthal, *Alice Roosevelt Longworth* (New York: G. P. Putnam's Sons, 1988), 119.

277 "I would go over": Alice Roosevelt Longworth, *Crowded Hours: Reminiscences of Alice Roosevelt Longworth* (New York: Charles Scribner's Sons, 1933), 67–68.

278 flight student: Pilots Log, J. M. Patterson Papers.

278 "Capt. Patterson's heart": *Time*, May 10, 1928.

278 "Mr. Patterson swiped": Pilots Log, J. M. Patterson Papers.

278 In 1928: *Time*, May 10, 1928.

278 Although awkward appearing: Ibid.

278 Gibbons contracted: *Chicago Tribune*, December 14, 1928.

278 It was a leisurely sampling: *Time*, January 14, 1929.

279 Charles Lindbergh's: Irwin Unger and Debi Unger, *The Guggenheims* (New York: HarperCollins, 2005), 254.

279 Both girls: *Time*, July 15, 1929.

279 bonus of a gold watch: Lieutenant Frederick H. Becker to Joseph Medill Patterson, thank-you note, J. M. Patterson Papers.

279 Alicia was: *Chicago Tribune*, October 31, 1930, and December 23, 1931.

279 But her flight history: *Chicago Tribune*, January 4, 1930.

279 By that year Josephine: Josephine Patterson obituary, *New York Times*, January 18, 1996.

280 They relieved the journey: *Chicago Tribune*, January 7 and 14, 1931.

280 From Australia: *Chicago Tribune*, February 7 and 13, 1931.

280 Next was Baghdad: *Chicago Tribune*, February 21, 1933.

280 "Alicia finished it off": *New York Times*, January 18, 1996.

281 Six months after: *Chicago Tribune*, April 23, 1931.

281 dubbing her "hunt lady": Ibid.

281 In researching: *Post*, May 12, 1951, 114.

281 She nevertheless triumphed: *New York Times*, January 18, 1996.

281 She also accompanied him: *Post*, May 12, 1951, 114.

281 "To live up to father": *Post*, February 21, 1959, 19.

282 "the best thing": Cover story, *Time*, September 13, 1954.

282 A onetime all-American: *Chicago Tribune*, December 23, 1931.

282 sportsman, aviator: Cover story, *Time*, September 13, 1954.

282 Physically he was everything: *Post*, May 12, 1951, 114.

282 top executive of Western Union: *Time*, November 9, 1931.

282 airfield at his trout-fishing camp: Alicia Patterson, "Flying for Fun," *Vogue*, May 10, 1930, 59.

282 When Brooks invited Joe: Keeler, *Newsday*, 33.

282 It was not: *Post*, May 12, 1951, 114.

282 After the ceremony: *Chicago Tribune*, December 24, 1931.

283 Among their stops: Ibid.

283 He settled an income: Unger and Unger, *The Guggenheims*, 306.

283 designed by Raymond Hood: Real Estate file, J. M. Patterson Papers.

283 one dollar a year in rent: Hofstra University biography of Alicia Patterson.

283 "could only have been built": *Arts & Decoration*, 1935.

283 Therefore the interiors: Ibid.

283 the ubiquitous Janet Chase: Ibid.

283 "The main thing is": *Newsday* biography.

284 she worked sporadically: Unger and Unger, *The Guggenheims*, 306.

284 Alicia truly enjoyed: Cover story, *Time*, September 13, 1954.

284 With Alicia's income: Keeler, *Newsday*, 34.

284 The simple building: Michael Dobbs, *Madeleine Albright: A Twentieth-Century Odyssey* (New York: Henry Holt, 1999), 189.

284 The natural simplicity: Ibid.

284 haven as long as she lived: Unger and Unger, *The Guggenheims*, 306.

284 Her one pregnancy: Ibid., 308.

284 Alicia was feeling: *Newsday* biography.

284 Concerned about lack: Unger and Unger, *The Guggenheims*, 250.

285 "When you get back": Ibid., 253.

285 Guggenheim believed: Ibid., 247.

285 He wanted to demonstrate: Ibid., 246.

285 Guggenheim Fund sponsored Lindy: Ibid., 258.

285 At any number of: Cover story, *Time*, September 13, 1954.

19: THE BITTERSWEET REVENGE OF ALICIA'S *NEWSDAY*

286 His Swiss grandfather: *Time*, July 1, 1929, 4.

286 The Midas-fingered: Stephen Birmingham, *Our Crowd: The Great Jewish Families of New York* (New York: Harper & Row, 1967), 69.

286 wealth came from smelting: Ibid., 268.

286 "amassed what may": Ibid., 65.

287 They pitted armed ruffians: www.encyclopedia.com.

287 Of Meyer Guggenheim's: Birmingham, *Our Crowd*, 318–19.

287 When the dynasty: www.encyclopedia.com.

287 Further riches: Irwin Unger and Debi Unger, *The Guggenheims* (New York: HarperCollins, 2005), 167.

287 largest private mining: www.encyclopedia.com.

288 1953 Kentucky Derby: Unger and Unger, *The Guggenheims*, 244.

288 Solomon R. Guggenheim Museum: Ibid., 385–86.

288 wary in guarding the family wealth: Alicia Patterson, official *Newsday* biography.

288 Helen Rosenberg: Unger and Unger, *The Guggenheims*, 145.

288 Caroline "Carol" Morton Potter: Ibid., 240.

288 Diane, was born in 1924: Ibid., 299.

288 It was a difficult marriage: Ibid., 277.

288 separated in 1937: Ibid., 304.

288 outwardly courtly Harry: Ibid., 305.

289 In the summer of 1939: Robert Keeler, *Newsday: A Candid History of the Respectable Tabloid* (New York: William Morrow, 1997), 49.

289 On July 1: Charles Wertenbaker, "The Case of the Hot-Tempered Publisher," *Saturday Evening Post*, May 12, 1951, 115.

289 The space scientist's: Keeler, *Newsday*, 3.

289 But Harry bankrolled: Ibid., 3–4.

289 never saw one of the rockets: Unger and Unger, *The Guggenheims*, 268.

289 "Goddamn old stuffed shirt": Keeler, *Newsday*, 47.

289 "Patterson didn't warm up": *Post*, May 12, 1951, 115.

290 "the most desirable home": Unger and Unger, *The Guggenheims*, 240.

290 An enclosed cobblestone-paved: Michael Dobbs, *Madeleine Albright: A Twentieth-Century Odyssey* (New York: Henry Holt, 1999), 172.

290 Also on the estate: Ibid.

290 not lost on Francis Ford Coppola: Madeleine Albright, *Madam Secretary: A Memoir* (New York: Hyperion, 2003), 49.

291 Harry lost interest: Keeler, *Newsday*, 148.

291 "Everybody ought to have a job": Alicia Patterson as told to Hall Burton, "This Is the Life I Love," *Saturday Evening Post*, February 21, 1959, 21.

291 At the time, Alicia thought: Hofstra University biography of Alicia Patterson.

291 *Nassau County Daily Journal: Newsday* biography.

291 The weak competition: Ibid.

291 "I favored a tabloid": Ibid.

292 Fred Hauck: Ibid.

292   The effect was: *Post*, February 21, 1959, 45.

292   "My job is to make": *Post*, February 21, 1959, 51.

292   September 3, 1940: Hofstra biography.

292   "I'm afraid it looks like hell": *Newsday* biography.

292   "The burning ambition": Ibid.

292   "People who knew her": Keeler, *Newsday*, 58.

293   Harry owned the paper: *Post*, February 21, 1959, 21.

293   "In lieu of salary": *Newsday* biography.

293   favoring Willkie, the Republican candidate: Ibid.

293   "Those were rugged days": *Post*, February 21, 1959, 50.

294   rationing ad space: Ibid.

294   commandant of Mercer Field: Ibid.

294   combat in the Pacific: Ibid.

294   action in both world wars: Unger and Unger, *The Guggenheims*, 286.

294   Patrick and Janka Koenigswarter: Keeler, *Newsday*, 99.

294   Harry "had girl friends": Unger and Unger, *The Guggenheims*, 319.

294   he had a liaison: Ibid., fn.

294   Alicia was spending: Keeler, *Newsday*, 101.

294   visited her regularly: Ibid.

294   They fished together: Ibid.

295   hoped she would leave Harry: Ibid.

295   a self-inflicted gunshot wound: *New York Times*, November 28, 1953.

295   staff became increasingly female: *Newsday* biography.

295   Fearlessly, she took on: Hofstra biography.

295   *Review-Star*'s days: *Newsday* biography.

295   Levittown, the famous postwar: *Newsday* biography.

295   thousands of new families: *Post*, May 12, 1951, 117–18.

295   Echoing her ancestor: Ibid., 117.

296   eighteen hundred newsboys: Ibid.

296   Garden City plant: *Newsweek*, March 28, 1949, 61–62.

296   "Alicia Patterson's *Newsday*": Author's observation.

296   carried more advertising: *Time*, November 1, 1948.

296   won the top Pulitzer Prize: *Time*, May 10, 1948.

296   "As you know": *Newsday* biography.

296   "Harry told me": Jeffrey Potter, *Men, Money & Magic: The Story of Dorothy Schiff* (New York: Signet, 1976), 239.

297   she would retreat alone to Kingsland: Keeler, *Newsday*, 235.

297   been in a youthful romance: Porter McKeever, *Adlai Stevenson: His Life and Legacy* (New York: William Morrow, 1989), 124.

297 Both were married: Jean H. Baker, *The Stevensons: A Biography of an American Family* (New York: Norton, 1996), 25.

297 Despite rumors to the contrary: John Bartlow Martin, *Adlai Stevenson of Illinois* (Garden City, NY: Doubleday, 1976), 647.

297 fueled by Ellen: Keeler, *Newsday*, 154.

297 After his marriage: Martin, *Adlai Stevenson of Illinois*, 318.

297 Dorothy Fosdick: McKeever, *Adlai Stevenson*, 164.

298 tragically disturbed: Ibid., 57.

298 a fabled professional explorer: *Chicago Tribune*, August 27, 1916.

298 rivaled Mrs. Potter Palmer: McKeever, *Adlai Stevenson*, 56.

298 a passionate affair: Jeff Broadwater, *Adlai Stevenson: The Odyssey of a Cold War Liberal* (New York: Twayne, 1994), 93.

298 "So you've made it": Baker, *The Stevensons*, 21.

298 "to whom more": McKeever, *Adlai Stevenson*, 272.

298 "Somewhere the sun": Martin, *Adlai Stevenson of Illinois*, 356.

299 "I brood about this": Ibid., 389.

299 "reveries of a drowsy": McKeever, *Adlai Stevenson*, 125.

299 columnist Marquis Childs: Martin, *Adlai Stevenson of Illinois*, 381–82.

299 present as a beard: Jeffrey Potter, *Men, Money & Magic*, 235.

299 "the fairy land of": Baker, *The Stevensons*, 23.

299 "As always it was a charmed": Martin, *Adlai Stevenson of Illinois*, 431.

299 "We feel that the country": *Newsday* biography.

299 When she gave a dinner: Marilyn Nissenson, *The Lady Upstairs: Dorothy Schiff and the New York Post* (New York: St. Martin's Press, 2007), 25.

299 "Tell Adlai how sorry": Martin, *Adlai Stevenson of Illinois*, 690.

300 Alicia insisted: Keeler, *Newsday*, 232, 238.

300 subject of a 1929 *Time:* Ibid.

300 Alicia backed Stevenson: *Newsday* biography.

300 "I have chosen": Keeler, *Newsday*, 242.

300 At one point she left: Ibid.

300 "Elisha dearest": Martin, *Adlai Stevenson of Illinois*, 477.

301 "but to say that": Ibid., 478.

301 didn't expect to survive: Unger and Unger, *The Guggenheims*, 320.

301 underwent exploratory surgery: Keeler, *Newsday*, 184–85.

301 further surgery uncovered: Ibid., 185.

301 "A letter from Josephine": Walter Johnson, *The Papers of Adlai E. Stevenson*, vol. 2 (Boston: Little, Brown, 1974), 149.

301 "sounds so tired": Ibid., 180.

301 "I completely lost": *Post*, February 21, 1959, 44.

301 divorced from Jay Frederick Reeve: Ann Blackman, *Seasons of Her Life: A Biography of Madeleine Korbel Albright* (New York: Lisa Drew/Scribner, 1998), 121.

302 "virtually fell apart": Keeler, *Newsday*, 276.

302 The marriage disintegrated: Blackman, *Seasons of Her Life*, 121.

302 Josephine took their children: Josephine Patterson obituary, *New York Times*, January 18, 1996.

302 painter Ivan Le Lorraine Albright: Ibid.

302 Adam, born in 1947: Keeler, *Newsday*, 276.

302 Dina, in 1949: Albright, *Madam Secretary*, 62.

302 "Life with Junior" for *Newsday:* Dobbs, *Madeleine Albright*, 171.

302 55 East Division Street: Ibid., 185.

302 Wyoming ranch: Ibid., 171.

302 "*The New York Times* with guts": *Time*, February 16, 1959.

302 While a Williams College student: Dobbs, *Madeleine Albright*, 165–68.

302 When they married: Ibid., 182.

302 "figure out how": Albright, *Madam Secretary*, 62.

303 "I never got used to": Ibid., 51.

303 "It was a very hard family": Blackman, *Seasons of Her Life*, 127.

303 "could be very impatient": Dobbs, *Madeleine Albright*, 186.

303 "a mixture of rebel and socialite": Albright, *Madam Secretary*, 51.

303 "after the wedding": Ibid., 59.

303 "She looked like": Ibid., 50.

303 "less than five feet tall": Ibid., 51.

303 Fortunately she accepted Madeleine: Ibid., 56–57.

303 "Wonderful idea": Ibid., 57–58.

304 "beneath them": Blackman, *Seasons of Her Life*, 121.

304 America's most profitable new: *Newsday* biography.

304 Alicia did more: *Newsweek*, March 28, 1949.

304 "Oh, she's all right": Keeler, *Newsday*, 96.

305 "I wouldn't give them": Ibid., 73.

305 "He walked in": Ibid., 96.

305 "When I started *Newsday*": *Newsday* biography.

20: HUBRIS: FDR AND THE MCCORMICK-PATTERSON AXIS

306 Between them they controlled: Wayne Andrews, *Battle for Chicago* (New York: Harcourt, Brace, 1946), 294–95.

306 By 1941 they were reaching: Ibid.

306 rivaled only: John Tebbel, *An American Dynasty* (1947; reprinted Westport, CT: Greenwood Press, 1968), 4.

306 long after much: Ibid.

306 As one of: Paul Healy, *Cissy: A Biography of Eleanor M. "Cissy" Patterson* (Garden City, NY: Doubleday, 1966), 275.

307 Cissy became: Ibid., 271–72.

307 traveled in her railroad car: Ibid., 272–73.

307 "on the shinbone": Ralph G. Martin, *Cissy: The Extraordinary Life of Eleanor Medill Patterson* (New York: Simon & Schuster, 1979), 322.

307 The discreet candidate: Ibid.

307 "the noblest woman": Ibid., 324.

307 rumor of a romance: Ibid., 360.

307 "I don't care": Ibid.

307 She appreciated: Ibid., 325.

307 giving her picture retoucher: Ibid., 359.

308 Cissy supported Roosevelt: Healy, *Cissy*, 276.

308 "drive out some day": Martin, *Cissy*, 381.

308 "when the nice weather starts": Ibid.

308 "spend a weekend": Marion Davies, *The Times We Had: Life with William Randolph Hearst* (New York: Ballantine Books, 1975), 236.

308 "All right": Healy, *Cissy*, 277.

309 "You have been": Ibid., 277–78.

309 Her next hostile move: Ibid., 279.

309 The cherry trees: Ibid., 282.

309 "another one of": Richard Norton Smith, *The Colonel: The Life & Legend of Robert McCormick 1880–1955* (Boston: Houghton Mifflin, 1997), xx.

309 "the NEWS was worth": John Chapman, *Tell It to Sweeney: The Informal History of the New York Daily News* (Garden City, NY: Doubleday, 1961), 198.

309 he and Mary King: Ibid.

309 the *News* was instrumental: Ibid., 199.

310 ambassador to the Court of St. James's: Ibid.

310 attempted to rationally explain: Smith, *The Colonel*, 365.

310 Alice's resistance: Ibid.

310 After buying: Real Estate file, J. M. Patterson Papers.

310 The provocative modernist: Christopher Gray, "Streetscapes," *New York Times*, November 12, 1995.

311 "Inside the owner": Fay Hines, "Steel for the Private Life of a Business Man," *Arts & Decoration*, November 1935, 18–20.

311 "I have often been": Real Estate file, J. M. Patterson Papers.

311 Butler and housekeeper: Ibid.

311 Among the automobiles: Correspondence and invoices in J. M. Patterson Papers.

311 further installations: Real Estate file, J. M. Patterson Papers.

311   it was only Jimmy: Robert Keeler, *Newsday: A Candid History of the Respectable Tabloid* (New York: William Morrow, 1997), 48.

311   Mary remained in Riverdale: Ibid.

311   "Dining in town": Joseph Medill Patterson correspondence, October 24, 1935, J. M. Patterson Papers.

312   work began at six: Tebbel, *An American Dynasty*, 290.

312   The *Daily News* printed: *Time*, June 20, 1938.

312   Alice's terms: Gwen Morgan and Arthur Veysey, *Poor Little Rich Boy: The Life and Times of Col. Robert R. McCormick* (Carpentersville, IL: Crossroads Communications, 1985), 351.

312   Onwentsia in Lake Forest: Joseph Medill Patterson correspondence, June 28, 1938, J. M. Patterson Papers.

312   Lake Bluff's Shoreacres Club: Joseph Medill Patterson correspondence, October 10, 1938, J. M. Patterson Papers.

312   Saddle & Cycle: Joseph Medill Patterson correspondence, December 27, 1935, J. M. Patterson Papers.

312   New York's Lotus Club: Joseph Medill Patterson correspondence, March 28, 1938, J. M. Patterson Papers.

312   the *News* played the story: *Time*, July 18, 1938.

312   attended Mary Immaculate School: J. M. Patterson Papers.

312   After Joe's morning exercise: Tebbel, *An American Dynasty*, 290.

313   produced some of his best ideas. Walter E. Schneider, "Fabulous Rise of N. Y. Daily News Due to Capt. Patterson's Genius," *Editor & Publisher*, June 24, 1939, 46.

313   driving to a movie house: Ibid., 7.

313   not up to academy requirements: James Patterson Education file, J. M. Patterson Papers.

313   sisters of the Dominican order: Ibid.

313   Joe enrolled his son: Ibid.

313   six-month West Point preparatory: Ibid.

313   did have flat feet: Ibid.

313   French lessons at Berlitz: Ibid.

313   accepted at West Point: Ibid.

313   He cheerfully ran errands: Leo E. McGivena and Others, *The News: The First Fifty Years of New York's Picture Newspaper* (New York: News Syndicate, 1969), 322.

313   Immediately following: Ibid.

314   Their grandfather: Martin, *Cissy*, 403.

314   Cissy's feelings: Ibid., 404.

314 the turning point: Frank Waldrop, *McCormick of Chicago: An Unconventional Portrait of a Controversial Figure* (Englewood Cliffs, NJ: Prentice-Hall, 1966), 233.

314 "gives the President": Chapman, *Tell It to Sweeney*, 203.

314 "make the President": Ibid.

315 "He lied to me": Martin, *Cissy*, 415.

315 Bert was already: Andrews, *Battle for Chicago*, 306.

315 the McCormick-Patterson Axis: Joseph Gies, *The Colonel of Chicago* (New York: Dutton, 1979), 163.

315 Marshall III, born in 1893: Stephen Becker, *Marshall Field III* (New York: Simon & Schuster, 1964), 49.

315 Henry, two years later: Ibid., 53.

315 Three-fifths was earmarked: Ibid., 65.

316 an elective tonsillectomy: Ibid., 87–88.

316 Ralph Ingersoll: Gies, *Colonel of Chicago*, 172.

316 "man bites underdog": Axel Madsen, *The Marshall Fields: The Evolution of an American Business Dynasty* (Hoboken, NJ: John Wiley & Sons, 2002), 236.

316 The publication: Gies, *Colonel of Chicago*, 172.

317 ominous overcast skies: *Chicago Tribune*, December 7, 2009.

317 He followed by directing: Smith, *The Colonel*, 420.

317 executive editor, Frank Waldrop: Martin, *Cissy*, 417.

317 when the bulletin came: Healy, *Cissy*, 287.

317 Cissy called her staff: Martin, *Cissy*, 417.

317 *Times-Herald* extra: Ibid.

317 ahead of the competition: Healy, *Cissy*, 287.

317 first in any city: Martin, *Cissy*, 417.

318 She turned to Chalmers Roberts: Ibid.

318 "Do you think *he* arranged this?": Smith, *The Colonel*, 420.

318 Patterson was with Alicia: McGivena, *The News*, 310.

318 "My God": Keeler, *Newsday*, 94.

318 Joe immediately drove: McGivena, *The News*, 310.

318 "Well, we're in it": Martin, *Cissy*, 418–19.

318 Fred Pasley: Chapman, *Tell It to Sweeney*, 182.

318 "in any capacity": Ibid., 183.

318 What he really hoped: Ibid., 182.

319 When Joe was admitted: Ibid., 184.

319 "I am here": Ibid.

319 "I remained standing": Ibid., 185.

319 "was to read over": Ibid.

319 "that as a result": Ibid., 185–86.

319 "It took balls": Martin, *Cissy*, 419.

319 "That man did things": Ibid.

319 "All I want to do now": Ibid.

319 "Until today the *News*": Morgan and Veysey, *Poor Little Rich Boy*, 377.

320 "Hiyi": Healy, *Cissy*, 289.

320 "America's No. 1 and No. 2": Healy, *Cissy*, 290–91.

320 "doing their best": Ibid., 291.

320 YOU'RE A LIAR: Gies, *Colonel of Chicago*, 199.

320 "SHIT ON ELEANOR": Martin, *Cissy*, 434.

320 accusations of anti-Semitism: Ibid., 434–35.

321 "news, editorials and cartoons": Gies, *Colonel of Chicago*, 198.

321 Soon after the meeting: Ibid.

321 McCormick received a letter: Ibid., 201.

321 "You do not know it": Ibid.

321 "And On the Seventh Day": Smith, *The Colonel*, 422.

321 "Whatta Man!": Ibid.

321 "I think we should": Ibid.

321 "The *Tribune* doesn't": Gies, *Colonel of Chicago*, 215.

322 a Nazi Iron Cross: Martin, *Cissy*, 434.

322 the love and esteem: Ibid., 438.

21: THE COUSINS IN WINTER

323 she and Drew Pearson: Ralph G. Martin, *Cissy: The Extraordinary Life of Eleanor Medill Patterson* (New York: Simon & Schuster, 1979), 427.

323 She also split: Ibid., 429.

323 "like a man honking": Bob Thomas, *Winchell* (Garden City, NY: Doubleday, 1971), 35.

323 Cissy's insomnia: Martin, *Cissy*, 439.

323 The urbane Russian: Ibid., 427.

323 blithely provided illicit: Ibid., 428.

324 Cissy was smoking: Richard Norton Smith, *The Colonel: The Life & Legend of Robert McCormick 1880–1955* (Boston: Houghton Mifflin, 1997), 463.

324 The copious alcohol: Martin, *Cissy*, 439.

324 She was advised: Ibid., 445.

324 De Savitsch solemnly: Ibid.

324 When Evie Robert: Ibid., 446.

324 "Get me a doctor": Ibid.

324 she published an exposé: Ibid.

324 "a nice little heart": Ibid.

325 she slapped him: Ibid., 450.

325 "You'll only hurt": Ibid., 451.

325 Bizarre stories: Ibid., 452.

325 caught up in another triadic: Smith, *The Colonel*, 450–51.

325 Amy viewed her: Smith, *The Colonel*, 451.

325 one of her best friends: Gwen Morgan and Arthur Veysey, *Poor Little Rich Boy: The Life and Times of Col. Robert R. McCormick* (Carpentersville, IL: Crossroads Communications, 1985), 390.

325 In November 1944: Ibid., 391.

326 "The ceremony was unpretentious": *Life*, January 10, 1945.

326 The new energy extended: Morgan and Veysey, *Poor Little Rich Boy*, 394.

326 "The whole nation": Ibid., 396.

326 "Don't serve champagne": Ibid.

327 "I don't know of anyone": Ibid.

327 His *Daily News:* Tebbel, *An American Dynasty*, 268.

327 "You don't need": Martin, *Cissy*, 453.

327 "He's the story now": Ibid.

327 proposed to live on money: Ibid., 453–54.

327 to an AA meeting: Smith, *The Colonel*, 463.

327 Ellen, married George Arnold: Martin, *Cissy*, 457.

327 Cissy's relationship: Ibid.

328 hoped to attend his fiftieth reunion: Alice Hoge, *Cissy Patterson: The Life of Eleanor Medill Patterson, Publisher & Editor of the Washington Times-Herald* (New York: Random House, 1966), 219.

328 New York's Doctors' Hospital: Smith, *The Colonel*, 464.

328 The women in his life: Ibid.

328 Joe, the center of silence: Ibid.

328 "strange and fearsome man": A. J. Liebling, "Mamie and Mr. O'Donnell Carry On," *New Yorker*, June 8, 1946.

328 "one of the greatest": Tebbel, *An American Dynasty*, 299.

328 "Everyone on the *Tribune*": Ibid., 301.

328 Joe's body: Paul Healy, *Cissy: A Biography of Eleanor M. "Cissy" Patterson* (Garden City, NY: Doubleday, 1966), 373.

329 advising her sister-in-law: Hoge, *Cissy Patterson*, 219.

329 When the limousines: Ibid.

329 usurping Mary's position: Ibid.

329 "It was the only time": Martin, *Cissy*, 455.

329 Joe had become a Catholic: Ibid.

329 There was no conversion: Ibid., 457.

329 Scarcely was Joe's body: Smith, *The Colonel*, 465.

329 control of the *Daily News:* Leo E. McGivena and Others, *The News: The First Fifty Years of New York's Picture Newspaper* (New York: News Syndicate, 1969), 320.

329 Mary and Joe's: Smith, *The Colonel*, 465.

329 Cissy, in a throwback: Ibid., 466.

329 to the displeasure of the Colonel: Ibid.

329 McCormick's relationship with Cissy: Hoge, *Cissy Patterson*, 220.

330 The two were made trustees: Ibid.

330 Maintaining the Patterson power balance: Ibid.

330 she suggested that Alicia: Ibid.

330 She also nominated Alicia: Ibid.

330 Cissy even returned: Martin, *Cissy*, 458.

330 Her paranoia was extreme: Healy, *Cissy*, 380.

330 "Received, one shoebox": Martin, *Cissy*, 460.

330 drinking returned: Ibid., 461.

331 amazingly magnanimous wife: Penelope Rowlands, *A Dash of Daring: Carmel Snow and Her Life in Fashion, Art, and Letters* (New York: Atria Books, 2005), 377.

331 lost her desire to live: Martin, *Cissy*, 463.

331 Cissy had planned: Healy, *Cissy*, 381.

331 On Friday night: Martin, *Cissy*, 465.

331 Her bedroom: Healy, *Cissy*, 383–84.

331 A watchman: Martin, *Cissy*, 465.

331 At approximately one o'clock: Healy, *Cissy*, 383.

331 Both spent: Ibid.

331 There was no: Martin, *Cissy*, 465.

331 staff waited: Healy, *Cissy*, 383.

331 Robert Lye: Ibid.

331 not yet awakened: Hoge, *Cissy Patterson*, 225.

331 Finally, around noon: Healy, *Cissy*, 384.

331 lying across the bed: Ibid.

331 "I think she's dead": Hoge, *Cissy Patterson*, 225.

331 Lye followed his abrupt: Healy, *Cissy*, 384.

331 death had occurred: Hoge, *Cissy Patterson*, 226.

331 servants remembered: Healy, *Cissy*, 384.

332 Waldrop and Dr. Walsh: Martin, *Cissy*, 465.

332 a short Episcopal service: Healy, *Cissy*, 385.

332 an estimated $35,000: Hoge, *Cissy Patterson*, 226.

332 blanket of yellow roses: Martin, *Cissy*, 466.

332 flowers filling two railroad: Healy, *Cissy*, 386.

332 Cissy's body was cremated: Ibid.

332 "A great lady died": Martin, *Cissy*, 466.

332 "I'm the last leaf": Smith, *The Colonel*, 474.

332 he publicly lauded her: Joseph Gies, *The Colonel of Chicago* (New York: Dutton, 1979), 232.

332 "They'll have a damned": Martin, *Cissy*, 474.

332 there were accusations: Hoge, *Cissy Patterson*, 229.

333 Felicia was outraged: Martin, *Cissy*, 472.

333 The Dupont Circle house: Ibid.

333 Mrs. Smith: Healy, *Cissy*, 394.

333 "aiding Polish refugee children": Martin, *Cissy*, 472.

333 She did not want to destroy: Ibid., 473–74.

334 four hundred thousand dollars: Ibid., 474.

334 In 1924 she was her mother's: Healy, *Cissy*, 397.

334 the wardrobe was put up for sale: Ibid., 410.

334 a trail of clues: Healy, *Cissy*, 398.

334 wanted to leave him: Ibid.

334 He declined: Ibid.

334 "But what do I care": Ibid., 399.

335 "great changes": Ibid., 402.

335 intensified rumors: Ibid.

335 he was certain Truman had won: Smith, *The Colonel*, 483.

335 "She left us a gold mine": Healy, *Cissy*, 411.

335 the predicted conflict: Ibid.

335 If they were to sell: Ibid., 412.

335 William Randolph Hearst Jr.: Smith, *The Colonel*, 491.

335 Eugene Meyer: Healy, *Cissy*, 412.

336 Ruth and Medill's only son: Kristie Miller, *Ruth Hanna McCormick: A Life in Politics 1880–1944* (Albuquerque: University of New Mexico Press, 1992).

336 Six days later: Miller, *Ruth Hanna McCormick*, 250–52.

336 "Now everything": Morgan and Veysey, *Poor Little Rich Boy*, 358.

336 The Colonel: Smith, *The Colonel*, 364.

336 contribute most of her inheritance: Morgan and Veysey, *Poor Little Rich Boy*, 352.

337 "I've always hated": Wayne Andrews, *Battle for Chicago* (New York: Harcourt, Brace, 1946), 318.

337 Asking for a higher price: Smith, *The Colonel*, 365.

337 It was an ideal fit: Morgan and Veysey, *Poor Little Rich Boy*, 408.

337 Despite her lack: Ibid.

337 "She's getting": Ibid., 424.

337 Garvin "Tank" Tankersley: Ibid.

338 raise Arabian horses: Ibid., 425.

338 now run by *Tribune* executives: Katharine Graham, *Personal History* (New York: Knopf, 1997), 217.

338 Kent Cooper: Waldrop, *McCormick of Chicago*, 278.

338 close enough to McCormick: Morgan and Veysey, *Poor Little Rich Boy*, 429.

338 he had become increasingly: Ibid.

338 "business matter": Graham, *Personal History*, 216.

338 "one of the most important": Ibid., 219.

338 "Dad arrived": Ibid., 216.

339 " 'Kent' ": Ibid.

339 terrified that Bazy: Smith, *The Colonel*, 517.

339 "Cooper told us": Graham, *Personal History*, 218.

339 "struck by a thunderbolt": Ibid., 219.

339 Mary Patterson stood up: Smith, *The Colonel*, 517.

339 "The time was": Graham, *Personal History*, 220.

340 toured in their own plane: Gies, *Colonel of Chicago*, 218.

340 The wartime aircraft: Smith, *The Colonel*, 470.

340 Wherever they went: Gies, *Colonel of Chicago*, 218.

340 They met with: Smith, *The Colonel*, 470.

340 Maryland was charmed: Morgan and Veysey, *Poor Little Rich Boy*, 417.

340 "Argentina": Ibid.

340 "about the size": Gies, *Colonel of Chicago*, 222.

340 "the father": Frank Waldrop, *McCormick of Chicago: An Unconventional Portrait of a Controversial Figure* (Englewood Cliffs, NJ: Prentice-Hall, 1966), 267.

340 "He's an awful man": Morgan and Veysey, *Poor Little Rich Boy*, 417.

340 sentimental afternoon: Gies, *Colonel of Chicago*, 234.

341 "rather courtly": Ibid., 228.

341 "with no little": Ibid.

341 "The fire-breathing": Ibid., 228–29.

341 "a great man": Smith, *The Colonel*, 467.

341 "I don't know": Ibid.

341 a spectacular hostess: Gies, *Colonel of Chicago*, 223.

341 The mammoth: Smith, *The Colonel*, 458.

342 reputation as a hostess: Morgan and Veysey, *Poor Little Rich Boy*, 423.

342 Three hundred and fifty: Ibid., 419–20.

342 his niece Bazy: Waldrop, *McCormick of Chicago*, 182.

342 "People ask": Ibid.

342 Maryland followed: Morgan and Veysey, *Poor Little Rich Boy*, 423.

342 "Sometimes at ninety": Ibid., 459.

342 "Good God!": Ibid.

343 After a disagreement: Ibid., 428–29.

343 She had written: Gies, *Colonel of Chicago*, 234.

343 "Be careful": Ibid., 235.

343 alcohol continued: Morgan and Veysey, *Poor Little Rich Boy*, 459.

343 "The only man": Ibid., 459–60.

343 "Young man": Ibid., 461.

343 His appetite: Ibid., 465.

344 In mid-December: Gies, *Colonel of Chicago*, 234.

344 Two years before: Ibid.

344 Maryland would: Smith, *The Colonel*, 514–15.

344 "pestering the life": Ibid., 514.

344 "As far": Ibid., 515.

344 Maryland was becoming: Ibid., 519.

344 On Christmas night: Gies, *Colonel of Chicago*, 235.

344 Maryland continually: Morgan and Veysey, *Poor Little Rich Boy*, 466.

344 "the tenement": Ibid.

345 Watchers of the Night: Ibid., 467.

345 He terrified: Waldrop, *McCormick of Chicago*, 5.

345 on March 10: Morgan and Veysey, *Poor Little Rich Boy*, 469.

345 He contacted Bazy: Ibid.

345 A nonflyer: Smith, *The Colonel*, 520.

345 silently held hands: Ibid.

345 On St. Patrick's Day: Smith, *The Colonel*, 521.

345 taken to Cantigny: Waldrop, *McCormick of Chicago*, 281.

345 Buster Boo: Ibid.

345 the Watch: Smith, *The Colonel*, 522.

345 "You know": Ibid.

345 she was sleeping: Ibid.

345 Official cause: Morgan and Veysey, *Poor Little Rich Boy*, 473.

EPILOGUE: AFTER THE MEDILL CENTURY

347 Joe's daughter: Robert Keeler, *Newsday: A Candid History of the Respectable Tabloid* (New York: William Morrow, 1997), 289–90.

347 three out of four: Museum of Broadcast Communications.

347 watched Jacqueline Kennedy: C. David Heymann, *A Woman Named Jackie* (New York: Lyle Stuart/Carol Communications, 1989), 334–35.

348 It was: Hofstra University biography of Alicia Patterson.

348 The former skydiver: Najeeb Halaby obituary, *New York Times*, July 3, 2003.

348 "Get me": Keeler, *Newsday*, 289.

348 "Jeeb, we don't": Ibid.

348 "It's closed": Ibid.

348 "She persuaded": Ibid., 290.

348 Although the ulcer: Madeleine Albright, *Madam Secretary: A Memoir* (New York: Hyperion, 2003), 70.

349 "Your children": Ann Blackman, *Seasons of Her Life: A Biography of Madeleine Korbel Albright* (New York: Lisa Drew /Scribner, 1998), 156.

349 Harry's 51 percent: Michael Dobbs, *Madeleine Albright: A Twentieth-Century Odyssey* (New York: Henry Holt, 1999), 277.

350 "This marriage": Albright, *Madam Secretary*, 120.

350 he had met: Dobbs, *Madeleine Albright*, 282.

350 She also emerged: Ibid., 29.

350 president and publisher: *Time*, March 26, 1984.

BIBLIOGRAPHY

Albright, Madeleine. *Madam Secretary: A Memoir*. New York: Hyperion, 2003.

————. *Read My Pins*. New York: HarperCollins, 2009.

Amory, Cleveland. *The Last Resorts*. New York: Harper & Brothers, 1948.

————. *Who Killed Society?* New York: Harper & Brothers, 1960.

Andreas, A. T. *History of Chicago*. Vol. 1, *To 1857*. Chicago: A. T. Andreas, 1975.

————. *History of Chicago*. Vol. 2, *1857 to 1871*. Chicago: A. T. Andreas, 1975.

————. *History of Chicago*. Vol.3, *From the Fire to 1885*. New York: Arno Press, 1885.

Andrews, Robert Hardy. *A Corner of Chicago*. Boston: Little, Brown, 1963.

Andrews, Wayne. *Battle for Chicago*. New York: Harcourt, Brace, 1946.

Arpee, Edward. *Lake Forest Illinois: History and Reminiscences 1861–1961*. Lake Forest, IL: Rotary Club of Lake Forest, 1963.

Auchincloss, Louis. *The Rector of Justin*. Boston: Houghton Mifflin, 1964.

Bach, Ira J. *Chicago's Famous Buildings*. Chicago: University of Chicago Press, 1965.

Baker, Jean H. *The Stevensons: A Biography of an American Family*. New York: Norton, 1996.

Beadle, Muriel. *The Fortnightly of Chicago: The City and Its Women: 1873–1973*. Chicago: Henry Regnery, 1973.

Becker, Stephen. *Marshall Field III*. New York: Simon & Schuster, 1964.

Birmingham, Stephen. *Our Crowd: The Great Jewish Families of New York*. New York: Harper & Row, 1967.

Bishop, Glenn A., and Paul T. Gilbert. *Chicago's Accomplishments and Leaders*. Chicago: Bishop, 1932.

Blackman, Ann. *Seasons of Her Life: A Biography of Madeleine Korbel Albright*. New York: Lisa Drew/Scribner, 1998.

Blood, Thomas. *Madam Secretary: A Biography of Madeleine Albright*. New York: St. Martin's, 1997.

Bluestone, Daniel. *Constructing Chicago*. New Haven, CT: Yale University Press, 1991.

Bowen, Louise de Koven. *Growing Up with a City*. New York: Macmillan, 1926.

———. *Open Windows*. Chicago: Ralph Fletcher Seymour, 1946.

Brinkley, Alan. *The Publisher: Henry Luce and His American Century*. New York: Knopf, 2010.

Broadwater, Jeff. *Adlai Stevenson: The Odyssey of a Cold War Liberal*. New York: Twayne, 1994.

Brough, James. *Princess Alice: A Biography of Alice Roosevelt Longworth*. Boston: Little, Brown, 1975.

Butcher, Fanny. *Many Lives—One Love*. New York: Harper & Row, 1972.

Carter, Miranda. *George, Nicholas and Wilhelm: Three Royal Cousins and the Road to World War I*. New York: Knopf, 2010.

Cassini, Marguerite. *Never a Dull Moment*. New York: Harper & Brothers, 1956.

Chapman, John. *Tell It to Sweeney: The Informal History of the New York Daily News*. Garden City, NY: Doubleday, 1961.

Chicago Tribune. *Chicago Days: 150 Defining Moments in the Life of a Great City*. Wheaton, IL: Cantigny-First Division Foundation, 1997.

Churchill, Allen. *Park Row: A Vivid Re-Creation of Turn of the Century Newspaper Days*. New York: Rinehart, 1958.

Ciccone, F. Richard. *Chicago and the American Century*. Lincolnwood, IL: Contemporary Books, 1999.

Clark, Herma. *The Elegant Eighties: When Chicago Was Young*. Chicago: A. C. McClurg, 1941.

Cohen, Stuart, and Susan Benjamin. *North Shore Chicago: Houses of the Lakefront Suburbs, 1890-1940*. New York: Acanthus Press, 2004.

Condit, Carl W. *The Chicago School of Architecture*. Chicago: University of Chicago Press, 1964.

Cook, Frederick Francis. *Bygone Days in Chicago*. Chicago: A. C. McClurg, 1910.

Coventry, Kim, Daniel Meyer, and Arthur H. Miller. *Classic Country Estates of Lake Forest*. New York: Norton, 2003.

Cronin, William. *Nature's Metropolis: Chicago and the Great West*. New York: Norton, 1991.

Darby, Edwin. *The Fortune Builders*. Garden City, NY: Doubleday, 1986.

Dart, Susan. *The Friday Club: The First Hundred Years 1887-1987*. Published privately, 1987.

Davies, Marion. *The Times We Had: Life with William Randolph Hearst*. New York: Ballantine Books, 1975.

Dedmon, Emmett. *Fabulous Chicago: A Great City's History and People*. New York: Random House, 1953.

Dobbs, Michael. *Madeleine Albright: A Twentieth-Century Odyssey*. New York: Henry Holt, 1999.

Donaldson, Scott. *Hemingway vs. Fitzgerald: The Rise and Fall of a Literary Friendship*. Woodstock, NY: Overlook Press, 1999.

Drury, John. *Old Chicago Houses*. New York: Bonanza Books, 1941.

Dwight, Eleanor. *The Letters of Pauline Palmer: A Great Lady of Chicago's First Family*. Milano: M. T. Train/Scala Books, 2005.

Edwards, Jerome. *The Foreign Policy of Col. McCormick's Tribune, 1929–1941*. Reno: University of Nevada Press, 1971.

Emery, Edwin. *The Press and America: An Interpretative History of Journalism*. Englewood Cliffs, NJ: Prentice Hall, 1962.

Farr, Finis. *Chicago: A Personal History of America's Most American City*. New Rochelle, NY: Arlington House, 1973.

Felsenthal, Carol. *Alice Roosevelt Longworth*. New York: G. P. Putnam's Sons, 1988.

Fitzgerald, F. Scott. *Ledger: A Facsimile*. Washington, DC: NCR, 1972.

Franch, John. *Robber Baron: The Life of Charles Tyson Yerkes*. Urbana: University of Illinois Press, 2006.

Gale, Edwin Oscar. *Reminiscences of Early Chicago and Vicinity*. Chicago: Fleming H. Revell, 1902.

Gardner, Virginia. *Friend and Lover: The Life of Louise Bryant*. New York: Horizon Press, 1982.

Gatewood, Worth. *Fifty Years: The New York Daily News in Pictures*. Garden City, NY: Dolphin/Doubleday, 1979.

Gies, Joseph. *The Colonel of Chicago*. New York: Dutton, 1979.

Gizycka, Eleanor. *Fall Flight*. New York: Minton, Balch, 1928.

———. *Glass Houses*. New York: Minton, Balch, 1926.

Graf, John. *Chicago's Mansions*. Charleston, SC: Arcadia, 2004.

Graham, Katharine. *Personal History*. New York: Knopf, 1997.

Greene, Virginia A. *The Architecture of Howard Van Doren Shaw*. Chicago: Chicago Review Press, 1998.

Grossman, James R., Ann Durkin Keating, and Janice L. Reiff. *The Encyclopedia of Chicago*. Chicago: University of Chicago Press, 2004.

Halberstam, David. *The Powers That Be*. New York: Knopf, 1979.

Hannigan, William. *New York Noir: Crime Photos from the Daily News Archive*. New York: Rizzoli, 1999.

Harris, Neil. *Chicago Apartments: A Century of Lakefront Luxury*. New York: Acanthus Press, 2004.

Harris & Morrow. *The Bon Ton Directory*. Chicago: Blakely, Brown & Marsh, 1879.

Harrison, Carter H. *Stormy Years: The Autobiography of Carter H. Harrison*. Indianapolis: Bobbs-Merrill, 1935.

Harrison, Mrs. Carter H. *Strange to Say—Recollections of Persons and Events in New Orleans and Chicago*. Chicago: A. Kroch & Son, 1949.

Healy, Paul. *Cissy: A Biography of Eleanor M. "Cissy" Patterson*. Garden City, NY: Doubleday, 1966.

Hecht, Ben. *Charlie: The Improbable Life and Times of Charles MacArthur*. New York: Harper & Brothers, 1957.

———. *A Child of the Century: The Autobiography of Ben Hecht*. New York: Simon & Schuster, 1955.

Hemingway, Ernest. *A Moveable Feast*. New York: Charles Scribner's Sons, 1964.

Heymann, C. David. *A Woman Named Jackie*. New York: Lyle Stuart/Carol Communications, 1989.

Hoge, Alice. *Cissy Patterson: The Life of Eleanor Medill Patterson, Publisher & Editor of the Washington Times-Herald*. New York: Random House, 1966.

Horowitz, Helen Lefkowitz. *Culture & the City: Cultural Philanthropy in Chicago from the 1880s to 1917*. Chicago: University of Chicago Press, 1976.

Hurlbut, Henry H. *Chicago Antiquities*. Chicago: Privately printed, 1881.

Jaher, Frederic Cople. *The Urban Establishment: Upper Strata in Boston, New York, Charleston, Chicago, and Los Angeles*. Urbana: University of Illinois Press, 1982.

Jensen, Peter. *Historic Chicago Sites*. Chicago: Creative Enterprises, 1953.

Johnson, Walter. *The Papers of Adlai E. Stevenson*. Vol 2. Boston: Little, Brown, 1974.

Kahn, E. J. Jr. *The World of Swope*. New York: Simon & Schuster, 1965.

Keeler, Robert. *Newsday: A Candid History of the Respectable Tabloid*. New York: Morrow, 1997.

Kinsley, Philip. *The Chicago Tribune: Its First Hundred Years*. Vol. 1, *1847–1865*. New York: Knopf, 1943.

———. *The Chicago Tribune: Its First Hundred Years*. Vol. 2, *1865–1880*. Chicago: Chicago Tribune, 1946.

———. *The Chicago Tribune: Its First Hundred Years*. Vol. 3, *1880–1900*. Chicago: Chicago Tribune, 1946.

Kinzie, Mrs. John H. *Wa-bun: The Early Days in the North-West*. New York: Derby & Jackson, 1856.

Kirkland, Caroline. *Chicago Yesterdays: A Sheaf of Reminiscences*. Chicago: Daughaday, 1919.

Kirkland, Joseph, and Caroline Kirkland. *The Story of Chicago*. Vol. 2. Chicago: Dibble, 1894.

Kogan, Herman, and Robert Cromie. *The Great Fire: Chicago, 1871*. New York: G. P. Putnam's Sons, 1971.

Koolhaas, Rem. *Delirious New York*. New York: Monacelli Press, 1994.

Leonard, John. *The Book of Chicagoans*. Chicago: A. N. Marquis, 1905.

Lewis, Lloyd, and Henry Justin Smith. *Chicago: The History of Its Reputation*. New York: Harcourt, Brace, 1929.

Liebling, A. J. *The Press*. New York: Ballantine Books, 1961.

Lindberg, Richard. *Chicago by Gaslight: A History of Chicago's Netherworld 1880–1920*. Chicago: Academy Chicago, 1996.

Longstreet, Stephen. *Chicago 1860–1919*. New York: David McKay, 1973.

Longworth, Alice Roosevelt. *Crowded Hours: Reminiscences of Alice Roosevelt Longworth*. New York: Charles Scribner's Sons, 1933.

Lowe, David. *The Great Chicago Fire in Eyewitness Accounts and 70 Contemporary Photographs and Illustrations*. New York: Dover, 1979.

———. *Lost Chicago*. Boston: Houghton Mifflin, 1978.

Madsen, Axel. *The Marshall Fields: The Evolution of an American Business Dynasty*. Hoboken, NJ: John Wiley & Sons, 2002.

Marcus, Geoffrey. *Before the Lamps Went Out: Britain's Golden Age, Christmas 1913–August 1914*. Boston: Atlantic/Little, Brown, 1965.

Marquis, Albert Nelson. *The Book of Chicagoans*. Chicago: A. N. Marquis, 1911.

———. *Who's Who in Chicago 1931*. Chicago: A. N. Marquis, 1931.

Martin, John Bartlow. *Adlai Stevenson of Illinois*. Garden City, NY: Doubleday, 1976.

Martin, Ralph G. *Cissy: The Extraordinary Life of Eleanor Medill Patterson*. New York: Simon & Schuster, 1979.

———. *Jennie: The Life of Lady Randolph Churchill*. Vol 2. Englewood Cliffs, NJ: Prentice-Hall, 1971.

Massie, Robert K. *Nicholas and Alexandra*. New York: Atheneum, 1967.

Massie, Robert K., and Jeffrey Finestone. *The Last Courts of Europe*. New York: Greenwich House, 1981.

Mayer, Harold M., and Richard Wade. *Chicago: Growth of a Metropolis*. Chicago: University of Chicago Press, 1969.

McCormick Tribune Foundation. *Robert R. McCormick: A Celebration of His Life and Legacy*. Chicago: McCormick Tribune Foundation, 2005.

McCullough, David. *Mornings on Horseback*. New York: Simon & Schuster, 1981.

McCutcheon, John T. *Drawn from Memory*. Indianapolis: Bobbs-Merrill, 1950.

McDonald, Forrest. *Insull*. Chicago: University of Chicago Press, 1962.

McGivena, Leo E., and Others. *The News: The First Fifty Years of New York's Picture Newspaper.* New York: News Syndicate, 1969.

McIlvaine, Mary, ed. *Reminiscences of Chicago During the Civil War.* New York: Citadel Press, 1967.

McKeever, Porter. *Adlai Stevenson: His Life and Legacy.* New York: William Morrow, 1989.

McLean, Evalyn Walsh. *Father Struck It Rich.* Ouray, CO: Bear Creek, 1981.

McNulty, Elizabeth. *Chicago Then and Now.* San Diego: Thunder Bay Press, 2000.

McPhaul, John J. *Deadlines & Monkeyshines: The Fabled World of Chicago Journalism.* Englewood Cliffs, NJ: Prentice-Hall, 1962.

McTaggart, Lynne. *Kathleen Kennedy: Her Life and Times.* Garden City, NY: Dial Press, 1983.

Meeker, Arthur. *Prairie Avenue.* New York: Knopf, 1949.

———. *Chicago, with Love.* New York: Knopf, 1955.

Mellow, James R. *Charmed Circle: Gertrude Stein & Company.* New York: Praeger, 1974.

Miliukov, Paul. *History of Russia.* Vol. 3, *Reforms, Reaction, Revolutions (1855–1932).* New York: Funk & Wagnalls, 1969.

Miller, Donald L. *City of the Century: The Epic of Chicago and the Making of America.* New York: Simon & Schuster, 1996.

Miller, Kristie. *Ruth Hanna McCormick: A Life in Politics 1880–1944.* Albuquerque: University of New Mexico Press, 1992.

Miller, Ross. *The Great Chicago Fire.* Urbana: University of Illinois Press, 2000.

Milton, Joyce. *The Yellow Kids: Foreign Correspondents in the Heyday of Yellow Journalism.* New York: Harper & Row, 1989.

Morgan, Gwen, and Arthur Veysey. *Poor Little Rich Boy: The Life and Times of Col. Robert R. McCormick.* Carpentersville, IL: Crossroads Communications, 1985.

Morris, Edmund. *The Rise of Theodore Roosevelt.* New York: Ballantine Books, 1979.

Mosolov, À. À. *At the Court of the Last Emperor: Memoirs of the Chief of the Minister's of the Court Office.* St. Petersburg, Russia: Nauka, 1992.

Mott, Frank Luther. *American Journalism: A History of Newspapers in the United States Through 250 Years, 1690 to 1940.* New York: Macmillan, 1941.

Mowry, George E. *Theodore Roosevelt and the Progressive Movement.* New York: Hill & Wang, 1960.

———. *The Twenties: Fords, Flappers & Fanatics.* Englewood Cliffs, NJ: Prentice-Hall, 1963.

Nash, Jay Robert. *People to See: An Anecdotal History of Chicago's Makers and Breakers.* Piscataway, NJ: New Century, 1981.

Nicolson, Nigel. *Mary Curzon*. New York: Harper & Row, 1977.

Nissenson, Marilyn. *The Lady Upstairs: Dorothy Schiff and the New York Post*. New York: St. Martin's Press, 2007.

Oates, Stephen B. *With Malice Toward None: The Life of Abraham Lincoln*. New York: Harper & Row, 1977.

Ogden, Christopher. *Legacy: A Biography of Moses and Walter Annenberg*. Boston: Little, Brown, 1999.

O'Sullivan, Shawn. *New York Exposed: Photographs from the Daily News*. New York: Abrams, 2001.

Pacyga, Dominic, and Ellen Skerrett. *Chicago: City of Neighborhoods*. Chicago: Loyola University Press, 1986.

Pares, Sir Bernard. *A History of Russia*. New York: Knopf, 1926.

Patterson, Joseph Medill. *A Little Brother of the Rich*. Chicago: Reilly & Britton, 1908.

Pierce, Bessie Louise. *As Others See Chicago: Impressions of Visitors 1673–1933*. Chicago: University of Chicago Press, 1933.

————. *A History of Chicago*. Vol 2, *1848–1871*. Chicago: University of Chicago Press, 1913.

Poole, Ernest. *Giants Gone: Men Who Made Chicago*. New York: Whittlesey House, 1943.

Potter, Jeffrey. *Men, Money & Magic: The Story of Dorothy Schiff*. New York: Signet, 1976.

Radzinsky, Edvard. *The Last Tsar: The Life and Death of Nicholas II*. New York: Doubleday, 1992.

Rascoe, Burton. *Before I Forget*. Garden City, NY: Doubleday, Doran, 1937.

Roderick, S. V. *Nettie Fowler McCormick*. West Rindge, NH: Richard R. Smith, 1956.

Rose, Kenneth. *Superior Person: A Portrait of Curzon and His Circle in Late Victorian England*. New York: Weybright & Talley, 1969.

Ross, Ishbel. *Ladies of the Press*. New York: Harper & Row, 1936.

Rowlands, Penelope. *A Dash of Daring: Carmel Snow and Her Life in Fashion, Art, and Letters*. New York: Atria Books, 2005.

Russo, Gus. *Supermob: How Sidney Korshak and His Criminal Associates Became America's Hidden Power Brokers*. New York: Bloomsbury USA, 2006.

St. Johns, Adela Rogers. *The Honeycomb*. Garden City, NY: Doubleday, 1969.

Salny, Stephen M. *The Country Houses of David Adler*. New York: Norton, 2001.

Schulze, Franz, Rosemary Cowler, and Arthur H. Miller. *30 Miles North: A History of Lake Forest College, Its Town, and Its City of Chicago*. Chicago: University of Chicago Press, 2000.

Seldes, George. *Lords of the Press*. New York: Julian Messner, 1938.

Singleton, Esther. *Romantic Castles and Palace as Seen and Described by Famous Writers*. New York: Dodd, Mead, 1901.

Smith, Bruce. *The History of Little Orphan Annie*. New York: Ballantine Books, 1982.

Smith, Liz. *Natural Blonde: A Memoir*. New York: Hyperion, 2000.

Smith, Richard Norton. *The Colonel: The Life & Legend of Robert McCormick 1880–1955*. Boston: Houghton Mifflin, 1997.

Spinney, Robert G. *City of Big Shoulders: A History of Chicago*. Dekalb: Northern Illinois University Press, 2000.

Squires, James. *Read All About It! The Corporate Takeover of America's Newspapers*. New York: Times Books, 1993.

Stamper, John W. *Chicago's North Michigan Avenue: Planning and Development, 1900–1930*. Chicago: University of Chicago Press, 1991.

Swanberg, W. A. *Citizen Hearst*. New York: Charles Scribner's Sons, 1961.

———. *Pulitzer*. New York: Charles Scribner's Sons, 1967.

Tallmadge, Thomas E. *Architecture in Old Chicago*. Chicago: University of Chicago Press, 1941.

Tebbel, John. *An American Dynasty*. 1947; reprinted Westport, CT: Greenwood Press, 1968.

———. *The Inheritors: A Study of America's Great Fortunes and What Happened to Them*. New York: G. P. Putnam's Sons, 1962.

———. *The Life and Good Times of William Randolph Hearst*. New York: E. P. Dutton, 1952.

———. *The Marshall Fields: A Study in Wealth*. New York: E. P. Dutton, 1948.

Thomas, Bob. *Winchell*. Garden City, NY: Doubleday, 1971.

Thorndike, Joseph J. Jr. *The Magnificent Builders and Their Dream Houses*. New York: American Heritage Publishing, 1978.

Tribune Company. *Pictured Encyclopedia of the World's Greatest Newspaper*. Chicago: Chicago Tribune, 1928.

Unger, Irwin, and Debi Unger. *The Guggenheims*. New York: HarperCollins, 2005.

Viskochil, Larry A. *Chicago at the Turn of the Century in Photographs*. New York: Dover, 1984.

Waldrop, Frank. *McCormick of Chicago: An Unconventional Portrait of a Controversial Figure*. Englewood Cliffs, NJ: Prentice-Hall, 1966.

Wendt, Lloyd. *The Chicago Tribune: The Rise of a Great American Newspaper*. Chicago: Rand McNally, 1979.

Wendt, Lloyd, and Herman Kogan. *Big Bill of Chicago*. Evanston, IL: Northwestern University Press, 2005.

———. *Chicago: A Pictorial History*. New York: Bonanza Books, 1958.

————. *Lords of the Levee*. Indianapolis: Bobbs-Merrill, 1943.

Wilner, Isaiah. *The Man Time Forgot: A Tale of Genius, Betrayal, and the Creation of Time Magazine*. New York: HarperCollins, 2006.

Zorbaugh, Harvey Warren. *The Gold Coast and the Slum: A Sociological Study of Chicago's Near North Side*. Chicago: University of Chicago Press, 1976.

BOOKLETS, MANUSCRIPTS, JOURNALS,
AND UNPUBLISHED THESES

Chicago Tribune. *Joseph Medill: A Brief Biography and an Appreciation*. Chicago: Chicago Tribune, 1947.

Glessner, Frances M. "Journals 1870–1921." Manuscript, Chicago Historical Society.

Maddock, Kathryn. *Joseph Medill: An Editor of the Old School*. Unpublished thesis, University of Illinois, 1916.

Moriarty, Frank Thomas. *The Life and Public Service of Joseph Medill*. Unpublished thesis, Northwestern University, 1933.

Rushton, Wyatt. "Joseph Medill & the Chicago Tribune." Manuscript, Chicago Historical Society.

PERIODICALS

Alexander, Jack. "Vox Populi I." *The New Yorker*, August 6, 1938, 16–21.

————. "Vox Populi II." *The New Yorker*, August 13, 1938, 19–24.

————. "Vox Populi III." *The New Yorker*, August 20, 1938, 19–23.

"Another Patterson." *Newsweek*, March 28, 1949, 61–62.

"The Boss Lady." *Newsweek*, July 15, 1963, 56.

Chicago Blue Book of Selected Names. Various years.

The Chicago Magazine of Fashion, Music and Home Reading. Monthly issues, April 1870–December 1874.

Childs, Marquis. "Squire of Washington." *Saturday Evening Post*, June 5, 1943, 14–15, 41–44.

"Cissie and Her Papers." *Newsweek*, February 6, 1939, 29–30.

"Cissy and the New Terror." *Newsweek*, November 10, 1945, 87.

Cleveland, H. I. "Booming the First Republican President, A Talk with Abraham Lincoln's Friend, the Late Joseph Medill." *Saturday Evening Post*, August 5, 1899.

Corinthus. "A Gentleman of the Old School." *Quest*, May 2008, 78–79.

The Elite Directory of Chicago. Various years.

Gertz, Elmer. "Joe Medill's War." *Lincoln Herald*, October–December 1945, 2–12.

Gizycka, Felicia. "Jackson Hole, 1916–1965, A Reminiscence." *Vogue*, April 1, 1965, 200–10.

Hartwell, Dickson. "No Prissy Is Cissy." *Collier's*, November 30, 1946, 21, 72–78.

Hines, Fay. "Steel for the Private Life of a Business Man." *Arts & Decoration*, 1935, 18–20.

"Hon. Joseph Medill." *The Graphic*, December 19, 1891.

"Jazz-Age Baby, Patterson's Tabloid Tops the All on Its 25th Birthday," *Newsweek*, July 3, 1944, 60.

Lewis, Russell. "From Shock City to City Beautiful." *Chicago History*, Fall 2010, 18.

"Lewis Exposed." *Newsweek*, December 6, 1937, 15–16.

Liebling, A. J. "Mamie and Mr. O'Donnell Carry On." *The New Yorker*, June 8, 1946, 30–34.

MacFarquhar, Larissa. "East Side Story: How Louis Auchincloss came to terms with his world." *The New Yorker*, February 25, 2008, 54–63.

"McCormick Weds." *Life*, January 10, 1945, 35–38.

"Mrs. Patterson Takes on Another Capital Job." *Newsweek*, August 14, 1937, 35.

Patterson, Alicia. "Air Yachting in the Caribbean." *Liberty*, March 30, 1929, 15–18, 21–22, 24–26.

———. "Flying for Fun." *Vogue*, May 10, 1930, 59–61, 154.

———. "This Is the Life I Love." *Saturday Evening Post*, February 21, 1959, 19–21, 44–51.

Patterson, Joseph Medill. "The Nickelodeons," *Saturday Evening Post*, November 23, 1907, 10–11, 38.

Pearson, Drew. "My Mother-in-Law Troubles." *Saturday Evening Post*, November 17, 1956, 44–45, 87–92.

———. "Our Leading Lady Publisher." *Redbook*, 1937, 24–25, 92–94.

"Prelude to a Chicago War." *Newsweek*, October 20, 1941, 58, 60.

Schneider, Walter E. "Fabulous Rise of the Daily News." *Editor & Publisher*, June 24, 1939, 5–7, 45–49.

Smith, Beverly. "Herald Angel." *American Magazine*, August 1940, 28–29, 110–11.

"Those Charming People." *Newsweek*, July 3, 1944, 62.

Thurman, Judith. "Missing Woman." *The New Yorker*, September 14, 2009, 103–8.

Walker, Stanley. "Cissy Is a Newspaper Lady." *Saturday Evening Post*, May 6, 1939, 21–23, 58–60.

———. "Symphony in Brass." *Saturday Evening Post*, June 5, 1938, 10–11, 69–73.

Wells, George Y. "Patterson and the Daily News." *American Mercury*, December 9, 1944, 671–79.

Wertenbaker, Charles. "The Case of the Hot-Tempered Publisher." *Saturday Evening Post*, May 12, 1951, 36–37, 113–18.

INDEX